Legal Risks in EU Law

Emilia Mišćenić • Aurélien Raccah
Editors

Legal Risks in EU Law

Interdisciplinary Studies on Legal Risk Management and Better Regulation in Europe

Springer

Editors
Emilia Mišćenić
Faculty of Law
University of Rijeka
Rijeka, Croatia

Aurélien Raccah
Law Faculty
Catholic University of Lille
Lille, France

ISBN 978-3-319-28595-5 ISBN 978-3-319-28596-2 (eBook)
DOI 10.1007/978-3-319-28596-2

Library of Congress Control Number: 2016935495

Printed on acid-free paper

This Springer imprint is published by Springer Nature
The registered company is Springer International Publishing AG Switzerland

This project was executed by

Centre sur les Relations entre le Risque et le Droit (C3RD)

International and European Law School (IELS) of the Faculté Libre de Droit, Université Catholique de Lille, 56, rue du Port, F-59016 Lille

Global Legal Network, 60 boulevard Vauban, F-59016 Lille, Official website: http://www.global-legal-network.eu/

Contributing Member of "Creative'Labs SHS" co-financed by the European Union

Preface

The Union of today is faced with numerous legal, economic, social and many other risks that are seriously affecting its economic development as well as growth. Excessive and inadequate legal regulation act restrictively upon the activity of entrepreneurs on the market, on the one hand, and lowers the confidentiality of consumers, on the other. This in turn affects the functioning of the Union's internal market and restrains economic growth of the European Union (EU) in comparison to other important players on the global market. The consequences are reflected upon societal prosperity. The features common to all social disturbances that are taking place in the world today are, firstly, the fact that they are caused by inadequate reactions to existing risks and, secondly, the fact that they affect the world globally. The strong interdependence between the mentioned risks creates a "magical circle" that is very difficult to break and leads to serious consequences, which contribute to financial instability as well as economic crises. The Union's awareness of these risks is demonstrated in numerous communications, reports and recommendations and particularly in the European Strategy for Smart, Sustainable and Inclusive Growth (Europe 2020).[1] Europe 2020 insists upon measures necessary to achieve the so-called smart growth, meaning upon measures that are going to strengthen knowledge and innovation as key drivers for future economic growth as well as progress of the Union. It also emphasises sustainable growth and promotes a more resource-efficient, greener and more competitive economy. Finally, it promotes inclusive growth fostering a high-employment economy delivering social and territorial cohesion. These are the three key ingredients necessary for Europe's social market economy of the twenty-first century.[2] From a legal point of view,

[1] Communication from the Commission, Europe 2020, A Strategy for Smart, Sustainable and Inclusive Growth, COM (2010) 2020, Brussels, 3.3.2010.

[2] Ibid., p. 3.

these goals require a significant improvement of the existing Union's regulatory framework, the ineffectiveness of which presents one of the most important barriers to the development of technology, industry and consequently of economic growth. As rightly emphasised by the European Commission, in an era of globalisation, in which barriers to movement of goods, services and people are falling, citizens expect from legal regulations to ensure their safety and welfare, while businesses expect that legal regulations enable a level playing field and boost competitiveness.[3] However, if a regulatory framework across the Member States is scattered, inconsistent, outdated or does not take the interests of its addressees adequately into account, legal regulations may do exactly the opposite. It is precisely due to these reasons that the Union insists upon the introduction of better or so-called smart regulations in all affected areas of EU legislation. This belongs to one of the key strategic goals of Europe 2020, according to which "to face up to the challenges we face inside and outside Europe, policies, laws and regulations need to adapt to the fast pace of technological change, to foster innovation, to protect the welfare and safety of Europeans".[4]

The book *Legal Risks in EU Law* addresses these serious issues from a horizontal and interdisciplinary perspective by observing and analysing primarily legal and consequently inseparable economic, societal, environmental and other risks in different areas of EU legislation. Legal regulation is always enacted in a public interest in order to achieve a variety of goals, such as to ensure a fair and competitive market, to protect health, to provide safety, to stimulate innovations, to preserve the natural environment, to protect climate, etc.[5] Therefore, the interdisciplinary analysis of risks deriving from legal regulation in various fields is the most appropriate approach to observe the legal risk issue from different angles. On the other hand, the horizontal approach indicates that despite of the diversity of the studied subject matters and EU policies as well as the differences in applied research and writing methodology, all of the contributions tend to offer similar results. It is common knowledge that legal regulation should deliver policies and meet expectations of those to whom it is addressed, by taking into account all of the effects the regulation might have on the addressee's interests. This should include a thorough examination of economic, social, environmental and other important impacts of their legislative drafts.[6] However, in today's global society characterised by an increasing speed of changes, fast technology and economic progress, this seems to be a difficult task for lawmakers to achieve. Here is where the risk management usually includes an invitation to all relevant stakeholders to engage

[3] European Commission, Better Regulation—Simply Explained, available at: http://ec.europa.eu/smart-regulation/better_regulation/documents/brochure/brochure_en.pdf, p. 3.

[4] Ibid., p. 1.

[5] Ibid., p. 3.

[6] Wiener (2004), pp. 483–500.

in a public consultation or elaboration of independent reports, i.e. impact assessments. Unfortunately, the decision to launch regulatory initiatives is very often taken before the publication of impact assessment reports. Since a lawmaker does not dispose with the expertise necessary to respond properly to developmental challenges in specific regulatory fields, this results in regulations either offering inadequate protection or restricting market freedom. As a consequence a legal risk occurs that by its definition "commonly refers to a situation where the applicable law does not provide for a predictable and sound solution" and "might also refer to situations where the answer provided by the applicable law does not fit the market reality, or where the law does unnecessarily complicates or burdens a transaction".[7]

Bearing all that was said in mind, it is the primary mission of the authors gathered under the single roof of the book *Legal Risks in EU Law* to identify and analyse the causes as well as consequences of legal risks in regulatory frameworks of various EU policies and beyond. Over several decades now, the Union has been faced with numerous legal risks that are adversely affecting the functioning of the EU and the development of EU law. Particularly, due to the constraints of the principles of subsidiarity and proportionality, it is getting more and more difficult to justify the Union's authority to regulate in a variety of competence areas. Internal market, consumer protection, social policy, foreign policy, environmental policy, etc. are only some of the areas to which this book dedicates its chapters and horizontally examines the Union's approach to regulation and management of legal risks. In doing so, the authors generally come to very similar conclusions concerning the inability of the Union's regulatory methods to respond properly to existing legal and consequently economic and other existing risks and challenges. Especially, approximation, i.e. harmonisation of different Member States' laws as the most extensively used means of EU legal regulation, at the end of the day resulted in overregulation and further differences at national levels. New differences in legal regulation caused by the Union's attempts to remove existing regulatory differences between Member States affected the realisation of the Union's supreme goal of the establishment and proper functioning of the internal market. Furthermore, discrepancies caused by departures in application and interpretation of harmonised national regulatory frameworks across the Union seriously affect the principle of effectiveness of EU law. This is getting even more complicated by the fact that every single EU legal act has to be translated into 24 EU official languages. Despite the principle of equal authenticity, according to which all language versions of the same EU legal act are presumed to be authentic and to have the same meaning, imperfections in legal translations often result in different meanings of the same legal rules. Consequently, by managing legal risks deriving from the diversity of Member States' laws presenting barriers to trade and to the Union's economy, the Union actually produced new legal risks that need management of their own. This serious failure contributed to the legal uncertainty of

[7] UNIDROIT Explanatory Notes on Preliminary Draft Convention on Harmonised Substantive Rules Regarding Securities Held With an n Intermediary, Rome, 2004, p. 7.

stakeholders acting on the internal market and lowered their economic activity and cross-border transactions. The improper response to the management of legal risks thus resulted in the creation of further legal, economic as well as other kinds of risks, and it also adversely affected the development and economic growth of the Union.

The book *Legal Risks in EU Law* is the first in a line of publications that will try to set a new and innovative path offering effective solutions to the here presented issues. The application of an original interdisciplinary approach to legal risk management should enable a better understanding of the interests of all stakeholders included in the complex regulatory processes. Both on the level of the EU and of the Member States, lawmakers need to apply a completely new regulatory approach that will, besides focusing on general legal issues, give more attention to the specific needs of a certain regulatory field (e.g. technology, industry) and to various impacts of enacting legal regulations on the future development of the concerned and other related areas. This requires the abandoning of a traditional discipline-oriented approach in favour of new alternative regulatory methods that will accentuate the role of the interdisciplinary approach in legal regulation. The initiative for the creation of a new and innovative regulatory approach for the management of legal risks was born within the international interdisciplinary network of excellent scientists named Global Legal Network (GLN).[8] This interdisciplinary network that was formed in November 2014 in Lille (France) gathers academic scholars and practitioners coming from more than 15 European countries, as well as from the USA, Canada, Brazil and many other countries who specialise in legal, economic, political, sociological, philosophical and other sciences. Such a joint venture of science and practice mixed with valid expertise and knowledge of experts coming from a variety of disciplines guarantees the invention of new and effective regulatory approaches. Bearing in mind the significant lack of similar scientific projects at the international level, the members of GLN started a long-lasting project "Interdisciplinary Studies on Legal Risk Management and Better Regulation in Europe" that can generally be divided in three main stages. The first stage, the results of which are presented in the book *Legal Risks in EU Law*, is dedicated to the thorough analysis of causes and consequences of failures in regulatory approaches and legal risks management. Since proposing of new and effective methods of legal regulation and risk management depends heavily upon the understanding of the current situation, this stage appears to be crucial. The second stage deals with the comparative analysis of a variety of regulatory and risk management methods existing in laws of European and other world countries that can offer valid lessons and insights to the EU. The research results of the first two stages will open the door to the third and most creative stage dedicated to the development of innovative regulatory approaches for the management of legal risks in EU law. By pursuing this interdisciplinary project, the GLN members aim to achieve scientific results that will significantly contribute to the accomplishment of

[8] Visit the Global Legal Network at: http://www.global-legal-network.eu/.

key EU strategic goals on better regulation and consequently on the smart, sustainable and inclusive growth of the EU.

Rijeka, Croatia
Lille, France
1 November 2015

Emilia Mišćenić
Aurélien Raccah

Acknowledgements

This contributed volume is a result of the initiative taken by Assoc. Prof. Aurélien Raccah, vice dean at the Law Faculty, Catholic University of Lille (France), who was in charge of the international scientific conference on "Legal Risks in Recent Developments of EU Law: Approach of Recent Legal Challenges Faced by the EU" held on 13 November 2014 in Lille. This conference brought together over 30 excellent scholars from various EU and other world countries, specialised in social fields, such as legal, economic, political, sociological, philosophical and other sciences. As a follow-up to this conference, a first meeting was organised on 14 November 2014 at the Catholic University of Lille, which resulted in the creation of an international and interdisciplinary network of scientists as well as practitioners named *Global Legal Network* (GLN). The work of the *Global Legal Network* is supported by the *Centre sur les Relations entre le Risque et le Droit* (C3RD) and the *International and European Law School* (IELS) attached to the Catholic University of Lille. While the C3RD has been working for many years on the concept of "legal risks" in national law, the *Global Legal Network* is now extending the research to European and international issues.

Therefore, we would like to take this opportunity to express our gratitude to all the members of the *Global Legal Network* who contributed to this book: Assoc. Prof. Dr. Harry Post, Assoc. Prof. Dr. Ioannis Panoussis, Assoc. Prof. Dr. Réka Somssich, Assoc. Prof. Dr. Claire Marzo, Assist. Prof. Dr. Darinka Piqani, Assist. Prof. Dr. Moritz Jesse, Dr. Alessandro Chechi, Dr. Leonardo Massai and Dr. Matteo Giuseppe Vacaro Incisa. We thank the authors for their valuable contributions providing multidisciplinary perspectives on the effects of legal risks upon the recent development of EU law. The editors are especially grateful to the Law Faculty, Catholic University of Lille, for its financial support, which made the publication of this book possible, mainly to Assoc. Prof. Dr. Ioannis Panoussis as dean of the Law Faculty and Assoc. Prof. Dr. Andra Cotiga-Raccah as IELS codirector, friend as well as wife. The editors also thank Ms Noémie Bomble for her support through the creation of the GLN website: http://www.global-legal-network.eu/. We are also grateful to those who participated in the preparation of the book, in particular to

Ms Dina Sušanj for the English revision of the chapter written by non-native speakers of English and to Ms Zuzana Babikova for her technical assistance. Finally, a special thanks goes to Ms Anke Seyfried and Mrs. Julia Bieler from Springer who guided us through the publication process.

October 2015

Contents

Notes on Contributors

Alessandro Chechi, Ph.D. (European University Institute), LL.M. (University College London), J.D. (University of Siena), is a postdoctoral researcher at the Art-Law Centre (Faculty of Law) of the University of Geneva (Switzerland) and lecturer at the Faculty of Law of the Université Catholique of Lille (France). He is reporter for Italy in the International Law in Domestic Courts project, Oxford University Press, consultant at the IDR Group's Art Law Section and member of the editorial committee of the Italian Yearbook of International Law. He is the author of the book *The Settlement of International Cultural Heritage Disputes*, Oxford, Oxford University Press, 2014.

Moritz Jesse, Dr., LL.M., Europa Institute, University of Leiden, the Netherlands, is associate professor of the European Union law at the Europa Institute of Leiden Law School. He joined the Law School in October 2010. His teaching and research focuses on the EU's internal market, the free movement of persons, European citizenship as well as EU migration law. Moritz Jesse teaches and coordinates courses at bachelor as well as master's level in English and Dutch at Leiden Law School, the Paris Branch of the Catholic University of Lille and the Academy for Legislation in the Hague. Since 2015, Moritz Jesse has been pursuing his research project "The Others Amongst Us: Immigration and Integration and the Law", which is funded by the Dutch Scientific Organization for 3 years. Before joining the Europa Institute, Jesse obtained his Ph.D. in European Union law at the European University Institute in Florence, Italy.

Claire Marzo is a lecturer (Maître de Conférences) at University Paris-Est Créteil (UPEC). She also teaches at several universities in France and in the UK. She is a European social lawyer. She wrote her Ph.D. on European social citizenship (published in 2010) at the European University Institute and focused on the EU law's potentials in the field of social security, education as well as labour law. She has since extended her research interests, projects and publications to other social and current issues such as women's inclusion, healthcare law and the financial crisis.

Leonardo Massai, Ph.D., is legal and policy advisor for the Coalition for Rainforest Nations (CfRN) (www.rainforestcoalition.org), where he provides direct counsel, assistance, advice and training for CfRN's participant countries on international environmental law, climate change governance, mitigation and adaptation, climate compatible development plans and multilateral negotiations. Recently, Massai has been hired as team leader to assist the government of Madagascar to prepare its INDC for Paris COP21. Massai is also senior lecturer in EU law, international and EU environmental law, climate change law, human rights and environments and UN multilateral negotiations at the Catholic University of Lille in France.

Emilia Mišćenić, Dr. Iur. (Graz), LL.M. (Saarbrücken), is assistant professor at the Chair of European and Private International Law, Faculty of Law, University of Rijeka (Croatia). After completing the postgraduate master's study programme at the Europa-Institut of Saarland University in Germany, she enrolled in the postgraduate doctoral scientific study programme of the Faculty of Law, Karl-Franzens University of Graz. Upon completing the doctoral study programme, she published a scientific monograph in German entitled *Der Verbraucherkreditvertrag in der EU und Kroatien aus materiell- und kollisionsrechtlicher Sicht* (LIT Verlag, 2010). In 2011, she received the Annual National Science Award for Junior Researcher in the field of social sciences from the National Science Awards Committee of the Croatian Parliament for her scientific monograph. In 2012, she received an award from the Foundation of the University of Rijeka for her special contributions to scientific research and teaching activities. In 2013, she was selected by the Ministry of Science, Education and Sports as one of the twenty most successful research assistants in the Republic of Croatia. Special recognition of her work came in the form of a quotation from Advocate General Trstenjak of the Court of Justice of the European Union in the Opinion to the Case C-453/10, *Pereničová et Perenič*, who cited her award-winning monograph. She is teaching at the Faculty of Law, University of Rijeka, Faculty of Law, Business and Economics of the University of Bayreuth and the Law Faculty of the Catholic University of Lille.

Ioannis K. Panoussis holds a Ph.D. in public international law (human rights). He is the dean of the Faculty of Law of the Catholic University of Lille (Lille and Paris Campuses), the president of the Administration Council of the University's Library and a visiting professor at the Political Science Institute as well as the IESEG Business School where he teaches public international law, human rights, law of armed conflicts, EU institutions, etc. He is also the academic director of the master's programme in international and European law, specialising in "human rights, security and development". His research primarily focuses on the relations between risk and law within the field of international human rights protection and public international law (obligation of the States to prevent violations of human rights, terrorism and human rights, migration, succession of States, etc.). He was chosen to be part of the selection committee for the Belgian National Fund for Research (FNRS). Finally, he has also been a UNHCR expert since 2011 (judge at the French National Court for Asylum representing the UNHCR) and accomplished, in 2013, an international mission for the Ministry of Foreign Affairs in Afghanistan (Human Rights Week) aiming to promote human rights and to educate Afghan nationals working for the government, NGOs and international organisations.

Darinka Piqani is assistant professor of EU law at Leiden University College the Hague and lecturer of EU law at Leiden Law School, the Netherlands. Darinka holds a Ph.D. from the Law Department of the European University Institute where she graduated in 2010. She researches and publishes on the relationship between EU law and national constitutional law and more specifically on the role of constitutional courts in construing constitutional reservations to the primacy of EU law.

Harry H. G. Post is retired professor of international law at the University of Exeter as well as currently visiting professor at the Law Faculties of the Catholic University of Lille and the University of Sassari. He was adjunct professor at the University of Victoria, Canada, the Paul Nitze School of Advanced International Studies, Johns Hopkins University, the University of Modena and Reggio Emilia as well as at LUISS Guido Carli in Rome. His research interests are international humanitarian law and (the future of) international criminal law, waste management in environmental law and territorial sovereignty and conflict. He is at present finalising a book entitled *Territorial Sovereignty: Its Acquisition and Loss in Modern International Law*.

Aurélien Raccah, Ph.D. (European University Institute, Florence), LL.M. (EUI, Sorbonne), is associate professor and vice dean at the Law Faculty of the Catholic University of Lille and barrister in Paris at ELEA AVOCAT. He wrote a Ph.D. thesis on the following topic: "The Direct Implementation of EU Law by the Devolved Bodies. Comparative Approach in Germany, the UK and France". Aurélien Raccah is codirector of the *International and European Law School* (IELS) where he teaches EU law. As researcher, he specialised in EU law and published articles relating to EU law and administrative, environmental and social law and a book on the Lisbon Treaty titled *Traité de Lisbonne: De nouvelles compé tences pour l'Union*, L'Harmattan, 2012. He is one of the founding members of the Global Legal Network.

Réka Somssich is associate professor at the Faculty of Law of Eötvös Loránd University, Budapest, where she works at the Department of Private International Law and European Economic Law. She obtained her Ph.D. degree in 2008. Her teaching and research cover internal market law, application of EU law by national courts and multilingual lawmaking. She was the research coordinator and co-author of the comprehensive studies *Lawmaking in the EU Multilingual Environment* (2010) and *Language and Translation in International Law and EU Law* (2012).

G. Matteo Vaccaro-Incisa, Ph.D. (University of Geneva and Bocconi University), LL.M. (IHEID and University of Geneva), M.Sc. (Bocconi University), Esq. (Florence, Madrid), senior research fellow in international public and investment law at Bocconi University (Milan, Italy), chargé de cours at the Law Faculty of the Catholic University of Lille (France). Previously, he was an early-stage Marie Curie researcher for the Dispute Settlement in Law and Economics (DISSETTLE) ITN programme as well as visiting scholar at the University of Buenos Aires (2015) and Melbourne (2013). Concurrently with his practice of law (international contracts and dispute settlement), he pursues academic research in the fields of public international law, international investment law and international arbitration.

Part I
Legal Risks in Developement of EU Law

Reframing Legal Risk in EU Law

Aurélien Raccah

Contents

Abstract Legal risk is an oxymora. Law creates predictable duties and rights protecting human relations and justice conciliates disagreements on law's interpretation. The high production of international, European and national legislations increases legal protection and thus legitimate expectations but paradoxically (or logically) makes interpretation more complex for three reasons. Firstly, legal provisions may be imprecise, unclear or uncertain. Secondly individuals, companies or even public authorities may not have the necessary knowledge. Thirdly, the concerned bodies may not have the structural and financial capabilities to fulfil their obligations. Due to its inherent complexity, EU law faces many legal risks. The Better Regulation policy has thus introduced risk management in the EU law making process. However, the Impact Assessments focus on economic, social and environmental hypothetic consequences and the legal ones remain subsidiary as long as fall into the national competences. For that purpose, the European Commission has recently adopted a culture of evaluation monitoring the implementation of EU law. However, it doesn't prevent against any infringement relating to legal uncertainty. The Court of Justice of the European Union plays a major role to stabilise the interpretation and to allocate the liabilities. This chapter aims at presenting an exhaustive review of the doctrine relating to legal risk management

A. Raccah (✉)
Faculty of Law, Catholic University of Lille, Lille, France
e-mail: Aurelien.RACCAH@univ-catholille.fr

E. Miščenić, A. Raccah (eds.), *Legal Risks in EU Law*,
DOI 10.1007/978-3-319-28596-2_1

and to connect it with the European Union in order to sketch few first elements of definition of what can be considered as legal risk in EU law.

1 Introduction

The European legal doctrine agrees that there is no common definition of legal risk.[1] From the point of view of legal science, there is no legal risk because the core of the law has to be predictable. Introducing risk in law would imply a value judgement opposing threats and security. In other words, it would introduce a subjective opinion on negative and positive consequences of the law, which is not the purpose of legal science. Thus, legal risks may be researched from economic, political, sociological or social perspectives, not from a legal one.

However, legal science may reframe legal risk as a metalanguage to describe and analyse the purpose as well as the impact of law on different components of society. In that sense, legal scientists participate in the interdisciplinary approach of social sciences, which is driven by the European Commission. It may help to explain how the EU legislative process anticipates the implementation of EU law and what the risks faced by public authorities, companies and individuals when they apply EU law are.

Risk has been taken into consideration as a scientific tool since the sociological studies of Ulrich Beck in the eighties.[2] He supports the idea that there is a plurality of risk definitions linked to our civilisation. Social modernity produces wide categories of risks, which may be identified by social science. He states that modernity is the cause of many damages to the environment (soils, forests, air, water, waste management, animals...), human health (new diseases caused by pollution, industrial foods, chemicals, pharmaceuticals...), private life (divorces, access to education, poverty...), economy (financial markets, exchange rates, liquidity, crises, unemployment...). In that sense, any social activity may create a risk of damages to certain people. According to Ulrich Beck, the new role of social sciences is to rationalise the objective constraints of each policy in order to manage their impacts on society.[3] Since these works, theories of risk management exist in natural and social sciences to identify, assess, anticipate as well as prioritise the risks before catastrophes happen. However, methods, definitions and objectives vary widely between the sciences.

The International Organization for Standardization (ISO) gives a standard definition of risk management as "risks affecting organizations can have consequences

---

[1] Mahler (2007), pp. 10–31; Moorhead and Vaughan (2015), p. 36; available at: http://www.ucl.ac.uk/laws/law-ethics/research/papers/erc-executive-report-legal-risk-definition-management-ethics.pdf.

[2] Beck (1986, 1988, 1991a, b, c, 1995a, b, 1999).

[3] Beck (1991a, b, c), pp. 155–182.

in terms of economic performance and professional reputation, as well as environmental, safety and societal outcomes. Therefore, managing risk effectively helps organizations to perform well in an environment full of uncertainty".[4] This international standard provides also principles and guidelines helping organisations to identify opportunities as well as threats in order to improve risk management. This approach has been already applied to companies,[5] legal firms[6] and EU institutions themselves[7] to organise their own internal structure as well as analysis. However, ISO is a non-governmental organisation setting international standards, not legal sources.

The Anglo-Saxon doctrines also adopted these theories to develop prospective studies. European doctrines are basically reluctant to those studies which are based on a hypothetical uncertain future that rarely happens. It explains why each social science opposes two schools: one presenting a new theory based on risk management,[8] and the other criticising the unrealistic purpose of prospective scientific studies.[9] Each social science tends, indeed, to define the risk(s) to justify its own scientific purpose.

Legal science has remained mostly apart from these developments. Consequently, there is neither a standard definition of legal risk, nor a clear definition of risk. Legal studies on risk management are only realised with corporate and business issues, mostly led by the Anglo-Saxon (overall American) doctrine.[10] The Basel Accords on banking supervision include many aspects of credit risk, operational risk and market risk.[11] The International Bar Association tried to define risk management for law firms as a result of a defective transaction, a claim, a legal failure or a change in law.[12] A few isolated German,[13] French[14] and Scandinavian[15] publications also relate to regulatory and liability risks. The recent works led by

---

[4] ISO, No. 31000, available at: http://www.iso.org/iso/home/standards/iso31000.htm.

[5] Baranoff (2003), p. 639; Collard et al. (2011), p. 285.

[6] Hopkins (2013), p. 2; Anderson and Black (2013); Whittaker (2003), pp. 5–7.

[7] Tracol (2014), pp. 711–744. See Communication of the European Commission on Customs Risk Management and Security of the Supply Chain, COM(2012)793 final.

[8] Dowd (2002), p. 274.

[9] Elliot (2002); Meric et al. (2009), p. 277; Grimaldi (2006), p. 996.

[10] Terblanché (2012); Mccormick (2008); Howard (2007–2008), p. 505; Viscuki (2000).

[11] Since 1988, the Basel Committee on Banking Supervision has adopted 3 major accords setting capital requirements for banks: Basel III: International framework for liquidity risk measurement, standards and monitoring, 2010; Basel II: International convergence of capital measurement and capital standards; Basel I: International convergence of capital measurement and capital standards, 1988. Hull (2012), pp. 257–278.

[12] International Bar Association, *The Management of Legal Risk by Financial Institutions*, Draft Discussion Paper, Working Party on Legal Risk, 2003.

[13] Wyss (2005); Pfohl (2002).

[14] Dekeuwer-Defossez (2015), p. 5; Moury (2012), p. 1020; Lasserre (2011), p. 1632; Barbier (2011); Millet (2001).

[15] Mahler (2007).

Alberto Alemanno in the *European Journal of Risk Regulation*[16] tend to approximate these interdisciplinary movements through the concept of risk regulation.[17] In these studies, legal risk management is seen through different steps: risks identification, risks classification, impact assessment, EU law-making process, risk regulation, risk management, legal monitoring, legal liabilities and sanctions.

EU law may paradoxically create threats to national public authorities, companies or individuals that shall be managed by competent authorities. Using legal science as a tool for risk management may help to be aware of the legal consequences. For that purpose, this chapter aims to define and identify the legal risks resulting from EU law (I) and then demonstrate how the legal risks are managed by EU law (II).

2 Looking for a Definition of Legal Risks in EU Law

In 2005, the European Central Bank (ECB) expressed its will to develop a legal risk definition as part of operational risk and the Bank considers that "a general definition of legal risk would facilitate proper risk assessment and risk management, as well as ensure a consistent approach between EU credit institutions. It would also be worthwhile examining the extent to which one should take into account the fact that legal risks are inherently unpredictable and do not generally conform to a pattern. In addition, the management of legal risk would have to be consistent with the management of operational risk as a whole. For these reasons, the ECB suggest that CEBS should carry out further work to clarify the definition of legal risk".[18] However, the final Directive only mentions legal risk as part of the operational risk relating to credit institutions, but does not define it properly.[19]

[16] European Journal of Risk Regulation, since 2010, 4 issues a year, available at: http://www.lexxion.de/en/zeitschriften/fachzeitschriften-englisch/ejrr/about-ejrr.html.

[17] Alemanno (2016), p. 224; Alemanno (2014); Alemanno et al. (2014), p. 338; Alemanno and Spina (2014); Alemanno (2012); Alemanno (2011), p. 320; Alemanno (2008), Series No. 6; Alemanno (2007).

[18] European Central Bank, Opinion of 17 February 2005 on a proposal for Directives recasting Directive 2000/12/EC of 20 March 2000 relating to the taking up and pursuit of the business of credit institutions and Directive 93/6/EEC of 15 March 1993 on the capital adequacy of investment firms and credit institutions (2005/C 52/10).

[19] Directive 2006/48/EC of the European Parliament and of the Council of 14 June 2006 relating to the taking up and pursuit of the business of credit institutions (recast), OJ L 177, 30.6.2006, pp. 1–200.

Indeed, neither the EU Treaties and Legislations, nor the European institutions and the Court of Justice[20] expressively refer, use or define "legal risk". The Treaties refer 14 times to the word "risk".[21] Every reference to risk in the Treaties is tied to respective liabilities of the European institutions and Member States. However, risk is taken into consideration in many EU Regulations and Directives as well as in many soft law documents.

The first purpose of this chapter is to reframe the concept of legal risk through existing general principles of EU law (Sect. 2.1) and then to identify which threats may be seen as "legal risks" (Sect. 2.2).

2.1 Legal Risks Through EU Law Principles

If the expression of "legal risk" is not expressively used in EU law, its concept is already implemented through a few general principles of EU law. Legal risk can be considered as already partly managed by existing EU law.

---

[20] The General Court mentioned it in two Judgments only to express the binding effect of EU Law in national legal orders and the consequence of an agreement between two Parties: Joined Cases T-425/04, T-444/04, T-450/04 and T-456/04, *France, France Télécom vs Bouygues e. a.* [2010] ECR II-02099, para. 187; Case T-271/04, *Citymo SA vs European Commission* [2007] ECR II-01375, para. 152.

[21] Art. 7, para 1 EU in case of "clear risk of serious breach by a MS of the [European] values"; Art. 121, para 4 TFEU provides a possibility for the European Commission to address a warning to a MS if its economic policies risk to jeopardise "the proper functioning of economic and monetary union"; Art. 126, para 3 TFEU permits the European Commission to prepare a report if "there is a risk of an excessive deficit in a Member State"; under Art. 196, para 1 a) TFEU, the Union supports the MS' action in risk prevention relating to civil protection; Art. 207, para 4 a) relating to the common commercial policy foresees (Who?), in case the agreements in the field of trade in cultural and audiovisual services risk prejudicing the Union's cultural and linguistic diversity, the Council shall also act unanimously, as well as, under b) in the field of trade in social, education and health services; Art. 256, para 2 TFEU provides Decisions given by the General Court in proceedings brought against Decisions of the specialised courts which may be subject to review by the Court of Justice "*where there is a serious risk of the unity or consistency of Union law being affected*", as well as for a preliminary ruling and in general the First Advocate General may propose it, on the basis of Art. 62 of the Protocol (No. 3) of the Statute of the Court of Justice of the European Union; Art. 7, para 3 of the Protocol (No. 5) of the Statute of the European Investment Bank specifying that "the Board of Directors shall [. . .] lay down the terms and conditions of any financing operation presenting a specific risk profile" and under para 6 "the Bank shall protect itself against exchange risks by including in contracts for loans and guarantees such clauses as it considers appropriate" and Art. 7 provides the same protection in referring to the risks. Finally Art. 19, para 2 states that "*No one may be removed, expelled or extradited to a State where there is a serious risk that he or she would be subjected to the death penalty, torture or other inhuman or degrading treatment or punishment*".

EU law *firstly* refers to risk management using the precautionary principle,[22] especially in the fields of environment,[23] public health[24] and food safety.[25] The European Commission itself expressively structures the precautionary principle around the analysis of risk "which comprises three elements: risk assessment, risk management, risk communication".[26] In the first Case relating to the Bovine Spongiform Encephalopathy (BSE), the Court first stated that "where there is uncertainty as to the existence or extent of risks to human health, the institutions may take protective measures without having to wait until the reality and seriousness of those risks become fully apparent".[27] This was confirmed in the other CJEU Cases for the refusal to end the ban on British beef and veal[28] and for emergency measures to combat BSE.[29] The precautionary principle then became a general principle of EU law which applies to any EU policy.[30]

In the area of food safety, the concept of risk has also been introduced to anticipate the potential negative impacts on human health.[31] The Regulation No. 178/2002 on Food Safety is, therefore, articulated around risk assessment, management and communication.[32] "Risk" is defined as "a function of the probability of an adverse health effect and the severity of that effect, consequential to a

---

[22] Craig and de Burca (2011), p. 549.

[23] Art. 191, para 2 TFEU refers to the precautionary principle. European Commission, Communication of 2 February 2000 on the Precautionary Principle, COM/2000/0001 final. Case C-246/07, *European Commission v. Sweden* [2010] (Sometimes you use vs and sometimes v. when referring to the different Cases and I think you should choose one so it is consistent.) applying the Stockholm Convention on Persistent Organic Pollutants.

[24] The 1st Case mentioning risk management was Case T-13/99, *Pfizer Animal Health SA v. Council* [2002], ECR II-3318 relating to risk assessment and management of transfer of resistance to antibiotics from animals to humans. See the website of the DG Public Health relating to risk management:

http://ec.europa.eu/health/preparedness_response/risk_management/index_en.htm.

[25] Case C-601/11 P, *France v. European Commission* [2013] EU:C:2013:465 relating to risk management of the transmissible spongiform encephalopathies; Joined Cases C-58/10 to C-68/10, *Monsanto SA v. Ministre de l'Agriculture et de la Pêche* [2011] ECR I-07763 relating to the risks of GMO dissemination; Case C-558/07, *S. P. C. M. SA e. a. v. Secretary of State for the Environment, Food and Rural Affairs* [2009] ECR I-05783 concerning the REACH Regulation; Case C-66/04, *UK v. EP and Council* [2005] ECR I-10553 concerning the Regulation on Smoke Flavourings; Case C-198/03 P, *European Commission v. CEVA Santé Animale SA e. a.* [2005] ECR I-06357.

[26] Communication on the Precautionary Principle, Brussels, 2 February 2000, COM(2000)1 final.

[27] Case C-180/96 *UK v. Commission* [1998] ECR I-2265, para. 99.

[28] Case C-1/00, *European Commission v. France* [2001] ECR I-09989.

[29] Case C-393/01, *France v. European Commission* [2003] ECR I-5405.

[30] Case T-13/99 *Pfizer Animal Health SA v. Council* [2002] ECR I-3305; Case T-74, 76, 83–85, 132, 137 and 141/00, *Artegodan GmbH v. Commission* [2002] ECR II-4945.

[31] Serratosa (2011), Weimer (2010), pp. 31–39.

[32] Regulation (EC) No. 178/2002 of the European Parliament and of the Council of 28 January 2002 laying down the general principles and requirements of Food Law, establishing the European Food Safety Authority and laying down procedures in matters of food safety.

hazard" and "risk management" as "the process, distinct from risk assessment, of weighing policy alternatives in consultation with interested parties, considering risk assessment and other legitimate factors, and, if need be, selecting appropriate prevention and control options".[33] In 2010, France has failed to fulfil its obligations by laying down prior authorisation for processing aids and foodstuffs qualified as a measure having equivalent effect to a quantitative restriction on imports.[34] The Court connected the risk management of food safety and the legal uncertainty resulting from the contradiction between the European regulation as well as the national measures.

However, the precautionary principle is not a proper legal risk management tool, but rather a social or environmental risk management tool through the law. In this case, the law appears much more as a form of medicine than a threat. The threats are here produced by social behaviours (overproduction of food, environmental pollution, human diseases. . .) managed by EU law.

Secondly, the most appropriate general principle of legal certainty has been recognised as the constitutional principle in most European States as well as in ECHR law[35] and in EU law.[36] According to the settled CJEU case law, "the principle of legal certainty requires that rules of law be clear and precise and predictable in their effect, so that interested parties can ascertain their position in situations and legal relationships governed by EU law".[37] In other words, the EU legal interpretation shall protect, in particular, public authorities, companies and individuals against uncertain EU law.[38] Those concerned by EU law shall know precisely their obligations and the overall financial consequences.[39]

In a Case relating to the protection of the financial interests of the European Union, the Court underlined that an EU Regulation can't apply "until the administration has discovered those irregularities could encourage inertia on the part of the national authorities in bringing proceedings in respect of irregularities, whilst exposing operators, firstly, to a long period of legal uncertainty".[40] The uncertainty of a legal provision shall in principle benefit the exposing operators.

---

[33] Art. 3, 9 of Regulation No. 178/2002.

[34] Case C-333/08, *European Commission v. France* [2010] ECR I-757.

[35] ECHR Case 6833/74, *Marckx v. Belgium* [1979], para. 58.

[36] Case 348/85, *Denmark v. European Commission* [1987] ECR 5225 (declaring void a Commission Decision cancelling financial compensation for agriculture).

[37] Case C-48/14, *EP v. Council* [2015] on protecting human health against radioactive substances in water intended for human consumption (action dismissed); Case C-147/13, *Spain v. Council* [2015] EU:C:2015:299, para. 79 (on the creation of unitary patent protection), Case C-81/10 P, *France Télécom v. Commission* [2011] ECR I-12899, para. 100; Case C-643/11, *LVK* [2013] EU:C:2013:55, para. 51; Case C-325/91, *France v. Commission* [1993] ECR I-3283, para. 26.

[38] Case C-98/14, *Berlington Hungary Tanácsadó és Szolgáltató kft e. a. v. Hungary* [2015] EU:C:2015:386, para. 77.

[39] Case C-348/85, ibid., para. 19.

[40] Case C-52/14, *Pfeifer & Langen GmbH & Co. KG v. Bundesanstalt für Landwirtschaft und Ernährung* [2015] EU:C:2015:381.

For that purpose, the Court may exceptionally restrict the opportunity of relying on EU law provisions for any person concerned if two criteria are fulfilled. On the one hand, they should have acted in good faith, on the other, there should be a risk of serious economic repercussions to a large number of legal relationships entered into in good faith.[41]

The principle of legal certainty shall, however, not be used by interested Parties to skirt around other general principles of EU law. In the *Belgacom* Case relating to public procurements passed without call of tenders, the Court specified that "that principle may not be relied on to give an agreement an extended scope which is contrary to the principles of equal treatment and non-discrimination and the obligation of transparency deriving therefrom".[42] The same conciliation has been applied regarding the protection of the rights of the defence and the proper conduct procedure.[43] Legal certainty shall therefore be conciliated with all existing general principles of EU law. Legal risk may subsist from this conciliation.[44] In the *Belgacom* Case, municipalities and indirectly the consumers would be affected by significant financial losses. The respect of the law may not necessarily protect the weaker Parties.[45]

Thirdly, qualified by the Court as corollary of the principle of legal certainty, the protection of legitimate expectations settles that a plaintiff may uphold that he acted with the belief that he got acquired rights to rely upon binding obligations.[46] In particular, it shall protect any person to which an EU institution has caused to entertain expectations, which are justified by precise assurances provided to him. The General Court defined three conditions to claim entitlement to the protection of legitimate expectations[47]:

- A precise, unconditional and consistent assurance originating from authorised and reliable sources given to the person concerned;

[41] Cases C-401/13 and C-432/13, *Vasiliki and Attila Balazs v. Casa Judeţeană de Pensii Cluj* [2015] EU:C:2015:26, para. 50, concerning social security for migrant workers; Case C-76/14, *Mihai Manea v. Instituţia Prefectului judeţul Braşov* [2015] EU:C:2015:216, paras. 54 and 55. Joined cases C-338/11 to C-347/11, *Santander Asset Management SGIIC and Others* [2012] EU: C:2012:286, paras. 59 and 60.

[42] Case C-221/12, *Belgacom NV v. Integan, Inter-Media, WVEM, PBE* [2013] EU:C:2013:736, para. 40.

[43] Case C-662/13, *Surgicare — Unidades de Saúde SA v. Fazenda Pública* [2015] EU:C:2015:89; Case C-312/93, *Peterbroeck* [1995] ECR I-04599, para. 14; Case C-2/08, *Fallimento Olimpiclub*, [2009] ECR I-07501, para. 27.

[44] See, in that sense, Joined Cases C-270/97 and C-271/97, *Deutsche Post AG and Elisabeth Sievers, Brunhilde Schrage* [2000] ECR I-933, para. 50.

[45] In that sense, Case C-362/12, *Test Claimants in the Franked Investment Income Group Litigation* [2013] EU:C:2013:834.

[46] Chalmers et al. (2010), p. 412.

[47] Case T-549/08, *Luxembourg v. Commission* [2010] ECR II-2477, para. 71; Case T-347/03, *Branco v. Commission* [2005] ECR II-255, para. 102; Case T-282/02, *Cementbouw Handel & Industrie v. Commission* [2006] ECR II-319, para. 77.

- These assurances must give rise to a legitimate expectation from the person concerned;
- The assurances given must comply with the applicable rules.

In the current practice, as Eleanor Sharpston already stated in 1990, "very few cases succeed on the legitimate expectations argument".[48] This limitation is due to the constant evolution of EU law. A broad interpretation of legitimate expectations would affect their effectiveness.[49] This principle is only used as extreme protection for affected operators facing legal obligations they couldn't objectively expect and which would be inequitable or financially unreliable.

In the *Europäisch-Iranische Handelsbank* Case concerning restrictive measures taken against Iran with the aim of preventing nuclear proliferation, the injured bank pleaded that the Council breached the principle of protection of legitimate expectations by failing to take into account the authorisations of the Bundesbank. However, the European courts held that the transactions were not authorised in accordance with the provisions of Regulation No. 423/2007. "If a prudent and alert economic operator could have foreseen the adoption of an EU measure likely to affect his interests, he cannot plead that principle if the measure is adopted", said the Court.[50] A national measure can thus not constitute a legitimate expectation toward EU obligations.

In that sense, in Cases relating to EU funds, the Court held that the principle of the protection of legitimate expectations does not apply if the beneficiary of a subsidy has not complied with one of the conditions to which the grant of the subsidy was subject.[51]

Moreover, Member States must also observe the principles of legal certainty and the protection of legitimate expectations in the exercise of the powers conferred on them under EU law.[52] In the Case *Salomie and Oltean*, the Court protected the individual rights against the Romanian tax authority imposing an unclear national provision for the implementation of the value added tax (VAT) to sales of immov-

[48] Sharpston (1990), p. 103.

[49] In that sense, see Cases C-288/09 and C-289/09, *British Sky Broadcasting Group plc, Pace plc v. The Commissioners for Her Majesty's Revenue & Customs* [2011] ECR I-2851, paras. 104–112.

[50] Case C-585/13, *Europäisch-Iranische Handelsbank AG v. Council* [2015] EU:C:2015:145, para. 95; Case C-194/09, *Alcoa Trasformazioni v. Commission* [2011] ECR I-6311, para. 71. In that sense: Case C-144/14, *Cabinet Medical Veterinar Dr. Tomoiagă Andrei* [2015] EU:C:2015:452, paras. 39–42.

[51] Case C-599/13, *Somalische Vereniging Amsterdam en Omgeving (Somvao) v. Staatssecretaris van Veiligheid en Justitie* [2014] EU:C:2014:2462, para. 52; Case 385/06, *Vereniging Nationaal Overlegorgaan Sociale Werkvoorziening and Others* [2008] ECR I-1561, para. 56.

[52] Case C-183/14, *Radu Florin Salomie, Nicolae Vasile Oltean v. Direcţia Generală a Finanţelor Publice Cluj* [2015] EU:C:2015:454, para. 29; Cases C-487/01 and C-7/02, *Gemeente Leusden and Holin Groep* [2004] ECR I-5337, para. 57; Case C-376/02, *Goed Wonen*, [2005] ECR I-3460, para. 32; Cases C-181/04 to C-183/04, *Elmeka NE* [2006] ECR I-8186, para. 31.

able property.[53] It concluded that the authority's practice shall not "give rise, in the mind of a prudent and well-informed trader, to a reasonable expectation that that tax would not be levied on such transactions".[54] The national judge remains, however, free to appreciate the clarity of the provision and the "mind" of the trader.

Therefore, any infringement of EU law by a Member State, even in the area of national competence, renders that Member State liable. The individuals have the right to obtain compensation for the damage suffered as a result of that infringement.[55] Consequently, damages from legal risk must be repaired.

2.2 *Identification of EU Legal Risks*

According to the previous statements, the following legal risks may be identified:

- The creation of new obligations in EU law;
- The change of the existing EU law;
- An unclear EU legislation;
- A failure to fulfil EU obligations;
- A claim based on EU law.

EU experts may join the public opinion considering that EU law is complex. This complexity arises from the regular *creation of new obligations* in a large legal corpus translated into 24 languages and concerning 28 Member States. The pace of legal and regulatory change at national as well as EU level increases the legal uncertainty. Each year, EU law creates a plethora of new obligations: over 1500 Regulations, 132 Directives and 1600 Decisions in 2014.[56] Public authorities and private entities are increasingly looking for effective monitoring of EU law. Legal risks for public authorities, individuals and private companies result from massive regulation.

New EU obligations may be applied differently with time. They usually refer to forthcoming situations, but may exceptionally be retroactive. According to the *principle of the non-retroactivity* of legal acts, a new EU law applies from the entry into force of the act introducing it,[57] and does not apply to legal situations that have arisen and become definitive under the old law which are covered by the

[53] Case C-183/14, *Radu Florin Salomie, Nicolae Vasile Oltean v. Direcţia Generală a Finanţelor Publice Cluj* [2015] EU:C:2015:454, para. 29.

[54] The same was concluded in the Case C-144/14, *Cabinet Medical Veterinar Dr. Tomoiagă Andrei* [2015] EU:C:2015:452. See O'Neill (2011), p. 1960, pt. 2.163.

[55] Case C-98/14, *Berlington Hungary Tanácsadó és Szolgáltató kft e. a. v. Hungary* [2015] EU: C:2015:386, paras. 111–115.

[56] According EUR-Lex database.

[57] Cases C-401/13 and C-432/13, *Vasiliki and Attila Balazs v. Casa Judeţeană de Pensii Cluj* [2015] EU:C:2015:26.

principle of acquired rights.[58] There can be, however, an exception only if special provisions accompany the new rule. In the *Moravia Gas Storage* Case,[59] the Court recalled that "procedural rules are generally taken to apply from the date on which they enter into force".[60] Nevertheless, "substantive rules, which are usually interpreted as applying to situations existing before their entry into force only in so far as it clearly follows from their terms, their objectives or their general scheme that such an effect must be given to them".[61] The companies shall be well informed to understand their EU obligations. In the *Moravia* Case, the General Court first annulled the Decision of the European Commission providing exemption of an underground gas storage facility in the Czech Republic from the internal market rules[62] and, then, the CJEU set aside the Judgment and referred it back to the General Court.

Most of EU law adopted each year are *amendments of the existing legislation*. Therefore, the concerned bodies must follow up the EU lawmaking process closely to anticipate new obligations arising out from these evolutions. The CJEU case law, however, protects shortterm amendments which create legal risks. In the famous *Strack* Case,[63] the Court stated that the "reliance on the principle of proportionality cannot allow the time-limits laid down by Regulation No 1049/2001 [on public access to EU documents] to be changed without creating a situation of legal uncertainty".[64] In that Case, the General Court first annulled a Decision of the European Commission for access to various EU documents before the Court dismissed all pleas of the plaintiff.

The principles of legal certainty and legitimate expectations demand that EU law shall be clear and foreseeable, consistent as well as coherent, which "requires the limitation of the possibilities of amendment of legal norms, the stability of rules imposed by these".[65] As we observed previously, in the practice, EU law—like any law—may contain *unclear provisions* leading to uncertainty. The respective legal liabilities shall therefore be distinguished.

In case of irregularities relating to the protection of EU's financial interests, the Court pointed out that the Member States must observe the general obligation of diligence when verifying the legality of payments, which implies rectifying irregularities promptly. In the context of tax enforcement order for the recovery of wine

[58] Case C-334/07 P, *European Commission v. Freistaat Sachsen* [2008] ECR I-9465; Case C-168/09, *Flos SpA v. Semeraro Casa e Famiglia SpA* [2011] ECR I-181.

[59] Case C-596/13, *European Commission v. Moravia Gas Storage a. s.* [2015] EU:C:2015:203, paras. 32 and 33.

[60] Case C-610/10, *Commission v. Spain*, [2012] EU:C:2012:781, para. 45.

[61] Cases 212/80 to 217/80, *Meridionale Industria Salumi and Others* [1981] ECR 2735, para. 9; Case C-201/04, *Molenbergnatie* [2006] ECR I-02049 para. 31; Case C-334/07, *Commission v. Freistaat Sachsen* [2008] ECR I-9465, para. 44.

[62] Case T-465/11, *Globula v. Commission* [2013] EU:T:2013:406.

[63] Related in the media: Beck (2011).

[64] Case C-127/13, *Guido Strack v. European Commission* [2014] EU:C:2014:2250, para. 29.

[65] Predescu and Safta (2009).

export refunds wrongly received by a company, the Court judged unlawful the inertia encouraged by the national administration in bringing proceedings in respect of 'irregularities' exposing "operators, firstly, to a long period of legal uncertainty and, secondly, to the risk of no longer being in a position to prove at the end of such a period that the transactions in question were lawful".[66] The legal risk comes here from the unclear application of EU law by national authorities, creating discrimination between the operators.

In another Case concerning the Directive 2002/46/EC on food supplements, the Court stated that the economic operators are exposed to the risks of changing circumstances[67] and may be affected by new EU obligations influencing the market. An economic operator cannot "claim an acquired right or even a legitimate expectation that an existing situation which is capable of being altered by measure taken by the Community institutions within the limits of their discretion will be maintained".[68]

The *intermediate conclusion* is that any person may be affected by a legal risk in EU law as long as his legal obligations are objectively unclear and unexpected. Managing this legal risk means providing legal protection against any legal threat by insuring, on the one hand, a stable legal implementation of EU law, and on the other hand, enough flexibility in the legal interpretation of EU law to appreciate the legal risk. The main roles belong, firstly, to European lawmakers to produce clear and predictable obligations and, secondly, to national and European judges to allocate the respective liabilities.

3 From Impact Assessment to Allocation of Liabilities in EU Law

Social disparities, financial crisis, digital economy, environmental pollution, human diseases, humanitarian and military conflicts... those factual risks caused by social modernity and described in Beck's work on *risk society* (*Risikogesellschaft*, 1984) influence the law decision-making. All the social disasters have in common that they have to be caused by human actions and affect the global world. According to the subsidiarity principle, in so far as the objectives cannot be sufficiently achieved by the Member States, the European Union is pressed to elaborate appropriate answers to this *globalisation of social disasters*.

Legal risk management may become a key scientific and practical approach for the European Union to assess the impact of its current as well as potential legislation. As part of the Better Regulation policy, the European Commission itself stated

[66] Case C-341/13, *Cruz & Companhia Lda v. IFAP* [2014] EU:C:2014:2230, para. 62.

[67] Case C-280/93 *Germany v. Council* [1994] ECR I-4973, para. 79, and *Swedish Match*, para. 73.

[68] Joined Cases C-154/04 and C-155/04, *Alliance for Natural Health e. a. v. Secretary of State for Health e. a.* [2005] ECR I-06451, para. 128.

that "decision-makers are often faced with the need to reduce or eliminate the risk of adverse effects to the environment or to health. When the problem you are dealing with is affected by risk, i.e. you can attach probabilities to different possible outcomes, the IA will have to include a risk assessment as a tool to determine the best policy to deal with this".[69]

Looking at EU law through the perspective of legal risk management may become a practical approach of the EU lawmaking process and it may be useful for the European institutions. Legal risk management may be conceived through two approaches. The first one relates to risk regulation through public policy. European legal risks may be solved by the law itself and the impact of the future shall be anticipated within the pre-legislative process; the law itself may create legal risks (A). The second one aims to distinguish the respective liabilities in case of legal risk causing an infringement of EU law (B).

3.1 Impact Assessment as Public Legal Risk Management

The European Commission considers that "judging what an acceptable level of risk is an eminently political responsibility".[70] According to the principles of precaution, legal certainty and legitimate expectations, the EU decisionmakers shall therefore take proportionate, precise, expectable, non-discriminatory, consistent, financially beneficial, and reviewable measures. Since the 2000s, this is the purpose of the Better Regulation policy.[71]

The Impact Assessments (IAs) are already an essential tool to motivate EU policy decisions.[72] IA fix additional rules to the pre-legislative process (planning rules, coordination, consultation, reporting and dissemination of results). In order to evaluate a potential EU policy before any legal act is adopted, the purpose of the IA is, *first*, to identify the problem and to define appropriate political objectives as well as, *second*, to analyse their economic, social and environmental impacts on the society. In other words, the European Commission applies a risk analysis in the lawmaking process.[73] Since 2010, many measures have been led by the Secretariat General to improve the policy evaluation: Smart Regulation, Cost/Benefit Analysis, Refit, Roadmaps, Regulatory Scrutiny Board (RSB) and the Cumulated Cost

[69] European Commission, *Impact Assessment Guideline*, 2009.

[70] Communication on the Precautionary Principle, COM(2000)1 final, pp. 3 and 15.

[71] European Commission, Better Regulation for Better Results – An EU Agenda, 19 May 2015, COM(2015)215 final. See the Better Regulation website: http://ec.europa.eu/smart-regulation/index_en.htm.

[72] IA Guidelines, 15 January 2009, SEC(2009) 92, updating the previous versions of 2005 and 2006.

[73] Smismans (2005), pp. 6–26.

Assessment.[74] The recent Better Regulation Guidelines encompass all these policies into a common "toolbox".[75]

The Cost/Benefit Analysis of EU action has introduced economic, social and environmental criteria in the EU lawmaking process which were essentially motivated by political necessity as well as legal proportionality. The main EU goal is to minimise the financial or administrative burden at all levels of government, economic operators and ultimately the citizens. To achieve this, efforts have been focused on broad consultations of public and private entities (stakeholders). Gradually, European institutions and Member States have used impact assessment methods to improve the quality of EU legislation.

In 2012, as part of the Smart Regulation agenda, the European Commission proposed a new methodology to improve risk regulation in EU law with the "Regulatory Fitness and Performance Programme" (REFIT).[76] The objective is to commit "to a simple, clear and predictable regulatory framework for business workers and citizens".[77] It includes the previous policy of reducing regulatory burdens measuring the costs of EU legislation in order to cut burdens on businesses.[78]

Lower costs and a minimum of administrative burdens have become the leitmotiv of the European Commission over the past 15 years. In assessing the efficiency and the effectiveness of EU law, the Commission aims to identify the problems faced by stakeholders. These studies are mostly based on national reports and consultations. Even if the number of consultations is usually very high,[79] they cannot be exhaustive and many concrete situations aren't assessed.[80] National exhaustive impact assessments are still missing to cover the economic, social and environmental risks of EU legislation in the Member States. The amount of EU legislations that shall be enforced in 28 Member States renders any exhaustive study of the potential impacts impossible. Moreover, of the over 1500 Regulations

---

[74] Smismans et al. (2015), p. 11; Smismans (2005), pp. 6–26.

[75] Commission staff working document, *Better Regulation Guidelines*, 19 May 2015, COM(2015) 111 final.

[76] European Commission, *Communication on EU Regulatory Fitness*, COM(2012) 746 final; *Communication on Regulatory Fitness and Performance (REFIT): Results and Next Steps*, COM(2013) 685 final; *Communication on Regulatory Fitness and Performance Programme (REFIT): State of Play and Outlook*, 18 June 2014, COM(2014) 368 final; *Decision of the European Commission Establishing the REFIT Platform*, 19 May 2015, C(2015) 3261 final.

[77] Idem, COM(2014) 368 final, p. 2.

[78] European Commission, *Action Programme for Reducing Administrative Burdens in the EU – Final Report*, 12 December 2012, SWD(2012) 423 final.

[79] For example, 670 stakeholders have been consulted for the proposal for a Directive amending Directives 2008/98/EC on waste, 94/62/EC on packaging and packaging waste, 1999/31/EC on the landfill of waste, 2000/53/EC on end-of-life vehicles, 2006/66/EC on batteries and accumulators and waste batteries and accumulators, and 2012/19/EU on waste electrical and electronic equipment. See Commission staff working document impact assessment accompanying the document Proposal of the Directive, 2 July 2014, SWD(2014) 207 final.

[80] In that sense, Smismans et al. (2015), p. 13.

and 132 Directives adopted in 2014, only 59 impact assessments have been produced.[81,82] Most of EU law, thus, enters into force without impact assessment.

The European Court of Auditors played down the importance attached to the impact assessments. Its 2010 reports stated that "*the Commission did not use impact assessments to decide to move closer or further away with proposal [for the simple reason that] the decision to launch an initiative is generally taken before the impact assessment report is completed*". It supports scientific critics from sociologists, to political scientists and lawyers pointing out the unpredictability of all future risks. In other words, prospective studies cannot be an efficient tool for social sciences because the latter focus on existing subjects. The impact assessment allows the EU Commission to justify its intervention on the basis of sufficiently flexible criteria. The Court of Auditors said this statement is even more obvious because the financial impact can hardly be calculated accurately due to national disparities.

We think that major improvements could be achieved by:

- Introducing the analysis of legal risks in the IA;
- Systematising national Impact Assessments of EU policy in each legal system;
- Formalising the EU pre-legislative procedure.[83]

Legal risk management may thus become an important tool to improve the quality of EU legislation, but still not an exhaustive one. For the advocates of risk management, "risk is not the same as catastrophe, but the anticipation of the future catastrophe in the presence".[84] In that sense, legal risk management anticipates social threats through precaution and prevention. The legal approach shall focus on respective legal responsibilities from the (EU) lawmaking process to the (EU) law compliance.

3.2 *Allocation of Liabilities in Legal Risk Management*

The few studies on legal risk management concern liabilities in corporate law and financial institutions, mostly led by management schools.[85] They want to reorganise companies around a *risk management strategy*. The recent financial crisis illustrates the occurrence of risks that were not foreseen. Companies have been deprived of their loans, financial institutions, rating agencies and banks have been blamed.

[81] Final Impact Assessment reports in 2014 available at: http://ec.europa.eu/smart-regulation/impact/ia_carried_out/cia_2014_en.htm.

[82] Only 25 of them have been examined by the Regulatory Scrutiny Board. Since 1st July 2015, the IA Board has been replaced by the Regulatory Scrutiny Board. It provides an independent quality control of the IA.

[83] Raccah (2008), pp. 543–558.

[84] Beck (2009).

[85] Moorhead and Vaughan (2015), p. 36; See Edhec Risk Institute, available at: http://www.edhec-risk.com/; Collard et al. (2011); Collard (2008).

Many international companies developed a risk management strategy including legal compliance: BNP Paribas, Microsoft, Total, Ikea... These wide strategies encompass safety programmes, insurance issues, claims management, contract management and human resources.

Managing legal risk aims to allocate the respective liabilities in case of legal uncertainty between public authorities taking appropriate measures to implement EU law, on the one hand, and companies as well as individuals towards their legal obligations, on the other hand.

As seen in the first part, legal uncertainty may be produced by EU law itself. Environment, agriculture, internal market, competition rules, public contracts, fiscal policy ... most legal fields conciliate the freedom to take risks and the necessity to secure a legal relationship. Ensuring a framework for legal risks may be the main task of current legal risk management. Shall EU law protect individuals and companies from excessive legal risks?[86] Shall EU law protect only vulnerable Parties? Legal risk management may be seen as an exception to freedom and it is strictly accepted if it is legally based and proportionate to its objective.

In case of legal risks leading to judicial conflicts, the Court of Justice of the European Union plays an important role in clarifying the respective liabilities, mostly in references for a preliminary ruling in case of miscellaneous interpretations of EU law at the national level and through the actions resulting in failure to fulfil EU obligations when the European Commission sues due to national infringements. Direct actions for annulment of EU measures may be engaged against any EU institution before the European courts on the basis of the principle of legal certainty,[87] but most of them are dismissed.[88]

Firstly, EU law mostly suffers from *miscellaneous legal interpretation* in the 28 national legal systems. Harmonising the interpretation of EU law is the main competence of the CJEU. On the basis of Article 267 TFEU, the reference for a preliminary ruling is the main tool for national judicial institutions to overcome any conflict of interpretation of EU law and to clarify legal uncertainty creating legal risks.[89]

In case of conflict creating a risk for a concerned Party, EU law provides the fundamental right to effective judicial protection. On the basis of the first paragraph of Article 47 of the Charter, "everyone whose rights and freedoms guaranteed by EU law are violated has the right to an effective remedy before a tribunal". The effective judicial protection implies reasonable time limits for the duration of proceedings. The Court stated that the time limits for proceedings must not make

[86] Example: Directive 2014/104/EU of 26 November 2014 on certain rules governing actions for damages under National Law for infringements of the Competition Law provisions of the MS and of the EU, OJ L 349, 5.12.2014, pp. 1–19.

[87] Case C-447/13, *Riccardo Nencini v. EP* [2014] EU:C:2014:2372.

[88] Case C-585/13, *Europäisch-Iranische Handelsbank AG v. Council* [2015] EU:C:2015:145; Case T-549/08, *Luxembourg v. European Commission* [2010] ECR II-02477.

[89] Case C-279/13, *C More Entertainment AB v. Linus Sandberg* [2015] EU:C:2015:199 relating to legal uncertainty regarding the nature and the level of protection of copyrights.

it impossible or excessively difficult to exercise the rights conferred by the EU legal order in practice.[90]

In fiscal policy, several Cases for preliminary ruling recently stated that an unclear tax shall not apply to any prudent and well-informed individual or professional having a reasonable expectation that it would not apply to his transactions.[91] An inappropriate implementation of EU law may cause a risk not only to individuals, but also to public authorities, which raise taxes.

Public procurement is also subject to the protection of tenderers against arbitrary behaviour on the part of the contracting authority.[92] With regard to the principle of non-discrimination, the interested Parties shall be informed in a reasonable time frame that a contract is signed so they can engage an action to protect their rights. In Italy, *Fastweb* complained that *Telecom Italia* got a public contract for the supply of electronic communications services, under a negotiated procedure without prior publication of a contract notice.[93] In order to limit "the legal uncertainty that may be engendered by the ineffectiveness of the contract", the Court of Justice referred to Directive 89/665/EEC on review procedures to the award of public contracts to remind about the right to bring pre-contractual proceedings for interim relief and the right to obtain annulment of an unlawful contract. Moreover, affected operators may bring an action for damages before the national jurisdictions.

In a similar Case in Belgium, *Belgacom* denounced public contracts signed without call of tenders between several municipalities and the company *Telenet* for television broadcasting service activities.[94] Two legal and financial risks have been underlined: on the one hand, heavy sanctions to which the municipalities would be exposed in case of infringement and, on the other hand, the "risk of depreciation of an economic activity carried on by a public entity under a pre-existing contractual framework which turns out to be unsuitable due to technical and commercial developments". Even if this Decision may have a negative impact on the existing contracts, "grounds of an economic nature, such as the wish to avoid the depreciation of an economic activity, are not overriding reasons in the public interest". In that sense, the legal and, therefore, economic risks may result from the illegality of the procedure.

Preliminary rulings before the CJEU are, thus, necessary to clarify the respective liabilities according to EU law obligations and interpret them in a way that would not cause an unexpected prejudice to the concerned Parties.

---

[90] Case C-603/10, *Pelati* [2012] EU:C:2012:639.

[91] Case C-183/14, *Radu Florin Salomie, Nicolae Vasile Oltean v. Direcţia Generală a Finanţelor Publice Cluj* [2015] EU:C:2015:454; Case C-144/14, *Cabinet Medical Veterinar Dr. Tomoiagă Andrei* [2015] EU:C:2015:452; Case C-76/14, *Mihai Manea v. Instituţia Prefectului judeţul Braşov* [2015] EU:C:2015:216; Case C-362/12, *Test Claimants in the Franked Investment Income Group Litigation v. Commissioners of Inland Revenue* [2013] EU:C:2013:834.

[92] Case C-212/02, *Commission v. Austria* [2004] EU:C:2004:386.

[93] Case C-19/13, *Ministero dell'Interno v. Fastweb SpA* [2015] EU:C:2014:2194, paras. 57–65.

[94] Case C-221/12, *Belgacom NV v. Integan, Inter-Media, WVEM, PBE* [2013] EU:C:2013:736, paras. 40 and 41.

Secondly, the European Commission is not only the EU lawmaker, but also the guardian of the Treaties. This double task requires the monitoring of the implementation of EU law by Member States.[95] On the basis of Article 258 TFEU, the European Commission may engage an *infringement procedure* if the legal uncertainty is caused by the national measures of implementation.

On the basis of that principle of legal certainty, the Court recently judged that Poland failed to fulfil obligations to transpose Directives relating to public health. The national measures adopted pursuant to EU rules were not sufficiently published "as to enable the persons concerned by such measures to ascertain the scope of their rights and obligations in the particular area governed by EU law".[96] Member States shall thus be responsible for not taking the appropriate measures ensuring the certainty of EU law.

In an opposite case, Portugal claimed that a Directive on access to the groundhandling market at Community airports contained a lacuna, which allowed the Member States to introduce freely a transitional regime.[97] On the basis of Article 288 TFEU, the Court repealed that Directives are to be binding, as to the result to be achieved, upon the Member States to which they are addressed. In the present case, since there was no suggestion from any EU institution, Portugal couldn't rely on any legitimate expectation that the previous system in place would be maintained.

The Member States cannot have legitimate expectations regarding international bilateral agreements if they don't comply with EU law. In this Case, Germany infringed Article 56 TFEU on the freedom to provide services by interpreting in a discriminatory way an agreement of 1990 between Germany and Poland on the posting of workers from Polish undertakings to carry out works contracts. The German interpretation excluded the possibility for undertakings established in other Member States to conclude works contracts with Polish undertakings for work to be carried out in Germany. The Court stated that "the principle of protection of legitimate expectations cannot [...] be relied on by a Member State in order to preclude an objective finding of a failure on its part to fulfil its obligations".[98]

Consequently, legal risk management requires knowledge, methodology, assessment and social acceptance. The objective is not necessarily to eliminate legal risks, but rather to anticipate their impact on public authorities and private entities.

To conclude, we may sketch a definition of *legal risk* as the prejudicial occurrence arising from an unclear, imprecise or uncertain normative provision imposing obligations to an individual, a company or an authority, which would be inequitable or financially unreliable. The legal risk management done by public authorities and companies consists, therefore, in identifying, assessing and anticipating any potential legal risk before it occurs. Once it occurs, it becomes an infringement that may

---

[95] Smith (2015), pp. 90–100.

[96] Case C-29/14, *European Commission v. Poland* [2015] EU:C:2015:379.

[97] Case C-277/13, *European Commission v. Portugal* [2014] EU:C:2014:2208.

[98] Case C-546/07, *European Commission v. Germany* [2010] ECR I-00439.

be judged by the competent jurisdictions to determine the respective liabilities. Decision makers are thus raising a major issue to ensure the compliance and effectiveness of EU law.

References

Alemanno A (2007) The shaping of the precautionary principle by European courts: from scientific uncertainty to legal certainty. In: Cuocolo L, Luparia L (eds) Valori costituzionali e nuove politiche del diritto. Cahiers Européens, Halley

Alemanno A (2008) Science & EU risk regulation: the role of experts in decision-making and judicial review. In: Vos E (ed) European risk governance – its science, its inclusiveness and its effectiveness, Connex Report, Series No. 6

Alemanno A (2011) Governing disasters: the challenges of emergency risk regulation. Edward Elgar Publishing Ltd

Alemanno A (2012) Public perception of risks under WTO law: a normative perspective. In: van Calster G, Prévost D (eds) Research handbook on environment, health and the WTO. Edward Elgar, UK

Alemanno A (2014) What role for a chief scientist in the European Union system of scientific advice? Eur J Risk Regul 3:1–17

Alemanno A (2016) EU risk regulation: towards a European government of health, safety and environmental risks, modern studies in European Law. Hart Publishing

Alemanno A, Spina A (2014) Nudging legally – on the checks and balances of behavioural regulation. Int J Const Law 12(2):1–27

Alemanno A, Den Butter F, Nijsen A (2014) Better business regulation in a risk society. Springer Verlag, New York

Anderson K, Black J (2013) Legal risks and risks for lawyers. Herbert Smith Freehills and LSE Regulatory Reform Forum

Baranoff E (2003) Risk management and insurance, 8th edn. Wiley

Barbier H (2011) La liberté de prendre des risques, thèse, PU Aix-Marseille

Beck U (1986) Risikogesellschaft. Auf dem Weg in eine andere Moderne, Suhrkamp

Beck U (1988) Gegengifte. Die organisierte Unverantwortlichkeit, Suhrkamp

Beck U (1991a) Risk society: towards a new modernity. SAGE Publications, pp 155–182, Chapter 7 on "Science Beyond Trust and Enlightenment?"

Beck U (1991b) Risk society: towards a new modernity. SAGE Publications

Beck U (1991c) Politik in der Risikogesellschaft: Essays und Analysen, Suhrkamp

Beck U (1995a) Ecological politics in an age of risk. Blackwell Publishers

Beck U (1995b) Ecological enlightenment, essays on the politics of the risk society. Atlantic Highlands, 1995

Beck U (1999) World risk society. Blackwell Publishers

Beck U (2009) Critical theory of world risk society: a cosmopolitan vision. Blackwell Publishing, Constellations vol 16, no 1

Beck S (2011) Ein Beamter kämpft gegen Brüssel. Süddeutsche Zeitung (online)

Chalmers D et al (2010) European Union law. Cambridge University Press

Collard Ch (2008) Le risque juridique existe-t-il? Contribution à la définition du risque juridique. Cahiers de droit de l'entreprise 24–29

Collard Ch et al (2011) Risque juridique et Conformité, Lamy Conformité

Craig P, de Burca G (2011) EU law, 5th edn. Oxford University Press

Dekeuwer-Defossez F (2015) Chronique Droit et Risque. Les Petites Affiches 5–13

Dowd K (2002) Beyond value at risk, the new science of risk management. John Wiley & Sons, New York

Elliot A (2002) Beck's sociology of risk: a critical assessment. SAGE Publications
Grimaldi M (2006) La promotion de notre système juridique s'organise: la constitution d'une Fondation pour le droit continental. Rec. Dalloz 996
Hopkins EB (2013) Legal risk management for in-house counsel and managers. Trafford Publishing, Singapore
Howard PK (2007–2008) The dynamics of legal risk. Drake Law Rev 56:505; Seminar organised by UNIDROIT on "Legal Risk and Market Efficiency", Rome, 2003; Conference on "Risk Management for Law Firms", 2007, Munich
Hull CfJC (2012) Risk management and financial institutions. Wiley Finance 257–278
Lasserre V (2011) Le risque. Rec. Dalloz 1632
Mahler T (2007) Defining legal risk. Proceedings of the conference "Commercial Contracting for Strategic Advantage - Potentials and Prospects". Turku University of Applied Sciences. Available at SSRN: http://ssrn.com/abstract=1014364
Mccormick R (2008) Legal risk in the financial markets, Round table organised by Herbert Smith on "Legal and Compliance Risk Management: Towards Principles of Best Practices". Oxford University Press, London
Meric J et al (2009) La «Société du Risque»: analyse et critique. Economica 277
Millet F (2001) La notion de risque et ses fonctions en droit privé, LGDJ
Moorhead R, Vaughan S (2015) Legal risk: definition, management and ethics, Executive Report of the UCL Center for Ethics and Law, p 36, available at: http://www.ucl.ac.uk/laws/law-ethics/research/papers/erc-executive-report-legal-risk-definition-management-ethics.pdf
Moury J (2012) Le droit confronté à l'omniprésence du risque. Rec. Dalloz 1020
O'Neill A (2011) EU law for UK lawyers. Hart Publishing
Pfohl HCH (2002) Risiko- und Chancenmanagement in der Supply Chain. Erich Schmidt Verlag GmbH & Co. KG
Predescu I, Safta M (2009) Principiul securităţii juridice, fundament al statului de drept repere jurisprudenţiale. Buletinul Curţii. Constituţionale, nr. 1/2009, pp 1–19
Raccah A (2008) Towards a formalisation of the EU's pre-legislative procedure. RFAP 543–558
Serratosa J (2011) Food safety risk assessment in the E.U. versus U.S., Optimizing Food Systems for Human Health, Healthy Food Summit. Available at: http://www.arboretum.umn.edu/2011healthyfoodssummit.aspx
Sharpston E (1990) European Community law and the doctrine of legitimate expectation: how legitimate, and for whom? N West J Int Law Bus 11(1):87–103
Smismans S (2005) Policy evaluation in the EU: the challenge of linking ex ante and ex post appraisal. EJRR, pp 6–26
Smismans S, Schreffer L, Luchetta G, Simonelli F (2015) A new tool in the box the cumulated cost assessment. EJRR 1:68–78
Smith M (2015) Evaluation and the salience of infringement data. EJRR 1:90–100
Terblanché JR (2012) Legal risk and compliance for banks operating in a common law legal system. J Oper Risk 7(2):67–79
Tracol X (2014) Legal risk management in EU organizations. Eur Public Law 20(4):711–744
Viscuki WK (2000) Risk equity. J Leg Stud XXIX:843–871
Weimer M (2010) The regulatory challenge of animal cloning for food – the risks of risk regulation in the European Union. EJRR 1:31–39
Whittaker AM (2003) Lawyers as risk managers. Butterworths J Int Bank Financ Law 5–7
Wyss L (2005) Juristisches Risk Management und Hedging als Mittel zur Risikokontrolle. Stämpfli Verlag AG

Legal Risks in the Relation Between National Constitutional Law and EU Law

Darinka Piqani

Contents

Abstract Already at the beginning of the existence of the EU Communities, the ECJ introduced direct effect and primacy of EU law as two fundamental principles of the EU legal order. These principles were based on a need for uniform and effective application of EU law. This development had a great impact on the organization of national constitutional orders, among other things, on the role of ordinary courts in the judicial architecture and the position of national constitutional courts. This chapter investigates potential legal risks for the national and EU legal orders and concludes that although not materialized, legal risks have shaped the relation between EU law and national law.

D. Piqani (✉)
Leiden University, Leiden, The Netherlands
e-mail: d.piqani@law.leidenuniv.nl

E. Miščenić, A. Raccah (eds.), *Legal Risks in EU Law*,
DOI 10.1007/978-3-319-28596-2_2

1 Introduction

This chapter provides a general overview of legal risks in the context of the relation between Constitutional Law and the European Union (EU) legal order. Often, constitutional courts in the Member States put forward constitutional limits to the full application of EU law. These limitations or reservations may constitute legal risks in that they may ultimately undermine the basic claim of the EU legal order, namely the necessity for uniform and effective application of EU law. Already at the beginning of the existence of the EU Communities, the Court of Justice of the EU (CJEU/ECJ) introduced direct effect and primacy of EU law as two fundamental principles of the EU legal order. Direct effect and primacy are based on the autonomy of the EU legal order and on a need for uniform and effective application of EU law. In order not to jeopardize the achievement of the objectives of the Union (or EU Communities at the time), EU law has to be applied in a uniform manner in all Member States. This implies that there is no space for Member States' claims questioning the application of EU law and ultimately the authority of the EU legal order.

Following these claims responses from national legal orders emerged. Whereas ordinary courts generally accepted the new role designed for them by the ECJ as part of the empowerment vis-à-vis other national institutions,[1] constitutional courts in certain Member States showed scepticism in accepting an unconditional version of primacy of EU law over national (constitutional) law. Some of these courts felt that they had to guard their standard of protection of fundamental rights as guaranteed in the Constitution, others claimed that they would declare EU law inapplicable in case it was adopted by EU institutions in excess of their powers. Thus, ECJ's claim of uniform and effective application of EU law was challenged by constitutional courts on grounds of adequate protection of fundamental rights, exercise of powers in accordance with the principle of conferral or protection of constitutional identity.

These two categories of claims do in fact reflect two categories of legal risks. Firstly, the EU claim for uniform and effective application of EU law bears the inherent legal risk of touching upon the core characteristics of statehood in the Member States and strongly impacting the national constitutional framework. Similarly, national constitutional claims bear the legal risk of affecting fundamental principles on the basis of which the Union functions such as uniform and effective application of EU law. The following parts of this chapter will give an overview of these risks. Limited space and the abundance of existing literature and case law do not allow for an in-depth analysis. The chapter will conclude by emphasizing that both actors, namely the ECJ and constitutional courts, have come up with solutions that so far have managed to reconcile their initial diverging positions and more generally have shaped the relation between the two legal orders.

---

[1] See for an overview on reactions from national courts Claes (2006).

2 The EU Legal Order: A New Legal Order in International Law

2.1 Setting the Scene: Direct Effect and Primacy of EU Law

According to the ECJ, "the founding treaties of the EU, unlike ordinary international treaties, established a new legal order, possessing its own institutions, for the benefit of which the Member States thereof have limited their sovereign rights, in ever wider fields, and the subjects of which comprise not only those states but also their nationals".[2] The EU legal order, referred to by the ECJ as the new legal order, is characterized by its autonomy, direct effect and primacy over the laws of the Member States.[3]

EU law stems from the Treaties and as a result it is independent although integrated into the national legal orders. The EU legal order is not isolated from international law as, for instance, fundamental rights guaranteed by the European Convention of Human Rights constitute general principles of EU law.[4] The autonomy of the EU legal order *vis-à-vis* national and international law implies the obligation to interpret EU law in the context of the constitutional principles and objectives of the EU.[5] For instance, in the *Kadi I* case the ECJ ruled that there is a constitutional obligation that EU acts, including acts which reflect international obligations, respect fundamental rights and the violation of these rights is not acceptable in the Union.[6] However, this respect will be guaranteed by the same court which has the power to review EU law for conformity with fundamental rights "in the framework of the complete system of legal remedies established by the Treaty".[7] Thus, the validity of EU law has to be assessed only by the ECJ and only by reference to the EU constitutional framework. The EU judicial system, based on cooperation between national courts and the ECJ, strives to "secure uniform interpretation of EU law [. . .] thereby serving to ensure its consistency, its full effect and its autonomy as well as, ultimately, the particular nature of the law established by the Treaties".[8]

The other two characteristics of the EU legal order are direct effect and primacy over the laws of the Member States. According to the Court, the EEC Treaty was more than an agreement that brings about obligations to States as contracting parties, it also gives rights to nationals of the EU Community. This was so,

---

[2] Opinion 2/13 [2014] para. 157.

[3] Opinion 2/13, para. 166.

[4] Article 6(3) TEU.

[5] Opinion 2/13, para. 170.

[6] Case C-402/05, *Kadi Yassin Abdullah Kadi and Al Barakaat International Foundation v. Council of the European Union and Commission of the European Communities* [2008] ECR I-06351, para. 284.

[7] Ibid., para. 285.

[8] Opinion 2/13, para. 176.

according to the Court, because the preamble of the Treaty refers not only to the governments of the Member States, but also to the peoples of Europe. Under the Treaty the peoples of Europe are given a say through the European Parliament, and the Economic and Social Committee. The preliminary reference procedure would be meaningless if it could not be invoked by individuals before courts at a national level.[9]

The necessary corollary element to direct effect in the EU legal order is the primacy of EU law, namely the ability of EU law norms to take precedence over conflicting norms of national law. The capacity of legal norms to produce direct effect that is translated into the ability of individuals to invoke EU law before national courts would be rendered meaningless in case national courts, after such an invocation, were unable to give precedence to EU law in a conflict between the latter and national provisions. In *Costa v ENEL* by using a 'functionalist argument' the Court argued that if EU law were to be really effective and applied without discrimination, it had to be applied in a uniform and equal manner all over the Union (Community at the time), notwithstanding national law.[10]

Van Gend en Loos and *Costa v ENEL* are of seminal importance for the EU legal order because they established two basic principles for the functioning of the Union. These two judgments represent the beginning of the constitutionalization of the EU and its legal order. They put forward two characteristics or principles of the EU legal order, namely direct effect and primacy of EU law, which constitute the backbone of the everyday and effective application of EU law in the Member States. The EU legal order was characterized by the ECJ as a new legal order in International Law, in a quest to distinguish it from international law and its modes of application, which are based on national constitutional law.

2.2 *Reinforcing the Claims: Simmenthal and Further*

Whereas in *Van Gend en Loos* and *Costa v ENEL*, the ECJ introduced direct effect and primacy, it was in later cases that these two constitutional principles of the EU legal order were further developed by the same Court. In *Simmenthal*, the ECJ endowed national courts of the Member States with the obligation to give full effect to EU law even if that would mean that conflicting provisions of national law would have to be set aside. According to the Court in *Simmenthal*, EU law provisions take precedence over national law even if the former predates national law.[11] Thus, a court outside national jurisdiction such as the ECJ authorizes national courts to set aside or to not apply provisions of national law if they conflict with EU law. The

[9] Case 26/62, *Van Gend en Loos* [1963] ECR 00001.

[10] Case 6/64, *Costa v ENEL* [1964] ECR 585 and for a classic see also Stein (1964–1965), pp. 491–518.

[11] Case C-106/77, *Amministrazione delle Finanze dello Stato v Simmenthal SpA* [1978] ECR 629. For an extensive analysis on these issues see Claes (2006).

classic rule of *lex posteriori derogat legi priori* is rendered ineffective. New remedies are created for national courts in order to ensure the application of EU law. National courts are authorized by the ECJ to set aside conflicting provisions of national law on their own motion, without waiting for repeal by parliaments or constitutional courts. Indeed, the message for other institutions is that national parliaments should refrain from adopting national law that conflicts with EU law. Moreover, they have the duty to remedy the inconsistency between the two legal orders through amendment or repeal of conflicting legislation.

By going even further, the ECJ extended the *Simmenthal* mandate to administrative authorities. It was initially in the *Costanzo* case that the Court elaborated the duty of administrative authorities to give full effect to provisions of Community law, and if necessary to disapply any contrary national provision. According to the ECJ, all administrative bodies, including decentralized authorities are under the *Simmenthal* obligation.[12]

Apart from extending the obligation to ensure compatibility between national law and EU law to all state institutions in their daily application of EU law, the ECJ opted for an unconditional primacy of EU law over national law. This meant that even in an event of a conflict between a provision of the national constitution and a provision of EU law, the latter would prevail. To rule differently would mean to put into question the effectiveness of the EU legal order. According to the Court in *Internationale Handelsgesellschaft*, "The validity of a Community measure or its effect within a Member State cannot be affected by allegations that it runs counter to either fundamental rights as formulated by the constitution of that State or the principles of a national constitutional structure".[13] The ECJ has reinstated its position on unconditional primacy of EU law over provisions of constitutional law, more recently in the *Melloni* case.[14]

3 Legal Risks Emanating from the EU Legal Order and Directed to National Constitutional Law

3.1 Legal Risks to the Constitutional Fabric of Member States

Since *Van Gend en Loos*, EU law pierces the veil of national law in a direct and supreme manner. Furthermore, national courts are mandated by the ECJ to directly

[12] Case C-103/88, *Fratelli Costanzo SpA v Comune di Milano* [1989] ECR I-1839 and as a further example Case C-224/97, *Erich Ciola v Land Vorarlberg* [1999] ECR I-2517.

[13] Case C-11/70, *Internationale Handelsgesellschaft v Einfuhr- und Vorratsstelle Getreide* [1970] ECR-1125.

[14] Case C-399/11, *Stefano Melloni v Ministero Fiscal* [2013] ECR nyr. See also Case C-409/06, *Winner Wetten* [2010] ECR I-08015; Case C-416/10, *Križan and Others* [2013] published in electronic reports of cases.

apply EU law and if necessary set aside conflicting national law, although they may not be empowered under national law to ignore national legislation. There are at least two features that make *Van Gend en Loos* a ground-breaking judgment that allegedly contains legal risks for the very constitutional foundations of Member States.

Firstly, whereas it was not unheard of that provisions of international treaties may be directly applicable (if certain conditions are fulfilled), the main novelty of *Van Gend en Loos* concerns the issue of who decides whether specific provisions of EU Treaties have direct effect.[15] In *Van Gend en Loos* the ECJ ruled that it would be that Court and not the courts in Member States to interpret EU law and decide whether existing EU law provisions had direct effect. This is understandable in the light of arguments such as effectiveness and uniform application of EU law. At the time, this did not go without objection from the Belgian and Dutch government who intervened in the *Van Gend en Loos* case: They opposed ECJ's jurisdiction on this matter arguing that the reference concerned the application of the Treaty "in the context of the constitutional law of the Netherlands".[16] Moreover, according to the same governments, the ECJ had no jurisdiction to decide whether the EEC Treaty provisions prevailed over national law: This issue falls "within the exclusive jurisdiction of the national courts...".[17] There is a clear difference in the views of Member States' governments and the ECJ regarding who can decide what, which in the end is a matter of conflicting authorities. The centralizing claim of the ECJ stood in stark contrast with the decentralizing claim of the intervening governments, and more importantly, with their view on the tasks of national courts according to the national constitution.

Secondly, with *Van Gend en Loos*, national courts were "drafted [...] into the immediate service of the Community".[18] According to Halberstam, this is different from international law in which "the corporate structure of the state remains intact".[19] Whereas under classic constitutional law, national courts have the obligation to apply the law adopted by the legislature, and therefore they must serve only one master, the domestic one, under the new formula as a result of *Van Gend en Loos* and *Costa v ENEL*, national courts, in situations where EU law applies, have the duty to serve another master, that is the EU legal order and the ECJ.[20] This "service" can take the form of asking a question for a preliminary ruling to the ECJ on the direct effect of existing EU law provisions, or in case of conflict, setting aside conflicting national law. Most importantly, this duty, according to *Van Gend en*

[15] De Witte (2011), p. 327.

[16] Case 26/62, Van Gend en Loos [1963] ECR 00001.

[17] Van Gend en Loos, p. 6.

[18] Halberstam (2010), p. 28.

[19] Halberstam (2010), p. 28.

[20] Halberstam (2010), p. 29.

Loos "is not mediated by the national political branches, national laws or even the national constitution".[21]

In this context, Halberstam speaks of "constitutional disaggregation" in that "'superior' Community law is directly infused into the national process of adjudication.[22]" Thus, hard lines between national and EU law blur and legal systems integrate, but at the same time loyalties multiply. In the context of EU law, national courts are mandated by the ECJ to disregard the outcome of the national legislature if that conflicts with EU law. This puts into question the foundations of constitutional law, at least its orthodoxy. In *Simmenthal*, national courts were transformed into courts of judicial review, independently of the domestic institutional choices. The ECJ transgresses the orthodoxy of national legal orders by ruling that judges can set aside, on their own motion, any conflicting national law, without waiting for the repeal of said national act by national parliaments, or for a declaration of unconstitutionality by a constitutional court.[23]

3.2 Legal Risks to National Constitutions: EU Law Trumps Constitutional Law of the Member States

The rulings in *Van Gend en Loos* and *Costa* challenge directly the authority of national constitutions in the Member States. The ideal of national constitutions as the highest law of the land was profoundly shaken in *Internationale Handelsgesellschaft*, where the Court of Justice ruled that the validity of EU law or its effect in a Member State cannot "be affected by allegations that it runs counter to either fundamental rights as formulated by the constitution of that State or the principles of a national constitutional structure."[24] In this specific case, the German referring Court had asked the ECJ about the validity of an EU system of import and export licences that in its view conflicted with fundamental rights protected by the German Constitution. For the ECJ the fact that the conflict was between a provision of EU law and a constitutional provision was not an argument to put into question the validity of the former. The legal risk for national constitutions is present and clear: In the context of EU law and in a case of conflict between national law and EU law, constitutions are not the supreme law and they must yield to EU law.

---

[21] Halberstam (2010), p. 29.

[22] Halberstam (2010), p. 29.

[23] Claes (2006), pp. 97–102.

[24] Case C-11/70, *Internationale Handelsgesellschaft v Einfuhr- und Vorratsstelle Getreide* [1970] ECR I-1125. In this case, the referring German Court asked the Court of Justice about the validity of the system of import and export licenses as established by two regulations, of the Council and the Commission respectively. The referring Court based the allegation on the invalidity of such Community Acts on the grounds that these acts were against some fundamental principles of the German Basic Law.

Unconditional primacy of EU law was confirmed more recently in the *Melloni*[25] judgment in which the ECJ was confronted with the issue of different levels of protection of fundamental rights in the context of the implementation of the Council Framework Decision on the European Arrest Warrant (EAW).[26] The reference for a preliminary ruling by the Spanish Constitutional Court boiled down to the following issue: Can Member States of the EU afford a higher level of protection of fundamental rights (as they are interpreted in national constitutional law) when they act within the scope of EU law? This question was warranted especially because Article 53 of the Charter of Fundamental Rights of the European Union provides that "Nothing in this Charter shall be interpreted as restricting or adversely affecting human rights and fundamental freedoms as recognized, in their respective fields of application, by Union law and international law and by international agreements to which the Union or all the Member States are party, including the European Convention for the Protection of Human Rights and Fundamental Freedoms and by the Member States' constitutions". This provision seems to allow for higher levels of protection of fundamental rights within the field of application of each legal order. In the concrete case of *Melloni* two standards were at stake: According to the Spanish constitutional law, the fair trial guarantee included the right of persons convicted *in absentia* to have their conviction reviewed on their request. The availability of a review of the judgment was a condition for surrender of individuals in situations of serious offences. On the other hand, according to the Council Framework Decision on EAW, the execution of an EAW may be refused in cases of trials *in absentia*, but not in situations such as that of Mr. Melloni in which the accused person was aware of the trial and had appointed his legal counsellors.[27] Thus, this was a clear case of a conflict in the standard of protection of fundamental rights at the EU and national level.

Dealing with the conflict, the ECJ discarded the reading of the national constitutional court with the following steps: Firstly, it reinstated *Internationale Handelsgesellschaft*.[28] Secondly, it accepted in principle the possibility that within the scope of application of EU law, "...national authorities and courts remain free to apply national standards of protection of fundamental rights", but the ECJ conditioned this by saying that "....the level of protection provided for by the Charter, as interpreted by the Court, and the primacy, unity and effectiveness of EU law are not thereby compromised."[29] Hence, the answer of the ECJ was: Yes, there can be a higher level of protection of fundamental rights, but only if that does not affect the level of protection in the Charter (as interpreted by the ECJ), and more importantly

[25] Case C-399/11, *Stefano Melloni v Ministero Fiscal* [2013] ECR nyr. For a comment see De Boer (2013), pp. 1083–1104.

[26] Council Framework Decision 2002/584/JHA on the European Arrest Warrant and the Surrender Procedures between Member States [2002].

[27] Art. 4a(1) of the Council Framework Decision 2002/584/JHA.

[28] Case C-399/11, *Stefano Melloni v Ministero Fiscal* [2013] ECR nyr, para. 59.

[29] Ibid., para. 60.

the primacy, unity and effectiveness of EU law. Thirdly, in the present case, a higher level of protection by the national constitution would not be acceptable because the respective provision of the EAW was very clear in which case surrender could be refused and in which not. The matter was clearly regulated by EU legislation and Member States had no discretion in this regard. Provisions of the Council Framework Decision on EAW in fact harmonized the conditions for the execution of EAW *in absentia* cases and they reflected "...the consensus reached by all the Member States regarding the scope to be given under EU law to the procedural rights enjoyed by persons convicted *in absentia* who are the subject of a European arrest warrant."[30] Thus, it seems that in cases when Member States have no discretion in implementing EU law, there is no possibility for them to apply their higher level of protection of fundamental rights. Apart from a direct challenge to constitutional law, the Melloni saga testifies for the existence of legal risks to the standard of protection of fundamental rights in Member States. After the preliminary ruling by the ECJ, the Spanish Constitutional Court[31] abandoned its extensive protection of fair trial rights in absence and followed the standard of protection offered by the Charter as interpreted by the ECJ.[32] Is effectiveness and uniform application of EU law acting as a force downgrading the standard of fundamental rights protection in the Member States?

3.3 Legal Risks to the Position of Constitutional Courts: The Fall of Giants?

The *Simmenthal* mandate had strong implications for national courts in the domestic legal order, especially in the judicial organization of Member States. As Claes rightly points out, ordinary primacy affects ordinary courts, which are more empowered vis-à-vis other institutions due to their duty to disapply conflicting national legislation.[33] On the other hand, unconditional primacy has implications for all courts, but especially for courts exercising constitutional jurisdiction, whose mandate upholding the constitution is tamed. This is so because primacy does not only imply the duty of national courts to set aside contrary national law, but also the duty of these courts to refrain from reviewing the validity or compatibility of EU law measures with national constitutional provisions or principles.[34] Any power related to the interpretation or validity of EU law is reserved to the Court of Justice. The rationale behind this claim is inherently related to concerns of uniform application of EU law. In this regard, the EU legal order provides for a centralized

[30] Ibid., para. 61.

[31] Spanish Constitutional Court, STC 26/2014 [2014].

[32] For an extensive analysis see Besselink (2014), pp. 531–552.

[33] Claes (2006), p. 102.

[34] Prechal (2007), p. 54.

judicial system in which, according to the Foto-Frost doctrine,[35] national courts cannot pronounce the invalidity of EU law. The lack of jurisdiction of national courts is compensated with the possibility to address the Court of Justice through the preliminary reference procedure.

Apart from the evident empowerment of national courts, the *Simmenthal* mandate may serve as a driving force in the decentralization of the system of constitutional review in Europe.[36] Victor Ferreres sees this as one of the external factors of a general trend of decentralization of the European model of constitutional review. The process of supranational integration in the context of the European Union and the Council of Europe constitutes, according to the author, external pressures toward the decentralization of the European system of constitutional review. The principle of primacy, apart from weakening the absolute primacy of the national constitution, brings an end to the exclusivity of the judicial review of laws by national constitutional courts.[37]

Yet, what usually happens in the practice of national constitutional courts is that validity of EU law (mainly secondary legislation) is assessed indirectly through the review of national implementing measures. This has been a ploy of national constitutional courts to reassert their jurisdiction as ultimate guardians of the national constitution and to elaborate their constitutional reservations with regard to the application of EU law within the national legal order.

4 Legal Risks from National Constitutional Claims to the EU Legal Order

4.1 National Constitutional Claims as a Legal Risk to the Unity and Effectiveness of the EU Legal Order

As it was analysed above, the legal issue in *Melloni* boiled down to the interpretation of Article 53 of the Charter and more specifically to whether it would be possible for Member States, when applying EU law, to afford a higher level of protection of fundamental rights to individuals. More concretely, if the Spanish Constitutional Court were to decide to apply its own standard of protection of fair trial rights *in absentia*, Mr. Melloni probably could have escaped surrender. This would mean that in fact Member States could disrupt, on the basis of their standards of fundamental rights protection, the application of the system of surrender set up by the Council Framework Decision on the EAW. In the words of the ECJ this would ultimately "...undermine the principles of mutual trust and recognition

[35] Case C-314/85, *Foto Frost v. Hauptzollamt Lübeck-Ost* [1987] ECR I-4199.

[36] Ferreres Comella (2004), pp. 477 et seq.

[37] Ferreres Comella (2004), pp. 477 et seq.

which that decision purports to uphold and would, therefore, compromise the efficacy of that framework decision."[38] In a bigger picture, this would put into risk and undermine the effectiveness of EU law.

Melloni is an illustration of the legal risks emanating from constitutional claims at the Member State level and which may potentially affect the EU legal order. Following the introduction by the ECJ of direct effect and primacy and after realizing the implications that the new legal order would have for the constitutions, constitutional courts in some Member States have come up with constitutional reservations. They are to be understood as claims put forward by constitutional courts either of constitutive value or at the level of *obiter dicta*, addressing and qualifying the version of primacy purported by the Court of Justice.[39]

Generally, it can be said that constitutional courts tend to align themselves with the ECJ's position on the autonomy of the EU legal order. They do not seem to oppose the view of the Court on the autonomous legal order. For instance, in the early days, the German Constitutional Court ruled that the Community had a special nature, and it represented "an intergovernmental institution" to which Germany and other Member States had transferred certain sovereign rights.[40] Later on, in *Lütticke*,[41] the obligation of German courts to apply Community provisions which "stem from an autonomous non-State sovereign authority" and which "have direct effect at the municipal level and superimpose themselves upon and displace conflicting national law"[42] was inferred. According to the Court, the rights of EU citizens can be effective only in this way. Similarly, in *Frontini*, the Italian Constitutional Court ruled that the Community's legal order and the national legal system were to be considered as autonomous and distinct, "albeit coordinated in accordance with the division of power laid down and guaranteed by the Treaty."[43]

Yet, it is the issue of review of EU law on constitutional grounds that was and still remains more problematic. Constitutional courts have insisted in reviewing EU acts or their implementation in the light of fundamental constitutional principles such as fundamental rights protection or constitutional identity. It is in fact this type of constitutional reservation that represents potential legal risks for the uniform and effective application of the EU legal order because constitutional courts claim that they would declare EU law within the Member States concerned inapplicable. The non-application of EU law in the Member States by constitutional courts has not

[38] *Case C-399/11, Stefano Melloni v Ministero Fiscal* [2013] *ECR nyr*, para. 63.

[39] For an elaboration on this see Piqani (2010). See also Kumm (2005); Alter (2001); De Witte (2001) in Kellermann, de Zwaan, Czuczai 2001.

[40] German Federal Constitutional Court, Case No. 1 BvR 248/63 and 216/67 [1967], in Oppenheimer (1994), p. 410.

[41] German Federal Constitutional Court, Case No. 2 BvR 225/69 [1971], in Oppenheimer (1994).

[42] Ibid.

[43] Italian Constitutional Court, Case 183/73 *Frontini* [1973] in Oppenheimer (1994), p. 629.

materialized which makes these constitutional reservations *potential* legal risks to the EU legal order.[44]

In this context, the Italian Constitutional Court is well-known for its doctrine of *controlimiti*. In Fragd[45] the Court affirmed that it had a legitimate competence in scrutinizing the constitutionality of the law implementing the treaty, in case a treaty provision, as interpreted and applied by Community institutions, would go against fundamental constitutional provisions. The French Constitutional Council has decided to suspend the review of national provisions that merely reproduce EU secondary legislation, by thus showing deference to the EU legal order and the doctrines of the ECJ, except for the case in which those provisions violate French constitutional identity.[46] The Czech Constitutional Court has ruled that in issues related to EU law, it interprets constitutional law by taking into account EU law principles. However, the Court has warned in the past that EU legal norms cannot be in conflict with "the principle of the democratic law-based state or that the interpretation of these factors may not lead to a threat of the democratic law-based state. Such a shift would come into conflict with article 9(2) or article 9(3) of the Constitution of the Czech Republic."[47] The same Court has taken a similar approach concerning the review of Czech acts implementing EU law: in cases in which the Czech implementation reflects EU law, following the principle of primacy, the Constitutional Court would be deprived from reviewing these acts in terms of their conformity with the Czech Constitution. The only exception to this would be the situations in which EU institutions exercise the transferred powers in a manner which is not compatible with the preservation of the foundations of state sovereignty, and in a way which threatens the very essence of the substantive law-based state.[48] The last two principles are given the status of paramount and inalienable principles of the Czech constitutional order.

---

[44] See the discussion below on Case C-399/09, *Landtová* [2011] ECR I-05573 and the response by the Czech Constitutional Court, Case Pl. ÚS 5/12 *Holubec* [2012] at http://www.usoud.cz/en/decisions/?tx_ttnews%5Btt_news%5D=37&cHash=f5c96e0e4789a7fc3b2eecaca01bc6b3. Accessed 20 August 2015.

[45] Italian Constitutional Court, Case No. 232/1989 *Fragd* [1989] in Oppenheimer (2003), pp. 653–662.

[46] See Article 88-I of the French Constitution and cases such as French Constitutional Council, Decision no. 2006-540 *Loi relative au droit d'auteur et aux droits voisins dans la societe de l'information* [2006], at www.conseil-constitutionnel.fr, and for an overview Millet (2014), pp. 195–218.

[47] Czech Constitutional Court, Case Pl. ÚS 50/04 *Sugar Quotas* [2006], part A-3 of the judgment.

[48] Czech Constitutional Court, Case Pl. US 66/04 *European Arrest Warrant* [2006], para. 53.

4.2 Examples of (yet) Unmaterialized Legal Risks to the EU Legal Order

Perhaps the most famous example here is the *So Lange* line of case law[49] by the German Constitutional Court. *So Lange I* can be seen as an open call for confrontation: As long as the Community did not have a democratically elected Parliament and no bill of rights guaranteeing fundamental rights at a level comparable to that guaranteed by the German Constitution, the application of Community law in Germany would be subject to the obligation to observe the basic structure of the German Constitution, including fundamental rights. This meant at least two things: Firstly, EU law would be assessed by reference to the German constitutional framework and secondly, any constitutional complaint or reference from lower courts, challenging the constitutionality of a German law implementing Community law, would be admissible and if necessary, the German court could declare its inapplicability within the German legal order. However, the legal risk of non-application of EU law in Germany in this case as in all the other cases to come before the German Constitutional Court did not materialize. In the specific case, the German Constitutional Court found that the contested EC Regulations did not breach fundamental rights. Whereas *So Lange I* in principle opened the door to confrontation, *So Lange II* represented a suspension of the German Constitutional Court's jurisdiction on the grounds of the EU legal order and especially the case law of the ECJ in general. It protected fundamental rights at a level which is "substantially similar" to that afforded by the German Constitution.[50] As a result, individual complaints brought on the grounds of violation by EU acts of fundamental rights would be declared inadmissible.

The *So Lange* line of cases is perhaps the most emblematic in the context of constitutional reservations and the alleged legal risks that they present for the EU legal order and effective application of EU law. Constitutional reservations were articulated by one of the most authoritative constitutional courts in Europe, a court of one of the founding Member States, and moreover, these reservations pointed at an unsatisfactory, according to the German court, level of protection of fundamental rights within the Communities at the time. However, these cases are not the only examples of constitutional reservations by the German Constitutional Court. They represent one line of constitutional reservations, namely fundamental rights. In the Maastricht Decision, the Court asserted its self-vested authority to examine whether legal acts of EU institutions are adopted within the limits of the sovereign

---

[49] German Federal Constitutional Court, Case No. 2 BvL 52/71 *Internationale Handelsgesellschaft Gmbh v. Einfuhr- und Vorratsstelle für Getreide und Futtermittel (Solange I)* [1974] in Oppenheimer (1994), p. 447 and German Federal Constitutional Court, Case No. 2 BvR 197/83 *Wünsche Handelsgesellschaft (Solange II)* [1986] in Oppenheimer (1994), p. 462.

[50] German Federal Constitutional Court, Case No. 2 BvR 197/83 *Wünsche Handelsgesellschaft (Solange II)* [1986] in Oppenheimer (1994), p. 494.

rights transferred to them.[51] More generally, in case EU institutions were to legislate by extending their competences, or exercising them in a way which was not provided for by the Treaty as ratified by law in Germany, these EU legal acts would not have any binding force in Germany. Further on in the Lisbon Judgment, the German Constitutional Court reintroduced its *ultra vires* and came up with the identity review, stating that "it must be possible within the German jurisdiction to assert the responsibility for integration if obvious transgressions of the boundaries take place when the European Union claims competences and to preserve the inviolable core content of the basic law's constitutional identity by means of an identity review".[52] This jurisdiction would be exceptional—'if obvious transgressions take place'—and subsidiary to legal protection at EU level—'if legal protection cannot be obtained at the Union level'. The consequences of such a review would be the inapplicability of EU law in Germany. In *Honeywell*,[53] the German Constitutional Court was called upon to apply these reservations. The legal question was whether the ECJ had acted *ultra vires* in its *Mangold*[54] ruling. According to the German Court, the ruling of the ECJ in *Mangold* did not entail a structurally significant shift in the allocation of competences and as a result it was not an *ultra vires* act of an EU institution.[55]

In the most recent episode of the troubled relation between EU law and the German Constitutional Court, the latter put itself again in the centre of attention. In January 2014 the German Constitutional Court, for the first time in its history, sent a reference for a preliminary ruling to the ECJ concerning the conformity with EU law of the Outright Monetary Transactions (OMT) Programme of the European Central Bank (ECB).[56] This programme provides for the purchase in the secondary market—for an unspecified amount—by the ECB of government bonds of selected Member States that are subject to an adjustment programme in the context of assistance received from the European Financial Stability Facility or the European Stability Mechanism. Although the OMT Programme has not been used so far, at least from a theoretical perspective its challenge by the German Constitutional Court adds to the debate on the relation between the ECJ and the German

[51] German Federal Constitutional Court, Case No. 2 BvR 2134 and 2159/92 *Maastricht Treaty 1992 Constitutionality Case* [1993] para. C/I/3 of the judgment in Oppenheimer (1994), pp. 555–556.

[52] German Federal Constitutional Court, Case 2 BvE 2/08, 5/08, 2 BvR 1010/08, 1022/08, 1259/08, 182/09 *Lisbon Treaty* [2009] https://www.bundesverfassungsgericht.de/SharedDocs/Entscheidungen/EN/2009/06/es20090630_2bve000208en.html. Accessed 25 September 2015.

[53] German Federal Constitutional Court, Case 2 BvR 2661/06 *Honeywell* [2010] at http://www.bundesverfassungsgericht.de/SharedDocs/Entscheidungen/EN/2010/07/rs20100706_2bvr266106en.html. Accessed 25 September 2015. For an analysis see Payandeh (2011), pp. 9–38.

[54] Case C-144/04, *Mangold* [2005] ECR I-09981.

[55] Case 2 BvR 2661/06 *Honeywell* [2010].

[56] German Federal Constitutional Court, Case 2 BvR 2728/13 [2014]. For a short comment on the ECJ case see Piqani (2015), at http://jog.tk.mta.hu/blog/2015/07/the-ecj-upholds-the-ecbs-bond-buying-programme. Accessed 25 September 2015.

Court and potential legal risks to the EU legal order in general and the Union monetary policy in that specific case. The German Constitutional Court in a rather suggestive reference asked the ECJ whether the OMT programme is *ultra vires* as it, according to the Court, allegedly goes beyond the monetary policy mandate of the ECB and whether it conflicts with the Treaties, more precisely with the prohibition of monetary financing as provided for in Article 123 of the TFEU. The German Constitutional Court seems to hold the position that the OMT programme should be considered illegal as an act encroaching upon the economic policy powers vested to the Member States and not the ECB, which on its own is responsible for the monetary policy. Thus, *prima facie* and "subject to the interpretation by the Court of Justice", the OMT would constitute a manifest violation of the distribution of powers.[57] It still has to be seen what the position of the German Constitutional Court on this matter will be after the recently issued preliminary ruling of the ECJ on this matter.[58] The ECJ did not surprise much: it upheld the validity of the OMT Programme by ruling that it falls within the mandate of the ECB, and that it is a proportionate measures and in line with Article 123 TFEU (prohibition of monetary financing). Only future will show what the position of the German Court will be: will it find ways to reconcile the ECJ's judgment and its assessment of the OMT Programme or will it pick a confrontational side and threaten with disapplication in Germany of a future, potential implementation of the OMT Programme?

In January 2012 the Czech Constitutional Court was under the spotlight for its judgment in *Holubec*[59] in which it declared that a June 2011 judgment of the ECJ[60] was to be considered *ultra vires* as it was taken outside of the powers transferred to the EU by the Czech Republic. This was the first time in which a Constitutional Court of a Member State declared an EU act—in this case a judgment of the ECJ—as *ultra vires*. The *Holubec* case was one case in a long line of cases concerning Czechoslovak pensions, more specifically the system of pensions to be applied to the Czech and Slovak citizens after the split of Czechoslovakia.[61] As a result of the solution found between the Czech and Slovak Republic, Czech citizens who had not lived in Slovakia received a pension from the Slovak State because their employer on 31 December 1992 resulted to be incorporated in Slovakia and not the Czech Republic.[62] So far so good, but the issue was that Slovak pensions were lower than Czech pensions and the category of these Czech citizens felt disadvantaged. In order to remedy their situation, the Czech Constitutional Court provided for a special supplement as a constitutional right.[63] One of these cases, namely *Landtová*,

[57] Case 2 BvR 2728/13 para. 36–42.

[58] Case C-62/14, *Gauweiler* [2015] n.y.r.

[59] Case Pl. ÚS 5/12 *Holubec* [2012].

[60] Case C-399/09, *Landtová* [2011] ECR I-05573.

[61] For an excellent analysis and background see Bobek (2014), pp. 54–90.

[62] Bobek (2014), p. 57.

[63] Bobek (2014), p. 58.

reached the ECJ in a reference for a preliminary ruling and the Luxembourg Court ruled that the supplements were in conflict with EU law. More specifically, according to the ECJ the granting of the supplement by the Czech Constitutional Court only to Czech citizens resident in the Czech Republic constituted discrimination based on nationality and residence.[64]

In the *Holubec* case[65]—concerning also a pension claim—the Czech Constitutional Court declared the ECJ judgment in *Landtová* as *ultra vires*. This was based on the allegation that the ECJ had transgressed its powers because Regulation 1408/71[66] "cannot be applied to entitlements of citizens of the Czech Republic arising from social security until 31 December 1992".[67] According to the Czech Court "...a situation occurred in which an act by a European body exceeded the powers that the Czech Republic transferred to the European Union under Art. 10a of the Constitution; this exceeded the scope of the transferred powers, and was ultra vires."[68] This decision of the Czech Constitutional Court will be remembered as the first judgment in which an act of EU institutions is declared *ultra vires*. At the same time no further concrete consequence for the application of EU law derived from the rebellion of the Czech Constitutional Court. On the one hand, the Czech Supreme Administrative Court—a Court directly involved in the pension saga—disqualified the judgment of the Constitutional Court as a judgment against a ruling of the ECJ.[69] On the other hand, the Czech Constitutional Court itself narrowed down considerably the scope of its own judgment, a judicial move that resembles a "silent retreat from Holubec".[70]

5 Concluding Remarks

This chapter gave an overview of legal risks in the context of the relation between national constitutions and EU law. In this regard two categories of legal risks were identified: legal risks emanating from the EU legal order and addressed to national constitutional law and conversely, legal risks emanating from national constitutional law and addressed to the EU legal order. Interestingly enough the EU legal order and national constitutional law serve at the same time as the source and target of legal risks. In the context of the constitutional architecture of the European Union it is the special nature of the EU legal order that represented the first instance

[64] Case C-399/09, *Landtová* [2011] ECR I-05573, para. 41–49.

[65] Case Pl. ÚS 5/12 *Holubec* [2012].

[66] Regulation (EEC) No. 1408/71 of the Council on the Application of Social Security Schemes to Employed Persons and their Families Moving within the Community [1971].

[67] Case Pl. ÚS 5/12 *Holubec* [2012] part VII.

[68] Case Pl. ÚS 5/12 *Holubec* [2012] part VII.

[69] Bobek (2014), pp. 63–66.

[70] Bobek (2014), p. 67.

of legal risks for the national constitutional order. For the EU legal order to be effective and produce effects in a uniform manner it has to be autonomous, applied directly and with precedence over conflicting national provisions. This has challenged the authority of the national legal orders and especially the authority of national constitutions. According to the ECJ, the EU legal order had to be applied with precedence over conflicting national law notwithstanding the status of the latter within the national legal system. Thus, as it was shown above, provisions of national constitutions had to yield to EU law provisions. This new reality provoked a series of chain reactions by national constitutions in the form of constitutional reservations to the unconditional version of the primacy of EU law. Although none of these reservations has materialized itself into non-application of EU law by the courts of Member States, one has to emphasize that the risk to the uniform and full application of EU law remains possible, albeit perhaps improbable.

One can see a common trend in constitutional reservations: Constitutional courts have raised concerns with regard to EU law instruments or acts that, according to these courts, do not respect the national level of protection of fundamental rights, violate constitutional identity or are adopted in transgression of conferred powers. Whereas these reservations display different concerns of national constitutional courts, the threat remains the same: non-application of the respective EU law provision. However, the situation is not as dramatic as it may seem and this is so primarily as a result of the willingness of the main actors to find a way out. For instance, the German Constitutional Court as the classic player in this field ruled that the EU Regulation in the case at hand did not infringe fundamental rights as protected by the basic law (*So Lange I*) and later on seemed satisfied with the level of protection of fundamental rights within the EU (*So Lange II*). The ECJ played its role as well. The Court of Justice already incorporated in *Internationale Handelsgesellschaft* fundamental rights as part of the general principles of EU law and later on in classic cases such as *Schmidberger*[71] or *Omega* recognized the protection of fundamental rights as a justification for restriction of the fundamental freedoms of the EU legal order. As is well-known, in *Schmidberger* the Court acknowledged the tension between the free movement of goods and the constitutionally guaranteed freedom of expression and freedom of assembly, the latter of which is common to the Member States, and is guaranteed by the European Convention of Human Rights. Later, in *Omega*,[72] human dignity was defined as a general principle of law, independent of the existence or non-existence of a shared conception on the precise way the fundamental right or legitimate interest was to be shared. This jurisprudential line shows that the Court of Justice tends to 'translate' fundamental rights, protected by national constitutions, into general principles of law, which would then serve as a limit to the absolute enforcement of the fundamental freedoms. As Claes puts it, the Court "re-phrased the issues from a conflict between

---

[71] Case C-112/00, *Schmidberger* [2003] ECR I-0000.

[72] Case C-36/02, *Omega Spielhallen-und Automatenaufstellungs-GmbH v. Oberbürgermeisterin der Bundesstadt Bonn* [2004] ECR I-0000.

European freedom and national constitutional rights, into a balancing of competing principles within the context of European law."[73] The core and the reconciling part of the general principles doctrine of the Court of Justice is that primacy of EU law is not construed as absolutely unconditional, and that, at times, the very basic pillars of the economic constitution are weakened for the benefit of the protection of fundamental rights within the Union.

In addition, the accommodation of national identities is an important step towards the rationalization of legal risks to both the national and EU legal order. The commitment of respect for national identities and fundamental constitutional structures of the Member States under Article 4(2) TEU and the case law of the Court of Justice show that in general elements of national identity are taken into account when a balance is struck between fundamental freedoms and legitimate interests which may serve as grounds to justify restrictions to these freedoms.[74]

References

Alter K (2001) Establishing the supremacy of European law – the making of an international rule of law in Europe. Oxford University Press, Oxford

Besselink L (2014) Parameters of constitutional conflict after Melloni. Eur Law Rev 39:531–552

Bobek M (2014) Landtova, Holubec, and the problem of an uncooperative court: implications for the preliminary rulings procedure. Eur Const Law Rev 10:54–90

Claes M (2006) The National Constitutional Mandate in the European Constitution. Hart Publishing, Oxford

Claes M (2007) The Europeanization of national constitutions in the constitutionalization of Europe: some observations against the background of the constitutional experience of the EU-15. Croat Yearb Eur Law Policy 3:1–38

De Boer N (2013) Addressing rights divergences under the Charter: Melloni. Common Mark Law Rev 50:1083–1104

De Witte B (2001) Constitutional aspects of European Union membership in the original six member states: model solutions for the applicant countries? In: Kellermann A, de Zwaan JW, Czuczai J (eds) EU enlargement: the constitutional impact at EU and national level. TMS Asser Press, The Hague

De Witte B (2011) Direct effect, primacy and the nature of the legal order. In: Craig P, De Burca G (eds) The evolution of EU law. Oxford University Press, Oxford, p 327

Ferreres Comella V (2004) The European model of constitutional review of legislation: toward decentralization? ICON 2:461–491

Halberstam D (2010) Pluralis, in Marbury and Van Gend. In: Maduro M, Azoulai L (eds) The past and future of EU law. Hart Publishing, Oxford, p 28

Kumm M (2005) The jurisprudence of constitutional conflict: constitutional supremacy in Europe before and after the Constitutional Treaty. Eur Law J 11:262–307

[73] Claes (2007), p. 11.

[74] See, for instance, cases such as Case C-208/09, *Ilonka Sayn-Wittgenstein* [2010] ECR I-13693; Case C-391/09, *Malgožata Runevič-Vardyn and Łukasz Paweł Wardyn v. Vilniaus miesto savivaldybes administracija and Others* [2011] ECR I-03787; Case C-202/11, *Anton Las v. PSA Antwerp NV* [2013].

Millet F-X (2014) How much lenience for how much cooperation? On the first preliminary reference of the French Constitutional Council to the Court of Justice. Common Mark Law Rev 51:195–218

Oppenheimer A (1994) The relationship between European Community Law and National Law: the cases. Cambridge University Press, Cambridge, p 410

Oppenheimer A (2003) The relationship between European Community Law and National Law: the cases, vol 2. Cambridge University Press, Cambridge, pp 653–662

Payandeh M (2011) Constitutional review of EU law after Honeywell: contextualizing the relationship between the German Constitutional Court and the EU Court of Justice. Common Mark Law Rev 48:9–38

Piqani D (2015) Supremacy of EU law and the jurisprudence of constitutional reservations in Central Eastern Europe and the Western Balkans: towards a ‘Holistic’ constitutionalism, PhD Thesis, European University Institute

Prechal S (2007) Direct effect, indirect effect, supremacy and the evolving constitution of the European Union. In: Barnard C (ed) The fundamentals of EU law revisited: assessing the impact of the constitutional debate. Oxford University Press, Oxford, p 54

Stein E (1964–1965) Toward supremacy of Treaty-Constitution by judicial fiat: on the margin of the Costa Case. Mich Law Rev 63:491–518

Human Rights Advocacy for an "International Society of Risk"

Ioannis K. Panoussis

Contents

Abstract The concept of risk in international human rights law is strictly connected to the idea of prevention. The problem is that international systems of protection are generally based on State responsibility for the violation of a human right guaranteed in the different conventions, which means that, in principle, prevention is not part of the attributions of international protecting bodies. Taking this into account, the development of the case-law of these organs is surprising. The concept of risk is actually present from the early beginning of the international procedures (even before examining the admissibility). The international bodies are facing questions related to risk and the obligation to prevent its realization at the stage of the precautionary or provisional measures. They are, at present, also examining the admissibility and the merits when dealing, for example, with the concept of "potential victim" or with the positive obligations to prevent violations of human rights. Issues such as asylum, counterterrorism, environment and others are the main areas of the development of this kind of case-law.

I.K. Panoussis (✉)
Faculty of Law, Catholic University of Lille, Lille, France
e-mail: Ioannis.PANOUSSIS@univ-catholille.fr

E. Mišćenić, A. Raccah (eds.), *Legal Risks in EU Law*,
DOI 10.1007/978-3-319-28596-2_3

1 Introduction

In recent years, the international society has been facing a number of issues relating to "security risks". On the one hand, the concept of "security risk" as we define it in the "international society of risk" is polysemic. It can identify the military risk, terrorist risk, environmental risk, economic risk, political risk, religious risk, human displacement risk... The human factor is becoming increasingly important, and this implies, therefore, taking into account the perspective of human rights. On the other hand, the fragility of States with regard to the multiplication of risks has emerged. However, this does not exempt States from a certain number of obligations under the international law of human rights. At most, this has the effect of changing the nature and the extent of their obligations by placing them before a possible violation of human rights.

The concept of risk, in principle, refers to the idea of a potential danger. How can one grasp this "potential"? In terms of temporality, is it possible to adopt a preventive approach? If doing so, how far do the State and Non-State actors have to go to achieve their goals? If the "potential" is realised, then what attitudes should international actors adopt both in order to repair the damage suffered by victims and to ensure, for example, the guarantee of non-repetition? This question assumes that the legal norms are interested to what happens upstream and downstream of the realisation of risks.

From the point of view of the international law of human rights, one of the structural issues we face is that the international systems of protection of human rights are, in principle, based on the logic of state responsibility and compensation for damages suffered (and, therefore, it is an *a posteriori* approach). This implies that the risk should be realized. Should prevention then be in our study? Can a controlling body have the function of preventing the realization of these risks? This is a major challenge, in our opinion, for the international law of human rights in the twenty-first century.

We cannot ignore that in the past 20 years several instruments and mechanisms aiming at the prevention of human rights violations have emerged. We can name, for example, the European Convention for the Prevention of Torture and Inhuman or Degrading Treatment or Punishment adopted in 1987, which established a European Committee for the Prevention of Torture,[1] or the Optional Protocol to the UN Convention against Torture adopted in 2002 that created the UN Sub-Committee for the Prevention of Torture.[2] These mechanisms, complementary to the general system of protection of human rights, are there to act as upstream systems compared to those based on State responsibility. Their declaratory impact

[1] Morgan and Evans (2002), p. 300; Nicolay (1996), p. 1.

[2] For an interesting approach to the prevention of human rights and the division of powers between the States and the subcommittee, see Steinerte (2013), p. 132.

is real, but the notion of obligation of States to prevent does not thereby become binding.[3]

It is interesting at this level to see how the general systems for the protection of human rights can until today and in the future take into account the risk(s). To achieve this goal, it is important to identify the means and techniques by which the risk integrates this branch of international law (I), before studying materially the most common themes faced by international monitoring bodies on this matter (II).

2 Risk Management in Human Rights: The Apparent Obligation to Prevent

Taking into account the risk of violation of human rights in judicial or quasi-judicial systems to protect human rights is, in principle, co-substantial to the appearance of an obligation of prevention that would weigh on States.[4] There is no doubt today that this obligation of prevention floods the litigation of human rights. It is necessary, however, to study this matter at different stages of the international procedure since differences exist concerning the existence of a State obligation whose possible consequence is the appearance of a subjective right for individuals. The issue of prevention is often prior to the examination of the merits, which is why its manifestation is fundamental in the context of emergency procedures/provisional measures (2.1). This, however, did not prevent the supervisory bodies to take it into account when examining a contentious case (2.2), which raises real legal problems at various levels.

2.1 Human Rights Violations: Interim Measures to Prevent Judicial Proceedings

The issue of emergency procedures is crucial in terms of prevention as it seeks to overcome the lack of suspensive effect of the international individual action to the

[3] It is particularly interesting that the writers of these texts did not want to compete with the existing control mechanisms of the prevention systems on the basis of the European Convention on Human Rights or the Convention of Nations against Torture, respectively. The goal was rather to enhance the complementarity of these mechanisms by giving the preventive bodies an investigative role and recommendations to prevent the occurrence or recurrence of a violation—they then play a warning role—then that controls them are part of a logic of responsibility.

[4] This link between the concept of risk and the obligation to prevent is always noticeable when trying to analyse the State's obligations. This overall theme is approached from very diverse angles in the book. See, e.g. Decaux and Touzé (2015), p. 230.

internal procedures.[5] This procedure has often been seen as a procedural issue, since, in parallel with the introduction of an application, the Parties may submit a request for protective/provisional measures, which will be decided ahead of the review of the merits.[6]

Although recent conventional and case-law developments have allowed the consecration of these measures in all protection systems, the instruments and the jurisdictional practices are still very different from one system to another. Article 63§2 of the American Convention on Human Rights and Article 27§2 of the Protocol to the African Charter establishing the African Court of Human Rights specifically provide the power to issue interim measures for both regional courts.[7] Conversely, the recognition of this power in favour of the European Court of Human Rights, the United Nations Committee or the American Commission finds its origin in a voluntary process of these bodies in their internal regulations[8] and refined in their jurisprudence.[9] This difference naturally has an impact in terms of legitimacy and on the binding nature of these measures, but also, on a more symbolic level, on the judicial formalism which will be devoted to them.[10]

To place this debate in terms of the challenges ahead, the major challenge here involves the possibility for interim measures to become a judicial tool for preventing risks and the potential emergence of a subjective right to the *international provisional protection*. The former President of the Inter-American Court of Human Rights and currently a judge at the International Court of Justice, A. A. Cançado Trindade, is a strong supporter of this favourable dynamic approach to the individual and emphasizes the importance of interim measures to prevent violations of human rights, as evidenced by a separate opinion on the order of the ICJ of 16 July 2013, *Certain Activities carried out by Nicaragua in the Border Area-*

---

[5] This issue is particularly highlighted by Professor Hélène Tigroudja in a recent study, which is relatively critical of the effectiveness of provisional measures as a means of prevention. See Tigroudja (2015), p. 141.

[6] For a study of this issue in terms of human rights, see the work of Rieter (2010), p. 1200; Rieter (2012), p. 165.

[7] Article 63§2 CADH provides specifically that "*In cases of extreme gravity and urgency, and when necessary to avoid irreparable damage to persons, the Court shall adopt such provisional measures as it deems pertinent in matters it has under consideration. With respect to a case not yet submitted to the Court, it may act at the request of the Commission*". In a shorter style, Article 27§2 of the Protocol establishing the African Court provides that "*In cases of extreme gravity and urgency, and when necessary to avoid irreparable harm to persons, the Court shall adopt such provisional measures as it deems necessary.*"

[8] To take the European example, the emergence of the possibility of the Strasbourg Court to adopt interim measures is grounded in Article 39 of the Rules of Procedure adopted by the latter itself.

[9] The absence of a conventional foundation casts doubts on the binding nature of the latter. The Strasbourg Court has decided to use its power of interpretation to establish the characteristic "normative" Interim Measures of its own. See e.g., App. No. 46827/99 and 46951/99, *Mamatkulov and Askarov v. Turkey* [2005] ECHR and the commentary of Frumer (2005), p. 799.

[10] As noted by Professor Tigroudja in her study, the ACHR is very formalistic in establishing criteria while the ECHR takes a much less formal and more confidential approach despite the real importance of these measures. See Tigroudja (2015), pp. 145–146.

Construction of a Road in Costa Rica along the San Juan River (Costa Rica v. Nicaragua).[11]

To illustrate the potential importance of this issue in the litigation of human rights, it is interesting to consider the case of *Belo Monte Dam* that faced the Inter-American Commission in April 2011.[12] Unlike the Court, the Commission has, we recall, not received the power to make interim measures,[13] this is often seen as a privilege granted to the Court. It is a prerogative the Court has arrogated in its rules. This sometimes explains the tensions that may exist with States, as was the case here.

In this matter,[14] the Commission requested the suspension of the construction of a hydroelectric plant in Brazil whose environmental impact seemed to have serious consequences on indigenous populations living in the Amazon rainforest. An area of 400 km^2 would be affected by the project. In order to prevent damage to life and to the physical integrity of the natives, the Commission issued provisional measures indicating the obligation of Brazil to implement a preliminary consultation procedure, to proceed and provide access in a language comprehensible by the natives to an environmental impact study and adopt positive measures to protect the life as well as personal integrity of the natives.

Such an approach to the prevention and to the obligations for the State is reminiscent of the positive obligations which may weigh on it in litigations before the European Court of Human Rights concerning environmental issues.[15] The parallelism with the obligation to inform that weighs on States in order to prevent possible damages to privacy and physical integrity is obvious.

What is particularly interesting here in terms of posture, is the fact that the Commission (as well as the Court for that matter) has a positive and dynamic vision of provisional measures. They aim to contribute to human security and not just to "freeze" a situation in time to decide the merits. The measures, therefore, extend the scope of international protection before the occurrence of a violation, and to the

---

[11] A degree of caution is needed in the analysis of this separate opinion. The dispute in question was an interstate dispute that Judge Cançado Trindade was called to overcome. Therefore, it was by no means a plea for the emergence of a subjective right for the individual. However, Judge Cançado Trindade recalled the appearance of a necessary independent legal regime, creating true obligations of prevention for upstream States of the substantive examination of the case. Applied to human rights, this reasoning can lead to the birth of a right to compensation in favour of the individual in case of non-compliance with this obligation by the State (see in particular paras. 69–76 of his dissenting opinion).

[12] Case MC 382/10, *Comunidades Indígenas da Bacia do Rio Xingu v. Brazil* [2011] IACHR.

[13] See, Hélène Tigroudja (2015), *supra*, pp.144–145.

[14] See the presentation of Neumann Das Neves N., "Barrage de Belo Monte: le droit des indigènes suspendu à une mesure provisoire (Commission IADH, 1er avril 2011, Comunidades Indígenas da Bacia do Rio Xingu c. Brésil)", available at:

http://combatsdroitshomme.blog.lemonde.fr/2011/04/21/barrage-de-belo-monte-le-droit-des-indigenes-suspendu-a-une-mesure-provisoire-commission-iadh-1er-avril-2011-comunidades-indigenas-da-bacia-do-rio-xingu-c-bresil/.

[15] Panoussis (2014), p. 17.

detriment of the sovereignty of the State. This is exactly the position of the Judge Cançado Trindade in his opinion of 16 July 2013 when he states that "*soon the recourse to provisional measures of protection, also at international level, had the effect of expanding the domain of international jurisdiction, with the consequent reduction of the so-called "reserved domain" of the State. This grows in importance in respect of regimes of protection, such as those of the human person as well as of the environment*".[16] It is, therefore, a contribution to the protection of the individual in a dynamic approach to prevention.

While it undeniably falls within a prevention approach, several questions arise, however, in this case that caused a diplomatic incident between the Inter-American Commission and Brazil.[17] Should the "potential" risk weighing on the human factor always trump economic, social and political considerations? Is it not wiser to seek a fair balance between theoretically divergent interests? Should there be strict ordering criteria? These questions are not unknown to European litigation in environmental matters. The search for the "fair balance" must nevertheless not be at the expense of the integrity of individuals.[18]

This case is largely responsible for changing the statute of the Inter-American Commission, which intervened in 2013, and which aims, *inter alia*, to formalize the conditions of the ordering of interim/provisional measures inspired from the work performed by the Inter-American Court. The new Article 25 contains elements inspired by the powers of the Inter-American Court and the case-law of the latter to regulate the operation of interim measures setting out a number of criteria such as

[16] Cançado Trindade A. A., dissenting opinion in the order of the ICJ of 16 July 2013, *Certain Activities carried out by Nicaragua in the Border Area - Construction of a Road in Costa Rica along the San Juan River (Costa Rica v. Nicaragua)*, para. 73.

[17] Dilma Rousseff, who originated the project, expressed strong criticism of the Commission. Brazil has taken a distance and openly challenged the legitimacy of the Commission to interfere in records management with a very important economic and social impact that has not been taken into account by the review body. We can estimate that changing the rules of the Commission is due largely to this case.

[18] App. No. 19234/04, *Bacila vs Romania* [2010] ECtHR, paras. 70–72 at the occasion of which she says that "*Certes, la Cour ne méconnaît pas l'intérêt que peuvent avoir les autorités internes à maintenir l'activité économique du plus grand employeur d'une ville déjà fragilisée par la fermeture d'autres industries.*

Cependant, la Cour estime que cet intérêt ne saurait l'emporter sur le droit des personnes concernées à jouir d'un environnement équilibré et respectueux de la santé. L'existence de consé quences graves et avérées pour la santé de la requérante et des autres habitants de Copşa Mică, faisait peser sur l'État l'obligation positive d'adopter et de mettre en œuvre des mesures raisonnables et adéquates capables de protéger leur bien-être.

Compte tenu de ce qui précède – et malgré la marge d'appréciation reconnue à l'État défendeur – la Cour estime que celui-ci n'a pas su ménager un juste équilibre entre l'intérêt du bien-être é conomique de la ville de Copşa Mică – celui de préserver l'activité du principal employeur de la ville – et la jouissance effective par la requérante du droit au respect de son domicile et de sa vie privée et familiale".

severity, urgency and irreparable damage.[19] Similarly, the reform has the effect of clarifying the roles of the two oversight bodies in this area. The Court remains mistress regarding the enactment of provisional measures, but the referral by the Commission is subject to the prior pronounced (and insufficient) precautionary measures. The question is whether the Commission, as in the case of *Belo Monte Dam*, will not benefit from this power to spill over that of the Court?

There can be no doubt that the challenges facing the Commission are strongly similar to those which the European Court and other international control bodies must also face. This dynamic approach of interim measures indicates the existence of a genuine need of protection in order to prevent, which might create a subjective right for individuals facing a State obligation. However, we cannot yet announce this as practices and legal effects are varying, depending on the organ who pronounces them. The problem is not really the same at the stage of reviewing the merits of a case.

2.2 Prevention as Core of Risk Management in Human Rights

During a substantive examination, issues change. To meet the admissibility requirements (specifically the jurisdiction of the organ examined at the admissibility stage), the individual must prove that he is the victim of a right guaranteed by the relevant Conventions.[20] This raises many questions, such as the existence of a subjective right to prevention/or a State obligation to prevent, the issue of the victim status, especially if the risk has not (yet) been achieved, the evidence for examining the "potential" and finally the reparation of the "potential".

---

[19] See in this brief commentary Lazarte (2013). The latter defines these concepts as follows:

- *La "gravité" : Impact sérieux qu'une action ou omission peut avoir sur le droit protégé ou sur l'effet éventuel d'une décision en suspens dans une affaire ou pétition face aux organes du système interaméricain;*
- *L'"urgence" : Risque ou menace imminentes qui peuvent se concrétiser au point de rendre né cessaire une action préventive ou de protection en référé;*
- *Le "dommage irréparable" : Atteinte aux droits qui, par sa nature même, n'est pas susceptible de réparation, de restauration ou d'indemnisation adéquate.*

[20] This is clear from Article 34 ECHR, which provides for the right of individual petition, conditioning the quality of a victim: "*The Court may receive applications from any person, non-governmental organisation or group of individuals claiming to be the victim of a violation by one of the High Contracting Parties of the rights set forth in the Convention or the protocols thereto. The High Contracting Parties undertake not to hinder in any way the effective exercise of this right.*"

2.2.1 State Responsibility for Risk Prevention

This question is fundamentally linked to the theory of positive obligations of the State.[21] There is no doubt that the main basis for these positive obligations (although one can make also reference to the direct consequences of certain provisions and the independent concepts) is the general obligation to protect human rights.[22] Today one can reasonably assert that there is a duality in these positive obligations, some manifesting upstream and others downstream of a violation of human rights.[23]

The nature of this obligation of prevention is such that it must be handled with great caution. A broad sense of this obligation would lead to State responsibility for the "risk" of a violation of human rights. We must not forget that one of the conditions of the admissibility of individual complaints before international bodies for the protection of human rights lies in the status of victim. Can potential victims receive protection before the international bodies concerned?[24] This is, in our opinion, a false problem. The difficulties that result are relative. As emphasized by Professor Hélène Tigroudja, referring to the terminology of the European Court of Human Rights, "said the potential victim is actually present victim of the violation of a positive obligation of the State".[25] This positive obligation is the obligation of prevention that weighs on States. The harm suffered by the victim is objective; in the absence of the development of the rights guaranteed by the various texts, the right concerned by the application cannot be exercised. Thus, as emphasized by Frédéric Sudre, the Convention does not stop with a defensive approach to human rights.[26] Thanks to this statement, for example, several requests have been considered saying that the realization of the damage has not yet occurred. This is, for example, the situation of the case-law on the Criminalization of Homosexuality in some European countries or the requests relating to the expulsion of an individual to a State where there is risk of torture or the death penalty.[27]

What exactly is this positive obligation of prevention then? States must ensure, as such, that their domestic legislation is in conformity with the Convention and as a

[21] Sudre (2000), p. 1359; Mowbray (2004), p. 239.

[22] See to that effect, Panoussis (2007), pp. 427–461.

[23] Panoussis (2007), pp. 427–461. When upstream of a violation, the duty of prevention is indeed in question. However, when one is downstream of a violation, that obligation essentially takes the form of a duty of investigation by State authorities.

[24] On the notion of a potential victim in the litigation of human rights, see Cançado Trindade (1987), pp. 243–299, especially pp. 92, 271–2. According to Professor Tigroudja, the terms "potential victim", "virtual" or "possible" are inappropriate. They ignore the positive obligations of the State. See, in this sense, Tigroudja (2001), pp. 32–40.

[25] Tigroudja (2001), p. 39.

[26] Sudre (2000), p. 1360.

[27] We can cite as examples: App. No. 22414/93, *Chahal v. UK*, [1996] ECtHR and App. No. 37201/06, *Saadi v. Italy*, [2008] ECtHR.

result of this that the authorities (police, justice, army...) behave in a way which ensures the effectiveness of the substantive provisions of the various texts.[28]

In a changing world, where security risks are increasingly felt, the issue of prevention is crucial. The cases concerning asylum, the fight against terrorism, and intervention in armed conflict zones are perfect illustrations for this. To prove the quality of victim issues are moving to the near certainty of the realization of risk—the potential becomes real. This method requires the adaptation of the vocabulary of the Court granting the conditional. The recent *Tarakhel* case,[29] concerning the return to the country of first entry into the European Union of a family of Afghan asylum seekers, offers us another perfect illustration of this.

Taking into account the risk of violation of their rights due to the alleged inability of Italy to provide dignified reception conditions, the Court "first reiterates its well-established case-law according to which the expulsion of an asylum seeker by a Contracting State may give rise to an issue under Article 3 where "substantial grounds have been shown for believing" that the person concerned faces a "real risk"[30] of being subjected to torture or inhuman or degrading treatment or punishment in the receiving".[31]

Although the risk is still not achieved, the conditional violations of positive prevention obligations imposed on the State were looked at. The Court stated in this case that "It follows that, *were the applicants to be returned to Italy* without the Swiss authorities having first obtained individual guarantees from the Italian authorities that the applicants would be taken charge of in a manner adapted to the age of the children and that the family would be kept together, *there would be a violation of Article 3* of the Convention."[32]

In the same vein, one can question the proof of the "real risk" and the possibility to repair it.

2.2.2 The Proof of the "Real Risk" in order to Repair the "Potential Damage"

In terms of evidence, the burden of proof is generally on the applicant. That said, when the applicant faces the risk he is, in principle, unable to prove the certainty of the damage (unless the risk will be realized). In the context of the breach of the duty of prevention and the consideration of risk, the supervisory bodies are therefore obliged to innovate. Monitoring bodies will often use *sufficiently strong, clear and*

[28] Panoussis (2014), pp. 447–452.

[29] App. No. 29217/12, *Tarakhel v. Switzerland,* [2014] ECtHR.

[30] This means that the danger must be predictable and sufficiently concrete. Moreover, the risk cannot be general, but individualized. In their dissenting opinion, Judges Casadevall, Berro-Lefèvre and Jäderblom rightly insist on the fact that *"The risk must be "real", meaning that the danger must be foreseeable and sufficiently concrete"*, and must demonstrate the existence of *"a sufficiently real and imminent risk of hardship severe enough to fall within the scope of Article 3"*.

[31] App. No. 29217/12, *Tarakhel v. Switzerland,* [2014] ECtHR, para. 102.

[32] Ibid., para. 122.

concordant inferences or of similar unrebutted presumptions of fact ... Moreover, in certain cases, by referring to the reports of international organizations, NGOs or any other useful source, we are witnessing a reversal of the burden of proof to the State,[33] or even an ex officio examination by the Court.

For example, in matters of asylum, the European Court stated consistently that in determining whether there are substantial grounds to believe that there is real risk of treatment contrary to Article 3, the Court based its decisions on all the information presented to it or, if necessary, examined *ex officio*. Given that in these cases the contracting States have a responsibility under Article 3 for exposing someone at risk of abuse, it is necessary to assess the existence of this risk, and to refer by priority to the circumstances in which the State in question had or should have knowledge of the moment of expulsion. That does not prevent the Court from taking into account further information, which can be used to confirm or disprove how the Contracting Party concerned considered the merits of an applicant's fears.[34]

Finally, an important element in the asylum process involves the consideration of risk at present, namely at the time of the lodging of the application.

Concerning cases where the risk is realised, a last important element to take into account is the obligation of State authorities to conduct an effective official investigation pursuant to positive obligations stemming from the general obligation of protection. This effective official investigation necessarily has implications with respect to evidence, and in particular for the respondent State in question.[35] The absence of positive behaviour on the State's part can cause the passive violation of the Convention.

---

[33] It is quite evident, for example, in a recent case concerning extraordinary renditions. See to that effect, App no 39630/09, *El-Masri v. the former Yugoslav Republic of Macedonia* [2012] ECtHR. In paras. 151–152, one can read: *"(...) In the proceedings before the Court, there are no procedural barriers to the admissibility of evidence or pre-determined formulae for its assessment. It adopts the conclusions that are, in its view, supported by the free evaluation of all evidence, including such inferences as may flow from the facts and the parties' submissions. According to its established case-law, proof may follow from the coexistence of sufficiently strong, clear and concordant inferences or of similar unrebutted presumptions of fact. Moreover, the level of persuasion necessary for reaching a particular conclusion and, in this connection, the distribution of the burden of proof, are intrinsically linked to the specificity of the facts, the nature of the allegation made and the Convention right at stake. The Court is also attentive to the seriousness that attaches to a ruling that a Contracting State has violated fundamental rights (...).152. Furthermore, it is to be recalled that Convention proceedings do not in all cases lend themselves to a strict application of the principle affirmanti incumbit probatio. The Court reiterates its case-law under Articles 2 and 3 of the Convention to the effect that where the events in issue lie within the exclusive knowledge of the authorities, as in the case of persons under their control in custody, strong presumptions of fact will arise in respect of injuries and death occurring during that detention. The burden of proof in such a case may be regarded as resting on the authorities to provide a satisfactory and convincing explanation (...)"*.

[34] In terms of evidence, see, e.g. App. Nos. 70073/10 and 44539/11, *H. and B. v. the United Kingdom*, [2014] ECtHR.

[35] Warolin Duteil (2005), p. 333.

Moreover, based on this positive obligation, the judge may relieve the existence of a "right to the truth" that goes beyond simple obligations *vis-à-vis* the applicant and may involve the society in its whole when it concerns facts/risks of particular gravity.[36]

In terms of reparation, the reparation of the "real risk", which is unrealized, is particularly difficult to grasp. That is why the Court considers, in general, that the mere finding of a potential violation is sufficient in order to afford just satisfaction to the victim (to repair the moral damage suffered by it). This, although it is intended as a measure of satisfaction, is interesting in the sense that the guarantee of non-execution of the harmful fact is likely to stop/eliminate the potential damage. We can see here the similarity with the provisional/interim measures, which help to stop the risk, not to repair it.

In terms of territory estrangement (extradition, expulsion, transfer of asylum seekers), such an approach may have the effect of the realization of potential, but under conditions imposed by the Court. Thus, for example, the role of the Court is not always to impose a State retention in its territory for the potential victim, but to impose the conditions to remove the risk. This is, for instance, the purpose of the requirement to obtain sufficient assurances from the receiving State relating to reception conditions, detention. . .[37]

To better understand all these aspects, it is now useful to look at some examples.

3 Illustrations of Risk Prevention in International Society

Although it is positioned in terms of the existence of an international obligation to prevent risks, the study of international case-law is also interesting concerning the control of excessive actions of government authorities when acting on that basis. Naturally, the extent of the obligations of the States and of the review by the supervisory bodies of the international law of human rights will vary depending on the issues involved.

Schematically, we can say that the supervisory bodies will tend to encourage States to adopt preventive measures when they are passive (Sect. 3.1) and control their behaviour when, on behalf of the obligation to prevent the violation of the rights of some persons subject to their jurisdiction, they will tend to interfere or to violate the rights of other individuals (Sect. 3.2).

---

[36] See below. Such was the case, for example, in the case of *El-Masri* cited above. See e.g. Panoussis (2013b), p. 5.

[37] See e.g. App. No. 29217/12, *Tarakhel v. Switzerland* [2014] ECtHR.

3.1 *The Incentive Obligation to Prevent*

3.1.1 Risk Prevention in Asylum Law

The litigation of asylum is based entirely on the concept of risk. Article 1A2 of the Geneva Convention rightly focuses on the obligation of States to assess "well-founded fear" of persecution.[38] In principle, when a case ends before the supervisory bodies, it affects the risk, the potential and the obligation of the State to prevent its occurrence.

Such an approach is recurrent in expulsion cases to the country of origin or, in some cases, to the country of first entry into the territory of the European Union (or a country associated with the asylum policy).[39] It is interesting to focus more specifically on a case that shows how the consideration of risk can impose heavy obligations on States where the risk assessment is not limited to the review of the situation in the country of return. An example for this is the case *Hirsi Jamaa*.[40]

The applicants of Somali/Eritrean nationalities were intercepted by the Italian authorities on the high seas and taken to Tripoli under an agreement ratified between Libya and Italy. In this case they were not only exposed to risks related to the security situation and the status of asylum seekers in Libya, but also to the risk of being expelled from Libya to their countries of origin where they feared persecution. In a so complex case, is it possible to impose on a State Party to the Convention to verify the deportation practices of a non-European third State? In a rather bold approach, the Court decided to weigh the responsibility of the State Party not only regarding the risk of expulsion to the "transit countries", but also the one incurred if returned by the latter to the likely final destination (delivery chain or cascade).[41] This is a quite original approach of being "indirectly responsible" because it implies an increased obligation vis-à-vis asylum seekers who often cross several countries before reaching their final destination. This enhanced duty is undoubtedly justified by the particular vulnerability of asylum seekers and the Court actually took some important precautions regarding it. To engage the responsibility of the State, the Court requires that the delivery from the third State to the State of origin seems plausible in the light of public information that the State Party has and that it is almost certain that

---

[38] According to the Convention, the term "*refugee*" *shall apply to any person who* "*(...) fear of being persecuted for reasons of race, religion, nationality, membership a particular social group or political opinion, is outside the country of his nationality and is unable or, owing to such fear, is unwilling to avail himself of the protection of that country; or who, not having a nationality and being outside the country of his former habitual residence as a result of such events, is unable or, owing to such fear, unwilling to return to it*".

[39] The European Court of Human Rights has dealt with abundant litigation in connection with the procedures of Dublin II as evidenced by the Judgments of the *M. S. S. v. Belgium and Greece* of 21 January 2011 or *Tarakhel v. Switzerland*, supra. Each time, the authorities, which were preparing to remove a person from their territory, were to conduct a risk analysis in the country of return using all the evidence described above.

[40] App. No. 27765/09, *Hirsi Jamaa and Others v. Italy*, [2012] ECtHR.

[41] Panoussis (2013a, b), p. 11.

the "transit countries" (in this case Libya) do not offer sufficient guarantees to prevent the risk to the end of the chain. This helps to understand that the European Court does not wish to insist on the State Party's obligation to monitor the situation of human rights in the State at the end of the chain, but rather evaluate the guarantees provided by the country to which the migrant is expelled.[42]

The evidence in this case was quite simple to provide, as, despite the existing public information, we were certain that Libya did not have a satisfactory asylum system.[43] All conditions were then fulfilled to fear a risk of arbitrary repression against which the State Party to the Convention must take all necessary measures to prevent the infringement of the rights of the applicants.

In view of the above, we understand that this case-law only reinforces the actual duty of prevention weighing on States to verify the state of the law and practices in the country of first delivery (in this case Libya). This enhanced obligation can, therefore, be accepted with favour, especially as it is justified by the particular vulnerability of asylum seekers.

Moreover, the issue of strengthened bonds is recurrent in the expulsion business whenever we are dealing with vulnerable groups. This was also evident in the case *Tarakhel* during which the Strasbourg Court has demonstrated once again extreme rigor/severity because children were involved.[44]

3.1.2 Risk Prevention in Environmental Law

As reported by Judge Cançado Trindade in his dissenting opinion, environmental issues are certainly among those, which generate the most questions when addressing the prevention obligations of States. Although the right to a healthy environment is still not among the rights protected by almost all texts on the protection of human rights, there are some particularly interesting case-law examples.

---

[42] See in particular paras. 147–148 which state that "*It is a matter for the State carrying out the return to ensure that the intermediary country offers sufficient guarantees to prevent the person concerned being removed to his country of origin without an assessment of the risks faced. The Court observes that that obligation is all the more important when, as in the instant case, the intermediary country is not a State Party to the Convention.*

148. In the instant case, the Court's task is not to rule on the violation of the Convention in the event of repatriation of the applicants, but to ascertain whether there were sufficient guarantees that the parties concerned would not be arbitrarily returned to their countries of origin, where they had an arguable claim that their repatriation would breach Article 3 of the Convention".

[43] Libya in this case had not even ratified the 1951 Refugee Convention.

[44] App. No. 29217/12, *Tarakhel v. Switzerland* [2014] ECtHR. More specifically, it points to para. 99 of its Judgment that "*With more specific reference to minors, the Court has established that it is important to bear in mind that the child's extreme vulnerability is the decisive factor and takes precedence over considerations relating to the status of illegal immigrant. Children have specific needs that are related in particular to their age and lack of independence, but also to their asylum-seeker status. The Court has also observed that the Convention on the Rights of the Child encourages States to take the appropriate measures to ensure that a child who is seeking to obtain refugee status enjoys protection and humanitarian assistance, whether the child is alone or accompanied by his or her parents.*"

The case, previously discussed, of *Belo Monte Dam* is certainly one such model in terms of the prevention of the obligation that weighs on the States when issues related to the preservation of the environment are addressed by international control bodies. The supervisory bodies tend to affirm strongly the positive obligations of investigation, impact assessment, and the information that results.[45]

Among the most interesting cases that have been the subject of a dispute review by a regional court, although not considered by the Grand Chamber, is in our view the case *Di Sarno*, which deals with waste management in the city of Naples and the region of Campania in Italy.[46] Three points deserve particular attention here.

Firstly, the Court adopted a particularly broad approach to the victim in that judgment in considering that a major environmental impact can affect the entire population of the region,[47] and calling into question partly the idea of the existence of a direct damage to qualify for victim status.[48] We stay on the logic of potential damage in respect of the entire population without switching to the *actio popularis*. This is a complex balance, but necessary to strike.[49]

Secondly, regarding the positive obligations arising for the State in terms of its obligation to prevent, the Court goes far enough along the lines of the Aarhus Convention. The Court decided in accordance with Article 8 CEDH to interact with this special text with the aim of enriching the obligations on States in environmental matters. The heart of these obligations lies still in the duty to inform the public of the risks they incur in order to prevent attacks on the integrity and home of the public. However, what is remarkable is that the Court is not limited to this. It also requires, on the part of the respondent State (in this case Italy) to take all necessary operational measures to provide an effective waste collection service.[50]

Finally, it is important to understand that even if States have wide discretion in how to implement their positive obligations (in the case of Italy to delegate the

---

[45] See Case MC 382/10, *Comunidades Indígenas da Bacia do Rio Xingu v. Brazil* [2011] IACHR.

[46] App no 30765/08, *Di Sarno and Others v. Italy* [2012] ECtHR.

[47] The Strasbourg Court does not distinguish in this matter between workers and residents thus expanding the number of individuals eligible to victim status under Article 8 ECHR and in particular under the protection of private life and home.

[48] To qualify for victim status, it is always important to demonstrate the direct damage to individualize grievances. In this case, it appears that the magnitude of the crisis was in itself sufficient to satisfy this requirement, which led the judge to establish a kind of existence of the presumption of direct damage to the benefit of all the applicants. See to that effect paragraph 81 of the Judgment: "*(...) les requérants dénoncent une situation affectant l'ensemble de la population de la Campanie, à savoir l'atteinte à l'environnement provoquée par le mauvais fonctionnement du système de collecte, de traitement et d'élimination des déchets mis en place par les autorités publiques. Toutefois, elle relève qu'il ressort des documents fournis par les parties que Somma Vesuviana a été frappée par la « crise des déchets (...) Dans ces conditions, la Cour estime que les dommages à l'environnement dénoncés par les requérants sont de nature à affecter directement leur propre bien-être. Partant, il y a lieu de rejeter l'exception du Gouvernement*". See Panoussis (2014), p. 17.

[49] Panoussis (2014).

[50] Panoussis (2014).

obligation to ensure the waste collection service to a private operator) they still remain responsible for the proper implementation of the international obligation of prevention. The Court is quite clear on this point by stating that "*Regard must also be had to the margin of appreciation the States enjoy in the choice of the concrete means they use to fulfil their positive obligations under Article 8 of the Convention... The fact that the Italian authorities handed over the management of a public service to third parties does not relieve them of the duty of care incumbent on them under Article 8 of the Convention.*"[51] A State cannot discard its obligations by delegating.

These examples could easily be multiplied. It is now common practice to remind States that they must be proactive to prevent violations of human rights. What about situations where States abuse their power to achieve some other objectives consistent with the international instruments they have ratified?

3.2 Supervision of Preventive Measures

Unlike the previous examples, there are areas in which States undertake risk prevention willingly. These are most often measures taken to manage "classic" safety risks. What is, however, the extent of their powers?

3.2.1 Risk Prevention in the Fight Against Terrorism

As part of the fight against terrorism, the difficulty lies in finding a balance between preventing terrorist risk and therefore the obligation to protect the population, and the prevention of the violations of the rights of the accused or suspected person of committing terrorist acts.[52] We are thus faced with two obligations of prevention that seem irreconcilable in theory.

[51] App. No. 30765/08, *Di Sarno and Others v. Italy* [2012] ECtHR, para. 110.

[52] Regarding the first requirement, the European Court of Human Rights had occasion to state that the State authorities were required to neutralize activists spreading terror. See to that effect App. No. 22535/93, *Mahmut Kaya v. Turkey* [2012] ECtHR, para. 85. In the case it is specified that "*the first sentence of Article 2 § 1 enjoins the State not only to refrain from the intentional and unlawful taking of life, but also to take appropriate steps to safeguard the lives of those within its jurisdiction. This involves a primary duty on the State to secure the right to life by putting in place effective criminal-law provisions to deter the commission of offences against the person, backed up by law-enforcement machinery for the prevention, suppression and punishment of breaches of such provisions. It also extends in appropriate circumstances to a positive obligation on the authorities to take preventive operational measures to protect an individual or individuals whose life is at risk from the criminal acts of another individual.*" On the second, namely the right of everyone, including alleged terrorists, to benefit from the protection of the State, the obligation to prevent resulted from the positive obligations studied above. The only question that remains is that of the ownership of rights even for *hostis humanis*. On this point, see Hennebel and Tigroudja (2009), p. 65, pp. 90 et seq.

Numerous examples exist today on this issue. Most of them deal either with the deportation of persons suspected of being terrorists to their countries of origin where they are at risk of ill-treatment, or with their "preventive detention".[53] The difficulty in these cases is mainly in the possible prioritization of the duties of the State. By preventing a security risk for the population, does the State take on the prevention of individual rights and freedoms of the suspect? For some, human rights are a domain where some kind of "collateral damage" is inevitable.[54]

That is not the approach of the international control bodies that will constantly confirm the fact that even the alleged terrorist cannot be deprived of his rights[55] and that, to the rights that are at stake—usually those related to the physical integrity of the person, namely the prohibition of torture or inhuman or degrading treatment, the right to life, the right to safety and security . . .—the margin of appreciation of States is almost non-existent. The case *A. and Others v. the United Kingdom* is particularly revealing in this regard, the Strasbourg Court refusing any possibility of the State to extend the scope of Article 5 ECHR (right to safety) by claiming to look for a balance between these two supposedly opposing duties.[56]

Among the most high-profile and resounding cases of importance in this matter is the case *El-Masri v. FYROM*.[57] At first, this case is part of the logical continuation of a series of cases relating to the transfer of a person to the authorities of another State where there would be a risk of violation of their human rights. The Court, therefore, had no difficulty in establishing the responsibility of the State Party in turn due to the real risk to which it submits the applicant. Where *El-Masri* differs, however, is that the other authorities concerned are the Intelligence Services of the United States of America (namely the CIA). As part of the "preventive measures" decided by the US Agency, the concept of "state secret" enhances the sense of a form of immunity which they would enjoy and which partially covers the behaviour of a European respondent State. The Strasbourg Court will oppose an obligation to shed light on what really happened that takes the form of a "right to the

[53] See, e.g., App. No. 22414/93, *Chahal v. the United Kingdom*, [1996], ECtHR. App. No. 37201/06, *Saadi v. Italy* [2008], ECtHR. App. No. 3455/05, *A. and Others v. the United Kingdom* [2009] ECtHR. Case 619-03, *Norin Catriman* and *Others v. Chile* [2007] IACHR.

[54] This is a stance adopted by several States, headed by the United States, as evidenced by the International Commission of Jurists in its 2009 report, *Assessing Damage, Urging Action*, pp. 17 et seq.

[55] See in this sense Hennebel and Tigroudja (2009), p. 22.

[56] App. No. 3455/05, *A. and Others v. the United Kingdom* [2009] ECtHR and particularly para. 171 of its Judgment which says that "*does not accept the Government's argument that Article 5 § 1 permits a balance to be struck between the individual's right to liberty and the State's interest in protecting its population from terrorist threat. This argument is inconsistent not only with the Court's jurisprudence under sub-paragraph (f) but also with the principle that sub-paragraphs (a) to (f) amount to an exhaustive list of exceptions and that only a narrow interpretation of these exceptions is compatible with the aims of Article 5. If detention does not fit within the confines of the sub-paragraphs as interpreted by the Court, it cannot be made to fit by an appeal to the need to balance the interests of the State against those of the detainee.*"

[57] App. No. 39630/09, *El-Masri v. the former Yugoslav Republic of Macedonia* [2012] ECtHR.

truth".[58] To achieve this, a very dynamic approach to proof will be used, as we have mentioned above, based on *sufficiently strong, clear and concordant inferences* and the reversal of the burden of proof.[59]

What conclusions should we draw? The first is that there is no hierarchy in the duties facing the State. Preventing a terrorist threat cannot be to the detriment of the suspect, especially when a *jus cogens* norm is at stake, namely the prohibition of torture. The second remark is that the duty of prevention, in particular the steps taken on this behalf, is also the subject of a rigorous European supervision. Finally, the international monitoring body will still evaluate the behaviour of the State with its obligation to respect the principles of necessity, proportionality, and non-discrimination, which will guide the State when acting on the basis of its obligation of prevention. Therefore, the conclusion to which we are inevitably led is not that of the impossible reconciliation of the divergent prevention obligations, but of the need to do that by respecting the framework imposed by the instruments of protection of human rights. The States, when they want to adapt a legal regime of human rights, they must do so through means such as derogations, restrictions or limitations provided in the texts.[60]

3.2.2 Risk Prevention in Armed Conflicts

Among the security risks that the European Court of Human Rights had to address recently was the question of the intervention of State Parties in international armed conflicts that take place outside the European geographical space. Although the issue of the jurisdiction of the State is already regulated by extensive case-law,[61] a fundamental question remains unanswered: What is the extent of the State's powers under the international law of human rights analysed in the light of the State's prerogative issues regarding international humanitarian law?

The judgment in the *Hassan v. the United Kingdom* case[62] is particularly relevant in the matter. It addresses the difficult issue of the reconciliation of international humanitarian law with the international law of human rights during armed conflict. The fundamental point in relation to the obligation to prevent lies in the possible control by the protection systems of the "preventive detention" and, in particular, the ability of States to take prisoners of war and detain civilians posing a

[58] See in particular para. 192 of the Judgment. Note, moreover, that this right has been explicitly enshrined by the Inter-American Court of Human Rights. See Case C No. 70, Bámaca-Velásquez v. Guatemala, [2000] IACHR, paras. 201 et seq. See e.g. Tigroudja and Panoussis (2003), p. 275.

[59] See in particular, paras. 151–152 of the Judgment.

[60] See, on this specific point Panoussis (2011), pp. 197–218.

[61] See App. No. 55721/07, *Al-Skeini and Others v. the United Kingdom* [2011] ECtHR and App. No. 27021/08, *Al-Jedda v. the United Kingdom* [2011] ECtHR and the analysis proposed by Panoussis (2012), p. 647.

[62] App. No. 29750/09, *Hassan v. the United Kingdom* [2014] ECtHR.

threat to security. This question is all the more interesting that, solely on the basis of international humanitarian law, it is lawful since it is one of the state attributes if the prisoner of war is still representing a certain degree of dangerousness.

The European Court wishes, by a very complex and debatable argument,[63] to assert that the preventive measures taken by States in the context of international armed conflict may be the subject of a control if the State has not used the mechanism provided for in Article 15 of the Convention on derogations in times of war or other public emergency threatening the life of the nation. To do this, the Court decided to extend the application of Article 5 of the European Convention in times of international armed conflict to include the deprivation of liberty under the 3rd and 4th Geneva Conventions. This resulted in offering jurisdiction to the Court on the rights and duties derived from International Humanitarian Law in the context of human rights.[64] In practice, this has a relative impact since the Court will use the criteria imposed by International Humanitarian Law in order to proceed to its control. Symbolically, however, this constitutes an additional way to control the behaviour of States and to fight against the excesses. This question, relatively old in substance, but new in its treatment by a court, constitutes, in view of the increasing number of international conflicts, an important challenge in the "international society of risk".

4 Conclusion

These examples are only illustrations to better understand the challenge of preventing violations of human rights. Beyond classical security risks, the relevance of this issue is pervasive in many other areas, such as the development of new technologies and in particular the "data records" of individuals[65] or that of domestic violence.[66] Therefore, without a doubt, this here is one step in a long road of twists and jurisprudential developments.

---

[63] See in particular the dissenting opinion on this one aspect of the Judgment of the Judges Spano, Nicolaou, Bianku and Kalaydjieva.

[64] The reasoning of the Court in paragraph 104 is: "*By reason of the co-existence of the safeguards provided by international humanitarian law and by the Convention in time of armed conflict, the grounds of permitted deprivation of liberty set out in subparagraphs (a) to (f) of that provision should be accommodated, as far as possible, with the taking of prisoners of war and the detention of civilians who pose a risk to security under the Third and Fourth Geneva Conventions. The Court is mindful of the fact that internment in peacetime does not fall within the scheme of deprivation of liberty governed by Article 5 of the Convention without the exercise of the power of derogation under Article 15 (see paragraph 97 above). It can only be in cases of international armed conflict, where the taking of prisoners of war and the detention of civilians who pose a threat to security are accepted features of international humanitarian law, that Article 5 could be interpreted as permitting the exercise of such broad powers*".

[65] See e.g. App. No. 21010/10, *Brunet v. France* [2014] ECtHR.

[66] App. No. 3564/11, *Eremia and Others v. the Republic of Moldova* [2013] ECtHR.

References

Cançado Trindade AA (1987) Co-existence and co-ordination of international mechanisms of protection of human rights (at global and regional levels). During the Collection of the Hague Academy of International Law 202(XI)

Decaux E, Touzé S (eds) (2015) La prévention des violations des droits de l'Homme. Pedone (Publications de l'Institut international des droits de l'Homme), Paris

Frumer P (2005) Un arrêt définitif sur les mesures provisoires: la Cour européenne des droits de l'homme persiste et signe. Revue trimestrielle des droits de l'Homme 16:799

Hennebel L, Tigroudja H (2009) Le juge, le terroriste et l'État de droit in Juger le terrorisme dans l'État de droit. Bruxelles, Bruylant

Lazarte BR (2013) Une réforme du système interaméricain des droits de l'Homme dans un contexte périlleux. La revue des Droits de l'Homme, in Lettre "Actualités Droits-Libertés" du Credof

Morgan R, Evans M (2002) Combattre la torture en Europe - Le travail et les normes du Comité Européen pour la Prévention de la Torture. Éditions du Conseil de l'Europe, Strasbourg

Mowbray AR (2004) The development of positive obligations under the European Convention on Human Rights by the European Court of Human Rights. Hart Publishing, Oxford

Nicolay C (1996) Une nouvelle approche des droits de l'Homme: la Convention européenne pour la prévention de la torture et des peines ou traitements inhumains ou dégradants. Revue pénitentiaire de droit pénal

Panoussis I (2007) L'obligation générale de protection des droits de l'Homme. RTDH 70:427–461

Panoussis I (2011) The control of European restrictions and derogations to human rights due to counter-terrorism measures. In: Hennebel L, Tigroudja H (eds) Balancing liberty and security: the human rights pendulum. Wolf Legal Publishers, The Netherlands

Panoussis I (2012) L'application extraterritoriale de la Convention européenne des droits de l'homme en Irak. In: Revue Trimestrielle des Droits de l'Homme, no 91, p 647

Panoussis I (2013a) L'interception de migrants en haute mer et les risques associés à leur refoulement immédiat vers un Etat tiers (Cour EDH, Grande chambre, arrêt du 23 février 2012, Hirsi Jamaa et autres contre Italie). Chronique Droit et Risque, Les Petites Affiches 11:7

Panoussis I (2013b) La pratique des "restitutions extraordinaires", comme moyen de prévention du risque terroriste, à l'épreuve de la Convention européenne des droits de l'homme (Cour EDH, Grande Chambre, arrêt du 13 décembre 2012, El-Masri c/ ex-République yougoslave de Macédoine). Chronique Droit et Risque, Les Petites Affiches 242:5

Panoussis I (2014) Waste management in the ECHR – an introduction. In: Panoussis I, Post H (eds) Waste management and European law. Eleven International Publishing, Den Haag/ Netherlands

Rieter ER (2010) Preventing irreparable harm: provisional measures in international human rights adjudication. Intersentia, Antwerp

Rieter ER (2012) Provisional measures: binding and persuasive? Enabling human rights adjudicators to follow up on state disrespect. Neth Int Law Rev 59

Steinerte E (2013) The changing nature of relationship of the United Nations between the subcommittee for the prevention of torture and national preventive mechanisms in search for equilibrium. Neth Q Hum Rights 31:132

Sudre F (2000) Les 'obligations positives' dans la jurisprudence européenne des droits de l'Homme. In: Protection des droits de l'homme: la perspective européenne. Mélanges en l'honneur de Rolv Ryssdall, Karl Heymanns Verlag KG, Köln

Tigroudja H (2001) Contributions à l'étude du statut de la victime en droit international des droits de l'homme, Thèse. DACT, Lille II

Tigroudja H (2015) L'(in)efficacité des mesures provisoires internationales en matière de prévention des violations des droits de l'homme. In: Decaux E, Touzé S (eds) La prévention des violations des droits de l'Homme. Pedone (Publications de l'Institut international des droits de l'homme), Paris

Tigroudja H, Panoussis I (2003) La Cour interaméricaine des droits de l'homme. Analyse de la jurisprudence consultative et contentieuse. Bruylant, Collection Droit et Justice, Bruxelles
Warolin Duteil L (2005) La Cour européenne des droits d l'homme aux prises avec la preuve de violations du droit à la vie ou de l'interdiction de la torture: entre théorie classique aménagée et innovation européenne. RTDH 62:333

Linguistic Equality and Language as a Legal Risk for Legislating in the European Union

Réka Somssich

Contents

Abstract Multilingualism is one of the core principles the European Union (EU) is based on. Much has been written in the legal literature on the risks arising out of eventual divergences between the different official language versions. However, less attention has been paid to the risks multilingualism entails for the practical enforcement and implementation of EU legislation as well as in certain cases even for its adoption. The present chapter will focus on these aspects with the aim of highlighting the most important cases where recent legislation was either faced with the problem of limiting linguistic equality for the sake of efficient functioning or where multilingualism made it necessary to enact special provisions on language use or translation requirements. It will be demonstrated, on the one hand, that even after more than six decades since the foundation of the first Community, the claim for equal or privileged status for a national language is still an issue being able to block the adoption of an EU measure. On the other hand, it will be shown that recent legislation adopted in the field of internal market law and judicial cooperation is more open to deal with language issues and see them as an obstacle to the smooth functioning of the Union that should be overcome or at least handled.

R. Somssich (✉)
Faculty of Law, Eötvös Loránd University, Budapest, Hungary
e-mail: somssichreka@ajk.elte.hu

E. Miščenić, A. Raccah (eds.), *Legal Risks in EU Law*,
DOI 10.1007/978-3-319-28596-2_4

1 Introduction

The EU—based since its foundation on the equality of the official languages of its Member States—is the only international organisation where the official languages of the members (at least one of the official languages) are at the same time official languages of the organisation.[1] Adopting legislation in 24 languages is already a risk if we take into consideration the budgetary implications[2] and the possible "translation" problems arising out of the linguistic equality.[3] One should also add that the number of languages is not only growing because of the subsequent accessions, but also because of the granting of official language status to second official languages of Member States. This is what happened in the case of Maltese as a result of a compromise reached at the very end of the accession negotiations[4] and in the case of Irish in 2007, 34 years after Ireland joined the EU.[5]

Languages having official status in a Member State form an inherent part of the cultural identity of the country concerned. They have both a symbolic and practical significance. As a symbol of national identity, they claim equal treatment with all other official languages of the other Member States in all respect when language use is regulated. This claim persists regardless of whether any restriction on this use would be justified. At the same time, official languages are the languages in which EU citizens are able to get informed about their rights and obligations as well as

[1] The EU's language system is exceptional, Luxembourgish being currently the only nationwide official language of a Member State, which is not at the same time an official language of the EU (Schilling 2008, pp. 1224–1225).

[2] In 2014, 64,265 legal texts were published in the HTML format in 24 languages (see: http://eur-lex.europa.eu/statistics/2014/eu-law-statistics.html?locale=en, last visited 14.04.2015).

[3] Although legal texts adopted by EU institutions are equally authentic in all languages, the different language versions are in fact translations of the language version in which the text is originally drafted, even if they thoroughly follow the changes and evolution of the draft (see: Somssich et al. 2010, pp. 18–38).

[4] The Commission's Comprehensive Monitoring Report of 2003 on Malta's preparation for membership notes that Malta started the process of translation of the acquis relatively late and faced a delay of 50,000 pages out of 70,000 to be translated into Maltese (see: http://ec.europa.eu/enlargement/archives/pdf/key_documents/2003/cmr_mt_final_en.pdf, last visited 14.04.2015). The Regular Report of 2001 on Malta's progress towards accession urges the Maltese administration to undertake additional efforts in the area of translating the acquis "without prejudice to the outcome of the accession negotiations", which suggests that the issue whether Maltese will in fact become an official language of the EU was still pending at that time (SEC (2001) 1751, p. 75). The first report including a separate chapter on the translation of the acquis was the Regular Report of 2000 underlining that no part of the acquis has been translated so far (Report of 8 November 2000, p. 63, see: http://ec.europa.eu/enlargement/archives/pdf/key_documents/2000/mt_en.pdf, last visited 14.04.2015).

[5] See Council Regulation (EC) No. 920/2005 of 13 June 2005 amending Regulation No. 1 of 15 April 1958 determining the language to be used by the European Economic Community and Regulation No. 1 of 15 April 1958 determining the language to be used by the European Atomic Energy Community and introducing temporary derogation measures from these Regulations.

enter into cross-border activities necessitating communication, understanding of information or self-expression.

In its second Communication on Multilingualism, the Commission underlined that the EU is committed to the harmonious co-existence of many languages in Europe and sees it as "a powerful symbol of the Union's aspiration to be united in diversity, one of the cornerstones of the European project."[6] However, multilingualism operating with so many languages cannot be limitless. As Theodor Schilling rightly points out: The obvious question that should raise is whether the very effort to legislate multilinguistically is self-defeating, by necessity or at least as practiced by the EU.[7]

The main challenge for the EU in this respect is thus to find the right balance between its endeavour to guarantee multilingualism and equality of languages on the one hand and practical, institutional and budgetary implications on the other. Thereby it is running several risks: If the EU puts forward a legislative proposal to limit multilingualism, it might be confronted with the national sensitivity of those Member States whose languages are disadvantaged by the proposal. If the EU extends the scope of multilingualism to new areas, it might interfere with national legislative competences or financial interests. The examples below demonstrate some of these risks and their side effects. These examples are in no way comprehensive, but rather illustrative.

2 Special Language Arrangements Restricting Linguistic Equality

The Treaties contain several references on the equal treatment of languages as far as the authenticity of the different language versions of the Treaties and the rights of citizens' to communicate with EU institutions are concerned[8] and the Charter of Fundamental Rights of the European Union obliges the EU to guarantee the respect of linguistic diversity.[9] Moreover, the very first Regulation adopted by the Council in 1958[10] is about the use of languages. It extends linguistic equality to the drafting and publication of regulations and other documents of general application[11] as well

[6] 'Multilingualism: An Asset for Europe and a Shared Commitment.' Communication from the Commission to the European Parliament, the Council, the European Economic and Social Committee and the Committee of Regions (COM (2008), 566 final.

[7] Schilling (2008), p. 1225.

[8] Article 55 TEU and Article 358 TFEU on the authentic languages of the Treaties, Article 20 and Article 24 TFEU on the rights to address institutions and bodies in any of the Treaty languages; see also Declaration No. 16 on the possibility to produce translations of the Treaty into official languages of the Member States which are not official languages of the EU.

[9] Article 22 of the Charter.

[10] Regulation No. 1 determining the languages to be used by the European Economic Community.

[11] Articles 4 and 5 of the Regulation.

as guarantees the use of any official language in any communication between Member States or a person subject to the jurisdiction of a Member State, on the one hand, and EU institutions on the other hand.[12] Article 6 of the Regulation authorises EU institutions to stipulate in their rules of procedure which of the languages are to be used in a specific case. It is however silent on the criteria to be taken into account when regulating internal language use of the institutions and on the use of procedural languages at EU agencies and bodies in charge of conducting administrative procedures at EU level.

The silence of the Regulation can also be explained by the fact that linguistic equality must have a logical limit in order to ensure the efficient functioning of not only the institutions themselves, but at the same time also of the EU policies and especially rules of the internal market. In some cases this kind of efficiency guided approach provokes resistance on behalf of Member States whose languages would be victims of the limitation. One of the most striking examples of the last years where this tension reached a degree that could not be handled anymore is without any doubt the Unitary Patent Regulation. The need for a unitary (or Community) patent system in the EU has already been in the focus of the European Commission since the 90's in order to enhance the competitiveness of European industry at the global level and reduce the costs of patent litigation.[13] However, differences of view between Member States over the linguistic regime have frustrated all previous unitary patent projects.[14] Lacking EU wide legislation the granting of European patents has been regulated by an international agreement—the European Patent Convention.[15] The shortcomings of that system are mainly due to the high transla-

[12] Articles 2 and 3 of the Regulation.

[13] See Kupzok (2014).

[14] See the reference in paragraph 25 of the opinion of Advocate General Bot in the Case C-147/13, *Kingdom of Spain v Council of the European Union* (EU:C:2014:2381).

[15] Under the European Patent Convention the content of the European patents taking effect in the particular States that signed the agreement is equivalent to the patents granted by the national offices. The Convention requires the validation of the granted patent separately in each and every signatory State. The European Patent Organisation (EPO) granting the patent has only three official languages (English, German and French) in which patent applications can be lodged and patents will be granted. Most countries require by virtue of Article 65 (1) of the Convention the complete text of the European patent to be translated into their national language as a precondition for the European patent taking effect in the territory of that country. In order to reduce translation costs a special agreement was signed in 2000 (London Agreement) for a simplified post-grant language regime. The simplified regime is based on the three procedural languages of the EPO where patent documentation would always be available in either of these languages and patent claims in all of these languages. Moreover, signatory States not having either of these languages as one of their official languages could ask for the translation of the documentation into one of the procedural languages in which it is not available and the translation of the patent claims into their own official language.

tion costs patenting entails in the countries where protection is sought.[16] Therefore, one of the cornerstones of the proposed EU legislation was to reduce the number of languages into which patent claims and descriptions should be translated. The sensitivity of the language issue was already underlined by the new legal basis enabling the adoption of acts on unitary titles and inserted into the TFEU by the Lisbon Treaty. The new Article 118 TFEU contains a distinct paragraph on language arrangements for European intellectual property rights foreseeing unanimity for the adoption despite the qualified majority voting necessary for the creation of such rights. In fact, the new Treaty rules mean that no Unitary Patent Regulation can be adopted without the support of all Member States because the system would be unworkable without the linguistic regime.

The languages chosen for the new Regulation were identical to the official languages of the European Patent Office (English, French and German)[17] in charge of granting the current European patents. Such a limitation is not foreign to European law given the fact that the Office for Harmonisation in the Internal Market (OHIM) responsible for registering European trademarks already has a restricted language system based on five procedural languages (English, French, German, Italian and Spanish).[18] In the *Kik* case,[19] the linguistic regime of the OHIM was approved by the European Court of Justice, which ruled that the EC Treaty contains "several references to the use of languages in the European Union. None the less, those references cannot be regarded as evidencing a general principle of Community law that confers a right on every citizen to have a version of anything that might affect his interests drawn up in his language in all circumstances".[20] Thus, Regulation 1/58, according to which any EU citizen can communicate with any EU institution in any of the official languages of the EU, is in the reading of the Court not applicable to procedural languages of EU bodies. Paragraph 92 of the judgment further explained that the language regime of the OHIM was created in order to achieve a proper balance between the interests of economic operators and the public interest in terms of the cost of proceedings, on the one hand, as well as, on the other hand, the interests of applicants for Community trademarks and those

[16] The European Commission considered in its Impact Assessment accompanying the proposal on a unitary patent that even if the London Agreement reduced the costs of validation requirements in some Member States, the overall cost of validation in the three Member States with the EPO official languages (GER, FR, UK) equals EUR 680. These costs reach EUR 12,500 in 13 Member States and over EUR 32,000 if a patent is validated in the whole EU. It is estimated that the actual validation costs are around EUR 193 million per year in the EU (SEC (2011) 483 final, para. 3.1).

[17] Proposal for a Council Regulation implementing the enhanced cooperation in the area of the creation of a unitary patent. Brussels, 13.4.2011, COM (2011) 216 final, 2011/0094 (CNS).

[18] Under Regulation (EC) 40/94 on Community trademarks, the application for a Community trademark shall be filed in one of the official languages of the European Community while the applicant must indicate a second language which shall be a language of the Office the use of which he/she accepts as a possible language of proceedings for opposition, revocation or invalidity proceedings.

[19] Case C-361/01, *Kik* (EU:C:2003:434).

[20] Paragraph 82 of the Judgment.

of other economic operators with regard to access to translations of documents which confer rights, or proceedings involving more than one economic operator.

By virtue of the *Kik* judgment, the Council is free to establish a language regime which is more restrictive than the one foreseen by Regulation 1/58. There is no consistent language policy to be followed when setting the frame for language regimes of bodies and agencies.[21]

Despite the clear guidance of the *Kik* judgment, Spain and Italy systematically refused since the release of the Commission proposal to adopt a regulation under which a unitary patent would not be authentic in their languages. This against the fact that the three language system under the unitary patent is not as radical as it seems at first sight. The proposal foresees a number of measures aimed at mitigating the potential harmful effects of restricting the language regime such as compensating translation costs or making the non-official translation of patent descriptions available in all official languages of the EU with the help of machine translation after a transition period of 12 years. The two countries, however, sought the same treatment for Spanish and Italian as the treatment granted to the other "big" languages.[22] It seems that the action taken by Italy and Spain fits into the general approach they follow with regard to language policy at European level.[23]

[21] Ó Reagen (2010), p. 111.

[22] Although it seems that later claims of the Spanish government against Regulation 1260/2012 were mainly based on the alleged breach of the principle of non-discrimination by creating a linguistic regime which is detrimental to persons whose language is not one of the official languages of the EPO, political declarations made during and after the negotiation phase demonstrate that the real reason behind the systematic refusal was in fact the unequal treatment of English, French and German on the one hand and Italian and Spanish on the other hand (see the speech of the Secretary of State of the Spanish Ministry of Foreign Affairs and Cooperation at the Council meeting on 30 May 2011). This is further underlined by the fact that according to the Spanish government the language regime for the Community trademark with five languages did achieve a balance between the interests of undertakings and those of the public while the Regulation 1260/2012 did not.

[23] Italy, supported by Spain and Latvia, lodged in 2005 an action against a decision of the Commission according to which external publications of the vacancy notices for senior management posts in the Official Journal of the European Union shall henceforth be in English, French and German for a period which shall in principle end on 1 January 2007 (Case T-185/05, *Italian Republic v European Commission* (EU:T:2008:519)). The decision was explained by the lack of translation capacity. At the same time the annulment of a vacancy notice published in the meantime was also sought by the Italian government. Italy pleaded that the Commission has breached the principles of non-discrimination on the grounds of nationality and respect for linguistic diversity. It submitted that adopting the *Kik* type of restrictions in language use is only permitted for the Council, not for the Commission. The Court of First Instance held that candidates for EU institution posts cannot benefit from the equal treatment provision of Regulation 1/58 since that Regulation does not apply to relations between the institutions and their officials and other servants since it only lays down the language rules applying between the institutions of the European Community and a Member State or a person coming under the jurisdiction of one of the Member States. Similar claims were lodged later by Italy (Joined Cases T-166/07 and T-285/07, *Italian Republic v European Commission* (EU:T:2010:393)), equally unsuccessfully.

The issue then became crucial: The Commission insisted on maintaining the original proposal arguing that the inclusion of any new language would undermine the added value of the new system that is raising cost effectiveness while the two Member States concerned saw the language issue as a *sine qua non* condition of the adoption.

The result is well-known: The Unitary Patent Regulations could only be adopted in the form of an enhanced cooperation[24] with the participation of 25 Member States where Italy and Spain not only refrained from the legislation, but at the same time attacked—although unsuccessfully—the decision on enhanced cooperation at the European Court of Justice.[25] In these actions, the pleas were based on the unlawfulness and misuse of the enhanced cooperation. The language issue appears in several pleas. Both countries based their second pleas on the misuse of powers. In this respect they claimed that the Council, by authorising the enhanced cooperation in question, circumvented the requirement of unanimity laid down by the second paragraph of Article 118 TFEU and brushed aside those two Member States' objections to the Commission's proposal on the language arrangements for the unitary patent. The Court rejected this claim by stating that the decision of the Council clearly proves that the rules on enhanced cooperation were not breached as the unitary patent and its language arrangements could not be established by the Union as a whole within a reasonable period.[26] Spain and Italy further argued that the Council could not adopt enhanced cooperation as a last resort as language arrangements had by no means been exhausted. The Court rejected this argument too as facts showed opposite findings. Finally, the applicants claimed that the enhanced cooperation in question is the source of the distortion of competition and of discrimination between undertakings because of the fact that trade in innovatory products is made easier for undertakings working in English, French or German. The Court, however, refused to rule on the compatibility of language arrangements with EU law arguing that they were at a preparatory stage when the contested decision was adopted and do not form part of it.[27]

Matthias Lamping claims that the Court was wrong in not examining whether the restricted language system as such would be able to distort competition in the internal market, regardless of the degree of elaboration of the rules, as language arrangements were the actual trigger for enhanced cooperation and thus the question of principle. He says that the exclusion of the issue of compatibility of the

---

[24] The decision on the enhanced cooperation was taken in March 2011 (2011/167 [2011] L 76/54), the two Regulations were adopted in December 2012: Regulation (EU) No. 1257/2012 of the European Parliament and the Council of 17 December 2012 implementing the enhanced cooperation in the area of the creation of unitary patent protection, Council Regulation (EU) No. 1260/2012 of 17 December 2012 implementing the enhanced cooperation in the area of the creation of unitary patent protection with regard to the applicable translation arrangements.

[25] Joined Cases C-274/11 and C-295/11, *Kingdom of Spain and Italian Republic v Council of the European Union* (EU:C:2013:240).

[26] See paragraphs 27–41 of the Judgment.

[27] See paragraph 76 of the Judgment.

language arrangements with the Union law from the subject matter of the proceedings testifies to the Court's lack of appreciation of the actual interests at stake and the only thing that should have been carefully assessed in connection with the authorising decision is the language arrangement and its effects.[28]

We can only agree with this analysis which is further underlined by the fact that after the two Regulations were published, Spain (this time alone) brought an action for annulment against the Regulation on the language arrangements[29] claiming that the linguistic regime creates an inequality between, on the one hand, EU citizens and undertakings that have the capacity to understand, with a certain level of expertise, documents drafted in the three official languages of the EPO and, on the other hand, those without that capacity who will have to have translations made at their own expense. All arguments submitted by Spain are focused on the detrimental effect of the language regime on citizens and undertakings.

In this case an extremely high number of Member States and institutions were intervening in order to support the Council.[30] The Court—in its judgment of 5 of May 2015—ruled recalling the *Kik* jurisprudence that the chosen linguistic regime differentiating between the official languages of the EU pursues a legitimate objective and does not go beyond what is necessary. First, it pointed out that European patent covering the territory of all Member States constitute an obstacle to patent protection within the European Union, and consequently it was essential that the translation arrangements for the Regulation should be demonstrably cost-effective.[31] Second, the Court underlined that a number of mechanisms designed to secure the necessary balance between the interests of applicants for the unitary patent and the interests of other economic operators in regard to access to translations were introduced by the Regulation such as compensation of translation costs, special translation arrangements during the transitional period and translation requirements in case of litigation.[32] The remaining four pleas of the Kingdom of Spain alleging the breach of the *Meroni* judgment, the principle of legal certainty, the autonomy of EU law and the lack of legal basis were also rejected by the Court.

Regardless of the recent judgment of the Court upholding the validity of language regime, the entry into force of the Patent Regulations is still dependent on the ratification by Member States of the third element of the so-called patent package, the Agreement on a Unified Patent Court,[33] which is not unproblematic either (but this time not for languages).

[28] Lamping (2015), pp. 6–7.

[29] Case C-147/13, Spain v Council (EU:C:2015:299).

[30] Belgium, the Czech Republic, Denmark, Germany, France, Luxembourg, Hungary, the Netherlands, Sweden, the United Kingdom, the European Parliament and the European Commission were granted leave to intervene.

[31] See paragraph 42 of the judgment.

[32] See paragraphs 44–46 of the judgment.

[33] The entry into force of the regulations is dependent of the ratification by at least 13 signatory states of the Agreement on a Unified Patent Court (OJ C 175/1, 2013.6.20.), an inseparable part of the so-called patent package. Interestingly Italy—not participating in the enhanced cooperation—signed this agreement, while Poland did not (Pila and Wadlow 2015, p. 46).

The Unitary Patent Regulation is the first legislative act where linguistic sensitivity was able to hamper the adoption of a European instrument and where language as well as the claim for linguistic equality (at least in the case of languages that were already included among the procedural languages of another EU organ) appeared to be a legal risk for the legislature that could not be handled in the process of ordinary lawmaking anymore and therefore an exceptional regulatory frame had to be chosen. Even if it is lawful under EU law, the restriction of internal language regimes within the EU has clearly reached its limits with the unitary patent saga making the adoption of an EU-wide regulation impossible and resulting in a system which will only be applicable in 25 out of 28 Member States (Croatia not having joined the enhanced cooperation) compromising the ultimate aim of any European act—that of having uniform rules throughout the whole EU. Thus, legal risks as a consequence of the impossibility of adopting an ordinary EU act because of the language issue still persist after the adoption of the regulations under the enhanced cooperation as this form of cooperation by its very nature generates risks of fragmented enforcement.

3 Information Requirements

The limitation of institutional or procedural use of languages is not the only risk for EU legislation arising out of multilingualism. Internal market rules that at first sight do not seem to have anything to do with language problems or requirements might well be compromised when not taking into account the fact that they are enforced in a multilingual legal area. Often these risks are not yet identified in the phase of elaboration, but at a later stage, in the quest for the reasons for the failure of the rules concerned to achieve their goals.

One of the problems here is the lack of information available to and understandable for EU citizens as well as undertakings on national provisions in non-harmonised areas. Providing information on its own legislation in other languages than its own official language(s) is in principle an issue that is reserved for national law and is not part of the EU's competences. However, the non-availability of information might amount to the hindering of rights individuals enjoy under internal market rules, especially the four freedoms. Citizens and SME's mainly might be prevented from efficiently exercising their rights under EU law as they are lacking the financial resources for legal advice or translation of the relevant legislation. Although it is quite questionable whether EU legislation can oblige Member States to provide information on their official website in a language or languages other than their own official language, it seems that recent EU legislation tries to solve this problem. This kind of intervention was made possible by the adoption in the 2000's of horizontal legal instruments aiming to foster the efficient functioning of certain economic freedoms. Given the fact that the main obstacles identified in the various fields of internal market law were linked to the lack of information on national provisions and procedures, the logical question arises whether the obligation of making such information available suffices or should it be accompanied by translations or multilingual display requirements as such information targets mainly those who do not understand the language in which the information is available?

The first legislative act in this line was the Services Directive of 2006.[34] Providing information on applicable national requirements covered by the Directive is an essential element of the act, this task being entrusted to the so-called Points of Single Contact. Recognizing that information requirements would be useless if they were not made available in other languages than the official language of the Member State concerned, especially if that language is not a widely spoken language, Article 7 (5) of the Directive urges both Member States and the Commission to take accompanying measures in order to encourage Points of Single Contact to make the information on the relevant national legislation available in other EU languages. The provision does not impose a clear obligation nor does it define the number of "other" languages. The prudent wording of the Directive demonstrates that the legislator entered an area of national competence. This is further supported by the last sentence of the provision making clear that this obligation does not interfere with Member States' legislation on the use of languages.[35]

Next, the Mutual Recognition Regulation of 2008[36] contains in its recital (30) an invitation for Member States according to which Product Contact Points responsible to provide information on their technical product requirements should be adequately equipped and resourced as well as also encouraged to make the information available through a website in other Community languages. Here, the requirement is even softer as it is not inserted among the legal provisions of the Regulation. It still draws the attention to the importance of the multilingual (or at least bilingual) display of information as a perquisite for the attainment of the objective of making technical requirements available.

Later, in 2011, the European Parliament and the Council adopted a Directive on patients' rights in cross-border healthcare[37] enacting and codifying the case law of the European Court of Justice elaborated in this field. As far as the information that

[34] Directive 2006/123/EC of the European Parliament and of the Council of 12 December 2006 on services in the internal market.

[35] While according to The Commission's report of 2010 only 11 Member States provided information on their applicable legislation in a language other than their own, the situation has slightly improved later. The current state of play in 2014 shows that most Member States have chosen to provide the information in English, but at the same time, we can see that some Member States have clearly gone beyond the Directive. The Czech website, for instance, is also available in Spanish and French, while the Danish website can be accessed in Polish and Lithuanian too.

[36] Regulation (EC) No. 764/2008 of the European Parliament and of the Council of 9 July 2008 laying down procedures relating to the application of certain national technical rules to products lawfully marketed in another Member State and repealing Decision No. 3052/95/EC.

[37] Directive 2011/24/EU of the European Parliament and of the Council of 9 March 2011 on the application of patients' rights in cross-border healthcare.

National Contact Points have to provide is concerned, Article 4 (5) states that Member States may choose to deliver information in other languages than those, which are official languages in the Member States concerned. At the same time, similarly to the previous legal acts, it confirms that the provision shall not affect laws and regulations in Member States on the use of languages. The language requirements of this Directive are less demanding as they do not encourage, but only authorise the making available of the relevant information in other EU languages. Interestingly that provision was not part of the original proposal of the Commission; it was inserted by the Council in its common position following the Parliament's proposal under the first reading. The Parliament would have gone further; its amendment required Member States to make the quality and safety standards in a language and format that is clear and accessible to all citizens public. It would have meant the translation of these standards by the Member States into all official languages of the EU, which would have, on the one hand, been excessive, and on the other, would have overpassed the competences of the Union.

However, in 2014 a shift in the approach can be seen in the case of the Workers' Right Enforcement Directive[38] and the Posted Workers' Rights Enforcement Directive.[39] Both acts were adopted in order to eliminate the obstacles to the effective exercise of rights for EU workers and bridge the existing gaps. The main obstacles identified by the Directives were the lack of awareness of EU rules among public and private employers as well as the difficulties faced by mobile citizens to get information and assistance in the host Member States. Providing information on worker's rights is thus an essential obligation of the Directives. Article 6 of Directive 2014/54/EU stipulates that the Member States shall provide information on workers' rights or information in other languages than their own official language. A similar provision is found in Directive 2014/67/EU as far as the information relevant for posted workers is concerned. For the first time one can witness a clear and enforceable obligation on multilingual information provision. However, in the case of the Workers' Right Enforcement Directive (the first Directive in line) this obligation was only inserted during the first reading in the European Parliament. It seems that the European Parliament plays a crucial role in enacting language requirements in relation to information obligations.

The second layer of communicating information in another language than the one from which the information emanates might be identified at the level of enforcement of EU rules when national authorities proceed to the checking of authenticity of certain official documents issued by other Member States or must

[38] Directive 2014/54/EU of the European Parliament and of the Council of 16 April 2014 on measures facilitating the exercise of rights conferred on workers in the context of freedom of movement for workers.

[39] Directive 2014/67/EU of the European Parliament and of the Council of 15 May 2014 on the enforcement of Directive 96/71/EC concerning the posting of workers in the framework of the provision of services and amending Regulation (EU) No. 1024/2012 on administrative cooperation through the Internal Market Information System ('The IMI Regulation').

cooperate with each other for other reasons in the course of national administrative procedures involving citizens or undertakings from other Member States.

Without the intervention of EU law to set up intelligent communication tools interconnecting national authorities, the implementation of certain crucial acts of the internal market law would cause major practical problems and delays in the national procedures. However, communication is impeded if there is no common language or at least language support, which makes real correspondence possible. While the above examples on multilingual information requirements are oriented towards the beneficiaries of internal market rules (citizens and undertakings), in this area bridging linguistic gaps emerges at the level of authorities, but again for the sake of enforcing the rights of the same beneficiaries.

The Internal Market Information System (IMI) was set up with the specific aim to enable communication and exchange of information between national authorities. The need to institutionalise and technically support such an exchange was closely connected with the accessions of 2004 when the 10 incoming States significantly enlarged the territory of the EU and raised the number of national authorities involved in the implementation of internal market legislation. It was, however, evident that administrative cooperation could only work if supported by a modern multilingual system.[40] IMI was envisaged under the Services Directive in 2006; the exchange of information between national authorities was not even unavoidable but a necessary, immanent feature of the implementation of the Directive, which would not have been possible without an institutionalised framework. Its test function started in 2008 for exchanges of information under the Professional Qualification Directive. The use of the system was later extended to other Directives where such cooperation was deemed to be useful for the implementation, like the Posting of Workers Directive, the Euro-Cash Transportation Directive, the Train Driving Licences Directive or the Patients' Right Directive. In all of these areas mainly concerned with the free movement of workers, facilitating information exchange was a way to overcome existing barriers.[41] The regulatory basis for IMI was laid down in 2008 in a Commission Decision repealed in 2012 when a legislative act[42] was adopted on the basis of Article 114 TFEU by the European Parliament and the Council on the establishment of the system which was transformed into a central as well as essential tool for the efficient functioning of the internal market. The IMI Regulation foresees the extension of the system to other areas of the internal market where it might be an effective tool to implement

[40] Communication from the Commission to the European Parliament, the Council, the European Economic and Social Committee and the Committee of Regions, Better Governance of the Single Market Through Greater Administrative Cooperation: A Strategy for Expanding and Developing the Internal Market Information System (IMI), COM (2011) 75 final, paragraph 1.2.

[41] See Joamets (2014), pp. 154–155.

[42] Regulation (EU) No. 1024/2012 of the European Parliament and of the Council of 25 October 2012 on administrative cooperation through the Internal Market Information System and repealing Commission Decision 2008/49/EC.

provisions for administrative cooperation.[43] The language barriers to be overcome under the cooperation are already mentioned in recital (2) of the preamble while recital (3) clearly states that in order to eliminate these barriers IMI should be available in principle in all official languages. This is based on predefined and pretranslated workflows and machine translation. However, legislative provisions of the Regulation do not confirm the clear commitment or endeavour to make the tool available (at least in principle) in all official languages. Article 8 of the Regulation only identifies the providing of a multilingual system as a task of the European Commission without referring to the scope of this multilingualism. Still it seems that in practice multilingualism is overall a core element of the system available in all official languages.[44]

The last decade has shown that there is a need for regulating the compulsory provision of information requirements and exchange as external as well as internal aspects of the efficient enforcement of internal market rules. In the course of this regulation, the language issue could not be avoided. Quite the contrary, it proved the most important aspect in order to make the information reach the recipients and be understood by them. Although we can witness the appearance of such provisions, they are far from being legal obligations. They are encouraging measures instead and reflect a rather hesitant attitude of the European legislator, trying most probably not to interfere with national competences, to burden national governments with translation tasks and to engage in a commitment that any multilingual tool managed by EU institutions should as such always be available in all EU languages.

This is one facet of language risks in this field. How far can EU legislation go in order to impose upon Member States the respect for multilingualism, where the obligations such as respect entails, have serious budgetary consequences? Alternatively, how far should the EU go in managing such tasks?

However, the main risk behind the linguistic implications of information requirements is if they are completely disregarded by the legislation, leaving their regulation or non-regulation to national law. This risk was clearly avoided by the legislator in the cases above, where the importance of multilingual (bilingual) availability is at least underlined.

4 Language and Translation Requirements Imposed by Member States

Exercising the rights under internal market law logically entails the involvement in national administrative procedures where often documents issued by authorities of other Member States have to be presented in order to be able to pursue an activity or

[43] Article 4 of the Regulation.

[44] IMI User Handbook (2012) point 2.2.

have a professional qualification recognised. As the language of the administrative procedure is the official language of the Member State concerned, national laws require, with justified reason, the translation of the documents submitted to the authorities into this language. However, in certain cases language requirements imposed by Member States might play down internal market provisions in an unjustified manner. This might be excessive translation requirements asking for the presentation of certified translations. Requiring certified translations raises significantly the administrative costs of the procedure given the fact that certification in general entails high fees. Therefore, even if the translation of such documents is seen as a necessity in administrative procedures, certified translation might be identified as an unnecessary administrative burden, unless justified by overriding reasons.

Although language use in administrative procedures is clearly a matter for regulation by Member States, there have been measures or recommendations taken at European level in order to reduce or at least neutralize administrative burdens due to certified translation requirements. The Services Directive is a pioneer in this respect. Its Article 5(3) states that Member States do not only have to mutually accept documents produced by another Member State's authority serving an equivalent purpose, but they also have to accept a simple (non-certified) translation of these documents. Certified translations can only be required in exceptional cases, if provided for in other Community instruments or where such a requirement is justified by an overriding reason relating to the public interest, including public order and security.[45] The Directive does not prejudice against Member States' rights to ask for translations, but their rights are limited by a prohibition on formality.

Although the translation of official documents is undoubtedly most required in procedures for the recognition of professional qualifications, the Directive on Professional Qualifications[46] did not foresee a similar prohibition as the Services Directive until its amendment in 2013.[47] The general rule followed by Member States in the field of recognition is still to require the provision of certified translations. This duty mainly concerns diplomas, certificates of nationality and diploma supplements. In some countries, the approach is somewhat more liberal: Requiring certified translations is the general rule with certain exemptions in favour of certain languages.[48] No legislative intervention was undertaken for quite a long time, but the Commission recognized the issue as a barrier. In 2009, the Commission drew up a (nonbinding) Code of Conduct for Member States. According to the Code,

---

[45] Case C-298/99, *Commission of the European Communities v Italian Republic* (EU:C:2002:194).

[46] Directive 2005/36/EC of the European Parliament and of the Council of 7 September 2005 on the recognition of professional qualifications.

[47] Directive 2013/55/EU of the European Parliament and of the Council of 20 November 2013 amending Directive 2005/36/EC on the recognition of professional qualifications and Regulation (EU) No. 1024/2012 on administrative cooperation through the Internal Market Information System.

[48] Somssich et al. (2012), p. 102.

translations may only be required if genuinely needed for processing an application and that certified or approved translations must be confined to essential documents. Certified translations of standard documents, such as identity cards or passports, may not be required. In addition, the Code foresees the mutual recognition of certified translations. In view of this, Member States must accept certified translations issued in another Member State and cannot insist on the presentation of certified translations prepared by sworn translators under their own jurisdiction.

In 2013, the Directive was amended in a significant way in order to lower administrative burdens. The recommendations of the Code of Conduct were not transposed into the amended text. However, a new instrument, the European Professional Card,[49] was introduced in order to ease the recognition process. By virtue of the newly inserted Article 4a, it is the Commission, which, by adopting implementing measures, will lay down rules on the translations to be provided by the applicant to support any application for a European Professional Card. In the end, it seems that, finally, the issue of translations and certified translations will be regulated if not in the legislative act itself, then in an implementing Regulation still being in the pipeline.

However, in 2013 a general reform was undertaken by the Commission in order to facilitate the free movement of public documents presenting a proposal for a Regulation on promoting the free movement of citizens and businesses by simplifying the acceptance of certain public documents in the European Union.[50] Certified translations are identified by the proposal as "other formalities" which must be simplified in order to enhance the establishment of the internal market. Article 5 foresees that authorities should accept non-certified translations of public documents issued by the authorities of other Member States. They may only require a certified translation of a document if they have reasonable doubt about the correctness or quality of its translation in an individual case.

As the legal basis of the Regulation and the legislative competence of the EU are being contested, the adoption of the Regulation is doubtful.[51] If adopted, it would have a major impact on the practice of national authorities and provisions requiring certified translations as it would, for the first time, enact a prohibition requiring certified translations in a general manner concerning a number of documents falling under the scope of the Regulation.[52]

However, some areas falling under national competence that are still important for individuals engaging in cross-border activities, like tax procedures, are not yet

[49] The European Professional Card is an electronic certificate proving either that the professional has met all the necessary conditions to provide services in a host Member State on a temporary and occasional basis or the recognition of professional qualifications for the establishment in a host Member State.

[50] COM (2013) 228 final.

[51] Boehm et al. (2014), p. 309.

[52] The Regulation would cover all "public documents" issued by an authority of a Member State and presented to the authorities of another Member State. Draft Article 3 enumerates twelve categories relating to which the document might have evidentiary value.

part of the simplification measures as well as requirements on certified translations and they might well cause a disproportionate burden on taxpayers.[53]

Not only translation requirements, but also aptitude tests in the official languages of the host Member States should be mentioned among those national provisions, which might hinder the proper functioning of the internal market. Regulation 1612/68 on the free movement of workers within the Community (replaced by Regulation 492/2011) authorised Member States to impose conditions relating to the linguistic knowledge required by the nature of the post to be filled. It was, however, to be specified what the level of knowledge that might be required in the admission process is. The Court had, already in the 80's, the opportunity to rule on the compatibility of language skills requirements with the free movement provisions of EU law. In the famous *Groener* case[54] the Court recognised that language requirements might be justified even in cases where the knowledge of language is not necessary for the performance of the duties the post in question entails, but is part of the official language policy of the Member State concerned in order to promote and protect the national language and are not disproportionate. Later in the *Angonese*[55] judgment it was confirmed that it is against proportionality to require an exclusive way to prove linguistic competence, such as a language diploma obtained in only one province of a Member State.

In 2002, the Commission issued a Communication on the free movement of workers[56] where it expressed its understanding of language requirements. It argued that "while very high level of language may, under strict conditions, be justifiable for certain jobs, a requirement to be mother tongue is not acceptable".[57]

Until recently, only a few secondary law instruments contained, beyond the basic regulation on the free movement of workers, specific rules on language requirements. Such are the provisions on train drivers whose language skills must be such that they can communicate actively and effectively in routine, adverse and emergency situations,[58] air traffic controllers who must demonstrate their ability to speak and understand English[59] or security staff of transporters of euro-cash by road where at least one member of the staff must know the language of local authorities of the country of transit of the host State.[60] The Professional Qualification Directive, however, setting the frame for any recognition of a qualification not falling

[53] Heidenbauer (2011), p. 221.

[54] Case C-379/87, *Groener* (EU:C:1989:599).

[55] Case C-281/98, *Angonese* (EU:C:2000:296).

[56] COM (2002) 694.

[57] See page 7 of the Communication.

[58] See Point 8 of Annex VI of Directive 2007/59 of the European Parliament and the Council of 23 October 2007 on the certification of train drivers operating locomotives and trains on the railway system in the Community as amended by Commission Directive 2014/82/EU.

[59] Article 8 of Directive 2006/23 of the European Parliament and the Council of 5 April 2006 on a Community air traffic controller licence.

[60] Regulation 1214/2011 of the European Parliament and the Council of 16 November 2011 on the professional cross-border transport of eurocash by road between euro-area Member States.

under special EU rules, only contains a general provision in its Article 53 stating that persons benefiting from the recognition of professional qualifications shall have the knowledge of language necessary for practising the profession in the host Member State. Despite an unequivocal obligation of having the necessary language skills, the provisions still remain at the level of a general clause leaving appreciable room of manoeuvre for the Member States in defining the scope and content of the requirements. A tendency to fine-tune provisions on language requirements and restrict Member States' competences in this field started to take shape in 2013 when the Professional Qualification Directive was revised. New paragraphs were added to Article 53 authorising Member States' authorities to carry out controls for compliance with language requirements in sensitive sectors where the profession concerned has patient safety implications or where there is a serious and concrete doubt about the sufficiency of the professional's language knowledge in respect of the professional activities that that professional intends to pursue. The provisions impose proportionality requirements on these controls and the possibility for the professional to appeal the authority's decision—a requirement stemming from the *Groener* case. Here, the aim of the legislator was not to eliminate language requirements, but to oblige Member States to apply strict language compliance tests for certain professions.

The reason behind the intervention of the EU legislator in the form of specific and rigorous provisions for the health sector is that during the evaluation of the Directive concerns have been raised in relation to the inefficiency as well as the insufficiency of the general language regime of the Directive.[61] Again, the non-regulation of language rules—at least in a specific sector—proved to be a legal risk, which had to be handled by new rules.

5 Language Rights as Procedural Guarantees in Court Proceedings

Language appears to be a legal risk for the proper implementation of EU measures in the area of freedom, security and justice. There are several risks, which might be identified. The first group of risks is closely connected to transnational litigation and enforcement of judicial decisions in other Member States. The second category of risks is linked to the language use in local procedures by EU citizens of other Member States.

[61] See Impact Assessment of the Proposal, SEC (2011) 1558 final, p. 17.

Regulations adopted in the field of judicial cooperation in civil matters eliminated occurring language risks by translation requirements concerning judicial acts to be enforced in other Member States or to be used in judicial proceedings.[62] The language into which documents have to be translated does not have to be necessarily the official language or one of the official languages of the Member States of enforcement. For the sake of flexibility, these States might indicate other languages, which they accept.[63] Some of these provisions require certified translations depending on the nature and importance of the document. These provisions are practice guided and rather unproblematic.

There are however other aspects where language issues need legislative intervention. The service of court documents to a citizen or firm of another Member State makes it necessary that the recipient understands the document because otherwise his or her rights to a fair hearing are violated. The Regulation on the service in the Member States of judicial and extrajudicial documents in civil or commercial matters was adopted in 2000[64] and replaced by a reformed version in 2007.[65] The original Regulation already had specific provisions on the language in which the document to be served must be drafted or translated although they were slightly amended during the reform. The non-respect of the language provision gives ground for the refusal to accept the document on behalf of the addressee, making the service invalid. The languages, which might be used under the current Regulation, are either a language the addressee understands or one of the official languages of the Member State addressed.[66] The Regulation of 2007 broadened the

---

[62] See Article 19 of Council Regulation 1346/2001 of 29 May 2000 on insolvency proceedings on the translation of the appointment decision of the liquidator or Article 42 on the translation of claims lodged by creditors of other Member States, Article 13 of Council Directive 2002/8 of 27 January 2003 to improve access to justice in cross-border disputes by establishing minimum common rules relating to legal aid for such disputes on the translation of applications for legal aid.

[63] See Article 20 of Regulation 805/2004 of the European Parliament and the Council of 21 April 2004 creating a European Enforcement Order, Article 21 of Regulation 1896/2006 of the European Parliament and the Council of 12 December 2006 creating a European Order for Payment Enforcement, Article 21 of Regulation 861/2007 of the European Parliament and the Council of 11 July 2007 establishing a European Small Claims Procedure, Article 41 of Regulation 2201/2003 of 27 November 2003 concerning the jurisdiction, recognition and enforcement of judgments in matrimonial matters as well as matters of parental responsibility, repealing Regulation (EC) No. 1347/2000, Article 20, Article 28, Article 38 and Article 59 of Regulation 4/2009 of 19 December 2009 on the jurisdiction, applicable law, recognition and enforcement of decisions and cooperation in matters relating to maintenance obligations.

[64] Council Regulation (EC) No. 1348/2000 of 29 May 2000 on the service in the Member States of judicial and extrajudicial documents in civil or commercial matters.

[65] Regulation (EC) No. 1393/2007 of the European Parliament and of the Council of 13 November 2007 on the service in the Member States of judicial and extrajudicial documents in civil or commercial matters (service of documents), and repealing Council Regulation (EC) No. 1348/2000.

[66] Article 8 of Regulation 1393/2007. The same approach is followed in the case of refusal by Regulation 861/2007 of the European Parliament and the Council of 11 July 2007 establishing a European Small Claims Procedure.

scope of languages that might be used as the previous Regulation only allowed the use of a language of the Member State of transmission that the addressee understands. The new version is more concerned with the real linguistic knowledge of the addressee, but objective criteria in order to assess his or her language skills are lacking which might give rise to divergent interpretations by national courts.[67]

Beyond the language requirements on safeguarding the right to defence of the addressee, Article 2 of the Regulation specifies language rules for communication between transmitting and receiving agencies competent for the transmission as well as receipt of judicial and extrajudicial documents. By virtue of this Article, Member States should identify languages that may be used for the completion of the standard form used for transmission. These languages are not necessarily (or exclusively) the official languages of the Member States. They are any additional language the Member States choose to accept forms to be completed in.[68] The aim of this provision was to bring flexibility into the system and encourage Member States to move away from the monolingual approach in the communication with the judiciary of other countries. As a result, all Member States except the United Kingdom, Ireland and Luxembourg, indicated one or several EU languages other than their own national language and all Member States, except Luxembourg, accepted English as a language of transmission.[69]

In 2014, a comprehensive study was presented on the implementation of the Regulation, which was prepared for the Commission.[70] The study concludes that language is the ever-recurring problem in the practical application of the Regulation and most delays as well as dysfunctions are directly connected with linguistic problems.[71] It seems that language risks have not been completely eliminated or adequately regulated by the Regulation, some of them still persist while new ones have occurred as a result of the legal rules adopted.

The study identifies problems both in the case of Article 8 on the refusal of documents and at the level of agencies. Article 8 proposes the fine-tuning of the text establishing a presumption that the addressee understands the official language of

---

[67] See the case report of Markus Würdinger on a Decision of 2010 of the Landgericht Bonn (Würdinger 2013). See also the Decision of the Court in the Case C-14/07, *Ingenieurbüro Michael Weiss* (EU:C:2008:264) in which the Court maintained, by interpreting Article 8 of the Regulation, that if the addressee of a document served has agreed in a contract concluded with the applicant in the course of his business that correspondence is to be conducted in the language of the Member State of transmission, that does not give rise to a presumption of knowledge of that language, but is evidence which the court may take into account in determining whether that addressee understands the language of the Member State of transmission.

[68] The same formulation is found in Article 5 of Council Regulation 1206/2001 of 28 May 2001 on cooperation between the courts of the Member States in the taking of evidence in civil or commercial matters.

[69] Commission's Report on the application of the Regulation (COM (2013) 585 final).

[70] Study on the application of Council Regulation (EC) No. 1393/2007 on the service of judicial and extrajudicial documents in civil or commercial matters, European Commission, Directorate-General for Justice, 2014.

[71] See point 4.1.3. of the study.

the Member State of receipt. In case of the agencies, the study submits that they often reject request forms not translated into the official language of the Member State even if the requests were drafted in the language chosen by the Member State. It seems that here the legal solution of the Regulation was not suitable to eliminate language risks and there might be room for a change either by moving away from flexibility or by appointing a single common language for communication as put forward by the study.

The second category of risks in the area of freedom, security and justice, is connected to language use in court proceedings by citizens of other Member States. The right to interpretation and translation for those who do not speak or understand the language of the proceedings is enshrined in Article 6 of the European Convention of Human Rights.[72] It is thus a fundamental right, which Member States being all Parties to the Convention must respect. However, at the level of the EU, there were no legal measures safeguarding the rights of defence of accused persons by setting minimum standards. For the first time in 2003, a Green Paper of the Commission envisaged setting such European minimum standards where the right to translation and interpretation was seen as a fundamental part of this project.[73] The risks identified in the national mechanisms were the lack of equivalent translation and interpretation standards in criminal proceedings throughout the EU.[74] The proposal for the Directive was presented in 2009 as part of the "Roadmap for Strengthening Procedural Rights of Suspected or Accused Persons in Criminal Proceedings" under the Stockholm Programme. In fact, two proposals were tabled, one prepared by a group of Member States setting lower standards and another lodged by the Commission, being more ambitious.[75] In the end, the Member States' version was taken as a basis for negotiations. Directive 2010/64/EU on the right to translation and interpretation was the first legal measure establishing minimum standards for the safeguarding of defence rights in criminal proceedings and as such it has a symbolic value.[76] The Directive aims to ensure that there is free and adequate linguistic assistance, allowing suspected or accused persons who do not speak or understand the language of the criminal proceedings to exercise fully their right of defence and safeguarding the fairness of the proceedings. Interpretation and

[72] Everyone charged with a criminal offence has the following minimum rights. . ...(e) to have the free assistance of an interpreter if he cannot understand or speak the language used in court.

[73] COM (2003) 75 final.

[74] Vogler (2015), p. 104. During the early preparatory phase of the proposal, the Commission identified in some States serious shortcomings like court interpretation provided by non-professionals, poor quality translation and interpretation due to low rates of pay, limitations on the documents translated for defendants (Morgan 2011, p. 6).

[75] Vogler (2015), p. 105. The Commission's proposal, still based on the pre-Lisbon legal basis, was accompanied by a Resolution encouraging Member States to promote measures on the involvement of bodies representing interpreters and translators, qualification of interpreters and translators, training, registration of qualified interpreters and translators, remote access to interpretation, and codes of conduct as well as guidelines on best practices (Morgan 2011, p. 7).

[76] Rafari (2012), p. 81.

translation under the Directive should be provided in the native language of the suspected or accused persons or in any other language that they speak or understand. Risks arising out of different national legislations and practices are circumvented by two requirements: compulsory translations of essential documents and ensuring high quality of translation as well as interpretation.

Still, the minimalist approach followed by the Member States left its footprint on the Directive. This is mostly because under the Directive translation and interpretation costs must be met by the Member States irrespective from the outcome of the procedure.[77] When negotiating the provisions, they were thus interested in reducing the number of documents to be translated to the minimum necessary. Translation requirements are limited to documents, which are essential to ensure that defendants are able to exercise their right of defence, and to safeguard the fairness of the proceedings. Essential documentary evidence is, however, not part of these documents. This already questions how the right of defence can be fully exercised without the translation of essential documentary evidence.[78]

The Directive is also unique for prescribing quality requirements. By virtue of Article 5, Member States shall take concrete measures to ensure that the interpretation and translation provided meet the adequate quality requirements. The quality of translations and interpretations should be monitored and a register of independent translators as well as interpreters, who are appropriately qualified, should be established. The Directive is, however, silent on what independency should mean and how the monitoring of quality should proceed or would be possible.[79] Article 2 (6) on remote interpreting, a novelty of the Directive, has been identified by many as not being without risks. Some consider it as irreconcilable with the nature of criminal proceedings and with the requirements of a fair trial[80] while others are of the view that by recognising and neutralising the risks videoconferencing might bring in legal interpretation, it could be developed into an efficient as well as cost effective tool.[81]

It seems that open issues unanswered by the Directive are left to European projects outside the legislative area. In 2013, a series of projects were launched to find practice oriented solutions to the challenges above.[82]

Despite the shortcomings above, the Directive is a major step in regulating through minimum standards language use in court proceedings, even if it is for the time being limited to criminal matters. Eliminating remaining or new language risks deriving from the Directive is open for future amendments or initiatives.

---

[77] Article 4 of the Directive.

[78] Vogler (2015), p. 106.

[79] Bajčić (2015), p. 226.

[80] Bajčić (2015), p. 221.

[81] Braun (2011).

[82] AVIDICUS 3: Assessment of Video-Mediated Interpreting in Criminal and Civil Justice – Assessing the Implementation; LIT, Search a database of legal interpreters and translators, is to be set up on the e-Justice portal. TraiLLD: Training in Languages of Lesser Diffusion.

The Directive does not apply to road traffic offences. One year later, in 2011 a Directive was adopted—and annulled since by the Court for its inappropriate legal basis[83]—on facilitating the cross-border exchange of information on road safety related traffic offences. The Directive not only established that the person suspected of committing the road safety related traffic offence should be informed in the language of the registration documents or the language most likely to be understood by the person concerned, but it also in its recital (14) urges Member States to apply the same quality standards to these translations as the ones laid down by Directive 2010/64/EU. There is no doubt that the new Directive to be adopted on the correct legal basis would not reproduce this recommendation showing the commitment of the Commission to extend its quality-guided approach to other areas apart from Criminal Law. Here again the issue of competences and legal basis might hinder or at least slow down progress.

6 Conclusion

The EU, when adopting legal acts, runs several risks closely related to language use or linguistic diversity. First, even if there is no general rule under EU law to guarantee equal treatment to all official languages if the subject matter to be regulated falls outside the scope of language rules applied between EU institutions and a Member State or individuals, any restriction of the number of languages that might be used in a given situation might provoke the refusal of the legislative act by certain Member States or result in actions for annulment against the act concerned. Second, if impediments caused by linguistic diversity in the enforcement phase of EU acts are disregarded and are not handled either by legislative provisions or by alternative language support tools as well as mechanisms, the European legislator risks having legal rules of doubtful efficiency. The above examples demonstrate that European institutions are aware of these risks or if they disregard them, they are immediately reminded of them by market forces or Member States.

References

Bajčić M (2015) The way forward for court interpreting in Europe. In: Šarčević S (ed) Language and culture in EU law: multidisciplinary perspectives. Ashgate, Farnham, pp 219–238

Boehm AS, Faetan N, Jäger-Maillet I (2014) Child maintenance and authentic instruments – a German perspective. In: Beaumont P et al (eds) The recovery of maintenance in the EU and worldwide. Hart, Oxford, pp 285–310

[83] Case C-43/12, *European Commission v European Parliament and Council of the European Union* (EU:C:2014:298).

Braun S (2011) Recommendations for the use of video-mediated interpreting in criminal proceedings. In: Braun S, Taylor JL (eds) Videoconference and remote interpreting in criminal proceedings. Intersentia, pp 265–287

Heidenbauer S (2011) Charity crossing borders: the fundamental freedoms' influence on charity and donor taxation. Kluwer, Alphen aan den Rijn

Joamets K (2014) Civil status registration – more than data collection: EU digital development in promoting the free movement of civil status documents. In: Kerikmäe T (ed) Regulating eTechnologies in the European Union. Normative realities and trends. Springer, Heidelberg, pp 154–155

Kupzok A (2014) Law and economics of the unitary patent protection in the European Union: the Rebels viewpoint. EIPR 36(7):418–427

Lamping M (2015) Enhanced cooperation in the area of unitary patent protection – testing the boundaries of the rule of law (6 February 2015). Published in Maastricht J Eur Comp L (2013), Max Planck Institute for Innovation and Competition. Research Papers. Available at http://papers.ssrn.com/sol3/papers.cfm?abstract_id=2561365, Accessed 1 April 2015

Morgan C (2011) The new European directive on the rights to interpretation and translation in criminal proceedings. In: Braun S, Taylor JL (eds) Videoconference and remote interpreting in criminal proceedings. Intersentia, pp 5–10

Ó Reagen F (2010) The linguistic regime and practice of the institutions of the European Union. In: Hanf D, Malacek K, Muir E (eds) Langues et construction européenne. Peter Lang, Bruxelles, pp 109–136

Pila J, Wadlow Ch (2015) The Unitary EU Patent System. Hart, Oxford

Rafari T (2012) The application of the principle of mutual recognition to decisions on supervision measures as an alternative to provisional detention. In: Ruggeri S (ed) Liberty and security in Europe. A comparative analysis of pre-trial precautionary measures in criminal proceedings. Universitätsverlag Osnabrück, Osnabrück, pp 67–86

Schilling T (2008) Language rights in the European Union. German Law J 9(10):1219–1242

Somssich R et al (2010) Lawmaking in the EU multilingual environment. OPOCE, Luxemburg

Somssich R et al (2012) Language and translation in international law and EU law. OPOCE, Luxemburg

Vogler R (2015) Lost in translation: language rights for defendants in European criminal proceedings. In: Ruggeri S (ed) Human rights in European criminal law. New developments in European legislation and case law after the Lisbon Treaty. Springer, Heidelberg, pp 95–110

Würdinger M (2013) Die Sprachen und Übersetzungsprobleme im Europäischen Zustellungsrecht – Ein Spannungsfeld zwischen Justizgewährung und Beklagtenschutz im Europäischen Justizraum. IPRax: 61–63

Legal Translation vs. Legal Certainty in EU Law

Emilia Mišćenić

Contents

Abstract This chapter primarily deals with the numerous and different challenges of legal translation in the process of legal approximation of the MS laws with the EU law. By using practical examples, the author demonstrates how and to what extent legal translation affects conceptual understanding of legal texts. Mistranslations of the EU *acquis* into different MS languages, problems with translation during MS accession negotiations, translation errors in language versions of directives, regulations, CJEU judgments and other sources of EU law published in the Official Journal of the European Union, different conceptual understanding and legal application of legal expressions arising from the EU *acquis* in the MS, different meanings of the "same" linguistic EU and MS legal terms etc., are only some of the issues in which language and law collide. Incorrect use of language in this context often leads to incorrect application of law and thus to wrong legal consequences, thereby bringing legal certainty seriously in question. This is why one should continue to raise the already existing awareness among both linguists and lawyers of the implications of these issues in legal practice and of the importance of the role of language in law in general.

E. Mišćenić (✉)
Faculty of Law, University of Rijeka, Rijeka, Croatia
e-mail: emiscenic@pravri.hr

E. Mišćenić, A. Raccah (eds.), *Legal Risks in EU Law*,
DOI 10.1007/978-3-319-28596-2_5

1 Introduction

The Union of today presents a complex multilegal and multilingual setting in which cultural and linguistic diversity is recognized as a fundamental right of European citizens.[1] At the moment, the European Union (EU) embraces 28 Member States (MS) and recognizes 24 official EU languages that all enjoy equal status.[2] Its legal texts are accessible to European citizens in all EU official languages and are presumed to have the same meaning in all authentic language versions.[3] The role of legal translation enabling the realization of EU multilingual lawmaking is thus of outmost importance for the functioning of the EU. As rightly emphasized by *Paunio*, "[...] translations are not really translations at all: they are equivalent official language versions [...]", what makes the "[...] translation (is) the official language of Europe".[4] Consequently, there is a strong and unbreakable bond between legal translation and legislative approximation and application of EU law. This is reflected in all aspects of the Union's lawmaking process, from the legislative drafting process and the legislative procedures on the adoption of EU legal acts, over the transposition of EU legislation into the laws of the MS and last but not least in decisions of the Court of Justice of the European Union (CJEU) ruling on uniform interpretation and application of EU law.

Nonetheless, there are numerous issues that can arise from the interaction between legal translation and legislative approximation and the application of EU law. Mistranslations of the EU *acquis* into different MS' languages, translation issues during MS accession negotiations, translation errors in language versions of directives, regulations, CJEU judgments and other sources of EU law published in the Official Journal of the European Union (OJ EU), different interpretation and legal application of legal expressions deriving from EU *acquis* in various MS,

[1] See Art. 22 of the Charter of Fundamental Rights of the European Union, OJ C 326/391 of 26 October 2012: "The Union shall respect cultural, religious and linguistic diversity". The respect for cultural diversity, which includes the respect for linguistic diversity is enshrined in Art. 167 (1) and (4) Treaty on the Functioning of the European Union, OJ C 326 of 26 October 2012 (TFEU). According to recital 4 of the Decision No 1934/2000/EC of the European Parliament and of the Council of 17 July 2000 on the European Year of Languages 2001, OJ L 232/1, 14.09.2000 "all the European languages, in their spoken and written forms, are equal in value and dignity from the cultural point of view and form an integral part of European cultures and civilisation." According to its recital 12 "the Council Conclusions of 12 June 1995 on linguistic diversity and multilingualism in the European Union emphasised that linguistic diversity must be preserved and multilingualism promoted in the Union, with equal respect for the languages of the Union and with due regard to the principle of subsidiarity".

[2] See the official website of the European Commission DG Translation, Official EU languages: http://ec.europa.eu/dgs/translation/translating/officiallanguages/index_en.htm.

[3] According to Biel (2007), p. 146, this principle is named differently by different scholars: "This approach is referred to as the principle of plurilinguistic equality (van Els 2001), the principle of equal authenticity (Šarčević 1997: 64), or the PEAT, i.e. the principle of equality of authentic texts (Doczekalska 2005)."

[4] Paunio (2013).

different legal meanings of linguistically equivalent EU and MS legal terms etc., are only some of the issues in which language and law collide. Incorrect use of language in these contexts often leads to incorrect application of law and thus to wrong legal consequences. This results in the paradox situation, where EU multilingualism instead of enforcing is actually undermining the legal certainty.

2 Issues of Legal Translation in Legislative Approximation and Application of EU Law

Legal translation plays a very important role within the process of EU approximation of MS laws.[5] The EU legislation resulting from the EU approximation process is to be drafted and adopted in all official languages of the EU, which was regulated for the first time by Council Regulation No. 1 determining the languages to be used by the European Economic Community of 15 April 1958.[6] On the other hand, the EU primary law guarantees to the EU citizens the right to communicate with the EU institutions in the official language of their choice, and to receive a reply in the same language.[7] By making the EU legislation, procedures and information "accessible" to all EU citizens in their own or other chosen official language,[8] the EU law

[5] According to Art. 114(1) TFEU "the European Parliament and the Council shall [...] adopt the measures for the approximation of the provisions laid down by law, regulation or administrative action in Member States which have as their object the establishment and functioning of the internal market". Art. 114 TFEU (ex Art. 95 TEC, ex ex Art. 100a TEEC) was introduced for the first time by the Single European Act, OJ 1987 L 169/14 of 29.6.1987. Besides this general approximation rule, further legal grounds for approximation are Art. 115 TFEU (ex Art. 94 TEC, ex ex Art. 100 TEEC), Art. 352 TFEU (ex Art. 308 TEC, ex ex Art. 235 TEEC) and numerous special approximation rules (e.g. social policy: Art. 153 TFEU (ex Art. 137 TEC); environment: Art. 192 TFEU (ex Art. 175 TEC); competition: Art. 103 TFEU (ex Art. 83 TEC); consumer protection: Art. 169 TFEU (ex Art. 153 TEC); fundamental freedoms: Arts. 46, 50, 53, 59 and 62 TFEU (ex Arts. 40, 44, 47, 52 and 55 TEC); area of judicial cooperation in civil matters: Arts. 67 and 81 TFEU (ex Arts. 61 and 65 TEC) etc.). In the wider sense, the approximation of laws can be achieved both by EU legislative activity, ECJ/CJEU case law and the work of scientific groups and legal doctrine. Within the TFEU the notion of "approximation" is equalized with the one of "harmonization", thought of different legal theories on the meaning of these terms. See Gutman (2014), pp. 27 et seq.

[6] OJ 017/385, 06.10.1958. Pursuant to Art. 4 "regulations and other documents of general application shall be drafted in the four official languages" and according to Art. 5 "the Official Journal of the Community shall be published in the four official languages". The Regulation was amended accordingly, upon accession of new MS.

[7] In accordance with Art. 24(4) TFEU "every citizen of the Union may write to any of the institutions or bodies referred to in this Article or in Article 13 of the Treaty on European Union in one of the languages mentioned in Article 55(1) of the Treaty on European Union and have an answer in the same language".

[8] Communication to the Council, the European Parliament, the European Economic and Social Committee and the Committee of Regions – A New Framework Strategy for Multilingualism, COM(2005)596 final, Brussels, 22.11.2005.

ensures the formal requirement of legal certainty.[9] Furthermore, according to the principle of equal authenticity, also called the principle of language equality, all language versions of the same EU legal act are presumed to be authentic and to have the same meaning in all the official EU languages.[10] With regard to the Treaties as the main source of EU primary law, this presumption is derived from the Vienna Convention on the Law of Treaties.[11] According to its Art. 33(3), dealing with the interpretation of treaties authenticated in two or more languages, "the terms of the treaty are presumed to have the same meaning in each authentic text".[12] Moreover, ex Art. 314 TEC that was repealed and in substance replaced by Art. 55(1) TEU confirms the MS' agreement on treating all language versions of the Treaties as single originals that are equally authentic.[13] Related to the sources of EU secondary law, the European Court of Justice (ECJ) has stated in the *CILFIT* case that the "Community legislation is drafted in several languages and [...] the different language versions are all equally authentic".[14] By enabling EU citizens to rely on the EU legal act to have the same meaning as those translated into other EU official languages, the EU approximation is thus contributing to uniform interpretation and application of EU law and guaranteeing a high level of legal certainty. However, the interpretation and application of EU law depends heavily upon the quality of legal translation of the *acquis communautaire*. As it will be demonstrated in the examples below, legal certainty can be undermined in cases of language discrepancies between authentic language versions of the same EU legal act.

For example, recital 19 of the Directive 2014/17/EU on credit agreements for consumers relating to residential immovable property,[15] also called Mortgage Credit Directive (MCD), requires for reasons of legal certainty, its consistency with other Union acts in the area of credit agreements and consumer protection on

---

[9] As confirmed by the ECJ in the case C-161/06, *Skoma Lux sro v Celní ředitství Olomouc* [2007] ECR I-10841, paras. 37–38, Unions' regulation not published in the language of a MS cannot be enforced against natural or legal persons of that MS.

[10] With regard to ECJ/CJEU judgments and other individual decisions, these are authentic only in their relevant language of procedure, even if published in all official EU languages in the OJ EU. See Case C-361/01, *P - Kik v OHIM* [2003] ECR I-8283, para. 87.

[11] United Nations, Vienna Convention on the Law of Treaties, 23 May 1969, United Nations, Treaty Series, vol. 1155, p. 331.

[12] See Šarčević (2013), p. 7.

[13] See Art. 358 TFEU and Art. 55 of the consolidated version of the Treaty on European Union (TEU), OJ C 326 of 26 October 2012. On the distinction between "Treaty languages" and "Official languages" see Urrutia and Lasagabaster (2007), p. 481.

[14] Case C-283/81, *CILFIT v Ministero della Sanità* [1982] ECR I-3415.

[15] Directive 2014/17/EU of the European Parliament and of the Council of 4 February 2014 on credit agreements for consumers relating to residential immovable property and amending Directives 2008/48/EC and 2013/36/EU and Regulation (EU) No 1093/2010 (Text with EEA relevance), OJ L 60/34 of 28 February 2014.

both the conceptual and terminological level.[16] Moreover, when transposing the MCD, MS should ensure that there is consistency of application and interpretation in relation to the essential definitions and key concepts arising from these related sources of Union law.[17] What stands in the way to this requirement is the existing conceptual incongruence between different language versions of the MCD, which occurred as a consequence of legal translation errors. For example, the English language version of Art. 4(5) of the MCD defines a credit intermediary as a "natural or legal person who is not acting as a creditor or notary and not *merely* introducing, either directly or indirectly, a consumer to a creditor or credit intermediary, and who, in the course of his trade, business or profession, for remuneration, which may take a pecuniary form or any other agreed form of financial consideration: a) presents or offers credit agreements to consumers; b) assists consumers by undertaking preparatory work or other pre-contractual administration in respect of credit agreements *other than as referred to in point (a)*; or c) concludes credit agreements with consumers on behalf of the creditor". By comparing English, German, French, Slovene and Italian language versions of the MCD with the Croatian one and by analyzing the goal and the content of this definition, the author comes to the conclusion that the latter contains errors in translation, which essentially affect the meaning of the credit intermediary definition. By omitting the word "merely" from the definition of credit intermediary, the Croatian language version of the MCD changed the conceptual meaning of the definition since, instead of emphasizing the strong interaction between the consumer and the credit intermediary, it ends up defining the credit intermediary as a person who does not introduce a consumer to a creditor or credit intermediary. Furthermore, one should notice the important discrepancy between the Croatian and other language versions of the MCD with regard to the *litera* (b) of the same definition. By using the words "other than as referred to in point (a)", the English and all other language versions actually speak about *other activities* linked with the conclusion of credit agreements than those referred to in point (a). On the other hand, the Croatian language version speaks about *other credit agreements* than those referred to in the point (a), or more precisely: "in respect of credit agreements, which are not those from point (a)". Such an error in legal translation affects significantly the content of a mentioned provision that aims at the encompassing of preparatory activities other than those

---

[16] Ibid., recital 19: "For reasons of legal certainty, the Union legal framework in the area of credit agreements relating to residential immovable property *should be consistent with and complementary to other Union acts, particularly in the areas of consumer protection* and prudential supervision. *Certain essential definitions* including the definition of 'consumer', and 'durable medium', *as well as key concepts* used in standard information to designate the financial characteristics of the credit, including 'total amount payable by the consumer' and 'borrowing rate' *should be in line with those set out in Directive 2008/48/EC so that the same terminology refers to the same type of facts* irrespective of whether the credit is a consumer credit or a credit relating to residential immovable property. *Member States should therefore ensure, in the transposition of this Directive, that there is consistency of application and interpretation in relation to those essential definitions and key concepts.*"

[17] Ibid.

mentioned in *litera* (a) that can occur in connection with the conclusion of the credit agreement. Due to this reason the definition explicitly excludes notaries, whose activities would otherwise fall under the *litera* (b).[18] Instead of referring to the assistance of a credit intermediary in all activities "other than as referred to in point (a)", due to the mistake in the legal translation of *litera* (b), the Croatian language version refers to the assistance of the credit intermediary "in respect of credit agreements, which are not those from point (a)".[19] The Croatian official language version of the MCD contains further legal translation errors, such as the one in Art. 18(4) dealing with creditworthiness assessment. Here the Croatian translation omitted an essential part regarding the prohibition for creditors to subsequently cancel or alter the credit agreement "to the detriment of the consumer" on the ground of an incorrectly conducted creditworthiness assessment. Moreover, while all other official language versions refer to "Article 20", the Croatian translation of the last sentence of the same provision refers to "Article 15".[20] Similar errors in legal translation can be found in key provisions of the MCD on the annual percentage rate of charge (APRC). One should bear in mind that one of the main goals of the EU's approximation of MS' consumer credit laws is the introduction of a uniform definition and formula for the calculation of the APRC in all the MS that would encompass most of the costs linked with the conclusion and execution of the credit agreement.[21] Nevertheless, instead of referring to the possibility of inclusion of "the costs referred to in Article 17(2)" into the calculation of the APRC, the erroneous Croatian translation of Art. 4(15) speaks about "the costs referred to in

[18] Pursuant to recital 74 of the MCD, MS "[. . .] should be able to provide that persons carrying out credit intermediation activities only on an incidental basis in the course of professional activity, such as lawyers or notaries, are not subject to the admission procedure [. . .]" set out in the MCD "[. . .] provided that such professional activity is regulated and the relevant rules do not prohibit the carrying out, on an incidental basis, of credit intermediation activities". For more details see Mišćenić (2014b), p. 224.

[19] Exactly the same error occurred in the legal translation of Art. 3(f) of the Directive 2008/48/EC of the European Parliament and of the Council of 23. April 2008 on credit agreements for consumers and repealing Council Directive 87/102/EEC OJ L 133/66, 22.5.2008 and its transposition into Art. 2(6) of the Croatian Consumer Credit Act, OG Nos. 75/09, 112/12, 143/13, 147/13-*corrigendum* and 9/15. See Čikara (2010b), p. 312.

[20] According to the English language version of Art. 18(4) of the MCD: "Member States shall ensure that where a creditor concludes a credit agreement with a consumer the creditor shall not subsequently cancel or alter the credit agreement *to the detriment of the consumer* on the grounds that the assessment of creditworthiness was incorrectly conducted. This paragraph shall not apply where it is demonstrated that the consumer knowingly withheld or falsified the information *within the meaning of Article 20*."

[21] According to recital 49 of the MCD, "in order to promote the establishment and functioning of the internal market and to ensure a high degree of protection for consumers throughout the Union, it is necessary to uniformly ensure the comparability of information relating to the APRC throughout the Union". See Mišćenić (2014b), pp. 243 et seq.

Article 12(2)".[22] The content of Art. 12(2) has nothing to do with the previous provisions and concerns regulation of tying and bundling practices. In another provision concerning the calculation of the AP, instead of using the term "additional" APRC, the Croatian translation uses the term "new" APRC, thereby affecting the conceptual meaning of the provision. On the other hand, the English term "additional" from the last sentence of the same provision was actually translated as "additional" into Croatian.[23]

These numerous errors in the legal translation of only one EU directive can have serious consequences both upon legislative approximation and application of the EU law. It should be noted that the aim of EU approximation is the removal of differences between national law provisions of the MS, which have as their object the establishment and functioning of the internal market.[24] Nevertheless, this goal is undermined when, due to the language discrepancies, the EU approximation measure has a different meaning in various MS. Contrary to the principle of equal authenticity, the Croatian language version of the MCD published in the OJ EU doesn't have the same meaning as those published in the rest of the official EU languages. Apart from this conflict with the general approximation rules in Arts. 114 and 115 TFEU (ex Arts. 95 and 94 TEC), one can also identify more specific conflicts arising from the requirements of the MCD itself. As already mentioned, there is direct conflict with the requirements of this approximation measure concerning terminological and conceptual consistency with other Union acts in the area of credit agreements and consumer protection.[25] Moreover, due to legal translation errors, MS cannot guarantee the required consistency of application and interpretation of essential definitions and key concepts when transposing the directive.[26] This brings us to the next level dealing with the uniform interpretation and application of EU law in the MS. Based on the principle of loyalty and sincere cooperation enshrined in Art. 4(3) TEU and on the definition of a directive given in Art. 288(3) TFEU, MS are obliged to correct and timely transpositions of EU directives. Once transposed into the law of the MS' by the relevant regulatory framework published in the Official Gazette (OG) of the MS, the content of the EU directive becomes legally binding for the MS citizens and authorities. However, the proper exercise of rights and obligations of MS' citizens deriving from

[22] According to the English language version of Art. 4(15) "'Annual percentage rate of charge' (APRC) means the total cost of the credit to the consumer, expressed as an annual percentage of the total amount of credit, where applicable, including the *costs referred to in Article 17(2)* and equates, on an annual basis, to the present value of all future or existing commitments (drawdowns, repayments and charges) agreed by the creditor and the consumer."

[23] Art. 17(6) of the MCD.

[24] See *supra* footnote no. 5. See Case C-120/78, *Rewe-Zentral v Bundesmonopolverwaltung für Branntwein* (*Cassis de Dijon*) [1979] ECR I-649, para. 8, where the ECJ speaks about "[...] obstacles to movement within the Community resulting from disparities between the national laws [...]".

[25] Recital 19 of the MCD.

[26] Ibid.

approximated MS legal acts is *inter alia* dependent upon the accuracy and reliability of legal translations. For example, recital 14 of the MCD demands from the MS "to transpose provisions of this Directive regulating the activity of persons acting as credit intermediary as defined in the Directive". Due to the above presented erroneous legal translation, the legal application of harmonized national law provisions could lead to misleading and undesired legal consequences, thereby bringing the legal certainty seriously in question. Pursuant to the principle of the EU consistent interpretation, national courts and all other state authorities are obliged to consider the whole body of national law and interpret it, as far as possible, in the light of the wording and purpose of the EU directive that was supposed to be achieved by its transposition (*effet utile*).[27] In doing so, they could either consult different language versions of the EU legal act published in the OJ EU, or rely on the text in their own language. In case of erroneous legal translation, the first approach would actually lead to the transfer of translator's duties to national judges and other applicants of law discovering legal translation errors affecting citizen's rights and obligations. However, the practice has shown that national courts and other MS authorities usually rely on the text of the EU legal act written in their own language.[28] Due to the fact that legal certainty is guaranteed through the principle of equal authenticity, they usually do not doubt the quality of legal translation of the EU legal act in their own language, unless it is unclear or ambiguous.[29] Such behaviour can and it often does lead to cases where erroneous legal translation results in the denial of rights to MS' citizens deriving from the EU law or in other forms of incorrect application of EU law in the MS. The risk of collision between the legal translation and legal certainty was recognized quite early by the established ECJ/CJEU case law. Within the framework of the preliminary rulings procedure, ensuring correct application and uniform interpretation of the EU law,[30] the ECJ/CJEU ruled on numerous occasions upon divergences between various language versions of EU legal acts.[31] It initially required from the national courts of the MS to consult other language versions of EU legal acts only "in cases of

---

[27] Legal basis for this duty existing also during the transposition period arises out of Art. 4(3) TEU and Art. 288(3) TFEU. See Case C-14/83, *Von Colson and Kamann v Land Nordrhein-Westfalen* [1984] ECR I-01891; Case C-106/89, *Marleasing v Comercial Internacional de Alimentación* [1990] ECR I-4135; Case C-91/92, *Faccini Dori v Recreb* [1994] ECR I-3325; Joined Cases C-240/98 to C-244/98, *Océano Grupo Editorial and Salvat Editores* [2000] ECR I-04941; Joined Cases C-397/01 to C-403/01, *Pfeiffer and Others* [2004] ECR I-08835; Case C-105/03, *Pupino* [2005] ECR I-05285.

[28] Derlén (2015), pp. 61 et seq.; Šarčević (1997), p. 218.

[29] Paunio (2007), p. 398.

[30] Art. 267 TFEU (ex Art. 234 TEC).

[31] For in depth analysis of ECJ/CJEU case law see e.g. Łachacz and Mańko (2013); Paunio and Lindroos-Hovinheimo (2010); Glézl (2007).

doubt",[32] later raising this requirement to the level of duty for the national courts to compare all language versions in all cases, and not merely in cases of doubt about linguistic discrepancies between different language versions.[33] Although, at the time, when there were only three/four official EU languages such a comparison was feasible, the realization of this rigid requirement today seems to be impossible in practice.[34] How is then legal certainty to be guaranteed to MS' citizens legitimately relying on their rights and obligations deriving from the EU law? In accordance with the *acquis communautaire*, as well as with constitutional prerequisites of the MS, it is the duty of national courts and other bodies to uniformly interpret and apply the harmonized national law consistent with EU law, thereby ensuring legal certainty for MS' citizens. In its established case law, the ECJ/CJEU requires from national courts to give preference as far as possible "to the interpretation which renders the provision consistent with the EC Treaty and the general principles of Community law [. . .] and, more specifically, with the principle of legal certainty".[35] Their eventual failure in the protection of individual's rights deriving from the EU law, for instance, by not consulting all 24 authentic language versions of the relevant EU legal act and by omitting to recognize essential translation errors affecting individuals' rights, would consequently lead to MS' liability for damage suffered by that individual.[36] Nonetheless, due to the complexity of the task

[32] Case C-19/67, *Van der Vecht* [1967] ECR I-445: "The need for a uniform interpretation of Community regulations prevents the text of a provision from being considered in isolation, but *in cases of doubt requires it to be interpreted and applied in the light of the versions existing in the other three languages*".

[33] See Šarčević (2013), p. 12. *Šarčević* invokes Case C-29/69, *Stauder* [1969] ECR I-419, under which para. 3: "When a single decision is addressed to all the Member States the *necessity for uniform application and accordingly for uniform interpretation* makes it impossible to consider one version of the text in isolation but *requires that it be interpreted* on the basis of both the real intention of its author and the aim he seeks to achieve, and *in the light in particular of, the versions in all four languages*." See also Case C-298/12, *Confédération paysanne* [1967] EU:C:2013:630, para. 22: "According to settled case-law, *the necessity of uniform application and, accordingly, of uniform interpretation of an EU measure makes it impossible to consider one version of the text in isolation, but requires it to be interpreted* on the basis of both the real intention of its author and the aim pursued by the latter, *in the light, in particular, of the versions in all the other official languages* (see, inter alia, Case C-569/08 *Internetportal und Marketing* [2010] ECR I-4871, paragraph 35, and Case C-52/10 *Eleftheri tileorasit and Giannikos* [2011] ECR I-4973, paragraph 23".

[34] See Derlén (2011), pp. 152 and 157.

[35] Case C-1/02, *Borgmann* [2004] ECR I-3219, para. 30. However, by analysing the case law of the ECJ/CJEU, *Šarčević* came to a conclusion that it prefers to give prevalence to the effectiveness of the EU law over legal certainty of individuals. According to her, "it is not reasonable to expect the Court to strike a balance between legal certainty and multilingualism if favouring the individual would undermine the effectiveness of EU law". See Šarčević (2013), p. 16.

[36] According to the EU principle of state liability MS are obliged to compensate loss and damage caused to individuals by breaches of EU law for which they can be held responsible. The criteria for state liability derive from Art. 246 TFEU (ex Art. 215 TEC) and established case law of the ECJ/CJEU. See Joined cases C-6/90 and C-9/90, *Francovich and Bonifaci v Italy* [1991] ECR I-05357; Joined Cases C-46/93 and C-48/93, *Brasserie du Pęcheur* [1996] ECR I-01029; Case

imposed on the national judges and other applicants of law concerning the consultation of all authentic language versions of the respective EU legal act, there is always a serious risk for legal translation errors to go unnoticed by the practice, which strongly endangers the legal certainty.

3 Issues of Legal Terminology in Legislative Approximation and Application of EU Law

Another important issue that should be addressed here is the extent to which legal terminology can affect legal translation and consequently legislative approximation and application of EU law. Although the European legal system is supranational, autonomous and independent from those of the MS, due to its continuous process of development, there is still a relatively small number of original EU terms and concepts. Within the process of legislative drafting, the EU legal terms are often created with the help of functional equivalents deriving from MS' legal terminology,[37] which many times leads to both terminological and conceptual incoherency between European and national legal terms. According to the *CILIFIT* case, the "[...] Community law uses terminology which is peculiar to it [...]" and "[...] legal concepts do not necessarily have the same meaning in Community law and in the law of the various Member States [...]".[38] In order to accommodate different national legal concepts and constructions, the legal terminology of the EU *acquis* is intentionally vague and open to a variety of interpretations.[39] However, this makes it extremely difficult for the MS' lawmakers to achieve coherency with the existing national legal terminology and concepts, when transposing the EU *acquis* into the laws of the MS. The recommendation to national lawmakers to use legal terms in national transposing provisions that correspond as closely as possible to the EU legal terminology is not always realizable and its strict observance can result in troublesome legal consequences, particularly if the EU legal term is incompatible

C-5/94, *Hedley Lomas* [1996] ECR I-02553; Case C-224/01, *Köbler* [2003] ECR I-10239; Case C-173/03, *Traghetti del Mediterraneo* [2006] ECR I-05177 etc.

[37] According to Biel (2007), p. 149 "[...] it is recommended to avoid system-specific terms of national law when drafting the EU legislation and replace them with more neutral terms [...] "in Community law it is often necessary to avoid a term of national law which has no satisfactory equivalent in one or more Member States and which does not cover exactly a given notion or corresponds to a more general notion. In such a case a more appropriate, term should be used in its place (even if it is perhaps less elegant)", (Manual of Precedents 2002:98). Similar recommendations are given to drafters in Principle 5 of the Joint Practical Guide of the European Parliament, the Council and the Commission [...]". On the contrary according to *De Groot* "[...] there are never one-to-one relations between the conceptual systems in different legal orders [...]", what renders the "[...] legal terminology always system-specific". See De Groot (2012), p. 140 as quoted by Strandvik (2013), p. 3.

[38] ECJ Case C-283/81, *CILFIT v Ministero della Sanità* [1982] ECR I-3415, para. 19.

[39] See Šarčević and Čikara (2009), p. 201.

with the national law.[40] For example, the definitions of "credit agreement" in so-called Consumer Credit Directives[41] or in Art. 4(3) of the MCD[42] intentionally do not correspond to legal concepts of credit agreements in contract laws of the MS. By combining elements of MS' legal concepts of both credit and loan agreement, the EU law creates a new legal concept that regardless of its linguistic equivalence does not conceptually correspond to the already existing national legal concepts of credit agreements.[43] Issues such as these, concerning the impact of the EU terminology on the content, understanding and application of legal terms in laws of the MS are however heavily dependent upon the level of harmonization of the relevant EU approximation measures. The minimum harmonization directives, which allow national legislators to adopt or maintain more favourable protection provisions, if they so decide, therefore leave more freedom with regard to legal terminology used in provisions transposed into national law. Hence, when transposing the definition of "credit agreement" from Art. 1(2)(c) of the now repealed minimum harmonization Directive 87/102/EEC on consumer credit[44] into the first and the second Croatian Consumer Protection Act (CPA),[45] the Croatian legislator used the linguistically different legal term "consumer loan".[46] This is not the case with maximum or targeted full harmonization that does not allow national legislators to keep or introduce into national law provisions diverging from those laid down in the relevant directive, including more or less stringent protection provisions, unless otherwise provided in it. The lack of flexibility inevitably affects the transposition technique used by national lawmakers, who often opt for the so-called "copy paste" method in order to avoid incorrect

[40] Šarčević and Čikara (2009), p. 203.

[41] "Credit agreement" is in Art. 1(2)(c) of the Directive 87/102/EEC defined as "an agreement whereby a creditor grants or promises to grant to a consumer a credit in the form of a deferred payment, a loan or other similar financial accommodation". Pursuant to Art. 3(c) of the Directive 2008/48/EC "credit agreement means an agreement whereby a creditor grants or promises to grant to a consumer credit in the form of a deferred payment, loan or other similar financial accommodation, except for agreements for the provision on a continuing basis of services or for the supply of goods of the same kind, where the consumer pays for such services or goods for the duration of their provision by means of instalments".

[42] Art. 4(3) of the MCD defines "credit agreement" as an agreement whereby a creditor grants or promises to grant, to a consumer, a credit *falling* within the *scope* of Art. 3 of the MCD in the form of a deferred payment, loan or other similar financial accommodation.

[43] More in detail Čikara (2010a), pp. 367 et seq.

[44] Council Directive 87/102/EEC of 22 December 1986 for the approximation of the laws, regulations and administrative provisions of the Member States concerning consumer credit, OJ L 042/48, 12/02/1987, as amended by Council Directive 90/88/EEC of 22 February 1990, OJ L 61/14 and Directive 98/7/EG of the European Parliament and of the Council of 16 February 1998, OJ L 101/17.

[45] Consumer Protection Act, OG No. 96/03; CPA, OG Nos. 79/07, 125/07, 75/09, 79/09, 89/09, 133/09, 78/12 and 56/13. Provisions on consumer loan ceased to apply with the transposition of Directive 2008/48/EC into the Croatian CCA. The CPA currently in force, OG Nos. 41/14, does not regulate consumer credits.

[46] Čikara (2010a), pp. 367 et seq.

approximation to the EU *acquis*.[47] When transposing the full targeted Directive 2008/48/EC on credit agreements for consumers (CCD) into the Consumer Credit Act (CCA),[48] the Croatian legislator opted for a verbatim transposition of all of the Directive's provisions, including the "credit agreement" definition. The definition of "credit agreement" transposed literally from Art. 3(c) of the CCD into Art. 2 (3) of the CCA differs by its content from the already existing national concept of "credit agreement" regulated in Art. 1021 of the Croatian Obligations Act (OA).[49, 50] As rightly emphasized by *Bajčić*, "translating EU legislation into Croatian can be difficult not only because of the absence of appropriate Croatian terminology for new EU terms, but also because the concepts to be transposed into the national law are new as well".[51] With its first approach, the Croatian lawmaker transposed the EU directive by actually "translating" its legal terms into national legal concepts and terminology,[52] therefore accomplishing conceptual congruency to the detriment of terminological consistency between EU and national legal terms. On the other hand, the second and prevailing approach of literal transposition of EU directives into national law was heavily criticized by Croatian scholars and practitioners.[53] A combination of these two completely different transposition techniques resulted in both terminological incoherence with the EU legal terms and conceptual incongruence between legal terms across different national legal acts. This opened the door to a serious risk that judges and other applicants of law will not be able to recognize the European origin of the harmonized national legal terms

[47] E.g., when transposing Directive 2005/29/EC of the European Parliament and of the Council of 11 May 2005 concerning unfair business-to-consumer commercial practices in the internal market and amending Council Directive 84/450/EEC, Directives 97/7/EC, 98/27/EC and 2002/65/EC of the European Parliament and of the Council and Regulation (EC) No 2006/2004 of the European Parliament and of the Council, OJ L 149/22 into the second Croatian CPA, the Croatian Parliament rejected the draft of the CPA in the first reading due to incomprehensibleness and unnatural sounding of provisions on unfair commercial practices and because the terminology was not adjusted to the Croatian one. See Čikara (2007), pp. 1100 et seq.

[48] Consumer Credit Act, OG Nos. 75/09, 112/12, 143/13, 147/13-corrigendum and 9/15.

[49] Obligations Act, OG Nos. 35/05, 41/08 and 125/11. According to Art. 1021 of the OA "by the credit contract, a bank undertakes an obligation to make available a certain amount of money funds to a borrower for a definite or indefinite period of time, for a certain purpose or without any certain purpose, and the borrower undertakes an obligation to pay the agreed interests to a bank and to return the used amount of money at a time and in a manner agreed upon".

[50] *Iorriati Ferrari* speaks about the "nomadic meaning" of linguistically identical expressions which have a different conceptual meaning. See Iorriati Ferrari (2010), p. 6.

[51] Bajčić (2010), p. 9.

[52] More in detail Šarčević and Čikara (2009), p. 199.

[53] Josipović (2013), p. 305; Miščenić (2014a), pp. 280 *et seq*. See also Łazowski and Blockmans (2014), pp. 119 et seq.

and interpret and apply them in the sense of EU law, thereby denying citizens their rights deriving from EU law and undermining legal certainty.[54]

A similar problem occurred with the transposition of the EU legal term "right of withdrawal" into the Croatian civil law. Regarding the chosen example, one should emphasize that problems started already at the EU level, where the term "right of withdrawal" was in various EU directives often used as a synonym with the terms "right of cancellation", "right of rescission", "right of renunciation" or "right of termination". For instance, the repealed Directive 85/577/EEC on contracts negotiated away from business premises used legal terms "right of cancellation" and "right of renunciation" as synonyms, while the repealed Directive 94/47/EC on timeshare contracts equalized the terms "right to withdraw" and "right of cancellation".[55] Transposition of these EU directives into the Croatian law thus resulted in the discrepancy between EU and Croatian legal terminology, where the Croatian legal term "right to terminate the contract" ['pravo raskinuti ugovor'] is used not only for the general contract terms "terminate a contract" ['raskinuti ugovor'] and "right of termination of contract" ['pravo na raskid ugovora'] in the OA, but also for the more specific EU legal terms to "withdraw from a contract" ['odustati od ugovora'] and "right of withdrawal" ['pravo na odustanak'].[56] While the Croatian first and second CPA used the terms "right to terminate the contract" ['pravo raskinuti ugovor'] and "right of unilateral termination of contract" ['pravo na jednostrani raskid ugovora'], the CPA currently in force uses the legal term "right of unilateral termination" ['pravo na jednostrani raskid'][57] to express this EU concept. On the other hand, the same EU legal term was in the CCA translated as a "right of withdrawal from a contract" ['pravo na odustanak od ugovora'].[58] Although it can be argued that withdrawal is a specific form of termination, one should bear in mind that "right of withdrawal" as one of the basic concepts of the EU consumer *acquis*, needs to be

[54] Pursuant to Art. 146 of the Constitution of the Republic of Croatia, OG Nos. 56/90, 135/97, 8/98 (consolidated text), 113/00, 124/00 (consolidated text), 28/01, 41/01 (consolidated text), 55/01 (correction), 76/10, 85/10 (consolidated text), Croatian citizens are EU citizens and enjoy the rights guaranteed by the *acquis*, which are to be exercised in compliance with the conditions and limitations laid down in the EU Founding treaties and the measures undertaken pursuant to these treaties. The enjoyment of all rights guaranteed by the *acquis* is in Croatia guaranteed to all EU citizens. Under Art. 145 of the Constitution the exercise of the rights arising from the *acquis* is made equal to the exercise of rights guaranteed by the Croatian law and the protection of subjective rights based on *acquis* is guaranteed by the Croatian courts. In addition to constitutional guarantees, the obligation of applying and observing the EU law arises from key EU principles, such as the principle of loyalty and sincere cooperation, the principle of direct applicability of EU law, the principle of supremacy of the Union law and the principle of consistent interpretation.

[55] Arts. 3–5 and 7 of the repealed Council Directive 85/577/EEC of 20 December 1985 to protect the consumer regarding contracts negotiated away from business premises, OJ L 372/31; Art. 5 of the repealed Directive 94/47/EC of the European Parliament and the Council of 26 October 1994 on the protection of purchasers regarding certain aspects of contracts relating to the purchase of the right to use immovable properties on a timeshare basis, OJ L 280/83.

[56] See Šarčević and Čikara (2009), p. 205.

[57] Arts. 57(1)(8–11), 61, 64, 70, 72–79, 84, 87–91, 93, 99–102, 104, 111, 138(1)(53–56), 140(1)(20), 147(1)(5).

[58] Arts. 5(1)(o), 10(1)(p), 14, 15(1), 26(1) of the CCA.

distinguished from the "right to terminate the contract" with regard to their goals, exercise and legal consequences.[59] The "right of withdrawal", as a fundamental instrument of consumer protection, enables consumers to withdraw from the contract in a certain period of time after its conclusion (so-called cooling-off-period), without giving any reason for doing so and without being liable for non-performance. In spite of conceptual differences between these two legal concepts and terms, the Croatian CPA insists upon using the legal term "termination of contract" extended by the word "unilateral". The latter word is supposed to indicate that this specific right enables the consumer to "terminate" the contract without citing any grounds or incurring any liability for non-performance. However, apart from the predominately used legal term "unilateral termination of contract", confusingly, the CPA still contains provisions using the term "termination of contract" for the EU legal term on withdrawal.[60] This inconsistent use of two similar but different legal terms standing for the EU legal concept of the "right of withdrawal" gets even more complicated when taking into account the fact that the CPA distinguishes them from the "actual" "termination of contract".[61] Such an incorrect use of EU legal terminology can actually lead to serious legal consequences and incorrect application of EU law. According to the principle of *lex specialis derogat legi generali*, if there are no relevant provisions within the special CPA or other relevant special legal acts, consumer contracts shall be subject to provisions of the OA as *lex generalis*.[62] As confirmed by the CJEU in the *Messner* case, the application of general contract law legal consequences of termination, such as payment of compensation for using goods until termination, makes the exercise of the right of withdrawal possible only against the payment, which is against *ratio* of this key consumer protection instrument.[63] Having said all that and by taking into account

[59] von Bar et al. (2009), Munich, p. 569, define the right to withdraw from a contract as "a right to terminate the legal relationship arising from the contract [. . .], without having to give any reason for so doing and without incurring any liability for non-performance [. . .]". Nevertheless, further provisions of the DCFR, as well as of the Directive 2011/83/EU of the European Parliament and of the Council of 25 October 2011 on consumer rights, amending Council Directive 93/13/EEC and Directive 1999/44/EC of the European Parliament and of the Council and repealing Council Directive 85/577/EEC and Directive 97/7/EC of the European Parliament and of the Council, OJ L 304/64, 22.11.2011 and of the Commission Proposal of 11 October 2011 for a Regulation of the European Parliament and of the Council on a Common European Sales Law (CESL), COM (2011) 635 final etc., make a clear distinction between the two legal concepts.

[60] Arts. 50(1)(6), 74, 75, 87, 92, 140(1)(19), 138(1)(39) of the CPA.

[61] Such as in Art. 44(2) of the CPA. On the other hand, there are provisions, such as Arts. 34(2)(5), 37(1)(4), 42(1)(8) of the CPA, where it is not clear whether the linguistical term "termination of contract" used therein, refers to termination or withdrawal.

[62] Art. 4(2) of the CPA.

[63] Case C-489/07, *Messner* [2009] ECR I-7315: "The provisions of the second sentence of Article 6(1) and Article 6(2) of Directive 97/7 [. . .] on the protection of consumers in respect of distance contracts must be interpreted as *precluding a provision of national law which provides in general that, in the case of withdrawal by a consumer within the withdrawal period, a seller may claim compensation for the value of the use of the consumer goods* acquired under a distance contract. If the consumer were required to pay such compensation merely because he had the opportunity to use the goods while they were in his possession, he would be able to exercise his right of withdrawal only against payment of that compensation."

the EU drafting guideline on consistency of terminology saying that "[. . .] the same terms are to be used to express the same concepts and identical terms must not be used to express different concepts [. . .]",[64] one comes to the conclusion that the legal terms "right to withdraw from a contract" and "right of withdrawal" should be used in the Croatian CPA. Terminological consistency between approximated legal acts of the MS regarding the same EU legal terms and concepts (e.g. between the CCA, CPA and COA) is crucial in order to avoid incorrect application and interpretation of the EU law and erroneous legal consequences which endanger the legal certainty of individuals.[65]

4 Conclusion

The relation between the legal translation and legislative approximation and application of EU law is multifarious. On the one hand, legal translation plays an important role in contributing to legal certainty guaranteed by the Union's multilingual *acquis*. On the other hand, it is precisely the legal translation that seriously undermines the presumption of equal authenticity of EU legal acts published in the EU official languages. Unfortunately, language discrepancies are the rule rather than the exception in EU legal acts and are today considered as one of the main impediments to the approximation of the EU law.[66] Nonetheless, even when legal translations are carried out by translators disposing of high level translation skills, language competences and legal knowledge, and even when revisions are made by highly competent lawyer-linguists, translation errors cannot be avoided. Moreover, within the complex process of legal translation into 24 official EU languages, divergences in meaning between various language versions of EU legal acts are

---

[64] Joint Practical Guide of the European Parliament, the Council and the Commission for persons involved in the drafting of European Union legislation, 2013, 6.2. available at: http://eur-lex.europa.eu/content/pdf/techleg/joint-practical-guide-2013-en.pdf: "[. . .] The aim is to leave no ambiguities, contradictions or doubts as to the meaning of a term. *Any given term is therefore to be used in a uniform manner to refer to the same thing, and another term must be chosen to express a different concept.*"

[65] According to distinguished Croatian scholars *Šarčević*, *Bratanić* and *Gačić*, terminological consistency is essential in translations of the EU *acquis* and can be achieved only by the standardization of EU terms in Croatian. Having this goal in mind Prof. Dr. Susan Šarčević and Prof. Dr. Milica Gačić guided a scientific project "Croatian Terminology for EU Legal Terms" the results of which are available in the STRUNA database of Croatian Special Field Terminology headed by Prof. Dr. Maja Bratanić at: http://struna.ihjj.hr/en/.

[66] Šarčević (2013), pp. 2 et seq.; Iorriati Ferrari (2013), pp. 153 et seq.

inevitable.[67] As rightly emphasized by *Šarčević*, "both lawyers and linguists are quick to concede that it is impossible to produce parallel texts of a single instrument which have the same meaning [. . .]".[68] This was recognized on numerous occasions by EU institutions themselves, through various Commission Communications, Joint Practical Guides of the European Parliament, the Council and the Commission and other documents aiming at the improvement of quality of legal drafting and translations and concerning legislative approximation.[69] It is upon the quality and reliability of legal translations that the realization of goals of EU approximation of MS' laws depends to a great extent. Different meanings of authentic language versions of the same EU legal acts which emerged from the imperfections in language translations are in direct conflict with the objectives of the EU approximation aiming at the removal rather than the creation of differences in MS' national laws. Legal application of the legal source of the EU *acquis* (e.g. regulation) or of the national law provisions approximated to the EU legal act (e.g. directive) having various meanings in different MS, leads to serious legal consequences and discriminatory effects upon the addressees of this EU approximation measure.[70] In order to

[67] By quoting Knox (1998), *Marí Isidor* and *Strubell Miquel* name five key problems concerning the authenticity of texts: "1) A version says something which is different from the others. 2) A version uses a word of unclear meaning, whereas the other versions use a word with a clear meaning. 3) A version uses the same word with different meanings, while the others use different words in each case. 4) The word used in one version has a broader meaning than the corresponding word used in the others. 5) A version uses a category which does not appear in the others." See Marí and Strubell (2002), p. 13.

[68] On the complex process of production of EU multilingual legislation see Šarčević (2013), pp. 8 et seq. Also Schilling (2010), pp. 49 and 51.

[69] E.g. Joint Practical Guide of the European Parliament, the Council and the Commission for persons involved in the drafting of European Union legislation, 2013; Communication to the Council, the European Parliament, the European Economic and Social Committee and the Committee of Regions – A New Framework Strategy for Multilingualism, COM(2005)596 final, Brussels, 22.11.2005; Communication from the Commission of 11 October 2004 to the European Parliament and the Council – European Contract Law and the revision of the acquis: the way forward, COM(2004)651 final; Interinstitutional agreement on better law-making, OJ C 321/1, 31.12.2003; Communication from the Commission of 12 February 2003 to the European Parliament and the Council – A more coherent European contract law – An action plan COM(2003) 68 final, OJ C 63; Manual of precedents for acts established within the Council of the European Union, 4th ed., General Secretariat of the Council of the European Union, 2002; Communication from the Commission to the Council and the European Parliament on European contract law, COM (2001) 398 final, OJ C 255; Interinstitutional Agreement of 22 December 1998 on common guidelines for the quality of drafting of Community legislation, OJ C 73/1; Council Resolution of 8 June 1993 on the quality of drafting of Community legislation, OJ C 166/1, 17.6.1993; 'Birmingham Declaration – A Community close to its citizens' in European Council Presidency Conclusions 16.10.1992, DN: DOC/92/6 and many others.

[70] Pursuant to Art. 21(1) of the EU Charter of Fundamental Rights "any discrimination based on any ground such as sex, race, colour, ethnic or social origin, genetic features, *language*, religion or belief, political or any other opinion, membership of a national minority, property, birth, disability, age or sexual orientation shall be prohibited". Numerous scholarly articles analyse the EU multilingualism from the perspective of human rights and principles of equality and non-discrimination. For example, Urrutia and Lasagabaster (2007), pp. 8 et seq.; Šarčević (2013), pp. 1 et seq.

deal with these important but obviously unavoidable risks, the EU law has several legal mechanisms in place, such as the *corrigendum* procedure, the application of general principles of EU law including the principle of EU consistent interpretation, the possibility to bring a request for a preliminary ruling and last but not least the MS' liability for breaches of EU law. The question remains, however, whether these mechanisms protecting the legitimate interests of legal acts' addressees are effective enough when it comes to legal translation issues? According to *Strandvik* each *corrigendum* bears a risk of creating legal uncertainty. "A term has to be seriously wrong or misleading to qualify for a *corrigendum*",[71] a procedure that sets very strict requirements. Thus, one can seriously question the effectiveness of a *corrigendum* procedure mechanism, if in protecting the formal legal certainty it actually contributes to the creation of substantive legal uncertainty for the Union's acts addressees. Furthermore, as seen in the examples presented above, the guarantee of legal certainty through the EU consistent interpretation or preliminary ruling procedure makes sense only where errors in legal translation are obvious enough to raise doubts about the content of applicable legal provisions. However, legal translation issues such as omissions of provisions referring to wrong article numbers, incorrect translation of one or two words etc. can many times pass unnoticed by legal applicants. The solution offered by the ECJ/CJEU case law establishing the duty of national courts and other applicants of law to consult all language versions of the relevant EU legal sources in all cases,[72] seems not only to be unrealizable, but also not respected by the practice. Namely, the observance of this duty in court proceedings contravenes some of the classical principles of procedural law dealing with the length and costs of procedures, therefore adversely affecting the parties' position with the goal of preserving the effectiveness of EU law.[73] Moreover, even if observed and applied by the legal applicants in practice, is there any guarantee that numerous legal translations of the relevant EU legal act into the language of the

[71] Strandvik (2013), pp. 10–11.

[72] See European Commission Summary Report, Seminars on Quality of Legislation, How to interpret legislation which is equally authentic in twenty languages, Lecture by Advocate General Francis Jacobs, Brussels, 20.10.2003, p. 2, available at http://ec.europa.eu/dgs/legal_service/seminars/agjacobs_summary.pdf.

[73] Apart from the uniform application and interpretation of the EU law by the CJEU, the effectiveness of EU law is guaranteed through the primary law duty of MS to provide remedies sufficient to ensure effective legal protection in the fields covered by Union law (Art. 19(1) TEU) and through the principle of effective protection developed by the ECJ/CJEU case law. According to the principle of effective protection that is now also enshrined in Art. 47(1) of the EU Charter of Fundamental Rights, national courts and other bodies must guarantee the protection of rights that individuals derive from EU law, whereby in the absence of EU legislation, the embodiment of procedural rules governing actions for safeguarding these rights falls within the internal legal order of the MS by virtue of the principle of the procedural autonomy of those MS. Those rules cannot however be less favourable than those governing similar domestic actions (principle of equivalence) or make it in practice impossible or excessively difficult to exercise the rights conferred by EU law (principle of effectiveness).

procedure, necessary for the purpose of its consultation within the national court or other dispute solving procedure, will be flawless and without translation errors?

On the other hand, it is not only legal translation that affects the EU approximation and application of EU law, it is also the other way around. As seen with the presented examples of legal terminology issues, the inconsistent use of legal terminology across the EU approximation measures mirrors itself upon the harmonized national law provisions, the application of which often leads to incorrect legal consequences, therefore undermining the legal certainty of individuals. Terminological inconsistency and incoherence in EU legal acts is in direct conflict with the general principles of the Joint Practical Guide requiring from the Union's legal acts to be drafted clearly, simply and precisely in order to guarantee the equality of citizens before the law and legal certainty.[74] Some of the recent EU approximation measures, such as the MCD, seem to even support the terminological inconsistency. According to recital 41, with the aim of using more simple and understandable language for consumers, "[...] the terms used in the ESIS (European Standardised Information Sheet) are not necessarily the same as the legal terms defined in this Directive but have the same meaning".[75] Similar numerous examples of incoherent use of legal terms and concepts that are spread all over various sources of EU law endanger considerably the realization of the EU approximation goals and the uniform application and interpretation of EU law. Therefore, it is often considered by scholars that the creation of uniform EU legal terms and concepts could significantly contribute to the improvement of the EU approximation process.[76] According to some, this work already began within the framework of European private law, with the creation of the Draft Common Frame of Reference (DCFR) and by proposing the Regulation of the European Parliament and of the Council on a Common European Sales Law (CESL), which both insist upon more neutral and uniform legal terms.[77] Although the legal efficiency of the CESL proposal can seriously be questioned, even if adopted, being the second and parallel legal regime existing besides MS' national civil law provisions, the CESL could never solve the already existing legal translation and terminology issues.[78]

[74] Joint Practical Guide of the European Parliament, the Council and the Commission for persons involved in the drafting of European Union legislation, 2013, 1.1. and 1.2. available at: http://eur-lex.europa.eu/content/pdf/techleg/joint-practical-guide-2013-en.pdf.

[75] According to *Mišćenić* there is no need for the introduction of linguistical discrepancy between the same concepts used in the main text and the annex of the MCD. The reasons for this approach of the EU legislator are even less understandable because of the prescribed possibility for creditors and credit intermediaries to offer advisory services (Art. 4(21) of the MCD) to consumers and duty to provide them with adequate explanations of pre-contractual and contractual terms (Art. 16 of the MCD). See Mišćenić (2015), p. 135.

[76] Šarčević (2010), pp. 23 et seq.

[77] Šarčević (2014), pp. 47 et seq.; Hargitt (2013), pp. 433 et seq.; Iorriati Ferrari (2013), pp. 5 and 10.

[78] Mišćenić (2012), pp. 729 et seq.

Legal translation and terminology issues causing significant differences between various authentic language versions of the respective EU legal acts affect adversely the EU approximation of MS laws and consequently the uniform application and interpretation of EU law. These EU methods aim at the removal of differences between national law provisions of MS that cause legal uncertainty for market participants and therefore present barriers to the establishment and proper functioning of the internal market. As a further guarantee of legal certainty the principle of equal authenticity provides for equal value and the meaning of all official language versions of EU legislation, including approximation measures aiming at the removal of differences between MS' national law provisions. Nonetheless, differences caused by imperfections of legal translations and by inconsistency and incoherence in EU legal terminology undermine the very essence of the principle of equal authenticity thereby contributing to the creation of legal uncertainty. The Union's motto "United in Diversity" referring to the *inter alia* respect of MS' linguistic diversity, can today be understood as referring to the diversities created by the Union itself. As stated by *Gotti* and *Williams* "terminological inconsistency and incoherence in EU directives [...] sometimes pose a threat to cross-border transactions".[79] Moreover, due to the EU approximation process of MS national law provisions, this threat also applies to pure domestic transactions. In attempting to strengthen the legal certainty for the purpose of the realization of the Union's supreme goal of the proper functioning of the internal market, the Union actually contributed to the strengthening of one of the barriers to cross-border trade. Differences in the meaning, understanding and interpretations of the various language versions of EU legislation contribute to the creation of legal uncertainty for addressees of EU legislation and act as barriers to the proper functioning of the internal market. For this reason, as rightly emphasised by *Šarčević*, "[...] efforts to remove the stigma of legal uncertainty from EU multilingual legislation remains a high priority on the agenda of linguists and lawyers [...]".[80]

References

Bajčić M (2010) Challenges of translating EU terminology. In: Gotti M, Williams C (eds) Legal discourse across languages and cultures. Peter Lang, Bern, pp 75–94

Biel Ł (2007) Translation of multilingual EU legislation as a sub-genre of legal translation. In: Kierzkowska D (ed) Court interpreting and legal translation in the enlarged Europe 2006. Translegis, Warszawa, pp 144–163

Čikara E (2007) Die Angleichung des Verbraucherschutzrechts in der Europäischen Gemeinschaft unter besonderer Berücksichtigung des Verbraucherschutzrechtes in der Republik Kroatien. ZPFR 28(2):1067–1112

[79] Gotti and Williams (2010), p. 9.

[80] Šarčević (2014), p. 68.

Čikara E (2010a) Gegenwart und Zukunft der Verbraucherkreditverträge in der EU und in Kroatien, Die Umsetzung der Richtlinie 87/102/EWG und Richtlinie 2008/48/EG in das deutsche, österreichische und kroatische Verbraucherkreditrecht. LIT Verlag, Berlin et al.

Čikara E (2010b) Otvorena pitanja potrošačkog kreditiranja u hrvatskome pravu (Open Issues of Consumer Crediting in Croatian Law). In: Zbornik 48. Susreta pravnika - Opatija '10 Hrvatskog saveza udruga pravnika u gospodarstvu, pp 305–335

De Groot G-R (2012) The influence of problems of legal translation on comparative law research. In: Baaij CJW (ed) The role of legal translation in legal harmonisation. Wolters Klüwer Law, Alphen aan den Rijn, pp 139–159

Derlén M (2011) In defence of (limited) multilingualism: problems and possibilities of the multilingual interpretation of European Union law in national courts. In: Kjær AL, Adamo S (eds) Linguistic diversity and European democracy. Ashgate, Surrey, pp 143–166

Derlén M (2015) A single text or a single meaning: multilingual interpretation of EU legislation and CJEU case law in national courts. In: Šarčević S (ed) Language and culture in EU law: multidisciplinary perspectives. Ashgate, Farnham, pp 53–72

Glézl A (2007) Lost in translation; EU law and the official languages – problem of the authentic text. Available at: http://www.cels.law.cam.ac.uk/events/Glezl.pdf

Gotti M, Williams C (2010) Introduction. In: Gotti M, Williams C (eds) Legal discourse across languages and cultures. Peter Lang, Bern, pp 7–20

Gutman K (2014) Constitutional foundations of European contract law: a comparative analysis. Oxford University Press, Oxford

Hargitt S (2013) What could be gained in translation: legal language and lawyer-linguists in a globalized world. Indiana J Global Leg Stud 20(1):425–447

Iorriati Ferrari E (2010) Linguistic precedent and nomadic meanings in EC private law. Revista General de Derecho Público Comparado 6:1–14

Iorriati Ferrari E (2013) Interpretazione comparante e multilinguilismo Europeo. CEDAM, Padova

Josipović T (2013) Enforcement activity in consumer protection regulation in Croatia. J Consum Policy 36(287):287–314

Knox SR (1998) Multiplicity of languages in the European Union: problems and proposals. Harvard Law School, Academy of European Law online, Advanced Issues in Law and Policy, Jean Monnet Seminar

Łachacz O, Mańko R (2013) Multilingualism at the Court of Justice of the European Union: theoretical and practical aspects. Stud Logic Grammar Rhetor 34(47):75–92

Łazowski A, Blockmans S (2014) Between dream and reality: challenges to the legal rapprochement of the Western Balkans. In: Roman Petrov R, Van Elsuwege P (eds) Legislative approximation and application of EU law in the eastern neighbourhood of the European Union: towards a common regulatory space? Routledge, New York, pp 108–134

Marí I, Strubell M (2002) The linguistic regime of the European Union: prospects in the face of enlargement. Workshop: Linguistic proposals for the future of Europe 'Europa Diversa'. Barcelona, pp 1–42

Mišćenić E (2012) Europsko ugovorno pravo na putu od soft prema hard law, Osvrt na opcionalno zajedničko europsko pravo prodaje (CESL) (European Contract Law on the Way from Soft to Hard Law, Review of the Optional Common European Sales Law (CESL)). ZPFR 33 (2):695–745

Mišćenić E (2014a) Consumer protection law. In: Josipović T (ed) Introduction to the Law of Croatia. Kluwer Law International, Alphen aan den Rijn, pp 279–290

Mišćenić E (2014b) Mortgage Credit Directive (MCD): are consumers finally getting the protection they deserve? In: Slakoper Z (ed) Liber Amicorum in Honorem Vilim Gorenc. Pravni Fakultet Rijeka, Rijeka, pp 219–260

Mišćenić E (2015) Novo europsko uređenje hipotekarnih kredita (New European Regulation of Mortgage Credits). Ann Fac Law - Univ Zenica 14(7):113–169

Paunio E (2007) The tower of Babel and the interpretation of EU law: implications for equality of languages and legal certainty. In: Wilhelmsson T, Paunio E, Pohjolainen A (eds) Private law and the many cultures of Europe. Kluwer Law International, Alphen aan den Rijn, pp 385–402

Paunio E (2013) Legal certainty in multilingual EU law: language, discourse and reasoning at the European Court of Justice. Ashgate, Aldershot

Paunio E, Lindroos-Hovinheimo S (2010) Taking language seriously: an analysis of linguistic reasoning and its implications in EU law. Eur Law J 16(4):395–416

Šarčević S (1997) New approach to legal translation. Kluwer Law International, The Hague

Šarčević S (2010) Creating a pan-European legal language. In: Gotti M, Williams C (eds) Legal discourse across languages and cultures. Peter Lang, Bern, pp 23–50

Šarčević S (2013) Multilingual lawmaking and legal (un)certainty in the European Union. Int J Law Lang Discourse 3(1):1–29

Šarčević S (2014) Legal translation and legal certainty/uncertainty: from the DCFR to the CESL proposal. In: Pasa B, Morra L (eds) Translating the DCFR and drafting the CESL, a pragmatic perspective. SELP, Monaco, pp 47–70

Šarčević S, Čikara E (2009) European vs. National Terminology in Croatian legislation transposing EU directives. In: Šarčević S (ed) Legal language in action: translation, terminology, drafting and procedural issues. Nakladni zavod Globus, Zagreb, pp 193–214

Schilling T (2010) Beyond multilingualism: on different approaches to the handling of diverging language versions of a community law. Eur Law J 16(1):47–66

Strandvik I (2013) EU translation – legal translation in multilingual lawmaking. FIT Forum. Available at: http://www.eulita.eu/

Urrutia I, Lasagabaster I (2007) Language rights as a general principle of Community law. German Law J 8(5):479–500

von Bar C et al (2009) Principles, definitions and model rules of European private law, Draft Common Frame of Reference (DCFR). Sellier, European Law Publishers, Munich

Part II
Legal Risks in Developement of EU Policies

Protection of Foreign Investment and the EU: Framework, Legal Risks, and First Fruits

G. Matteo Vaccaro-Incisa

Contents

Abstract The protection of foreign investment is undergoing profound modifications worldwide, in light of the new agreements currently under negotiations as well as the reaction of States and public opinion (for only partly coinciding reasons) to certain arbitral decisions. The synthetic model of investment agreement of European origin is being largely substituted, especially in the context of broader FTA negotiations with major or regional players, by the more analytic North American model, strong of 20 years of NAFTA experience. In its negotiations with Singapore and Canada, the EU associated to this trend, and endeavoured to build texts that are believed to represent the foundation of its international investment law policy and programme. Internal differences within the EU constitutional organs and Member States about the interpretation of the new regime of competences designed by the Lisbon Treaty have, nevertheless, stalled the process. The path to entry into force of the agreement with Singapore awaits a preliminary pronouncement of the European Court of Justice, while several Member States

G.M. Vaccaro-Incisa (✉)
School of Law, Luigi Bocconi University, Milan, Italy
e-mail: gm.vaccaroincisa@unibocconi.it

E. Miščenić, A. Raccah (eds.), *Legal Risks in EU Law*,
DOI 10.1007/978-3-319-28596-2_6

currently oppose that with Canada because of its Investor-State Dispute Settlement Mechanism. In the meantime, the Commission pursues negotiations with the US and China, in the attempt not to leave EU investors less protected than their counterparts, in either State.

1 The European Roots of the International Framework for the Protection of Foreign Investment

At their origin, Bilateral Investment Treaties (BITs) were conceived as instruments for major European capital-exporting States to 'promote and protect' their businesses in poor capital-importing States.[1] Their main purpose '. . .was historically that of protecting investments from the industrialized party into the developing one, thereby (hopefully) attracting capital into the latter's economy'.[2]

The first BIT was signed between the Federal Republic of Germany and Pakistan on 25 November 1959. Between 1959 and 1963, BITs have been a monopoly of Germany (and Switzerland).[3] The influence of Germany in shaping investment law and treaty models may be inferred by looking at the stipulations concluded around 'peak' moments in the course of international investment law history.[4]

In 1963, the Netherlands first (in March, with Tunisia) and France soon afterward (in August, also with Tunisia) signed their first BIT. Italy followed in 1964, with Guinea. While the Netherlands and Italy continued their BIT programmes over the subsequent years—the Netherlands with Côte d'Ivoire and Cameroon (1965), Indonesia (1968), Tanzania, Uganda, Sudan and Kenya (1970), Italy with Malta (1967), Gabon (1968), Chad and Côte d'Ivoire (1969)—France halted its own for almost a decade.[5] Sweden figures among the early starters as well, as its first BIT was concluded in 1965 (with Côte d'Ivoire).[6] The United Kingdom—more

[1] Cf., Dolzer and Stevens (1995), p. 1: 'BITs are European in Origin'.

[2] Sacerdoti (1997), pp. 327–328.

[3] Switzerland has been the second State to begin a BIT programme; it signed its first BIT in 1961, with Tunisia. By the time the Netherlands signed its first BIT, in 1963, Switzerland was party to 7 BITs already.

[4] See Table 1, below; for a review of the evolution of the model investment discipline of Germany, see Dolzer and Kim (2013), pp. 289–320.

[5] There will not be another French BIT until 1972—which was a renegotiation of that with Tunisia.

[6] Côte d'Ivoire appears to have represented at the time for BITs what Chile is today with regard to FTAs: by 1966, it enjoyed agreements with Switzerland, the Netherlands, Italy, Sweden and Germany.

focused on treaties of 'Friendship, Commerce and Navigation' (FCN)[7] and on intra-Commonwealth trade and investment privileges—signed its first BITs in 1975 (with Egypt and Singapore)[8]; nevertheless, it has subsequently proceeded at a fast pace (Romania and Indonesia in 1976, Thailand in 1978, Jordan in 1979, Sri Lanka, Senegal, Bangladesh and Philippines in 1980).

Some scholars, however, consider most of the early stipulations only as forerunners of current BITs. The actual first instance of a modern investment treaty is considered to be the 1969 Italy-Chad BIT[9]—the first combining substantive investment protection with binding ICSID investor-State arbitration.[10] In the 1990s, this type of BIT will represent by far the majority of those stipulated. By 1979, however, States had concluded only approximately 100 BITs, most of which between major Western European States and developing States. BITs were, back then, expanding at a slow pace (and the ICSID was a dormant system).[11] It was perhaps too early, for often newly independent States, to consent to the sovereign restraints a BIT implies (especially, vis-à-vis ex-colonizers).[12]

Non-European major economies mostly started their BIT programmes at a later stage. Among the traditional capital exporters, Japan's customary emphasis on trade, rather than foreign investment,[13] explains why it entered into its first BIT

[7] Despite being primarily concerned with trade, FCNs are considered the forerunners of BITs as they feature, *inter alia*, guarantees on property rights and business interests of foreigners. According to Dolzer and Stevens (1995), p. 11, however, '...the broad spectrum of close political, economic and cultural cooperation which was envisaged by FCNs (such as unrestricted right to entry and the unqualified right of national treatment) were thought to be incompatible with the new political realities [of the late 1950s]', and this brought to the end of the stipulation of FNCs in 1966 (with the conclusion of the last two: US-Togo and US-Thailand).

[8] The first BIT the UK signed with a Commonwealth State was in 1980, with Sri Lanka.

[9] Newcombe (2013), p. 17.

[10] Art. 7 of the 1969 Italy-Chad BIT reads: 'Tout différend concernant les investissements, objet du présent Accord, qui s'élèverait entre un Etat contractant (ou n'importe quelle Institution ou Organisation dépendante ou contrôlée par le même Etat) et une personne physique ou morale, ayant la nationalité de l'autre Etat, sera soumis à la juridiction du Centre International pour le règlement des différends relatifs aux investissements, conformément à la Convention Internationale de Washington du 18 mars 1965. Toute contestation ou tout différend entre les deux Etats, portant sur l 'interprétation ou l'application du présent Accord, seront réglés par la voie diplomatique'.

[11] The first publicly known ICSID Award was rendered on 29 August 1977, in the case involving the Italian investor *Adriano Gardella S. p. A. v. Côte d'Ivoire*, ICSID Case No. ARB/74/1.

[12] Such resistance on the part of developing States is exemplified by Resolution A/RES/S-6/3201, Declaration for the Establishment of a New International Economic Order, adopted by the General Assembly of the United Nations in 1974; also of 1974, General Assembly Resolution A/RES/29/3281, Charter of Economic Rights and Duties of States.

[13] Already noted back in 1995 by Dolzer and Stevens, p. 3, and maintained until nowadays (cf., Table 1).

in 1977 (with Egypt),[14] and today it is party to 19 of them only.[15] The US, even more than the UK, attempted to keep its long-standing policy based on bilateral FCN treaties.[16] It consequently signed its first BITs in 1982 (with Egypt and Panama), the same year as China (with Sweden). While the US developed its first model text a few years later (in 1987), its strategy first shifted for the conclusion of over sixty 'Trade and Investment Framework Agreements',[17] instruments primarily serving the purpose of providing for an annual bilateral forum '...to meet and discuss issues of mutual interest with the objective of improving cooperation and enhancing opportunities for trade and investment'.[18] Systematic BIT negotiations would take place only in the course of the 1990s.[19] Canada signed its first BIT with a dusking USSR in 1988.[20]

Looking at more recently established capital exporters, China is the only early starter (1982, with Sweden) with a robust BIT network (132 agreements). Brazil signed its first BIT in 1994 (with Portugal) and 13 other BITs subsequently, but ratified none of them[21] (and it looks unwilling to do so any time soon). Russia signed its first BIT in 1989 (as USSR, with the Belgium-Luxembourg Economic Union); it signed 76 further agreements, 61 of which are currently in force.[22] India signed its first BIT in 1994 (with the UK); today, it is signatory to other 84 agreements and has ratified 69 of them.[23] South Africa signed its first BIT in 1994 as well (also with the UK); it further signed 46 agreements and ratified 23 (at least six of which, however, it has denounced already).[24] Of these States, only China (since 1984) and India (since 1993) adopted a model BIT. In addition, Brazil, South Africa, and India currently display, to different extents, a negative attitude toward agreements for the protection of foreign investment: Brazil refuses to sign new BITs, and never ratified any of those it signed; South Africa is pursuing a rather

[14] Since its first BIT with Switzerland (1973), Egypt has rapidly concluded BITs with all major capital-exporters: Germany and France in 1974, Italy in 1975, the Netherlands in 1976, Japan in 1977 and the US in 1982; notably, Egypt appears also to be the first developing State to have signed a BIT with another developing State (*i.e.*, the Egypt-Morocco BIT, of 1976).

[15] ICSID n.d.

[16] The US entered into over 100 of such treaties (starting with the Treaty of Amity and Commerce with France, in 1782, and ending, in 1966, with the agreements with Togo and Thailand).

[17] Still today, the US appears continuing to conclude these agreements; for instance, in 2006 it signed a Trade and Investment Framework Arrangement with the ASEAN (the text of the arrangement is available via http://www.ustr.gov/sites/default/files/uploads/agreements/tifa/asset_upload_file932_9760.pdf).

[18] According to the US Trade Representative n.d.

[19] For a review of the early US BIT programme, see Vandevelde (1988), pp. 208–211.

[20] In that year the USSR also concluded BITs with Germany, France, Italy, Canada, the UK, the Netherlands, the Belgium-Luxembourg Economic Union, and Finland.

[21] Cf., UNCTAD n.d. at http://investmentpolicyhub.unctad.org/IIA/CountryBits/27#iiaInnerMenu.

[22] Id. at http://investmentpolicyhub.unctad.org/IIA/CountryBits/175#iiaInnerMenu.

[23] Id. at http://investmentpolicyhub.unctad.org/IIA/CountryBits/96#iiaInnerMenu.

[24] Id. at http://investmentpolicyhub.unctad.org/IIA/CountryBits/195#iiaInnerMenu.

Table 1 BITs concluded/selected states (selected years/*total number of BITs*)

	1967 [27] / *63*	1983 [28] / *220*	1994 [29] / *>700*	2014 [30] / *>2860*		
Germany	29 *(>50 %)*	54 *(>25 %)*	92 *(>10 %)*	155	131	17
Switzerland	16	34	68	130	115	10
France	1	25	62	109	95	4
UK	0	22	71	107	95	1
The Netherlands	3	14	48	107	92	10
Italy	1	7	30	106	79	14
Belgium-Lux	2	14	35	104	68	8
Sweden	3	13	31	73	66	4
US	0	3	33	47	40	1
Canada	0	2	10	45	31	5
Japan	0	2	4	25	19	0

steady policy of termination of its BITs[25]; and India has recently frozen all on-going negotiations, pending the adoption of the new model text.[26]

With regard to the size and content of BITs, there are two principal traditions. European model investment agreements are synthetic, counting no more than 15 provisions. The North American models, since 2004,[27] are instead more structured and extensive arrangements, divided into 3–5 sections, and comprising a number of provisions ranging between 30 and 50.[28] A notable conceptual difference

[25] Notwithstanding the release of the SADC Model BIT, in September 2012, South Africa has terminated the agreements with the Belgium-Luxembourg Economic Union, in November 2013 with the Netherlands and Switzerland, in December 2013 with Spain, and, in October 2013, with Austria and Germany.

[26] See, e.g., Mehdudia (2013).

[27] Despite the late start, since joining the trend of modern BITs the US is found to have been '. . .at the forefront of varying the BIT pattern started by Germany by the way of dramatically extending its length, and also by deviating from the basic pattern by way of combining matters of trade and investment in Free Trade Agreements instead of concluding solely investment-focused agreements', see Dolzer and Kim (2013), p. 290.

[28] The US Models of 2004 and 2012 (which are, for the most part, identical, substantially, when not outright literally), are both composed of 3 sections featuring 37 Articles in total, plus 4 draft Annexes; both Canadian Models are divided into 5 sections, but that of 2004 contains 52 Articles (and 7 draft Annexes), while in that of 2006 the number of provisions is reduced to 42.

between Europe and North America (especially, since 2004) is that, through BITs, the latter emphasizes the aspect of investment liberalization and free movement of capital flows, while the former seeks to first secure the 'promotion and protection' of investments. Nevertheless, still in 2006, investment liberalization was perceived as a '*per se* newly contentious global issue'[29] and, besides wider and deeper forms of integration among States (*e.g.*, EU, NAFTA or ASEAN), many—especially, developing States—still oppose it.[30]

2 The EU Treaty Framework and Competence to Negotiate Investment Protection Regimes with Third Parties

Between 1957 and 1994, the European Community (EC) external economic policy focused on trade. The 1957 Treaty of Rome, instituting the EC, provided for exclusive competence for trade policy; investment was left, instead, in the sovereign hands of the Member States. In 1991 an exception was made, with the Energy Charter Treaty signed in the form of a mixed agreement by both Member States and the Community (with the former competent for investment, and the latter for the trade aspects of the agreement). Seeds of involvement of EC institutions in investment protection began, in general terms, with the EC being partly competent for the WTO's investment regime (the TRIMs Agreement)[31] and, between 1996 and 2003, the EC participation in the Working Group on Trade and Investment. Subsequently, some EC-negotiated FTAs featured a chapter on investment liberalization, including commercial presence in services and investment in goods production (*e.g.*, 2009 EU-CARIFORUM EPA, 2011 EU-Korea FTA, 2013 EU-Central America FTA, 2013 EU-Colombia/Peru FTA). Nevertheless, all mandates (and most negotiations) for these agreements were granted prior to the entry into force of the Treaty of Lisbon, in 2009.

The entry into force of the Lisbon Treaty, on 1 December 2009, brought significant changes to the constitutional architecture of the European Union (EU) and its functioning. Synthetically, the Treaty of Lisbon consolidated the previous EC three-pillar system into one entity, the EU (also succeeding in the former's legal personality). In spite of the amendments and reorganizations introduced, the Lisbon system continues to pivot on two Treaties: the 1993 Treaty of Maastricht, or 'Treaty on the European Union' (TEU); and the 1958 Treaty of

[29] Huiping (2006), p. 144.

[30] E.g., ASEAN Member States accepted investment liberalization in the Framework Agreement on ASEAN Investment Area, but strictly limited to the ASEAN area; singular ASEAN Members—such as Malaysia, Indonesia, Thailand and the Philippines—along many other States such as, *e.g.*, India and China, still oppose it; nevertheless, ASEAN insisted for liberalization within the China-ASEAN FTA framework (cf., Chapter IV, Section D1).

[31] Agreement on Trade-Related Investment Measures; conversely, the EC did not participate in the negotiations for GATS Mode 3 (on commercial presence).

Rome, once officially 'Treaty Establishing the European Community', and now retitled 'Treaty on the Functioning of the European Union' (TFEU).

Through the Lisbon Treaty, the Union's powers and scopes have been redesigned (or clarified) along the lines of three 'exclusive', 'shared', and 'supporting' areas of competence. Among the amendments introduced, the Treaties now feature an express mention of 'foreign direct investment'. To retrieve a general clear attribution of competence on the matter of protection of foreign investment, let alone foreign direct investment, would be, however, uneasy for those unused to EU diplomatic and legalese phraseology.

Title V TEU, labelled 'General Provisions on the Union's External Action and Specific Provisions on the Common Foreign and Security Policy', features, in Chapter 1 (comprised of two provisions, Arts. 21 and 22), the 'General Provisions on the Union's External Action'.[32] The Chapter (thus, the general principles it features) is expressly recalled in the TFEU, in Part V ('The Union's External Action'), in Art. 205 (the sole provision of Title I, labelled 'General Provisions on the Union's External Action'): 'The Union's action on the international scene, pursuant to this Part, shall be guided by the principles, pursue the objectives and be conducted in accordance with the general provisions laid down in Chapter 1 of Title V of the Treaty on European Union.' However, it is only with the first of the two provisions of Title II ('Common Commercial Policy'), in Art. 206, that the first explicit mention of foreign direct investment emerges:

> By establishing a customs union in accordance with Articles 28 to 32, *the Union shall contribute,* in the common interest, to the harmonious development of world trade, *the progressive abolition of restrictions on* international trade and on *foreign direct investment,* and the lowering of customs and other barriers.[33]

Lastly, and most importantly, the other provision of Title II, Art. 207 (a dense and complex norm spanning through six paragraphs), constitutes a firmer ground for the EU competence on the matter of protection of foreign investment. Here, paragraph 1 specifies that:

> The *common commercial policy shall be based on uniform principles, particularly with regard to* changes in tariff rates, the conclusion of tariff and trade agreements relating to trade in goods and services, and *the commercial aspects of* intellectual property, *foreign direct investment...*[34]

Art. 207 is subject to the general principles and objectives of the Union's external actions. These are non-trade values, identified in overarching Arts. 21–22 TEU (such as, *e.g.*, protection of health, safety and environment, promotion of the rule of law, human rights, and sustainable development).

Paragraphs 3 and 4 of Art. 207 provide for some elements of the internal procedural rules to be followed with regard to 'agreements in the field of... foreign

[32] Chapter 2 dealing with the Specific Provisions on the Common Foreign and Security Policy.

[33] Emphases added.

[34] Emphases added.

direct investment'. According to the seeds of procedure there contained, and the others developed so far, the Commission makes a recommendation to the Council that, by qualified majority, authorizes the Commission to open the negotiations with the selected counterpart. The Commission hence conducts the negotiations and reports regularly to the Council and the Parliament. In any event, it is established that for the negotiation and conclusion of agreements in the fields of foreign direct investment, the Council shall act unanimously where such agreements include provisions for which unanimity is required for the adoption of internal rules. Paragraph 6 further stresses that 'the exercise of the competences conferred by [Art. 207] in the field of the common commercial policy shall not affect the delimitation of competences between the Union and the Member States'.

Having briefly illustrated the EU legal framework with regard to the regime of protection of foreign investments, the following section reviews its interpretation by the principal organs of the EU.

3 Interpreting the Treaty Framework: EU's 'Three Heads' and the New Regulations

The Lisbon Treaty framework briefly outlined above, by providing limited explicit reference yet enough room for interpretation on the matter of the protection of foreign investment, generated different readings, among the EU principal organs, about the extent of the newly acquired powers, or about the competence to sign EU-negotiated investment treaties (let alone, ratify them).

The Commission interpreted Arts. 206 and 207 TFEU as allocating exclusive competence to EU institutions for Foreign Direct Investment (FDI), investment liberalization and investment protection, covering the Member States' 'best and widest' practices. According to this early interpretation, an extensive reading based on the doctrine of implied powers,[35] granted the EU the power to conclude investment agreements also covering portfolio investment and Investor-State Dispute Settlement (ISDS).[36] Moreover, according to the Commission, Arts. 21–22 TEU provided the EU with the power to autonomously improve the already existing protection framework, most notably expanding into the investment admission regime.[37]

---

[35] Based on Art. 3.2 TFEU (competence to conclude agreements when necessary to exercise EU internal competence), and Art. 63 TFEU (free movement of capital within the EU extending to third countries).

[36] Communication of 7 July 2010 from the European Commission to the Council, the European Parliament, the European Economic and Social Committee and the Committee of the Regions, Towards a Comprehensive European International Investment Policy, pp. 2, 8 and 10, available via http://trade.ec.europa.eu/doclib/docs/2010/july/tradoc_146307.pdf.

[37] Ibid.

The Council, at first at least, adopted a similar approach, even though through more diplomatic wording such as 'the main focus of international investment agreements should continue to be effective and ambitious investment protection and market access'.[38] Moreover, the prevailing view in the Council was that portfolio investment remained within the domain of the Member States. Therefore, an understanding appears to have ultimately been reached by considering EU investment agreements covering both direct and indirect investments as 'mixed agreements', thus negotiated by the Commission on behalf of all Member States, yet upon unanimous authorization of the Council, which subsequently must sign the negotiated text. While it appears plain that the signed text must pass also in the European Parliament, it is unclear whether it is also supposed to be ratified by all 28 Member States, in accordance with the legislative process of each of them. Such an articulated arrangement, unsurprisingly, is proving uneasy for the negotiated treaties to actually get signed (let alone, ratified) as it will be illustrated in the subsequent sections.

By making the codecision mechanism the EU ordinary legislative procedure, Art. 294 TFEU provides for a significant strengthening of the competences of the Parliament of the European Union. The Parliament has thus become co-legislator, on an equal footing with the Council, in all matters the latter decides with simple and qualified majorities (except specific cases where it only retains a consultative role).[39] In the field of foreign investment protection, the Parliament exercised its new powers by expressing concerns about the perceived investor-oriented treaty-regime and arbitral practice, emphasizing the need to protect the right of Member States to regulate in the public interest.[40] In this respect, the Parliament requested a specific clause aimed at protecting the values enshrined in Arts. 21–22 TEU, and considered that EU investment agreements should only feature prohibitions on discriminatory treatment, direct and indirect expropriation (provided that such definitions balance in a 'clear and fair manner' public welfare objectives and investors' interests). Moreover, it requested for a specific clause to prevent the watering down of social and environmental legislation, and sector-specific reservations and exceptions aimed at carving out culture, education, public health, and national defence interests and legislations from potential actions by foreign investors.

---

[38] See the Conclusions adopted by the Council of the European Union on 25 October 2010 on a Comprehensive European International Investment Policy, available via https://www.consilium.europa.eu/uedocs/cms_data/docs/pressdata/EN/foraff/117328.pdf.

[39] I.e., in all matters covered by Art. 16 TEU and Art. 238 TFEU: under the ordinary legislative procedure, the Council acts by qualified majority, in co-decision with the European Parliament. The qualified majority mechanism introduced with the Lisbon Treaty requires at least 55 % of the Council to vote in favour of any topic, corresponding to at least 15 Members representing at least 65 % of the EU population. This notwithstanding, a block of at least four Members may veto the adoption of the debated measure.

[40] European Parliament Resolution of 6 April 2011 on the Future European International Investment Policy, 2010/2203 (INI), available via http://www.europarl.europa.eu/sides/getDoc.do?type=TA&language=EN&reference=P7-TA-2011-141.

In this framework, with Reg. (EU) No. 1219/2012, Parliament and Council have 'establish[ed] transitional arrangements for bilateral investment agreements between Member States and third countries', by which Member States have, in sum, accepted to halt further negotiations and expansions of their own BIT programmes.[41] Moreover, while pursuing EU negotiations with third parties, Reg. (EU) No. 912/2014 established a 'framework for managing financial responsibility linked to investor-to-state dispute settlement tribunals established by international agreements to which the European Union is party'.[42] Both regulations reflect the centralizing attempt of the EU executive over the foreign investment protection discipline, especially with regard to prospective EU-wide investment agreements.

No legislative attempt has been made, on the other hand, to regulate the problem of the around 190 intra-EU BITs mostly signed between Western 'old' Member States and Eastern 'new' Member States before their accession (*i.e.*, between 1991 and 2004).[43] The Commission, which for its part is responsible for having overly cautiously addressed the matter before it materially emerged,[44] subsequently repeatedly called upon Member States to terminate these agreements, as establishing a privileged relationship between investors and some Member States, at odds with both the EU-wide principle of non-discrimination and the nature of the EU common market.[45] The reaction on the part of Member States has been mixed,[46] even though many of these agreements have been effectively terminated to date.[47] In the meantime, the Commission has progressively adopted a policy of discouraging intra-EU investment arbitration, by intervening in many of these instances

[41] The text of the Regulation is available via http://eur-lex.europa.eu/legal-content/EN/ALL/?uri=CELEX:32012R1219. Currently, in principle Member States no longer have the competence to conclude new investment agreements, while those concluded before the entry into force of the Lisbon Treaty remain in force, but shall be notified to the Commission (Art. 3 Reg. 1219/2012). Under certain conditions, nevertheless, Member States can still amend existing agreements, or even conclude new BITs (Art. 7).

[42] The text of the Regulation is available via http://eur-lex.europa.eu/legal-content/EN/TXT/?uri=uriserv:OJ.L_.2014.257.01.0121.01.ENG.

[43] Cf., European Commission Report of 2012 on Monitoring Activities and Analysis, Bilateral Investment Treaties Between Member States (Intra-EU BITs), available via http://ec.europa.eu/internal_market/capital/analysis/monitoring_activities_and_analysis/index_en.htm#maincontentSec5.

[44] Cf., the unassertive attitude displayed by the Commission (as opposed to the rather firm view of the arbitral panel) in the first intra-EU investment arbitration, *Eastern Sugar B. V. v. Czech Republic*, SCC Case No. 088/2004, Partial Award, available via: http://www.italaw.com/cases/documents/369.

[45] See the latest European Commission Report of 17 October 2014, available via http://ec.europa.eu/internal_market/capital/analysis/monitoring_activities_and_analysis/index_en.htm#maincontentSec5.

[46] Cf., Vis-Dunbar (2009).

[47] Cf., Table 1, above; in any case, transition periods of validity (5–10 years) still maintain the vast majority of intra-EU BITs valid; see also Hepburn and Peterson (2015).

and advancing arguments along the lines of contrariness to the EU constitutional regime and public order.[48]

Ultimately, the final texts negotiated by the Commission with Singapore and Canada show that most of the Parliament's concerns had been taken into account. In order to do so, the Commission expanded considerably the detail of the Members States' traditional investment agreements, resulting in both texts acquiring a North American character, in both size and content. Nevertheless, as the political climate toward international investment agreements changed, the Council as a whole, and some Members States in particular, expressed, first, concerns about the Lisbon Treaty regime of competences; subsequently, with regard to the negotiation for the US-EU Transatlantic Trade and Investment Partnership (TTIP), the need for ISDS. Thus, both the ratification process of the two concluded texts, and the negotiations for the TTIP, are currently stalled. The subsequent sections will briefly analyse the relevant parts of the negotiated texts, and the reasons underlying the current state of affairs in greater detail.

4 EU-Led Negotiations for Investment Agreements with Third Parties

Since the entry into force of the Lisbon Treaty, the Council has granted the Commission negotiating mandates covering investment chapters within FTA arrangements with Canada (2009), Russia (2010),[49] India (2011),[50] Singapore (2011),[51] Japan (2012), Thailand (2013), and the US (2013).[52] Moreover, the Council has authorized the Commission to negotiate stand-alone investment agreements with China (2013), and Burma (2014).[53]

[48] *E.g.*, the observation of the Commission in the *amicus curiae* brief for the *European American Investment Bank (EURAM) AG v. Slovak Republic*, available via http://www.italaw.com/cases/1706; also, see the still on-going Micula case saga (*Ioan Micula, Viorel Micula, S. C. European Food S. A, S. C. Starmill S. R. L. and S. C. Multipack S. R. L. v. Romania*, ICSID Case No. ARB/05/20, available via http://www.italaw.com/cases/697).

[49] The original negotiating directive, aiming at a comprehensive FTA, is of 2008; in 2010 its scope has been narrowed down to trade and investment only.

[50] Building on negotiating directives granted by the Council in 2007 for the negotiation of a Comprehensive Free Trade Agreement, the Commission obtained an additional mandate to also negotiate investment protection in 2011.

[51] Additional mandate, based on the 2007 ASEAN negotiating directive.

[52] In this category, the Commission also includes Egypt, Tunisia, Morocco, Jordan, Malaysia, and Vietnam (see: http://ec.europa.eu/trade/policy/accessing-markets/investment/). Nevertheless, the investment protection regime therein featured or negotiated is not comparable to a typical BIT, nor do these agreements feature the Investor-State Dispute Settlement Mechanism.

[53] European Commission Overview of 5 May 2015 of FTA and Other Trade Negotiations, available via http://trade.ec.europa.eu/doclib/html/118238.htm.

To date, negotiations with Russia and India are stalled (for different reasons), and those with Japan are still at an early stage (and focused on trade). Only the negotiations with Singapore and Canada have been concluded. What follows is an outline of the characterizing policy and textual choices made in these two agreements.

4.1 Investment Chapter IX of the EU-Singapore FTA

Based on the Council's 2007 EU-ASEAN negotiating directives, negotiations for the EU-Singapore FTA were concluded on 17 October 2014. The agreement was, for the most part, initialled on 20 September 2013, and made public henceforth. The draft investment protection chapter is currently being reviewed by the respective legal teams. The text subsequently needs to be formally approved by the Commission and the Council, and then ratified by the Parliament. However, a different interpretation between the Commission and the Council emerged about whether the ratification process ends here or it must involve also domestic approval by all 28 Member States' parliaments. On 30 October 2014, the then outgoing Commission decided to request to the European Court of Justice (ECJ) an opinion on the competence to sign and ratify the FTA with Singapore.[54]

Investment Chapter IX of the EU-Singapore FTA features 30 provisions, divided into two Sections: Section A (Arts. 1–10) comprises the investment protection standards; Section B (Arts. 14–33)[55] disciplines ISDS mechanisms. Three Annexes (on expropriation, mediation, and arbitrators' code of conduct) are attached. The agreement builds on the experience with investment agreements of both Singapore and EU Members States; it also draws from the US model BIT, as well as adapts (or reacts) to some arbitral case law that shaped subsequent interpretive trends (generally unwelcome to States).

The definition of 'juridical person' is imported from Singapore's practice (mostly, matured within the ASEAN framework)[56]; typical of ASEAN's Comprehensive Investment Agreement (ACIA), and that concluded between ASEAN and China (CAIA), both signed in 2009, is that Chapter IX mentions the exceptions to the operation of the substantive clauses (national treatment, standard of treatment, expropriation) already in the provision of scope (Art. 2) and national treatment (Art. 3). Moreover, the National Treatment (NT) clause is phrased synthetically, with the same terms adopted in the CAIA, and the structure of the expropriation provision follows the typical Chinese practice (adopted in the CAIA as well).

---

[54] After the review of the initiative, on 4 March 2015, the newly installed Commission decided to go ahead with the request for the Court's opinion.

[55] The numbering is still provisional (that is why it is not perfectly consequential between the two Sections).

[56] Through the ASEAN Comprehensive Agreement on Investment (ACIA), signed in 2009.

Out of the Member States' practice, it is possible to see that Chapter IX applies to 'investment' (as opposed to 'measures affecting investments', as per the typical US model formulation, followed in ACIA and CAIA). Furthermore, in accordance with the UK standard criterion, the expropriated investment's value is determined on the basis of that held before 'the impending expropriation becomes of public knowledge'.[57] Lastly, drawing from both the German and British tradition, the expropriation is explicitly made subject to 'judicial review'; the addition appears, nevertheless, redundant, as it is conceptually included in the preceding notion of 'due process' (absent, as such, in both German and British practice), already listed as one of the four qualifying elements for a legitimate expropriation.

Striking is the change, for the Europeans, with regard to the notion of investment. The definition draws in its entirety from the US model and practice, thus expanding both the chapeau and the list of investment instances. In the latter, for the first time a European investment agreement mentions the so-called 'objective criteria' to better define the notion of investment (*i.e.*, commitment of capital, expectation of profit, assumption of risk). These changes, already accepted in ASEAN[58] and Chinese[59] practice, appear also to respond to some inconsistency about the interpretation of the notion of investment witnessed in the arbitral case law.[60]

Always responding to contrasting interpretive trends that emerged within the Investor-State Dispute Settlement Mechanism, the Parties agreed to a novel formulation of the Fair and Equitable Treatment (FET) and Full Protection and Security (FPS) clauses. Also, they agreed to expunge from the Chapter the Most Favoured Nation (MFN) and Minimum Standard of Treatment (MST) provisions.

---

[57] 2006 UK model BIT, Art. 5.2; the wording was already adopted by China since the adoption of the 1989 model BIT (Art. 4.2).

[58] Cf., footnote 2 to Art. 4.c of the ACIA.

[59] Cf., Art. 1 of the Supplementary Agreement on Investment of the China-Chile FTA (2012), and Art. 1.4 of the China-Canada BIT (2012).

[60] *Fedax N. V. v. The Republic of Venezuela*, ICSID Case No. ARB/96/3, Decision on Objections to Jurisdiction, 11 July 1997; *Salini Costruttori S. p. A. and Italstrade S. p. A. v. Kingdom of Morocco*, ICSID Case No. ARB/00/4, Decision on Jurisdiction, 23 July 2001; *Joy Mining Machinery Limited v. Arab Republic of Egypt*, ICSID Case No. ARB/03/11, Award on Jurisdiction, 6 August 2004; *Mr. Patrick Mitchell v. Democratic Republic of the Congo*, ICSID Case No. ARB/99/7, Decision on the Application for Annulment of the Award, 1 November 2006; *Saipem S. p. A. v. The People's Republic of Bangladesh*, ICSID Case No. ARB/05/07, Decision on Jurisdiction and Recommendation on Provisional Measures, 21 March 2007; *Malaysian Historical Salvors, SDN, BHD v. The Government of Malaysia*, ICSID Case No. ARB/05/10, Award on Jurisdiction, 17 March 2007; *M. C. I. Power Group L. C. and New Turbine, Inc. v. Republic of Ecuador*, ICSID Case No. ARB/03/6, Award, 31 July 2007; *Biwater Gauff (Tanzania) Ltd. v. United Republic of Tanzania*, ICSID Case No. ARB/05/22, Award, 24 July 2008; *Malaysian Historical Salvors, SDN, BHD v. The Government of Malaysia*, ICSID Case No. ARB/05/10, Decision on the Application for Annulment, 16 April 2009; note, however, the dissenting opinion of Judge M. Shahabuddeen; *Saba Fakes v. Turkey*, ICSID Case No. ARB/07/20, Award, 14 July 2010; *Abaclat and Others v. Argentine Republic*, ICSID Case No. ARB/07/5, Decision on Jurisdiction, 4 August 2011.

The umbrella clause is narrowly reformulated (and brought into Section A, dealing with the standard of treatment). The formulation of direct and indirect expropriation is highly detailed (also considering the dedicated Annex on 'guiding principles' on expropriation). Lastly, to reduce interpretive exercises, footnote 21 provides for a definition of both 'owned' and 'controlled' investments.

With regard to the dispute settlement mechanism, Section B of Chapter IX of the EU-Singapore FTA builds, in principle, on the ACIA and the US model BIT. As with the text agreed in the ASEAN-Australia-New Zealand FTA (AANZFTA), the Section features a dedicated 'scope and definitions' provision (Art. 14).[61] As of the scope, it is worth noting that the EU-Singapore text applies to '*a dispute concerning treatment* alleged to breach the provisions of Section A . . . which breach allegedly causes loss or damage to the claimant'.[62] Such a formulation is more precise than the one featured in the ACIA (where the Section applies to '*an investment dispute* between a Member State and an investor of another Member State that has incurred loss or damage *by reason of an alleged breach of any rights*'). Lastly, the dedicated list of definitions highlights the autonomous character of the Section B (distinct from Section A).[63]

A significant proceduralization of all stages of arbitration, and of the path to initiate it, is evident. The procedure is mandatory in all of its steps: Art. 20.3 makes explicitly clear that 'the tribunal shall decline jurisdiction where the claimant fails to respect any of the requirements or declarations [indicated prior to the submission of a claim to arbitration]'. What in all European model BITs used to be contained in one provision, the EU-Singapore FTA develops into a regime of 7 norms (spanning 8 pages). Firstly, Arts. 15 through 17 appear actually designed to *avoid* arbitration. Several are, indeed, the 'roadblocks'. Art. 16, for instance, features an articulated consultation procedure (structured similarly to the *iter* to initiate arbitration featured in the US model),[64] as a mandatory 6-month preliminary step to arbitration. Secondly, two provisions then separate the mandatory 3-month 'Notice of intent to arbitrate' (Art. 18) from the 'Submission of claim to arbitration' (Art. 19), otherwise listed under a single provision in the US model.

A brief review of the salient points of the substance of Section B must highlight:

- The anti-forum-shopping clause (Art. 20.6);
- With regard to the interpretive concerns that may arise on Chapter IX, the role reserved to the Trade Committee, which 'should exercise due restraint in recommending interpretations of any provision already submitted to a tribunal in a dispute . . . where a final award has yet to be made' (Art. 22) needs to be pointed out. Such 'restraint' is a countertrend to other recent treaties, which

[61] A provision of 'scope' in this Section is also present in ACIA and CAIA; together with that in the AANZFTA, it may thus be assumed that such a provision constitutes a solid practice of ASEAN.

[62] Art. 14.1 (emphasis added).

[63] Such a separation may ease possible future amendments of the text.

[64] Art. 24.2 US model BIT.

impose on the panel the application of the interpretation of the Parties (or Committees) *ipso facto*[65];

- Drawing from ACIA,[66] the struck-down provision on 'Claims manifestly without legal merit' (Art. 23);
- The original exception (apparently drawing from the *prima facie* case test adopted by the International Court of Justice in the *Oil Platform* case)[67] to challenge 'Claims unfounded as a matter of law': '... the tribunal shall address and decide as a preliminary question any objection by the respondent that, as a matter of law, a claim, or any part thereof ... is not a claim for which an award in favour of the claimant may be made under [the conditions dictated for the submission of claim to arbitration], even if the facts alleged were assumed to be true ...' (Art. 24.1);
- The provision on the arbitration costs (Art. 29) which, contrary to current practice, establishes that all costs shall be borne by the losing party, unless there are circumstances of exceptional (with regard to the arbitration *per se*) or inappropriate (with regard to legal representation and assistance) character. Independently from the arbitral procedure and venue adopted, paragraph 5 caps arbitrators' fees and expenses to those of the ICSID regime (significantly lower than most others);
- Similarly to the US model, Art. 33 (outlining the role of the Trade Committee) envisages the possibility of the establishment, if the Parties so agree, of an appellate mechanism. Moreover, always drawing from the US and NAFTA practice, the Committee is in charge to appoint the list of arbitrators—whose use, however, is not mandatory on the Parties.

4.2 Investment Chapter X of the EU-Canada FTA

The Council authorized the Commission to negotiate a comprehensive FTA with Canada in April 2009. On 26 September 2014, negotiations were concluded. Currently, the text is undergoing the legal review process on both sides; it is subsequently supposed to be submitted to the Council and EU Parliament for approval. Political opposition from several Member States about the entry into force of the agreement has however emerged. Same as in the preceding subsection, the analysis will first briefly focus on the text of the Treaty.

The foreign investment protection regime is featured in Chapter X, and comprises 43 Provisions divided into 6 Sections, plus three Annexes, one 'declaration'

---

[65] Cf., e.g., Art. 40 ACIA; Art. 19 China-Chile Supplementary Agreement on Investment; Arts. 18.2 and 30 China-Canada BIT.

[66] The first two paragraphs of Art. 23 EU-Singapore reproduce Art. 36.2 ACIA.

[67] *Oil Platforms (Islamic Republic of Iran v. United States of America)*, Preliminary Objection, ICJ Reports 1996, p. 822.

and one 'joint declaration' (for an overall length of 40 pages). The order and distribution of provisions appear original, despite the apparent influence of the North American models of investment agreement.

Firstly, by replicating the US model first provision's structure and wording, Chapter X applies to '*measures* ... relating to' investors and investments[68] (as opposed to 'investment', traditional of all European models). Such wording, a novelty for the European States, is close to the choice made by Canada in its 2012 BIT with China.[69] As per the EU-Singapore FTA, exceptions to the investment regime are already listed in the definition of scope (in Art. 1): here, they actually constitute the bulk of the provision, as they span through four of its five paragraphs. Displaying a very cautious attitude toward potential claims of investors, or expansive interpretation of investment tribunals, Art. 1.4 refers to Art. 17 already, reaffirming that 'claims may be submitted by an investor ... *only* in accordance with Section 6 Art. 17 (Scope of a claim to arbitration), and in compliance with the procedures otherwise set out in that Section'.[70] In the same paragraph a specification, present as well in the EU-Singapore FTA, by which the procedural steps set out in the Treaty are mandatory is also mentioned; the disposition is thereafter repeated in Art. 21.4. Signs of caution are represented as well by explicitly excluding the operation of ISDS on the establishment and performance requirements. The list of definitions draws from the (overly) comprehensive Canadian tradition, featuring 29 elements (as opposed to the traditional three of European models: investment, investor, and returns). Following the US practice, the notion of investment is preceded by that of 'covered investment'. To the latter traditional features (*i.e.*, *rationes loci*, *temporis* and *legis* of the agreement) the EU-Canada FTA adds that of 'direct' or 'indirect' ownership or control (redundantly so, as the same locution is already present in the notion of investment proper). The definition of investment is, instead, based on the Canadian model (for the most part, it was retained also in the 2012 China-Canada BIT: it may thus be inferred for Canada's insistence in this respect), nevertheless simplified in several parts through the British and German model texts. Somewhat surprisingly, in the definition of investor that of 'juridical person' is missing, replaced by the British (and Canadian) derived 'enterprise'.

Regarding the treatment of investment, it may be noted that NT and MFN clauses are gathered under Section 3, 'Non-discriminatory Treatment', separated from the FET (systematized in Section 4, 'investment protection'). The NT clause (Art. 6) is formulated as in the EU-Singapore FTA, but for the fact that here the provision protects also establishment, acquisition, expansion and conduct of the investment. The formulation is synthetic, limited to a single paragraph covering both 'investors' and 'investments'. Another novel element, shared with the subsequent MFN clause (Art. 7), is the multi-government-layers clause. Such a clause

[68] Art. X.1 (emphasis added).

[69] Art. 2 China-Canada BIT (2012).

[70] Emphasis added.

'federalizes' or 'regionalizes' both NT and MFN, understood here as treatments granted *within* specific sub-units of the EU and Canada, respectively.[71] It is also noteworthy that the MFN provision is indeed featured in the investment regime of the EU-Canada FTA (as opposed to the EU-Singapore FTA, where it has been expunged). The protection offered is limited in its scope by (1) the exceptions already featured in Art. 1, (2) the anti-*Maffezini*[72] clause (thus excluding MFN application to ISDS),[73] and (3) an original anti-expansive interpretation clause, that recites: 'Substantive obligations in other international investment treaties and other trade agreements do not in themselves constitute *treatment*, and thus cannot give rise to breach of this article, absent measures adopted by a Party pursuant to such obligation'.[74] Similar limitations are usually featured in the FET clause. As of this latter, the provision appears modelled on the EU-Singapore norm, and sets forth a closed list of treatments that may be deemed a breach of the granted standard. Among a list of relatively traditional instances, a new element has been agreed upon, including 'targeted discrimination on manifestly wrongful grounds, such as gender, race or religious belief'.[75] Significantly, the 'legitimate expectation', referred in varying extents by several arbitral tribunals,[76] is here explicitly downgraded to a criterion to determine a breach of one of the instances provided in the closed list (as opposed to a self-standing ground for breach). Also significant is that the reference to customary international law, typical of North American models, to determine violations of the standard of treatment of aliens, has been here discarded (similarly, instead, to the Chinese and Southeast Asian practice in this respect). Ultimately, it appears that, also in light of the EU Parliament's concerns, the Commission managed to reach a compromise text featuring, *inter alia*, a closed list for the FET clause, and a narrow definition of indirect expropriation.[77]

With regard to ISDS, in principle the agreed text draws on both Canadian models, integrated (or simplified) with the regime featured in the EU-Singapore FTA: here as well, the articulated provisions on consultation and mediation are followed by a series of 'roadblocks' to arbitration; the preliminary struck-down

---

[71] Art. 7.2 recites: 'For greater certainty, the treatment accorded by a Party under paragraph 1 means, with respect to the a government in Canada other than at the federal level or, with respect to a government of or in a European Member State, treatment accorded, in like situation, by that government to investors in its territory, and to investment of such investors, of any third country'.

[72] *Emilio Agustín Maffezini v. The Kingdom of Spain*, ICSID Case No. ARB/97/7, Decision of the Tribunal on Objections to Jurisdiction, 25 January 2000.

[73] Art. 7.4, first sentence.

[74] Art. 7.4, second sentence. The wording is original in that it pre-emptively excludes expansive interpretations of the MFN clause. In the past, doubts have arisen as to whether the FET clause would be violated by a breach of other obligations (whether in the same or another Treaty) of the host State. Never before, however, did such an issue emerge with regard to the MFN clause.

[75] Art. 9.2.

[76] See, in this respect, Potestà (2012); see also, Yost (2009).

[77] Annex on Expropriation, para. 2.

provisions are also present here (Arts. 29 and 30), as well as those for the apportionment and determination of the arbitration costs (Arts. 36.5 and 38). Also similarly to the agreement with Singapore, that with Canada features a mechanism to create a non-binding roaster of arbitrators (Art. 25.4), by a Committee granted with analogous functions. The EU appears also to have insisted on the insertion, in Art. 42, of a text equivalent to that featured in Annex 9 of the agreement with Singapore, in that it tasked the Committee to adopt a code of conduct for arbitrators, and rules for mediation. In this respect, however, there are three differences with respect to the EU-Singapore investment regime, all of them apparently representing an improvement to that text.

The first, in Art. 20, is the provision for the determination of the respondent (*i.e.*, the EU or a Member State); firstly, the investor must deliver a 'notice requesting the determination of the respondent' to the EU,[78] which shall inform the investor within 50 days.[79] A subsidiary regime comes into play where the EU does not timely respond: it will then fall upon the investor to identify the respondent, and the norm provides for the following guiding directive: 'where the measures identified in the notice are exclusively measures of a Member State of the EU, the Member State shall be respondent; where the measures identified in the notice include measures of the European Union, the European Union shall be the respondent'.[80] Such determination, of the EU in the first case, and of the investor in the second, is binding upon the tribunal,[81] and either respondent is barred from challenging it at any stage of the arbitral proceedings.[82] The outlined provision may be perceived as byzantine, as it imposes on the investor a forceful additional cooling-off period of up to 50 days (*i.e.*, the time the EU disposes of to identify who is the respondent), while alternatively calling upon the same investor for an autonomous determination, on the basis of a relatively simple criterion. The same effect—yet with a simpler procedure—would have perhaps been for the investor to be left the choice to make the first determination, which would become effective unless a different one is provided by the EU (possibly, within a term less hefty than 50 days).

The second addition in the EU-Canada investment regime, compared to that featured in the EU-Singapore FTA, is entirely and literally drawn from Canada's model,[83] and consists in the possibility for the tribunal to issue *interim* measures. The provision casts clarity on a power whose limits and opportunity of use otherwise rest on the doctrine of implied powers (hence, less certain in its content). Furthermore, this appears entirely appropriate in light of the

[78] Art. 20, para. 1.

[79] Art. 20, paras. 3 and 4.

[80] Art. 20, para. 4.

[81] Art. 20, para. 7.

[82] Art. 20, para. 6.

[83] Art. 43 Canada model BIT of 2004 (not the slightly different formulation featured in Art. 35 Canada draft model BIT of 2006).

varying degree of acceptance of measures as such from arbitral panels throughout the EU.[84]

The third novel provision deals with the transparency of proceedings.[85] The norm appears to respond to the concerns raised by the EU Parliament.[86] The first four paragraphs rely on the UNCITRAL Transparency Rules. Paragraph 5, however, brings in the text a novelty by providing that 'hearings shall be open to the public', and that the tribunal shall facilitate public access.

4.3 *Roadblocks to the Entry into Force of the Newly Negotiated Investment Regimes*

As briefly mentioned above, the two agreements have stumbled upon roadblocks on their way to signature and entry into force, both times due to the EU.

With regard to the agreement with Singapore, as noted earlier, a different interpretation between the Commission and the Council emerged about whether the ratification process ends here, or it must also involve approval by all 28 Member States, according to the domestic procedure of each. On 30 October 2014, the Commission decided to request to the ECJ an opinion on the competence to sign and ratify the FTA with Singapore,[87] which to date is still to be delivered.

With regard to the agreement with Canada, concerns have been expressed soon after the text was finalized, in the first place by Germany. Such concerns, primarily of a political nature, pivot on the current debate against ISDS, and the opportunity to allow foreign investors to eschew domestic courts in the context of an agreement between advanced OECD nations. The concern may also dwell on the (legal) fact that such a possibility is at odds with the EU founding principle of trust between domestic judicial systems of the Member States (among which, from 1958 up to the enlargement of 2004, no investment treaties existed[88] nor, consequently, ISDS had ever been an issue). Be that as it may, the framework as currently understood requires the Council to unanimously approve the text; as, along with Germany,

[84] E.g., in Italy, arbitral panels do not have the power to adopt enforceable provisional measures (cf., Art. 818 of the Italian Code of Civil Procedure).

[85] Art. 33 Chapter X EU-Canada FTA.

[86] Cf., European Parliament Resolution of 6 April 2011 on the Future European International Investment Policy, 2010/2203 (INI), available via http://www.europarl.europa.eu/sides/getDoc.do?type=TA&language=EN&reference=P7-TA-2011-141.

[87] After the review of the initiative, on 4 March 2015, the new Commission decided to go ahead with the request of the Court opinion.

[88] The only exceptions were the BITs concluded by Germany with Spain, Portugal and Greece, due to the later accession of these States to the EU.

other States subsequently expressed similar concerns, it appears that approval of the EU-Canada FTA as it stands rests either on a change in the political climate and attitude towards ISDS, or some effects of the opinion of the ECJ will cast on this agreement too. There is also a third possibility, namely that to expunge the investment protection chapter, or at least ISDS, from the Treaty; such an option, however, is not well received by Canada (which already pushes for ratification),[89] and, therefore, unfeasible.

5 Concluding Remark: The Negotiations for the EU-US Transatlantic Trade and Investment Partnership and the EU-China Investment Agreement

The issues mentioned above, and the pronouncement of the ECJ, will affect the current negotiations for the investment regime of the EU-US TTIP, and the EU-China BIT.

By negotiating first investment regimes with regional peers (*i.e.*, Canada and Singapore) of the current counterparts (*i.e.*, US and China), the EU is believed to have acquired both a preliminary grasp of the regional customs, as well as built a relatively uniform standard, to preserve the prospective consistency of its investment policy. Nevertheless, as opposition for ISDS grows both in the EU Council and Parliament, the way forward appears uphill in this respect. On the other side of the table, the US seems adamantine in its support to ISDS; and with China, with its relatively recent turn in favour of ISDS (even though with some significant limitations) and freshly acquired status of major capital exporter, it may not be beneficial for EU investors to give up their possibility to avoid local courts.

With the aim to conclude an agreement providing for the highest levels of liberalization and standards of protection that both Parties have negotiated to date,[90] the Council's negotiating mandate to the Commission for the TTIP is quite broad in principle, providing for investment liberalization and protection, including areas of mixed competence, such as portfolio investment, property and expropriation aspects. The mandate includes also ISDS, subject to prior consultation with the Member States and depending on the satisfaction of the Parliament's concerns on (1) exclusion of public policy measures, (2) protection of cultural diversity, (3) transparency and predictability of the mechanism, and (4) independence of arbitrators, suggesting also for the possibility of (5) the Parties' binding interpretation.

---

[89] Cf., e.g., Blanchfield (2015).

[90] Council of the European Union Directives of 17 June 2013 for the Negotiation on the Transatlantic Trade and Investment Partnership between the European Union and the United States of America, Doc. ST11103/13, paras. 22–23.

With regard to China, the EU Parliament, in the Resolution adopted on 9 October 2013,[91] voiced concerns on human rights, and on ISDS. On the former, it stressed that 'whereas goods for export to the EU which are produced in forced labour camps, such as under the Re-education through Labour system, generally known by the name *Laogai*, should not benefit from investments made under this bilateral investment agreement'.[92] On the latter, it expressed 'deep concern regarding the level of discretion of international arbitrators to make a broad interpretation of investor protection clauses, thereby leading to the ruling-out of legitimate public regulations; demands that the arbitrators appointed by the parties in the context of a dispute be independent and impartial, and that the arbitration provided follow a code of conduct based on the rules adopted by [UNCITRAL], on those of [ICSID] or on any other international agreements and standards recognized and agreed to by the parties'.[93] Moreover, the Commission's effort to entertain negotiations with a fast pace has been felt as some 'sort of bureaucratic sense of urgency, from Karel De Gucht [former Commissioner for Trade], who signed up for so many negotiations and FTAs, and then he had to deliver'.[94] The Chinese, conversely, appear more interested in negotiating a comprehensive FTA, rather than a stand-alone investment agreement,[95] and seem to show no hurry[96]; moreover, despite recent openings, China is still hostile to unrestricted market access clauses.

The parallel negotiations between the world's three largest economic players undoubtedly create expectations on their final outcomes. As noted, the EU is currently in a standstill, waiting for the ECJ's authoritative interpretation about the regime of competences between its internal organs and States. In the meantime, the Commission continues its negotiations with both counterparts, in order not to leave the EU lagging behind the US in the standards agreed with China, yet facing a multiplicity of concerns its constituents (Parliament, Council, and Member States) pose. Such restraints and concerns are shared only in part by the mandate and powers the US President's 'fast track' negotiating authority endures. The issue is particularly delicate when it comes to ISDS, as support from the US administration

[91] European Parliament Resolution of 9 October 2013 on the EU-China Negotiations for a Bilateral Investment Agreement, Doc. 2013/2674 (RSP), lett. N and points 23 and 36.

[92] E.g., lett. L.

[93] Id., point 41.

[94] David Fouquet, Senior Associate at the European Institute for Asian Studies of Brussels, statement as reported by Borderlex 2014.

[95] The EU-China trade is in excess of 480 billion euros; conversely, only 2.1 % of EU FDI lands in China, and 6 % of Chinese FDI is destined to the EU area.

[96] Cf., Borderlex 2015; also, European Commission Overview of 5 May 2015 of FTA and Other Trade Negotiations, available via http://trade.ec.europa.eu/doclib/html/118238.htm.

has not diminished—despite criticisms,[97] while China appears now comfortable with the mechanism (as long as it is corroborated with a series of treaty checks-and-balances to 'guide' the process and limit extensive interpretations).

The EU finds itself in the unsavoury position where it would welcome ISDS much more in the agreement with China than in that with the US. The arguments in support of this approach are several and understandable (despite unmentionable in the face of China): *e.g.*, relative trust in the counterpart's judiciary, relative similarity of (or acquaintance with) the judicial system, cautiousness towards the fairly aggressive litigation stance and standards of certain international law firms.[98] If implemented, however, a choice as such would result in the adoption of a double-standard approach, unpalatable in international political terms (vis–àvis China, but also other States further ahead), as defining a certain standard for some States, from which others would be excluded. Moreover, this solution seems incompatible, as a matter of principle, with China's wish to see its international standing recognized as equal to that of the US.[99]

In the intertwine of negotiations, then, the EU might well either be pushed to accept ISDS with both counterparts, or postpone the issue on both tables. On the one side, several actors are currently pushing to leave the investment chapter out of the TTIP; on the other, it has been noted that China does not seem in a hurry to conclude the investment agreement with the EU (having already 26 BITs in force with EU's 28 Member States, only two of which—UK and Italy—are in serious need of an update).

Acknowledgments The author gratefully acknowledges the valuable editing support of Alessandra Moroni and Piero Gregori.

References

Berger A, Skovgaard Poulsen LN (2015) The transatlantic trade and investment partnership, investor-state dispute settlement and China. Columbia FDI Perspective 140

---

[97] Cf., in the context of the negotiations for the US-Korea FTA, Letter of 22 July 2010 on the Korea Free Trade Agreement to President Obama from 110 Members of Congress (available via http://www.citizen.org/documents/KORUSLetterJuly2010.pdf), and Letter of 22 September 2010 on the Korea Free Trade Agreement to President Obama from 550 Organizations (available via http://www.citizenstrade.org/pdf/Korea_Opposition_Final.pdf), both requesting to discard from the Treaty the Investor-State Dispute Resolution Mechanism.

[98] Cf., Berger and Skovgaard Poulsen (2015).

[99] For instance, in 2013 Australia refused to grant to Chinese investors the same treatment accorded to US investors (US and New Zealand investments are the only ones not subject to review from the Australian Foreign Investment Review Board up to a value of 1 billion AUS dollars; all other States—including China—are subject to a much lower threshold, set at 258 million AUS dollars); this is considered to have contributed to the failure of the negotiations for an Australia-China FTA. Cf., Wallace (2013).

Blanchfield M (2015) G7 Summit: Harper Pushes Canada-EU Trade Pact. In: The Canadian Press. Available at: http://www.huffingtonpost.ca/2015/06/07/harper-pushes-canada-eu-t_n_7529500.html

Dolzer R, Kim Y (2013) Germany. In: Brown C (ed) Commentaries on selected model investment treaties. Oxford University Press, pp 289–320

Dolzer R, Stevens M (1995) Bilateral investment treaties. Martinus Nijhoff Publishers

Hepburn J, Peterson LE (2015) Italy is the EU's model citizen, when it comes to following European Commission demands to terminate intra-EU investment treaties. In: Investment Arbitration Reporter. Available at: http://www.iareporter.com/articles/investigation-italy-is-the-eus-model-citizen-when-it-comes-to-following-european-commission-demands-to-terminate-intra-eu-investment-treaties/

Huiping C (2006) China-ASEAN investment agreement negotiations: the substantive issues. J World Invest Trade: Law Econ Polit 7(1):143–163

Mehdudia S (2013) BIPA talks put on hold. In: The Hindu. Available at: http://www.thehindu.com/business/Economy/bipa-talks-put-on-hold/article4329332.ece

Newcombe A (2013) Developments in IIA treaty-making. In: De Mestral A, Lévesque C (eds) Improving international investment agreements. Routledge, pp 15–24

Potestà M (2012) Legitimate expectations in investment treaty law: understanding the roots and the limits of a controversial concept. Paper presented at the 3rd Biennial Global Conference, Society of International Economic Law, 9 July 2012. Available at: http://ssrn.com/abstract=2102771

Sacerdoti G (1997) Bilateral treaties and multilateral instruments on investment protection. Recueil des Cours de l'Académie de Droit International de la Haye 269:251–460

Vandevelde KJ (1988) The bilateral investment treaties program of the United States. Cornell J Int Law 21(2):201–276

Vis-Dunbar D (2009) EU Member States reject the call to terminate intra-EU bilateral investment treaties. In: Investment Treaty News. Available at: https://www.iisd.org/itn/2009/02/10/eu-member-states-reject-the-call-to-terminate-intra-eu-bilateral-investment-treaties/

Wallace R (2013) Free-trade push may open door to China. In: The Australian. Available at: http://www.theaustralian.com.au/national-affairs/policy/free-trade-push-may-open-door-to-china/story-fn59nm2j-1226681027576#

Yost C (2009) A case review and analysis of the legitimate expectations principle as it applies within the fair and equitable treatment standard. ANU College of Law Research Paper No. 09-01. Available at: http://ssrn.com/abstract=1364996

Legal Risks in Development of EU Consumer Protection Law

Emilia Mišćenić

Contents

Abstract The chapter analyses the legal development of the EU consumer protection law from the perspective of legal risks. It focuses on chosen key issues such as the variations in the level of harmonization across different EU consumer protection directives, the effectiveness of consumer protection instruments, the fragmentary approach to the legislative regulation of the EU consumer protection *acquis* etc. All these important issues affect adversely two main goals accentuated by the preambles of the EU consumer protection directives, namely, the achievement of a high level of consumer protection and the establishment and functioning of the internal market. The development of the EU consumer protection law demonstrates that the EU institutions engaged in the management of legal risks in the area of consumer protection attributed significantly to a development of new risks thereby increasing legal uncertainty in B2C relations.

E. Mišćenić (✉)
Faculty of Law, University of Rijeka, Rijeka, Croatia
e-mail: emiscenic@pravri.hr

E. Mišćenić, A. Raccah (eds.), *Legal Risks in EU Law*,
DOI 10.1007/978-3-319-28596-2_7

1 Introduction

When analysing the European Union (EU) consumer protection law from the perspective of legal risks, one comes to the conclusion of walking through a "minefield". This is certainly not the goal that the EU legislator had in mind in 1975 when the first Preliminary Programme of the European Economic Community for a Consumer Protection and Information Policy was adopted and when five key consumer rights that needed special and enhanced protection were determined.[1] It is unquestionable that consumer protection is of outmost importance for the development of EU law. The EU primary law provisions require its observance in defining and implementing any other Union policy or activity (Art. 12 TFEU)[2] and the EU Charter of Fundamental Rights demands insurance of a high level of consumer protection in all Union policies (Art. 38).[3] Moreover, consumer protection law is considered to be one of the most effective means to affect establishment and functioning of the internal market.[4] The European Court of Justice (ECJ), nowadays the Court of Justice of the European Union (CJEU), recognized quite early that the existing differences between national provisions of the Member States (MS) actually do represent barriers to trade and consequently infringe the accomplishment of the internal market.[5] In its famous *Cassis de Dijon* case, dealing *inter*

[1] Council Resolution of 14 April 1975 on a Preliminary Programme of the European Economic Community for a Consumer Protection and Information Policy, OJ C 92/1 established five key consumer rights: the right to protection of health and safety; the right to protection of economic interests; the right of redress; the right to information and education; the right of representation (the right to be heard).

[2] According to Art. 12 of the consolidated version of the Treaty on the Functioning of the European Union (TFEU), OJ C 326 of 26 October 2012 consumer protection is a horizontal policy, which "requirements shall be taken into account in defining and implementing other Union policies and activities".

[3] See Art. 38 of the Charter of Fundamental Rights of the European Union, OJ C 326/391 of 26 October 2012: "Union policies shall ensure a high level of consumer protection". See also the commentary to this provision in EU Network of Independent Experts on Fundamental Rights/ Réseau UE d'Experts Indépendants en Matière de Droits Fondamentaux 2006, pp. 318 et seq. See comments of Weatherill (2013), p. 252 on the relevance of Case C-544/10, *Deutsches Weintor*, EU:C:2012:526.

[4] According to Art. 26(2) TFEU "the internal market shall comprise an area without internal frontiers in which the free movement of goods, persons, services and capital is ensured in accordance with the provisions of the Treaties".

[5] Initially, the Founding Treaties were focused on public law aspects linked with the removal of obstacles to the internal market and not to private law aspects dealing with the relations of private parties acting on the internal market. For example, the concept of prohibition of measures having an effect equivalent to quantitative restrictions was primarily reserved for MS public law provisions (e.g. import inspections and controls, national type approvals, advertisement campaigns for national products (Case C-249/81, *Commission v Ireland* (*Buy Irish*) [1982] ECR 04005), sectoral prohibition on road transport, labelling of products (Case C-470/93, *Verein gegen Unwesen in Handel und Gewerbe Köln e.V. v Mars* [1995] ECR I-01923), language requirements etc.). However, the ECJ/CJEU case law and legal theory confirm that numerous differences between

alia with consumer protection, the ECJ speaks about "[. . .] obstacles to movement within the Community resulting from disparities between the national laws [. . .]".[6] These barriers can be removed by prohibitions contained in EU law i.e. by "negative integration", but also by the way of "positive integration", meaning by the adoption of EU legal acts approximating different laws presenting barriers to trade with the goal of the establishment and proper functioning of the internal market.[7] However, as proven in the *Cassis de Dijon* case, negative integration can under certain circumstances allow differences of the MS national law provisions, if this is necessary for the protection of so-called "mandatory requirements" to which consumer protection also belongs.[8] Therefore, in the field of consumer protection law, the EU legislator decided to put an emphasis on the removal of existing differences between MS provisions by introducing the legislative framework with common provisions, standards and rules for all the MS. Particularly in the field of consumer contract law relations it is considered that harmonized national consumer protection laws can boost the confidence of both consumers and traders who will then enter into cross-border legal transactions more willingly and conclude more

---

MS private law provisions can also violate fundamental freedoms and consequently represent a serious barrier to the goal of the establishment and functioning of the internal market of the EU (e.g. Case C-302/97, *Konle* [1999] ECR I-3099 or Case C-222/97, *Trummer and Mayer* [1999] ECR I-1661). As stated by Lando (2000), p. 61: "The existing variety of contract laws in Europe may be regarded as a non-tariff barrier to trade."

[6] Case C-120/78, *Rewe-Zentral v Bundesmonopolverwaltung für Branntwein* (*Cassis de Dijon*) [1979] ECR I-649, para. 8.

[7] The common goal of both means of integration is the establishment and functioning of the internal market. Negative integration is established by the EU primary and secondary law, including the ECJ/CJEU case law and consists of therein contained prohibitions to violations of the EU law. To such provisions belong for example the EU primary law provisions on prohibition of discrimination, provisions on the customs union and fundamental freedoms and provisions on fair market competition. Rodin and Ćapeta (2010), p. 84, define negative integration as a removal of trade barriers between the MS by non-application of national legal rules creating these barriers. A violation of fundamental freedoms through national provisions of the MS is prohibited by the primary law itself, without the regulation of special prohibitions in secondary law of the EU. Exceptions can be found in Arts. 36, 51–52, 62 in connection with 51–54 TFEU. According to the *Dassonville* formula "[. . .] all trading rules enacted by Member States which are capable of hindering directly or indirectly, actually or potentially, intra-Community trade are to be considered as measures having an effect equivalent to quantitative restrictions" and are prohibited by the TFEU provisions on the free movement of goods. See Case C-8/74, *Dassonville* [1974] ECR I-837. Thereby, the negative integration is limiting the legislative freedom of the MS. On the other hand, the positive integration concerns the adoption of legal acts having impact on the internal market.

[8] In the *Cassis de Dijon* case the ECJ clarified that "obstacles to movement within the Community resulting from disparities between the national laws relating to the marketing of the products in question must be accepted in so far as those provisions may be recognized as being necessary in order to satisfy mandatory requirements," i.e. to satisfy "requirements [that] serve a purpose which is in the general interest and such as to take precedence over the requirements of the free movement of goods, which constitutes one of the fundamental rules of the Community". To these interests belong among others tax surveillance, protection of public health, fairness in commercial transactions but also consumer protection. See Case C-120/78, *Rewe-Zentral v Bundesmonopolverwaltung für Branntwein* (*Cassis de Dijon*) [1979] ECR I-649, paras. 8 and 14.

contracts cross-border thereby contributing to the establishment and functioning of the internal market.[9] The result of such EU legislative activity is a rich consumer protection *acquis* with an emphasis on the secondary law adopted from the early 1980s until today and the case law on its application and interpretation.[10] The following pages will demonstrate that precisely these two main instruments of EU legal development opened the door to numerous legal risks in the field of consumer protection law at both the EU and MS level.

2 Legal Risks in EU Consumer Protection Law

Prior to the analysis and identification of existing and of eventual future legal risks in EU consumer protection law one should certainly define the notion of legal risk. However, despite plenty of scholarly writings on the topic, there is no uniform or general definition of legal risk.[11] Between numerous existing concepts on legal risk, the author accepts the one implying that the risk can *inter alia* come from the law itself. According to this concept, a legal norm can belong to sources of legal risk.[12] Following such an approach, the chapter focuses on risks deriving from legal uncertainty that is in the EU consumer protection law caused primarily by over- and inconsistent regulations, by legal fragmentation and inadequate interpretation of legal regulations.

When speaking about legal risks, one should bear in mind that removal and mitigation of legal uncertainty belongs to the primary tasks of EU consumer protection law. Related to this statement there are three important questions that need to be answered. The first question is why that is so. The answer is because of the establishment and functioning of the internal market. The main purpose of both the above described integration methods is the removal or minimizing of

---

[9] See Lando (2000), p. 61: "The Union of today is an economic community. Its purpose is the free flow of goods, persons, services and capital. (. . .) All of these move by way of contracts. It should, therefore, be made easier to conclude and perform contracts and to calculate contract risks. [. . .] Foreign laws are often difficult for the businessmen and their local lawyers to understand. They may keep him away from foreign markets in Europe."

[10] Consult the official web-page of the European Commission, Consumers at: http://ec.europa.eu/consumers/index_en.htm and the EU Consumer Law Acquis Database at: http://www.eu-consumer-law.org/.

[11] For numerous definitions of legal risk see Mahler (2007), p. 4: "some writers argue that legal risk is a rather loose category, which does not need to be defined, and which is essentially context-dependent".

[12] Mahler (2007), p. 21. According to UNIDROIT Explanatory Notes on Preliminary Draft Convention on Harmonised Substantive Rules Regarding Securities Held With An Intermediary, Rome, 2004, p. 7 "legal risk commonly refers to a situation where the applicable law does not provide for a predictable and sound solution" and "might also refer to situations where the answer provided by the applicable law does not fit the market reality, or where the law does unnecessarily complicates or burdens a transaction".

differences between MS provisions that cause legal uncertainty and thereby endanger the realization of the supreme goal of the EU. As stated in the ECJ's *Schul* case, "elimination of all obstacles to intra-Community trade in order to merge the national markets into a single market [bringing about conditions as close as possible to those of a genuine internal market]", is important not only for commerce but also for private persons who are conducting an economic transaction across national frontiers and who should be able to enjoy the benefits of that market.[13] The latter quotation leads us to the second question concerning the kind of risks causing legal uncertainty. These include for example the consumer's lack of knowledge, ignorance on the content of foreign law or general lack of confidence into the substantive and procedural level of protection as well as many other risks arising for consumers and traders when concluding contracts cross-border.[14] In order to remove or at least mitigate these risks causing legal uncertainty in cross-border business-to-consumer (B2C) relations over the years EU institutions developed an abundant legal framework in the area of consumer protection. Their activity opened up a third question about the ways in which they were dealing with legal risks. For the removal of legal barriers causing legal uncertainty and having restrictive effect upon the development of cross-border legal transactions and the internal market the approximation of MS' laws was used to a great extent. And within the broader notion of approximation,[15] an emphasis was put on the activity of the EU legislator.

[13] Case C-15/81, *Schul* [1982] ECR I-1409, para. 33.

[14] The results of the Eurobarometer Analytical Reports on European contract law in consumer transactions and on European contract law in business-to-business transactions of 2011 demonstrate that 49 % of participants consider that contract law differences are affecting them less than practical difficulties. To the latter belong administrative and formal requirements (e.g. licensing, registration procedures), language barriers (e.g. communication problems, translating documents, etc.), cultural differences, tax regulations, cross-border delivery problems etc. To the most important contract law related obstacles belong the difficulties in finding out about the provisions of a foreign consumer contract law and the need to adapt to the diverse consumer contract laws across the EU. According to the Expert Group's Feasibility Study on European Contract Law of 3 May 2011 available at http://ec.europa.eu/justice/contract/files/feasibility_study_final.pdf: "Businesses and consumers wishing to carry out cross-border transactions must reckon with the existence of different national contract laws when operating in the internal market. This can lead to additional transaction costs, increased legal uncertainty for businesses and lack of consumer confidence and thus cause obstacles to cross-border trade". On the contradictory results of the Eurobarometer Analytical Reports see Halson and Campbell (2013), pp. 112–113.

[15] Although there is no unique definition, the approximation of laws can be understood as the approximation of MS legal acts to standards established at the Union level both by removal or minimizing of the differences between effective national acts and by adoption of new proposals not existing in national law. It can be achieved by legislative activity, ECJ/CJEU case law and the work of scientific groups and the legal doctrine. Within the TFEU, the notion of "approximation" is equalized with the one of "harmonization", despite different legal theory approaches about the meaning of these terms. The approximation of laws is to be distinguished from the unification of laws which aims at the uniformity of MS legal acts. Examples of the unification of laws at the Union level are the Brussels I Convention on jurisdiction and the enforcement of judgments in civil and commercial matters, 27.9.1968, OJ L 1972/299 and the Rome Convention on the law applicable to contractual obligations, 9 October 1980, OJ L 266, that were both taken over into

Regrettably, the latter was conducted in an inconsistent manner and without following any kind of structured plan or strategy at the EU level. The result was an inexhaustible source of legal acts that are dealing with problematic issues separately and fragmentarily and without taking into account each other's contents. Consequently, the sources of EU consumer protection *acquis* differ in notions, definitions and protection instruments.[16] In answering the third question one comes to a conclusion that the efforts of the EU institutions regarding the removal of legal uncertainty actually led to its deepening. As it will be demonstrated in the chapter below, legal development in the area of the EU consumer protection law indicates that the management of legal risks actually resulted in their reinforcement.

2.1 Legal Grounds and Functionality Criterion

Initially, there was no reference to consumer protection in the Founding Treaties besides incidental references to consumers concerning agricultural and competition policies in the Treaty of Rome.[17] The approximation of MS laws in the area of consumer protection started to intensify with the adoption of the Single European Act (SEA) in 1986.[18] Until then the EU legislator disposed with two legal grounds appropriate for approximation: ex ex Art. 100 TEEC (ex Art. 94 TEC, Art. 115 TFEU) and ex ex Art. 235 TEEC (ex Art. 308 TEC, Art. 352 TFEU). Both of these provisions suffered from one important shortage namely from a unanimity rule as a precondition for the adoption of legal acts. Moreover, ex ex Art. 100 TEEC allowed the adoption of directives only,[19] while ex ex Art. 235 TEEC was and still

Council Regulation (EC) No 44/2001 of 22 December 2000 on jurisdiction and the recognition and enforcement of judgments in civil and commercial matters, OJ EC L 2001/12 and Regulation (EC) No 593/2008 of the European Parliament and of the Council of 17 June 2008 on the law applicable to contractual obligations (Rome I), OJ L 2008/177. On the complexity of these terms see Gutman (2014), pp. 27 et seq.

[16] Reich (2000), pp. 504 et seq. divides arguments existing in legal doctrine into "Systemargument", "Inkonsistenzargument" and "black-box-Argument". The first one criticises the fragmentary character of European consumer law, the second one the contradictions in the EU legislators' work and the third one the disintegrative function of the ECJ interpretation of EU law in relation to national traditions.

[17] Treaty Establishing the European Economic Community, 25.3.1957, not published in OJ.

[18] Single European Act, OJ 1987 L 169/14 of 29.6.1987.

[19] This legal ground received less attention in EU consumer protection law. Examples of directives adopted upon it are Council Directive 85/374/EEC of 25 July 1985 on the approximation of the laws, regulations and administrative provisions of the Member States concerning liability for defective products, OJ L 21/29 and repealed Council Directive 87/102/EEC of 22 December 1986 for the approximation of the laws, regulations and administrative provisions of the Member States concerning consumer credit OJ L 42/48. The Treaty of Lisbon, OJ C 306, 17.12.2007, reordered positions of ex Arts. 94 and 95 TEC and by renummerating ex Art. 94 TEC into Art. 115 TFEU it placed it behind the more important ex Art. 95 TEC that became Art. 114 TFEU.

is used as a subsidiary legal basis for fulfilling regulatory loopholes.[20] These restrictions to the approximation of MS laws motivated the EU institutions to rethink possible new solutions. New proposals came in the Commission's White Paper on Completing the Internal Market of 1985[21] in the form of a "new strategy" insisting upon speeding up the process of harmonization. As a result the SEA introduced a new legal ground for the approximation of MS laws: ex ex Art. 100a TEEC (ex Art. 95 TEC, Art. 114 TFEU). The latter provision facilitated the approximation i.e. harmonization by introducing qualified majority voting and by referring to "approximation measures" regarding the form of legal acts to be adopted. Moreover, in its para. 3 it requires the Commission to depart from the high level of protection in proposals concerning health, safety, environmental protection and consumer protection. Once the special provision on consumer protection policy was introduced with the Treaty of Maastricht,[22] ex Art. 95 TEC/today's Art. 114 TFEU being the main legal ground for the adoption of approximation measures in EU consumer protection law. This was enabled by ex ex Art. 129a TEC (ex Art. 153 TEC, Art. 169 TFEU) itself in its para. 1(a) that referred to the primary law provision on the approximation of laws in the context of the completion of the internal market, meaning to ex Art. 95 TEC.[23] In doing so it only reaffirmed the existing practice of adoption of EU consumer protection directives conditionally upon contribution to the establishment and functioning of the internal market and upon the observance of a high level of consumer protection. This so-called "functionality criterion" allowing approximation only if it concerns the establishment and the functioning of the internal market, is a common characteristic of all the mentioned legal grounds.[24] Previously, it was also reflected in ex Art. 3

[20] According to the current wording of this provision "if action by the Union should prove necessary, within the framework of the policies defined in the Treaties, to attain one of the objectives set out in the Treaties, and the Treaties have not provided the necessary powers, the Council, acting unanimously on a proposal from the Commission and after obtaining the consent of the European Parliament, shall adopt the appropriate measures.[. . .]" (Art. 352(1) TFEU). See Case C-436/03, *Parliament v Council* [2006] ECR I-03733, para. 36: "In that regard, Article 308 EC may be used as the legal basis for a measure only where no other provision of the Treaty gives the Community institutions the necessary power to adopt it [. . .]".

[21] Completing the Internal Market: White Paper from the Commission to the European Council, Milan, 28–29 June 1985, COM(85) 310, June 1985. See Part Two: The Removal of Technical Barriers, No. 1, pp. 18 et seq.

[22] Treaty on European Union, OJ C 191, 7.2.1992.

[23] According to the current wording of Art. 169(2) TFEU "the Union shall contribute to the attainment of the objectives referred to in paragraph 1 through: (a) measures adopted pursuant to Article 114 in the context of the completion of the internal market; (b) measures which support, supplement and monitor the policy pursued by the Member States". Objectives protected under para. 1 include the protection of health, safety and economic interests of consumers, the promotion of their right to information, education and to organise themselves in order to safeguard their interests.

[24] According to Art. 114(1) TFEU "save where otherwise provided in the Treaties, the following provisions shall apply for the achievement of the objectives set out in Article 26" i.e. in the provision regulating the internal market. In accordance with the ordinary legislative procedure and

(h) TEC, according to which Community activities intended for realisation of its tasks set out in ex Art. 2 TEC, included among others "the approximation of the laws of the Member States to the extent required for the functioning of the common market".

The functionality criterion was further elaborated in the ECJ's *Tobacco Advertising* cases,[25] where the ECJ accentuated that ex ex Art. 100a TEEC/today's Art. 114 TFEU does not give the Community a general power to regulate the internal market, but rather deals with situations where the adoption of measures is necessary to improve the conditions for the establishment and functioning of the internal market.[26] In the *Tobacco Advertising I* case it interpreted the functionality of approximation measures by developing a so-called *Tobacco Test* requiring from approximation measures to "genuinely have as its object the improvement of the conditions for the establishment and functioning of the internal market"[27] and to actually contribute to the elimination of obstacles to fundamental freedoms and to the removal of competition distortions that must be appreciable.[28] Further on, according to the ECJ the "recourse to Art. 100a as a legal basis is possible if the aim is to prevent the emergence of future obstacles to trade resulting from multifarious development of national laws", but in such a case the emergence of such obstacles must be likely and the measure in question must be designed to prevent them.[29] By interpreting the approximation provision from ex ex Art. 100a TEEC, in a way, the *Tobacco Test* established criteria for removal of certain risks causing legal uncertainty and therefore threatening the realization of the internal market. The question remains, however, whether the over the years adopted EU consumer protection directives "really" fulfil prerequisites out of ex ex Art. 100a TEEC/ex Art. 95 TEC/Art. 114 TFEU, in a way required by the *Tobacco Test* demanding them to "genuinely" follow the goal of the establishment and functioning of the internal market and to "actually" contribute to the removal of trade barriers? The EU approximation measures, whether in the form of directives or regulations usually contain explanations in their preambles, according to which legislative

after consulting the Economic and Social Committee the European Parliament and the Council adopt approximation measures which have as their objective the establishment and functioning of the internal market. Pursuant to Art. 115 TFEU directives will be issued unanimously in accordance with a special legislative procedure if directly affecting the establishment or functioning of the internal market. Different than the Art. 352 TFEU, ex Art. 308 TEC and ex ex Art. 235 TEEC provided for the adoption of approximation measures "if action by the Community should prove necessary to attain, in the course of the operation of the common market, one of the objectives of the Community [. . .]".

[25] Case C-376/98, *Germany* v *Parliament and Council* [2000] ECR I-8419 (*Tobacco Advertising I*) and Case C-491/01, *British American Tobacco (Investments) and Imperial Tobacco* [2002] ECR I-11453 (*Tobacco Advertising II*).

[26] Case C-376/98 *Germany* v *Parliament and Council* [2000] ECR I-8419, para. 83.

[27] Ibid., para. 84.

[28] Ibid., paras. 95 and 106. Under para. 107 the Community legislature may not rely on Art. 100a for elimination of the smallest distortions of competition.

[29] Ibid., para. 86.

differences cause obstacles to the exercise of fundamental freedoms and distort competition.[30] But, is such a justification enough for the adoption of approximation measures?[31] As stated by the ECJ in the *Tobacco Advertising I* case "if a mere finding of disparities between national rules and of the abstract risk of obstacles to the exercise of fundamental freedoms or of distortions of competition liable to result there from were sufficient to justify the choice of Art. 100a as a legal basis, judicial review of compliance with the proper legal basis might be rendered nugatory".[32] This leads to a conclusion that if the criteria developed by the ECJ on the application of today's Art. 114 TFEU would not actually be fulfilled by a certain approximation measure, the latter could be rendered null and void. For example, there are many doubts regarding Art. 114 TFEU as a chosen legal ground for the adoption of the Proposal for a Regulation on a Common European Sales Law (CESL).[33] These concern mainly the question whether the CESL represents an "approximation measure" at all[34] and whether it fulfils the *Tobacco Test* preconditions.[35] The same applies to the recently adopted Directive 2014/17/EU on credit agreements for consumers relating to residential immovable property also called Mortgage Credit Directive (MCD).[36] Although the preamble of the MCD insists upon contribution to the realization of the internal market, a more detailed analysis

---

[30] See recital 3 of Directive 1999/44/EC of the European Parliament and of the Council of 25 May 1999 on certain aspects of the sale of consumer goods and associated guarantees, OJ L 171/12, 7.7.1999; recitals 2 and 3 of Council Directive 93/13/EEC of 5 April 1993 on unfair terms in consumer contracts, OJ L 095/29, 21.4.1993; see recital 4 of Directive 2008/48/EC of the European Parliament and of the Council of 23. April 2008 on credit agreements for consumers and repealing Council Directive 87/102/EEC OJ L 133/66, 22.5.2008; see recitals 4 and 5 of Directive 2011/83/EU of the European Parliament and of the Council of 25 October 2011 on consumer rights, amending Council Directive 93/13/EEC and Directive 1999/44/EC of the European Parliament and of the Council and repealing Council Directive 85/577/EEC and Directive 97/7/EC of the European Parliament and of the Council, OJ L 304/64, 22.11.2011 etc.

[31] The same doubts are expressed by many authors. See also the analysis by Schütze (2014), pp. 228 et seq.

[32] Schütze (2014), para. 84.

[33] Proposal for a Regulation of the European Parliament and of the Council on a Common European Sales Law, COM(2011) 635 final, Brussels, 11 October 2011.

[34] According to Case C-436/03, *Parliament v Council* [2006] ECR I-3733, para. 44: "[...] the contested regulation, which leaves unchanged the different national laws already in existence, cannot be regarded as aiming to approximate the laws of the Member States [...]". See also Hesselink et al. (2007), p. 7.

[35] In that sense the Communication from the Commission to the European Parliament and the Council European Contract Law and the revision of the *acquis*: the way forward, COM(2004) 651 final, Brussels, 11.10.2004, Annex II: "An optional instrument should only contain those areas of contract law, whether general or specific to certain contracts, which clearly contribute to addressing identified problems, such as barriers to the smooth functioning of the internal market." A more detailed analysis by Mišćenić (2012), pp. 729 et seq.

[36] Directive 2014/17/EU of the European Parliament and of the Council of 4 February 2014 on credit agreements for consumers relating to residential immovable property and amending Directives 2008/48/EC and 2013/36/EU and Regulation (EU) No 1093/2010 (Text with EEA relevance), OJ L 60/34 of 28 February 2014.

of its provisions demonstrates that, in reality, these are not capable of removing "substantial differences in the laws of the various Member States" with regard to credit agreements relating to residential immovable property.[37] The same reasoning can be found in legal theory and practice with regard to many other EU consumer protection directives and beyond. The EU institutions themselves admit that approximation resulted with "divergent solutions in the Member States even in areas which were harmonised at Union level"[38] and that these solutions "deter the exercise of fundamental freedoms [...] and represent a barrier to the functioning and continuing establishment of the internal market".[39] With regard to legal risks, such acknowledgment of failure in fulfilling the functionality criterion inseparably brings the protection of not only consumers', but also traders' interests in question. In private law relations, particularly contractual ones, where the parties require a high level of legal certainty, the latter should not be undermined by a possibility of an annulment of the approximation measures by the CJEU. Through similar statements that can be found in the preambles of numerous EU consumer protection directives the Union is actually indirectly accepting the responsibility for failing at the management of legal risks arising out of MS's private law provisions diversity.

2.2 *Principle of Subsidiarity*

The argument of MS' contract law diversity being a hindering factor upon traders and consumers who want to engage in cross-border transactions within the internal market is, on the other hand, the Union's main ground of justification for the adoption of new approximation measures. The acceptance of responsibility for generating further differences between MS' consumer protection provisions does not discourage the Union's legislator in his further attempts of their removal. The Union's legislator considers himself to be most suitable for completing this task because "action by Member States alone is likely to result in different sets of rules, which may undermine or create new obstacles to the functioning of the internal market".[40] That is why the main goals of the EU consumer protection directives, namely, the establishment and functioning of the internal market and the achievement of a high level of consumer protection, "can" allegedly be better achieved by

[37] Recital 2 of the MCD recognises the differences of the MS' laws regarding the conduct of business in the granting of credit agreements and in the regulation and supervision of credit intermediaries and of non-credit institutions providing such credit agreements. Further on, it argues that "[...] such differences create obstacles that restrict the level of cross-border activity on the supply and demand sides, thus reducing competition and choice in the market, raising the cost of lending for providers and even preventing them from doing business" [...]. See also Mišćenić (2014b), pp. 219 et seq.

[38] See Explanatory Memorandum of the CESL, p. 5, No. 2.

[39] Recital 1 of the CESL.

[40] Recital 82 of the MCD.

the Union.[41] Justifications such as this one are however decisive since both the internal market and consumer protection areas belong to the shared competences between the Union and the MS.[42] As a consequence of the division of competences, the Union's actions in these areas are restricted by its duty to observe the principles of subsidiarity and proportionality.[43] According to the principle of subsidiarity "in areas which do not fall within its exclusive competence, *the Union shall act only if and in so far as the objectives of the proposed action cannot be sufficiently achieved by the MS*, either at central level or at regional and local level, *but can rather*, by reason of the scale or effects of the proposed action, *be better achieved at Union level*".[44] Pursuant to the principle of proportionality, "the content and form of Union action shall not exceed what is necessary to achieve the objectives of the Treaties".[45] Although, in practice, the compliance with the principle of subsidiarity is observed *ex ante* through national parliament's scrutiny and *ex post* through monitoring of the CJEU,[46] there are serious doubts as to whether EU consumer

---

[41] Ibid.: "Since the objective of this Directive, namely the creation of an efficient and competitive internal market [...] whilst ensuring a high level of consumer protection, cannot be sufficiently achieved by Member States and can therefore, by reason of the effectiveness of the action, be better achieved at Union level, the Union may adopt measures, in accordance with the principle of subsidiarity as set out in Article 5 of the Treaty on European Union".

[42] According to Art. 4(2) TFEU the Union shares competences with the MS in the area of internal market (lit. a) and of consumer protection (lit. f). This means that the Union and the MS may legislate and adopt legally binding acts in these areas (Art. 2(2) TFEU). However, the MS shall exercise their competence to the extent that the Union has not exercised or has decided to cease exercising its competence (Art. 2(2) TFEU).

[43] Pursuant to Art. 5(1) TEU "the limits of Union competences are governed by the principle of conferral", while "the use of Union competences is governed by the principles of subsidiarity and proportionality".

[44] Art. 5(3) TEU. The provision goes further on by prescribing the duty of the Union's institutions to apply the principle as laid down in the Protocol on the application of the principles of subsidiarity and proportionality and of national Parliaments to ensure compliance with the principle in accordance with the procedure set out in that Protocol. See Protocol (No. 2) on the application of the principles of subsidiarity and proportionality, OJ C 83/206, 30.3.2010.

[45] Art. 5(4) TEU.

[46] The Treaty of Lisbon has strengthened the role of both the national parliaments and the CJEU in monitoring compliance with the principle of subsidiarity. Under Arts. 5(3) and 12 TEU national parliaments monitor compliance with the principle of subsidiarity in accordance with the procedure set out in Protocol No 2. on the application of the principles of subsidiarity and proportionality. Under this procedure national parliaments have 8 weeks from the date of forwarding of a draft legislative act to submit a reasoned opinion why they consider that a draft legislative act does not comply with the principle of subsidiarity by using so-called yellow ('negative' opinions represent at least one-third of the votes allocated to the national parliaments) or red/orange (in the context of the ordinary legislative procedure, 'negative' opinions represent at least a simple majority of the votes allocated to national parliaments) card procedure. Compliance with the principle of subsidiarity may also be reviewed after adoption of the legislative act by means of a legal action brought before the CJEU (e.g. Art. 263 TFEU on action for annulment). Consult Fact Sheets on the European Union – 2015, The Principle of Subsidiarity, http://www.europarl.europa.eu/ftu/pdf/en/FTU_1.2.2.pdf.

protection directives really satisfy its conditions. The latest tendency of over accentuating the observance of the subsidiarity principle in preambles of the EU consumer protection directives would indicate rather the opposite.[47] Enhanced reasoning is evidently a logical consequence of the strengthened control of the subsidiarity principle after the Treaty of Lisbon.[48] However, one can argue that many EU consumer protection directives failed in the adequate fulfilment of so-called necessity and efficiency preconditions of the subsidiarity principle. Differences between MS consumer protection provisions that occurred due to the Union's minimum harmonization approach are in direct conflict with these two conditions of the subsidiarity principle. By enabling the national legislator the retention or introduction of more stringent provisions than those prescribed by directives the EU legislator actually enabled the creation of "different sets of rules, which may undermine or create new obstacles to the functioning of the internal market".[49] In following the goal of ensuring a maximum degree of protection for consumers it contributed to the development of a fragmented regulatory framework that offers everything but legal certainty for contract parties who want to engage in cross-border transactions.[50] Being aware of the negative implications of the described approach upon both the internal market and the consumer protection approximately 15 years ago the EU legislator started redirecting the minimum towards the maximum or full (targeted) harmonization.[51] The latter should prevent

[47] E.g. recital 65 of the Directive 2011/83/EU on consumer rights, recital 82 of the MCD, Explanatory Memorandum (p. 10) and recital 10 of the CESL, recital 23 of the Directive 2008/122/EC of the European Parliament and of the Council of 14 January 2009 on the protection of consumers in respect of certain aspects of timeshare, long-term holiday product, resale and exchange contracts, OJ L 33/10 etc.

[48] Schütze (2009), pp. 525 et seq.

[49] Recital 82 of the MCD. See Explanatory Memorandum of the CESL, p. 5: "There are significant differences between the contract laws in the MS. The Union initially started to regulate in the field of contract law by means of minimum harmonisation Directives adopted in the field of consumer protection law. The minimum harmonisation approach meant that Member States had the possibility to maintain or introduce stricter mandatory requirements than those provided for in the *acquis*. In practice, this approach has led to divergent solutions in the Member States even in areas which were harmonised at Union level."

[50] See Explanatory Memorandum of the CESL, p. 2: "Differences in contract law between Member States hinder traders and consumers who want to engage in cross-border trade within the internal market." The obstacles which stem from these differences dissuade traders, small and medium-sized enterprises (SME) in particular, from entering cross border trade or expanding to new Member States' markets. Consumers are hindered from accessing products offered by traders in other Member States."

[51] Although the European legislation and literature are often treating them as synonyms, there is an essential difference between the notion of "maximum" harmonization concerning the level of harmonization and the one of "full" harmonization concerning its scope. According to *Josipović* different than maximum harmonization, "harmonization is full when the directive covers all possible aspects of some legal concept or legal domain". See Josipović (2010), p. 209. Due to this reason the EU legislator and theory nowadays speak about "targeted full harmonization" directives that are "targeting" the regulation and fully harmonizing only certain chosen matters presenting barriers to traders and consumers willing to enter cross-border transactions.

fragmentation and diversification of MS consumer protection provisions by prohibiting maintenance or introduction of provisions into MS national laws that diverge from those laid down in directives.[52] From the perspective of the subsidiarity principle the full harmonization clauses contained in this "new wave" of EU consumer protection directives serve as a more appropriate ground of justification of the Union's action *versus* MS' that is considered to result in fragmentary solutions. Still, the prohibition contained in the full harmonization clauses does not mean that the directives do not contain different options for the MS or even certain minimum harmonisation provisions thus opening the door to further diversities at the national level.[53] For instance, Directive 2008/48/EC on credit agreements for consumers (CCD) or Directive 2011/83/EU on consumer rights (CRD) are both allowing the MS the application of provisions of these directives also to areas excluded from their scope.[54] The result of such a way of approximation are not only incidental differences resulting from options for the MS but also essential differences between MS' provisions on the personal and material scope of application. Whereby, it is understandable that absolute full i.e. maximum harmonization would be neither efficient nor acceptable in practice due to its lack of flexibility

[52] The shift from minimum to full harmonization was announced in the Communication from the Commission of 7 May 2002 to the European Parliament, the Council, the Economic and Social Committee and the Committee of the Regions – "Consumer Policy Strategy 2000–2006", COM (2002) 208 final, OJ C137/2 and the first results came in form of Directive 2002/65/EC of the European Parliament and of the Council of 23 September 2002 concerning the distance marketing of consumer financial services and amending Council Directive 90/619/EEC and Directives 97/7/EC and 98/27/EC, OJ L 271/16 and Directive 2005/29/EC of the European Parliament and of the Council of 11 May 2005 concerning unfair business-to-consumer commercial practices in the internal market and amending Council Directive 84/450/EEC, Directives 97/7/EC, 98/27/EC and 2002/65/EC of the European Parliament and of the Council and Regulation (EC) No 2006/2004 of the European Parliament and of the Council, OJ L 149/22. However, in Case C-52/00, *Commission v France* [2002] ECR I-3827 and Case C-183/00, *González Sánchez* [2002] ECR I-3901 the ECJ confirmed the full harmonization character of Council Directive 85/374/EEC of 25 July 1985 on the approximation of the laws, regulations and administrative provisions of the Member States concerning liability for defective products, OJ L 210/29.

[53] See Directive 2011/83/EU on consumer rights. Pursuant to Art. 3(4) "Member States may decide not to apply this Directive or not to maintain or introduce corresponding national provisions to off-premises contracts for which the payment to be made by the consumer does not exceed EUR 50. MS may define a lower value in their national legislation." Art. 5(3) contains an option for the MS regarding information requirements for contracts other than distance or off-premises contracts according to which "Member States shall not be required to apply paragraph 1 to contracts which involve day-to-day transactions and which are performed immediately at the time of their conclusion." Art. 5(4) contains a minimum harmonisation clause pursuant to which "Member States may adopt or maintain additional pre-contractual information requirements for contracts to which this Article applies."

[54] It is important to notice that this was done by recitals of the directives preambles. See recital 10 of the CCD or recital 13 of the CRD. As to the question of legal force and of the hierarchy between provisions contained in preambles and main regulatory texts of directives, the CJEU stated in Case C-602/10, *SC Volksbank România* EU:C:2012:443, para. 40, that "is also clear from recital 10 in the preamble to Directive 2008/48, the Member States may, in accordance with European Union law, apply provisions of that directive to areas not covered by its scope".

and numerous other deficiencies.[55] However, having in mind that the action of the Union is also resulting in different sets of rules at MS level one cannot rely on full harmonization as being one of the main arguments justifying compliance with the subsidiarity principle. The Union is indirectly confirming this reasoning in a renewed shift in the level of harmonization in the recent MCD. Different than the other EU consumer protection directives the MCD is combining minimum harmonization as a main principle with a few full (targeted) harmonization provisions.[56] Apart from this mixed harmonization approach the MCD is leaving the regulation of certain matters completely in the hands of MS thereby actually avoiding the approximation of national provisions.[57] It seems that irrespective of the applied harmonization approach the action of the Union is still resulting in different solutions at the MS level that may affect adversely the functioning of the internal market. This raises serious doubts as to whether the Union can really achieve the objectives set out in the EU consumer protection directives better than the MS in accordance with the subsidiarity principle. Although one can always invoke prior and post control mechanisms of the subsidiarity principle, according to the CJEU/ ECJ case law the approximation does not require (scientific) proof to be produced for every adopted measure.[58] From the aspect of legal certainty this brings us to a place where the adoption of the EU approximation measure of disputable efficiency becomes a reality.

---

[55] See the chapter "Regelungsintensität der Verbraucherrichtlinien: Mindest *v* Maximalharmonisierung" in: Čikara (2010), pp. 36 et seq.

[56] Art. 2(1) of the MCD prescribes that "this Directive shall not preclude Member States from maintaining or introducing more stringent provisions in order to protect consumers, provided that such provisions are consistent with their obligations under Union law". According to Art. 2(2) of the MCD the "Member States shall not maintain or introduce in their national law provisions diverging from those laid down in Article 14(2) and Annex II Part A with regard to standard pre-contractual information through a European Standardised Information Sheet (ESIS) and Article 17(1) to (5), (7) and (8) and Annex I with regard to a common, consistent Union standard for the calculation of the annual percentage rate of charge (APRC)". However, MS should be allowed to maintain or introduce more stringent provisions with regard to instructions for completing the ESIS and for areas not covered by the MCD. MS are free to maintain or introduce national law provisions (e.g. concerning validity of credit agreements, property law, land registration, contractual information and post-contractual issues) (recitals 7 and 9 of the preamble).

[57] With regard to foreign currency loans, pursuant to Art. 23(1) of the MCD, MS shall ensure the existence of an appropriate regulatory framework at the time of the credit agreement conclusion to at least ensure that the consumer has a right to convert the foreign into an alternative currency under specified conditions *or* that there are other arrangements in place to limit the exchange rate risk to which the consumer is exposed under the credit agreement. The following paragraph further elaborates the alternative currency, while there is no explanation or suggestion of possible other arrangements for limiting the exchange rate risk.

[58] Case C-84/94, *United Kingdom v Council* [1996] ECR I-5755, para. 79 and Case C-233/94, *Germany v Parliament and Council* [1997] ECR I-2405. The ECJ found that compliance with the principle of subsidiarity was one of the conditions covered by the requirement to state the reasons for Community acts which is met if it is clear from reading the recitals that the principle has been complied with. On the topic of the analytical framework of ECJ/CJEU judicial review of the principle of subsidiarity very detailed are Groussot and Bogojević (2014), pp. 244 et seq.

2.3 Consumer Protection Instruments

The aspect of efficiency can very well be observed and questioned regarding consumer protection instruments presenting common elements of EU consumer protection directives and aiming at protection and strengthening of consumers as weaker parties in contractual relationship with traders. Consumer protection instruments concern, for example, trader's information duties, consumer's right of withdrawal, mandatory interventions in contractual stipulations, formal requirements in consumer contracts, binding nature of consumer protection rules, essential elements of consumer contracts, shifting the burden of proof upon the trader, special conflict of law rules, rules on collective redress and alternative dispute resolution etc.[59] Within the EU consumer protection law these are considered to be a tool for the achievement of proper balance in B2C relationships that can be disturbed by inequality in contract parties positions to the detriment of consumers. The main reasons causing the imbalance in B2C relations are information asymmetry between the parties, differences in their bargaining powers, level of knowledge, understanding and experience, and last but not least, economical and structural inferiority of consumers as weaker parties.[60] All these circumstances are having a restrictive effect upon the consumer's true will when entering B2C transactions which are in reality often given no choice but to agree to the conditions offered by traders. The role of consumer protection instruments is thus twofold: They are managing numerous legal and economical risks that consumers are exposed to and regaining true and material balance between the parties in B2C transactions. In doing so consumer protection instruments are actually enabling the proper realisation of consumer's private autonomy and of its emanation, freedom of contract, which from the perspective of EU contract law represent main tools for the accomplishment of the internal market.[61]

---

[59] See the chapter "Schutzbestimmungen der Verbraucherrichtlinien" in: Čikara (2010), pp. 39 et seq.

[60] Both legal theory and CJEU/ECJ case law recognize intellectual and economic inferiority of consumers towards traders. See Case C-89/91, *Shearson Lehmann Hutton v TVB* [1993] ECR I-139, para. 18: "[. . .] the consumer as the party deemed to be economically weaker and less experienced in legal matters than the other party to the contract [. . .]". See Joined Cases C-240/98 to C-244/98, *Océano Grupo Editorial and Salvat Editores* [2000] ECR I-04941, para. 25: "[. . .] the consumer is in a weak position vis-à-vis the seller or supplier, as regards both his bargaining power and his level of knowledge [. . .]". See Case C-168/05, *Mostaza Claro* [2006] ECR I-10421, para. 25; Case C-137/08, *VB Pénzügyi Lízing* [2010] ECR I-10847 para. 22; Case C-26/13, *Kásler Káslerné Rábai*, EU:C:2014:282, para. 39. and numerous other cases. See also Kemper (1994), pp. 32 et seq.

[61] Pursuant to Grundmann et al. (2001), p. 325, the core of private or party autonomy lies in the capacity to enter into contracts and to negotiate for specific contract terms and in this sense it is closely related to freedom of contract being an institutional freedom granted to both parties and free from state interventions against their intent. These two basic civil law principles are in ECJ/CJEU case law recognized as principles common to MS legal traditions and in accordance with EU goals. Due to different MS' legal traditions regarding some of the principles (such as

On the contrary, consumer protection instruments are often criticised as being in direct conflict with the traditional formal understanding of private autonomy in MS' civil law systems that is based on the formal acknowledgment of equality of the parties to contractual relationships.[62] Consequently, it is considered that the strengthening of the protection of one contract party through special consumer protection instruments is having restrictive effects upon the private autonomy of the other contract party, namely of the trader.[63] The Union's functional approach to private autonomy and freedom of contract reflected in consumer protection instruments is thus colliding with the traditional understanding of these basic civil law principles in MS laws.[64] Further critiques concern inconsistent regulation of consumer protection instruments across different EU consumer protection approximation measures. Over the years consumer protection instruments became rather "different" than "common", which strongly affects MS laws when transposing "similar", but again "different" definitions of consumers and traders or when transposing different withdrawal periods and rules and so on.[65] Terminological and conceptual incongruence between EU consumer protection directives is attributed to the fact that for a long time EU approximation in the area of consumer protection was pursued unsystematically and without a common legislative strategy. This reflects itself particularly upon the effectiveness of consumer protection instruments in practice. In situations where a person is a consumer pursuant to the

"*pacta sunt servanda*" in the continental or common law system) it is not quite clear which understanding of the concept is considered to be common. See Case C-162/96, *Racke v Hauptzollamt Mainz* [1998] ECR I-3655. For example, private autonomy and freedom of contract are explicitly recognized in Art. 1 of the Annex I of the CESL. The EU Charter of Fundamental Rights recognizes them indirectly by Art. 15 on freedom to choose an occupation and right to engage in work, Art. 16 on freedom to conduct a business and Art. 17 on right to property.

[62] See Case C-26/13, *Kásler and Káslerné Rábai*, EU:C:2014:282, para. 82: "[...] objective of Article 6(1) of Directive 93/13, since, according to settled case-law, that provision is intended to substitute for the formal balance established by the contract between the rights and obligations of the parties real balance re-establishing equality between them [...]". See also Case C-453/10, *Pereničová and Perenič*, EU:C:2012:144, para. 31; CJEU Case C-618/10, *Banco Español de Cré dito*, EU:C:2012:349, para. 40.

[63] Nowadays it is widely accepted that private autonomy cannot be understood in mere formal, but also in a material sense. In situations where the self-determination of private parties is prevented due to certain economic or intellectual conditions the legislator can intervene in contractual relations if this is necessary for the protection of the weaker party to the contract and for the achievement of a true and material balance of the parties' rights and obligations. See Čikara (2009), pp. 45 et seq.

[64] Leczykiewicz and Weatherill (2013), p. 7: "[...] it comes as no surprise that arguments against the intervention of EU law into national private laws are really arguments for the protection of private autonomy [...]".

[65] With regard to fundamental concepts of consumer and trader as instrumental for the application of the consumer directives there is no uniform definition of either term in EU consumer protection directives. Depending on the subject matter some of them use the term consumer, person, main contractor etc. or trader, seller, supplier, vendor, retailer etc. With regard to different terminological and conceptual definitions and rules on basic consumer rights, such as the right of withdrawal, consult the EU Consumer Law Acquis Database at: http://www.eu-consumer-law.org.

definition of one legal act and is not a consumer pursuant to the definition of another legal act and where consequently a person may or may not enjoy special consumer rights, such as the right of withdrawal, legal certainty may be questioned.[66] On the other hand, ineffectiveness may result from the consumer protection instruments themselves rather than from the inconsistency of the approximation measures regulating them. For instance, one of the main consumer protection instruments on information duties should strike a balance between a consumer and a trader by bringing a consumer into a position where he can reach an informed decision on the conclusion of a contract with a trader.[67] However, due to the extensiveness of the information to be given to consumers in both the pre-contractual and contractual stage for consideration "in good time" before being bound by contract or offer or within the withdrawal period after the conclusion of a contract, the consumer often ends up being more confused than enlightened. This so-called "information overload" effect is therefore not only undermining the protection that should be guaranteed to consumers by information duties, but it also overburdens traders by the amount of information they have to provide. Since the consumer is according to established ECJ/CJEU case law "reasonably well informed and reasonably

[66] The fact that the consistency was needed both at the conceptual and terminological level was recognized by numerous EU communications and resolutions. In 2004 the Commission initiated the process of reviewing the EU consumer protection *acquis* intending to achieve its rationalization, clarification and modernization. One of its results is the CRD, based on the horizontal and full targeted harmonization approach, which amends Directives 93/13 and 99/44 and repeals and replaces Directives 85/577 and 97/7. See the Communication from the Commission of 7 May 2002 to the European Parliament, the Council, the Economic and Social Committee and the Committee of the Regions – "Consumer Policy Strategy 2000–2006", COM (2002) 208 final, OJ C137/2 explicitly mentioning "a need to review and reform existing EU consumer protection directives". See also the Communication from the Commission to the Council and the European Parliament on European contract law, COM(2001) 398 final, OJ C 255 containing four options for contract law approximation and for increasing the quality of consumer protection legislation. Further on: Communication from the Commission of 12 February 2003 to the European Parliament and the Council – A more coherent European contract law – An action plan COM(2003) 68 final, OJ C 63; Communication from the Commission of 11 October 2004 to the European Parliament and the Council – European Contract Law and the revision of the acquis: the way forward, COM(2004)651 final; Commission Report of 23 September 2005: First Annual Progress Report on European Contract Law and the Acquis Review, COM(2005)456 final; European Parliament Resolution of 23 March 2006 on European Contract Law and the Revision of the Acquis: The Way Forward [2006] OJ C292E/109; European Parliament Resolution of 7 September 2006 on European Contract Law [2006] OJ C305E/247; Commission Report of 25 July 2007: Second Progress Report on the Common Frame of Reference, COM(2007) 447 final; Commission Green Paper on Revision of the Consumer Contract Law Acquis of 7 February 2007, COM (2006) 744 final; Green Paper from the Commission of 1 July 2010 on Policy Options for Progress Towards a European Contract Law for Consumers and Businesses, COM(2010)348; Expert Group's Feasibility Study on European Contract Law of 3 May 2011 and many others.

[67] See Martinek (2000), p. 518: "Ein aufgeklärter Konsument kann sich, sofern er nur hinreichende Informationen erhalten hat, weitgehend selbst schützen und seine Privatautonomie sowohl beim Abschluss wie auch beim Inhalt des Vertrages wahren". See also the chapter "Informationspflichten" in: Čikara (2010), pp. 41 et seq.

observant and circumspect",[68] one also speaks about the "information paradigm" resulting from over informing the reasonably well informed consumer. According to Directive 2002/65/EC concerning the distance marketing of consumer financial services,[69] there is more than forty pre-contractual information to be given to the consumer (Art. 3) that can be widened by MS's additional prior information (Art. 4). In its Art. 5 the CCD is enumerating pre-contractual information from *litera* a) to s) that should be given to the consumer by means of the Standard European Consumer Credit Information form with a possibility of provision of additional information in a separate document. The MCD is going even further by differentiating between general (*litera* a) to n) in Art. 13) and personalized pre-contractual information (Art. 14). The latter shall be provided to consumers by means of the European Standardised Information Sheet whereby additional information may be given in a separate document annexed to it. The purpose of these extensive provisions on information duties is nevertheless often undermined in practice where standard contract terms contain the consumer's acknowledgment of the trader's fulfilment of its information obligations without such terms being supported by documents issued by the trader and supplied to the consumer. According to the recent case law of the CJEU, such contract terms cannot be considered as being proof of the trader's performance of pre-contractual obligations and are thus not undermining the effectiveness of the rights conferred by the directive.[70] Pursuant to the authors view, it is precisely due to the effectiveness of consumer protection instruments that such standard terms should be prohibited since the trader's behaviour supported by such clauses is in direct conflict with the *ratio* of information duties as a consumer protection instrument. Otherwise what will happen to the effectiveness of consumer protection instruments if in reality the consumer has to resort to procedural enforcement mechanisms as a last line of defence to actually enjoy a guaranteed legal certainty?

[68] Case C-210/96, *Gut Springenheide and Tusky v Oberkreisdirektor des Kreises Steinfurt* [1998] ECR I-4657, para. 31; Case C-470/93, *Verein gegen Unwesen in Handel und Gewerbe Köln e.V. v Mars* [1995] ECR I-01923, para 24; Case C-220/98, *Estée Lauder* [2000] ECR I-117; Case C-446/07, *Severi* [2009] ECR I-08041, para 62. The image of the average consumer differs when it comes to financial services. See Case C-15/78, *Société générale alsacienne de banque v Koestler* [1978] ECR I-1971, para. 2; Case C-384/93, *Alpine Investments v Minister van Financiën* [1995] ECR I-1141. See Stuyck (2014).

[69] Directive 2002/65/EC of the European Parliament and of the Council of 23 September 2002 concerning the distance marketing of consumer financial services and amending Council Directive 90/619/EEC and Directives 97/7/EC and 98/27/EC, OJ L 271/16.

[70] Case C-449/13, *CA Consumer Finance*, EU:C:2014:2464, para. 32: "[. . .] the provisions of Directive 2008/48 must be interpreted to the effect that [. . .] they preclude a court from having to find that, as a result of a standard term, a consumer has acknowledged that the creditor's pre-contractual obligations have been fully and correctly performed, with that term thereby resulting in a reversal of the burden of proving the performance of those obligations such as to undermine the effectiveness of the rights conferred by Directive 2008/48".

2.4 Transposition of EU Consumer Protection Acquis in the Member States

When transposing EU consumer protection *acquis* into the laws of the MS numerous issues arise that can seriously endanger the legal certainty of both consumers and traders. To this endless list belong, for example, matters of mistranslations of EU consumer protection directives to be transposed, terminological and conceptual inconsistency between legal terms of EU directives and MS laws, introduction of new and alien legal institutes into MS' laws, structural questions on how and where to transpose EU legislation in MS' laws, dynamic changes of EU *acquis* requiring constant amendments of MS legal acts, incorrect transposition of EU legal acts into the MS laws and so on. Many of these problems are reflecting previously analysed issues of EU consumer protection *acquis* that deepen even more at the level of MS.

Thus, inconsistent use of legal terminology across EU consumer protection directives leads to serious legal consequences at the national level of MS. Perfect examples are the inconsistent use of the legal notion "right of withdrawal", that was in EU consumer protection directives often used as a synonym to a "right of cancellation", "right of rescission" or a "right of termination".[71] This resulted in cases where the national legislator transposed the "right of withdrawal" by using the legal term "right to terminate" or by referring to the legal consequences of contract termination prescribed by national law.[72] Although it can be argued that withdrawal is a specific form of termination, these two concepts are to be distinguished according to their goals, exercise and legal consequences.[73] As confirmed by the CJEU case law, the application of the legal consequence of termination in case of withdrawal, such as payment of compensation for using goods until termination, makes the exercise of the right of withdrawal possible only against the payment, which is against the *ratio* of this key consumer protection instrument.[74]

---

[71] Repealed Council Directive 85/577/EEC of 20 December 1985 to protect the consumer with respect to contracts negotiated away from business premises, OJ L 372/31, used the term "right of cancellation" (Arts. 3–5). Art. 5 of the repealed Directive 94/47/EC of the European Parliament and the Council of 26 October 1994 on the protection of purchasers with respect to certain aspects of contracts relating to the purchase of the right to use immovable properties on a timeshare basis, OJ L 280/83, used "right to withdraw" and "right of cancellation" as synonyms.

[72] Croatian first Consumer Protection Act (CPA), OG No. 96/03 and second CPA, OG RC Nos. 79/07, 125/07, 75/09, 79/09, 89/09, 133/09, 78/12 and 56/13 used the term "right to terminate the contract", while the third and currently in force CPA, OG Nos. 41/14 uses the term "right of unilateral termination". On the other hand, Art. 14 of the Consumer Credit Act (CCA), OG Nos. 75/09, 112/12, 143/13, 147/13-corrigendum and 9/15 uses the term "right of withdrawal". More in detail Šarčević and Čikara (2009), pp. 204–205.

[73] Bar et al. (2009), p. 569, define the right to withdraw from a contract as "a right to terminate the legal relationship arising from the contract [. . .], without having to give any reason for so doing and without incurring any liability for non-performance [. . .]". Nevertheless, DCFR makes a clear distinction between the two concepts in further provisions (2008: 120–124, 163–165) as does the CRD in its Art. 12.

[74] Case C-489/07, *Messner* [2009] ECR I-7315, paras. 23 and 24.

Consumer protection across the MS is further affected by the level of harmonization of different EU consumer protection directives to be transposed. As explained the minimum harmonization approach led to numerous differences at the MS level by enabling the national legislator the adoption or retention of the most stringent provisions *in favorem consumentis*. On the other hand, due to its inflexibility the maximum or full harmonization could lower the MS' level of consumer protection in certain aspects that are fully harmonized by EU consumer protection directives. It also seriously affects the national legislators' transposition technique since it does not allow them to maintain or introduce in their national law provisions diverging from those laid down in directives. Namely, they will usually opt for a literal or so-called "copy-paste" transposition technique in order to guarantee the required standard of maximum protection. However, this technique opens the door to numerous issues of both conceptual and terminological nature.[75] Full targeted harmonization places even higher demands on national legislators by requiring them to distinguish between full, minimum and optional directives' provisions. In practice, transposition of full targeted harmonization directives often leads to failures caused by the inability to recognize these different standards united in one EU directive. For instance, the CCD as a full targeted harmonization directive contains, among others, minimum harmonization provisions on credit intermediaries and options regarding its scope of application.[76] Further on, besides the matter on how to transpose, the level of harmonization has also an effect on where to transpose EU consumer protection directives. This important question particularly concerned the transposition of the CRD repealing Distance and Doorstep Selling Directives and amending the Unfair Contract Terms Directive (UCTD) and Consumer Sales Directive (CSD). Since standard contract terms and conformity with the contract being subject matters of the UCTD and of the CSD, are in most MS regulated by their civil law codifications these directives were regularly transposed excessively by the same provisions. Nevertheless, the full targeted harmonization approach hampered the approximation of the civil law codifications with the CRD and resulted in the creation of two different but similar sets of rules, one concerning B2C and the other concerning the rest of the civil law relations.[77] Beyond that the approximation with the EU consumer protection

[75] As rightly pointed out by Šarčević and Čikara (2009), p. 209 "if an adequate national term exists, translators are obliged to use it, instead of creating a meaningless literal translation". On negative implications of the copy-paste transposition technique see Łazowski and Blockmans (2014), pp. 119 *et seq.*

[76] Pursuant to Art. 22(1) "insofar as this Directive contains harmonised provisions, Member States may not maintain or introduce in their national law provisions diverging from those laid down in this Directive". However, under recital 17 of the CCD "Member States should therefore remain free to maintain or introduce additional obligations incumbent on credit intermediaries [. . .]". According to recital 10 of the CCD "A Member State could thereby maintain or introduce national legislation corresponding to the provisions of this Directive or certain of its provisions on credit agreements outside the scope of this Directive [. . .]".

[77] On the transposition of these directives in the EU MS consult the EU Consumer Law Acquis Database at: http://www.eu-consumer-law.org. See also Čađenović et al. (2010), pp. 557 et seq.

directives led to a variety of regulatory solutions across the MS transposing them either by special consumer law or general civil law codifications or even separately by single legal acts corresponding to relevant EU directives.[78] Some legal systems took an even more disintegrative approach by combining all of the above mentioned solutions.[79] Whereby it is beyond all questions that the sheer number of applicable legal acts and the complexity of their legal relations adversely affects the protection of consumer rights at both the EU and MS level. In cases of fragmented directives transposition the practical applicability and effectiveness of the harmonized consumer protection provisions is hindered not only by their inconsistency, but also by their intransparency for consumers and traders as well as for competent authorities in charge of their application and consumer protection.

2.5 *CJEU Interpretation of EU Consumer Protection Acquis*

The CJEU plays a particularly important role in the approximation of MS' laws. To its primary tasks belongs the duty to ensure that in the interpretation and application of the Treaties the law is observed.[80] The CJEU contributes to the development of EU law by ensuring its correct application and uniform interpretation. To this end, within the framework of a preliminary rulings procedure, the CJEU gives rulings on the interpretation of the Treaties or on the validity and interpretation of acts of the institutions, bodies, offices or agencies of the Union.[81] Unlike "direct actions" these proceedings begin and end before national courts refer questions on the validity or interpretation of EU law to the CJEU therefore creating a strong interaction between the CJEU and MS national courts. Together they are providing for a uniform interpretation and uniform and correct application of EU law and ensuring the protection of rights that individuals derive from it. Since the protection of consumer rights can be endangered by incorrect transposition or application of the EU consumer protection directives within the MS' laws, here is where the role of the CJEU comes into focus. Although the CJEU is not deciding upon national laws of the MS, it can decide whether the EU consumer protection directives do or do not preclude certain national law provisions. Moreover, since the direct effect of directives between private individuals was consistently denied in the CJEU/ECJ established case law,[82] the application and enforcement of individual's rights and

[78] Schulte-Nölke (2009), p. 133.

[79] On the similar approach of the Croatian legislator see Mišćenić (2014a), p. 279.

[80] Art. 19(1) TEU. Pursuant to Art. 2 TEU, the Union is founded on the values of respect for *inter alia* "rule of law". See also Case C-294/83, *Les Verts v Parliament* [1986] ECR I-1339, para. 23: "[. . .] the European Economic Community is a Community based on the rule of law, inasmuch as neither its Member States nor its institutions can avoid review of the question whether the measures adopted by them are in conformity with the basic constitutional charter, the Treaty [. . .]".

[81] Art. 267 TFEU (ex Art. 234 TEC).

[82] The principle of direct effect enables natural and legal persons the protection of rights deriving from EU law before courts and other state authorities by invoking the provisions of EU law having

obligations deriving from the EU consumer protection directives before the national courts is particularly guaranteed through the mechanisms of supremacy, direct effect, consistent interpretation and state liability.[83] Pursuant to the principle of supremacy of the Union law, in case of collision of the provision of the Union law and of the national law, the latter must be excluded from the application and replaced either with some other compliant national law provision or with the Union law provision having direct effect.[84] On the other hand, the principle of consistent interpretation requires from national courts and all other public authorities to interpret the national law consistent to EU law, thus making an indirect third party effect of directives possible.[85] Consequently, in cases where consumers would be denied their rights deriving from EU law, due to the incorrect transposition of the EU consumer protection directive, all state authorities would be obliged to interpret national law in conformity with the provisions and goals of the directive or obliged not to apply national provisions contradicting it. If the incorrect transposition or application of the EU consumer protection directive would result in

---

direct effect. The established CJEU/ECJ case law developed criteria for the vertical direct effect of Treaty provisions, regulations and directives, however, denying the horizontal direct effect of directives. According to this concept, individuals should not suffer due to MS violation of the EU law in form of late or erroneous transposition of directives. See Case C-41/74, *Yvonne Van Duyn v Home Office* [1974] ECR I-1337; Case C-152/84, *M.H. Marshall v Southampton and South-West Hampshire Area Health Authority* [1986] ECR I-723; Case C-91/92, *Faccini Dori v Recreb Srl* [1994] ECR I-3325; Case C-192/94, *El Corte Inglés SA v Cristina Blázquez Rivero* [1996] ECR I-1281; Case C-80/06, *Carp* [2007] ECR I-4473 etc. A detailed analysis on the *pro* and *contra* of the horizontal direct effect of directives is provided by Craig (2009), pp. 349 et seq.

[83] Moreover, particular attention is to be given to the principle of autonomy of the EU legal order that demonstrates that the EU legal order is an autonomous one and is separated from the legal orders of the MS existing parallel to it. According to C-26/62 *Van Gend en Loos v Administratie der Belastingen* [1963] ECR 1: "[. . .] the Community constitutes a new legal order of international law for the benefit of which the states have limited their sovereign rights, albeit within limited fields, and the subjects of which comprise not only Member States but also their nationals. Independently of the legislation of Member States, Community law therefore not only imposes obligations on individuals but is also intended to confer upon them rights which become part of their legal heritage. [. . .]".

[84] See Case C-6/64, *Costa v. E.N.E.L.* [1964] ECR I-585; Case C-106/77, *Amministrazione delle finanze dello Stato v Simmenthal* [1978] ECR I-629; Case C-11/70, *Internationale Handelsgesellschaft mbH v Einfuhr- und Vorratsstelle für Getreide und Futtermittel* [1970] ECR I-1125.

[85] Pursuant to the principle of the EU consistent interpretation national courts and all other public authorities are obliged to consider the whole body of national law and interpret it, so far as possible, in the light of the wording and purpose of the EU directive that was supposed to be achieved by its transposition (*effet utile*). The legal basis for this duty existing also during the transposition period arises from Art. 4(3) TEU and Art. 288(3) TFEU. See Case C-14/83, *Von Colson and Kamann v Land Nordrhein-Westfalen* [1984] ECR I-01891; Case C-106/89, *Marleasing v Comercial Internacional de Alimentación* [1990] ECR I-4135; Case C-91/92, *Faccini Dori v Recreb* [1994] ECR I-3325; Joined Cases C-240/98 to C-244/98, *Océano Grupo Editorial and Salvat Editores* [2000] ECR I-04941; Joined Cases C-397/01 to C-403/01, *Pfeiffer and Others* [2004] ECR I-08835; Case C-105/03, *Pupino* [2005] ECR I-05285.

damage for the consumer, the vertical direct effect and principle of state liability[86] would guarantee consumer protection and damage compensation.

This comprehensive protection of consumer rights guaranteed through principles and institutes developed by ECJ/CJEU case law would nevertheless be undermined in case of an inadequate or inconsistent interpretation of the EU consumer protection *acquis*. Though the task of the CJEU is to interpret EU law uniformly, in its case law on consumer protection one can observe certain inconsistencies that could bring legal certainty in question. For example, in the recent case *Kásler and Káslerné Rábai*,[87] the CJEU concluded that the UCTD provision on invalidity of unfair contract terms is not precluding the national law provision allowing the amendment of an unfair contract term although it concluded exactly the opposite in its previous case *Banco Español de Crédito*.[88] In interpreting Art. 6(1) of the UCTD the CJEU stated in *Banco Español de Crédito* that the first part of the provision expressly requires MS to provide that unfair contract terms "shall [. . .] not be binding on the consumer", without authorising national courts to revise its content.[89] It also interpreted the second sentence of the provision on the possible continued existence of the contract by saying "that contract must continue in existence, in principle, without any amendment other than that resulting from the deletion of the unfair terms, in so far as, in accordance with the rules of domestic law, such continuity of the contract is legally possible".[90] Contrary than expected such reasoning of the CJEU was not substantiated by arguments on the intrusions of national courts into parties' autonomy and freedom of contract. Instead the CJEU concluded that the national courts power to revise the content of unfair terms would compromise the long-term objective of Art. 7 of the UCTD and have adverse effect on sellers or suppliers regarding the application of unfair terms since they "would remain tempted to use those terms in the knowledge that, even if they were declared

[86] It is a principle of EU law pursuant to which MS are obliged to compensate loss and damage caused to individuals by breaches of EU law for which they can be held responsible. Criteria for state liability derive from Art. 246 TFEU (ex Art. 215 TEC) and established CJEU/ECJ case law. See Joined cases C-6/90 and C-9/90, *Francovich and Bonifaci v Italy* [1991] ECR I-05357; Joined Cases C-46/93 and C-48/93, *Brasserie du Pęcheur* [1996] ECR I-01029; Case C-5/94, *Hedley Lomas* [1996] ECR I-02553; Case C-224/01, *Köbler* [2003] ECR I-10239; Case C-173/03, *Traghetti del Mediterraneo* [2006] ECR I-05177 etc.

[87] Case C-26/13 of 30 April 2014, *Kásler and Káslerné Rábai*, para. 86: "Article 6(1) of Directive 93/13 must be interpreted as meaning that, in a situation such as that at issue in the main proceedings, in which a contract concluded between a seller or supplier and a consumer cannot continue in existence after an unfair term has been deleted, that provision does not preclude a rule of national law enabling the national court to cure the invalidity of that term by substituting for it a supplementary provision of national law".

[88] Case C-618/10, *Banco Español de Crédito*, EU:C:2012:349, para. 89: "Article 6(1) of Directive 93/13 must be interpreted as precluding legislation of a Member State [. . .] which allows a national court, in the case where it finds that an unfair term in a contract concluded between a seller or supplier and a consumer is void, to modify that contract by revising the content of that term".

[89] Ibid., paras. 62 and 65.

[90] Ibid., para. 65.

invalid, the contract could nevertheless be modified".[91] On the contrary, in the *Kásler and Káslerné Rábai* case, the CJEU argued that "[. . .] it does not follows, *in a situation such as that in the main proceedings*, that Article 6(1) of Directive 93/13 precludes the national court, in accordance with the principles of the law of contract, from deleting an unfair term and substituting for it a supplementary provision of national law".[92] In this case the CJEU reckoned that the annulment of the unfair clause would render the entire contract null and void thus exposing the consumer to particularly unfavourable consequences.[93] Consequently, it concluded that "the substitution of an unfair term for a supplementary provision of national law is consistent with the objective of Article 6(1) of Directive 93/13, since, according to settled case-law, that provision is intended to substitute for the formal balance established by the contract between the rights and obligations of the parties real balance re-establishing equality between them, not to annul all contracts containing unfair terms".[94] Nevertheless, factual and legal circumstances of the case do not indicate clearly enough, whether the contract would be annulled in its entirety,[95] and as rightly pointed out by Advocate General (AG) *Trstenjak* in the CJEU case *Pereničová and Perenič* such a decision is subject to an objective assessment conducted by an impartial body,[96] namely the national court deciding in a concrete case. As reasoned by AG *Trstenjak*, Art. 6(1) of the UCTD is to be "understood to mean that, where an unfair term is found, the Member States are not in principle obliged to order the invalidity of the entire contract" and the invalidity of the contract as a whole is limited to a few exceptional cases.[97]

Apart from the uniform application and interpretation of EU law by the CJEU, effective legal protection of consumer rights is guaranteed at the forefront by the national judiciaries of the MS. Art. 19(1) TEU, introduced by the Treaty of Lisbon, requires from the MS, the provision of remedies sufficient to ensure effective legal protection in the fields covered by Union law. Together with the principle of effective protection developed by the CJEU case law this primary law provision

[91] Ibid., para. 69. Further on, the CJEU argued in para. 70 that that power could neither be based on Art. 8 of the UCTD, which leaves MS the option to adopt or retain, in the area covered by that directive, more stringent provisions compatible with EU law, inasmuch as they ensure a higher level of consumer protection.

[92] Case C-26/13 of 30 April 2014, *Kásler and Káslerné Rábai*, para. 80.

[93] Ibid., paras. 83 and 84.

[94] Ibid., para. 82.

[95] Ibid., para. 17. In the *Kásler and Káslerné Rábai* case concerning the mortgage loan denominated in a foreign currency, namely Swiss francs, secured by a guarantee *in rem*, the CJEU was deciding upon the unfairness of a not individually negotiated contract term stipulating the calculation of monthly repayment installments due on the basis of the selling rate of exchange, whereas the amount of the loan advanced was determined on the basis of the buying rate of exchange for that currency. The unfairness of the contract term in the case *Banco Español de Cré dito* concerned the high rate of interest on late payments (29 %).

[96] Opinion of Advocate General *Trstenjak* delivered on 29.11.2011, EU:C:2011:788 in Case C-453/10, *Pereničová and Perenič*, EU:C:2012:144, para. 59.

[97] Ibid., paras. 51 and 58.

guarantees to consumers effective protection of their rights deriving from EU law in a uniform and equal manner thereby ensuring a high level of legal certainty. According to the principle of effective protection that is now also enshrined in Art. 47 of the EU Charter of Fundamental Rights,[98] national courts and other bodies must guarantee the protection of rights that individuals derive from EU law, whereby in the absence of EU legislation, the embodiment of procedural rules governing actions for safeguarding these rights falls within the internal legal order of the MS by virtue of the principle of procedural autonomy of these MS.[99] These rules cannot however be less favourable than those governing similar domestic actions (principle of equivalence) or make it in practice impossible or excessively difficult to exercise the rights conferred by EU law (principle of effectiveness). In this way the EU principle of effective protection guarantees effectiveness of procedural protection to be afforded to relevant substantive rights of consumers deriving from EU consumer protection *acquis* before national courts and other dispute resolution bodies of the MS. Lately, one can notice obvious conflicts between the principle of effective protection and some fundamental principles of MS' procedural laws, such as *non ultra petita* and *res judicata*, in the CJEU case law on consumer protection. For instance, in the *Duarte Hueros* case, the CJEU concluded that these principles make the enforcement of the consumer protection deriving from the CSD excessively difficult, if not impossible, because there is a significant risk that the consumer will not use the other existing options under national procedural law, either due to its rigid requirements or because the consumer is unaware of, or does not appreciate, the extent of his rights.[100] Although, in a concrete case the consumer was able to seek an appropriate reduction of the price of non-conforming goods in a claim alternative to the main one seeking rescission of the sale contract, the CJEU considered that due to the aforesaid reasons such an option contained in the Spanish civil law procedure cannot guarantee an effective protection of consumer rights deriving from the CSD.[101] This quite disputable argumentation stands in opposition to the ECJ/CJEU developed concept of

[98] Under Art. 47(1) of the EU Charter of Fundamental Rights "everyone whose rights and freedoms guaranteed by the law of the Union are violated has the right to an effective remedy before a tribunal in compliance with the conditions laid down in this Article".

[99] Heinze (2009), pp. 337 et seq.

[100] Case C-32/12, *Duarte Hueros*, EU:C:2013:637, para. 38: "[. . .] because there is a significant risk that the consumer in question will not put forward an alternative claim which would seek, moreover, relief inferior to that sought in the principal claim, either on account of the particularly rigid requirement that the alternative claim be presented at the same time as the principal claim or because the consumer is unaware of, or does not appreciate, the extent of his rights [. . .]".

[101] Ibid., para. 37: "It thus follows from those indications that, under the Spanish procedural system, a consumer who brings proceedings seeking only rescission of the contract for the sale of goods is definitively deprived of the possibility of benefitting from the right to seek an appropriate reduction in the price of those goods pursuant to Article 3(5) of Directive 1999/44 in the event that the court dealing with the dispute were to find that, in fact, the lack of conformity of those goods is minor, except where that application contains an alternative claim seeking that such a price reduction be granted."

"reasonably well informed and reasonably observant and circumspect" consumer. Moreover, it opens the door to a possible conflict between two kinds of legal certainty guarantees, one at the EU and another at the MS level. Namely, the primary goal of national procedural law provisions on *non ultra petita*, *res judicata*, main and alternative claims etc., is to ascertain legal certainty of the parties protecting their substantive rights in the civil law procedure. On the other hand, from the point of view of the CJEU these mechanisms are not effective enough in protection of the substantive rights deriving from EU law because they make the protection provided for the consumer under the CSD "completely uncertain in nature" and thereby render that protection inadequate.[102] Seen in a wider perspective it seems that the CJEU reasoning just confirms the existence of a complex issue of EU vs MS legal certainty.

3 Conclusion

The development of EU consumer protection law is all about the removal and management of legal risks. The approximation of MS' laws in this area was consistently pursued with the goal of the removal and management of legal risks standing in the way of the realization of an internal market. Therefore, the focus was on the achievement of a high level of legal certainty for consumers, but also traders, whose common domestic and cross-border economic transactions contribute to the proper functioning and realization of the internal market. As demonstrated in the chapter, this difficult task brought many challenges, some of which were hard to conquer. On the one hand, the efforts of the EU institutions resulted with an abundancy of soft and hard laws in the area of consumer protection offering a high common standard of protection to consumers across the Union. On the other hand, walking an unknown path opened the door to numerous new legal risks that seriously affect the development of the EU consumer protection law and mirror themselves on EU private law in general. This is particularly apparent with regard to some of the elaborated issues such as the fulfilment of the conditions of the principle of subsidiarity or effectiveness of the consumer protection instruments. Combined with the fragmentary character of the EU consumer protection *acquis* these issues lead to separate legal risks that need to be managed on their own. At the breaching point when newly developed risks started to actually diminish the achieved results of the EU institutions, the latter were forced to react. An initiative for the resolution of the problems came in 1999 during the European Council

[102] Ibid., para. 40. See also para. 39: "In those circumstances, it must be held that such procedural rules are liable to undermine the effectiveness of the consumer protection intended by the European Union legislature in so far as they do not allow the national court to recognise of its motion the right of the consumer to obtain an appropriate reduction in the price of the goods, even though that consumer is not entitled to refine his initial application or to bring a fresh action to that end."

meeting in Tampere and the realization started with the process of reviewing the consumer *acquis* in 2004.[103] The results came first in form of the CRD and later in form of the full targeted harmonization directives such as the CCD, MCD, TSD etc., which in fact do demonstrate more consistency on both a conceptual and terminological level. These are nevertheless undermined by the fact that, as argued, neither minimum nor full targeted harmonization are "really" and "actually" removing differences between important harmonized private law provisions of MS. Irrespective of the question who produces them differences between the private law provisions of MS do present barriers to cross-border trade and distort market competition thereby affecting adversely the proper functioning of the EU internal market. As confirmed by the CESL Proposal in 2011 which remains unchanged until today, we are confronted with a reality in which "[. . .] the majority of European consumers shop only domestically [. . .] because of the differences of national laws consumers are often uncertain about their rights in cross-border situations".[104] Consequently, it seems that over the years of the development of EU consumer protection law the EU institutions not only failed in the management of risks creating legal uncertainty for consumers and traders, but moreover, came to a point where they are managing legal risks they produced themselves during the management of legal risks by means of the approximation of MS' laws. Nevertheless, one should acknowledge that the efforts and work invested in the approximation of MS' laws resulted with the creation of a special area of EU consumer protection law characterised by its own special features and protection instruments. Whether this special features and characteristics fit into MS' laws is another question and the crucial one. Issues that emerged at EU level were a consequence of the implementation of the EU consumer protection *aquis* transferred to MS' level. This led to the creation of harmonized regulatory frameworks of MS in the area of consumer protection with regard to which one can seriously raise the question whether the MS could have done it better than the EU? Having in mind the constraints imposed by the subsidiarity principle and the need to present evidence that consumers are not adequately protected by the MS laws, it is getting more and more difficult to justify the EU's authority to regulate in the name of consumer protection.[105] The conclusions reached with regard to the approximation of MS laws in the area of consumer protection raise far more important questions concerning EU approximation in general. Having presented the results one cannot help, but question whether an approximation of MS laws is the most appropriate means for the removal of risks causing legal uncertainty? Is it really necessary to achieve the same or at least similar regulatory solutions across the MS for the realization and proper functioning of the internal market? Maybe one should reconsider the Union's original approach of treating the differences as a main barrier to cross-border trade that is so deeply enshrined in the whole body of EU

[103] See supra, footnote 67.

[104] See Explanatory Memorandum of the CESL, p. 3.

[105] See Leczykiewicz and Weatherill (2013), p. 7.

law. As some of the legal theories and developed EU principles tend to suggest, the acceptance of differences could present a more acceptable and reasonable approach based on tolerance between the MS. Maybe the "common" market could better be achieved by accepting and tolerating differences.

References

Bar C et al (2009) Principles, definitions and model rules of European private law, Draft Common Frame of Reference (DCFR). Sellier, European Law Publishers, Munich

Čađenović Z et al (2010) Transposition of proposed directive on consumer rights into the national laws of the participating states. In: Čađenović Z et al (eds) EU consumer contract law, civil law forum for South East Europe-collection of studies and analyses. Jugoslovenski pregled, Denona d.o.o., Beograd et al., pp 557–562

Čikara E (2010) Gegenwart und Zukunft der Verbraucherkreditverträge in der EU und in Kroatien, Die Umsetzung der Richtlinie 87/102/EWG und Richtlinie 2008/48/EG in das deutsche, österreichische und kroatische Verbraucherkreditrecht. LIT Verlag, Berlin et al.

Čikara E (2009) Consumer protection in the light of private autonomy. In: Dávid R, Necká J, Sehnálek D (eds) Abstracts of the COFOLA Conference for Young Lawyers (COFOLA 2009): key points and ideas. Masaryk University, Muni Press, Brno, pp 45–46

Craig P (2009) The legal effect of directives: policy, rules and exceptions. Eur Law Rev 34 (3):349–377

EU Network of Independent Experts on Fundamental Rights/Réseau UE d'Experts Indépendants en Matière de Droits Fondamentaux (2006) Commentary of the Charter of Fundamental Rights of the European Union

Groussot X, Bogojević S (2014) Subsidiarity as a procedural safeguard to federalism In: Azoulai L (ed) The question of competence in the European Union. Oxford University Press, Oxford, pp 234–252

Grundmann S, Kerber W, Weatherill S (2001) Party autonomy and the role of information in the internal market. Walter de Gruyter, Berlin et al.

Gutman K (2014) Constitutional foundations of European contract law: a comparative analysis. Oxford University Press, Oxford

Halson R, Campbell D (2013) Harmonisation and its discontents: a transaction costs critique of a European contract law. In: Devenney J, Kenny M (eds) The transformation of European private law: harmonisation, consolidation, codification or chaos? Cambridge University Press, Cambridge et al., pp 100–130

Heinze C (2009) Effektivitätsgrundsatz. In: Basedow J, Hopt KJ, Zimmermann R (eds) Handwörterbuch des Europäischen Privatrechts, vol I. Mohr Siebeck, Tübingen, pp 337–341

Hesselink MW, Rutgers JW, de Booys T (2007) The legal basis for an optional instrument on European contract law. Centre for the Study of European Contract Law, Working Paper Series 4:1–83. Available at SSRN: http://ssrn.com/abstract=1091119

Josipović T (2010) Challenges to civil law harmonization by way of directives. In: Civil law forum for South East Europe, collection of studies and analyses, First Regional Conference, vol I. Cavtat, Beograd, pp 205–221

Kemper R (1994) Verbraucherschutzinstrumente. Nomos-Verl.-Ges., Baden-Baden

Lando O (2000) Optional or mandatory Europeanisation of contract law. ERPL 8:59–69

Łazowski A, Blockmans S (2014) Between dream and reality: challenges to the legal rapprochement of the Western Balkans. In: Roman Petrov R, Van Elsuwege P (eds) Legislative approximation and application of EU law in the eastern neighbourhood of the European Union: towards a common regulatory space? Routledge, New York, pp 108–134

Leczykiewicz D, Weatherill S (2013) Private law relationships and EU law. In: Leczykiewicz D, Weatherill S (eds) Involvement of EU law in private law relationships. Hart, Oxford, pp 1–8
Mahler T (2007) Defining legal risk. Proceedings of the conference "Commercial Contracting for Strategic Advantage - Potentials and Prospects". Turku University of Applied Sciences. Available at SSRN: http://ssrn.com/abstract=1014364
Martinek M (2000) Unsystematische Überregulierung und kontrakontinentale Effekte im Europäischen Verbraucherschutzrecht oder: Weniger wäre mehr. In: Grundmann S (ed) Systembildung und Systemlücken in Kerngebieten des Europäischen Privatrechts. Mohr Siebeck, Tübingen, pp 511–558
Mišćenić E (2012) Europsko ugovorno pravo na putu od soft prema hard law, Osvrt na opcionalno zajedničko europsko pravo prodaje (CESL) (European contract law on the way from soft to hard law, review of the optional Common European Sales Law (CESL)). ZPFR 33(2):695–745
Mišćenić E (2014a) Consumer protection law. In: Josipović T (ed) Introduction to the law of Croatia. Kluwer Law International, Alphen aan den Rijn, pp 279–290
Mišćenić E (2014b) Mortgage Credit Directive (MCD): are consumers finally getting the protection they deserve? In: Slakoper Z (ed) Liber Amicorum in Honorem Vilim Gorenc. Pravni Fakultet Rijeka, Rijeka, pp 219–260
Reich N (2000) Verbraucherrechte als- unverzichtbare – subjektive Rechte passive Marktbürger. In: Grundmann S (ed) Systembildung und Systemlücken in Kerngebieten des Europäischen Privatrechts. Mohr Siebeck, Tübingen, pp 481–509
Rodin S, Ćapeta T (2010) Osnove prava Europske unije (Fundamentals of the European Union law). Narodne novine, Zagreb
Šarčević S, Čikara E (2009) European vs. National Terminology in Croatian legislation transposing EU directives. In: Šarčević S (ed) Legal language in action: translation, terminology, drafting and procedural issues. Nakladni zavod Globus, Zagreb, pp 193–214
Schulte-Nölke H (2009) The transposition of European consumer directives into the national laws of the EU-Member States. Tijdschrift voor Consumentenrecht en handelspraktijken 4:133–138
Schütze R (2009) Subsidiarity after Lisbon: reinforcing the safeguards of federalism? Camb Law J 68(3):525–536
Schütze R (2014) Limits to the Union's 'Internal Market' competence(s): constitutional comparisons. In: Azoulai L (ed) The question of competence in the European Union. Oxford University Press, Oxford, pp 215–233
Stuyck J (2014) Consumer concepts in EU secondary law. Presented at an interdisciplinary workshop on "Consumer Images" organised by professors Klinck F. and Riesenhuber K. at the Law Faculty of the Ruhr Universität Bochum
Weatherill S (2013) EU consumer law and policy. Elgar European Law, Cheltenham et al.

Legal Risks in EU Social Law

Claire Marzo

Contents

Abstract This chapter aims at applying the new understanding of legal risks to the field of European Union (EU) social law. Understanding "Legal Risks in EU Law" implies to turn upside down the usual legal perspective on a given field of law. Instead of taking a given legal object and describing it, this is a new scientific and practical approach on EU law based on a prospective analysis, which can lead to a rationalised law-making process for the EU institutions and its partners. In other words, legal risk management may be introduced through two approaches: Social risks may be solved by the law, but the law itself may create legal risks. This approach calls for a study of the context and the actors: On the one hand, it is the multiplication of legal orders which leads to legal risks in the field of EU social law (1). On the other hand, it is the actors' choices and first of all the choice of the judge of Luxembourg (2).

C. Marzo (✉)
Université Paris Est, Paris, France
e-mail: claire.marzo@u-pec.fr

E. Mišćenić, A. Raccah (eds.), *Legal Risks in EU Law*,
DOI 10.1007/978-3-319-28596-2_8

1 Introduction

This chapter aims at applying the new understanding of legal risks to the field of European Union (EU) Social Law. This requires to beforehand define legal risks and the new approach they support as well as EU social law. Understanding "Legal Risks in EU Law" implies to turn upside down the usual legal perspective on a given field of law. Instead of taking a given legal object and describing it, this is a new scientific and practical approach on EU law based on a prospective analysis, which can lead to a rationalised law-making process for the EU institutions and its partners.

The legal definition of risk is not clearly defined. It is intrinsically linked to law or, in other words, the regulation of human behaviour. According to British sociologist Anthony Giddens, a risk society is a society increasingly preoccupied with the future (and also with safety), which generates the notion of risk,[1] whilst the German sociologist Ulrich Beck defines it as "a systematic way of dealing with hazards and insecurities induced and introduced by modernization itself".[2] Tackling legal risks involves an anticipation of social, environmental and economic phenomena.

It can be understood in several ways:

- First, it is a will to act in the face of potential dangers, to foresee and prevent risks. Legal texts will be a way to allow for this process of anticipation, to imagine the realisation of dangers and prepare for a solution to tackle them. Securitising society, sometimes too much, is a goal in this,
- A second understanding leads to attaining legal certainty. It is a softer version of the first approach. This meaning is often used by multinational companies that try to identify where legal risks are lower and where the law will be less likely to change unexpectedly.

First (1), legal risks can be created by any factual happening. Second (2), legal uncertainty can be tackled by the law. The precautionary principle, the agreement on risks in legal contracts, legal responsibility... It is one of the main objects of law: the necessity to secure a legal relationship. If the goal is not to attain certainty, it is at least to provide for more stability and security. Third (3), legal risks may be produced by the law itself (which takes us back to 1° as well as being a consequence of 2°). To summarise, legal risk management may be introduced through two approaches: Social risks may be solved by the law, but the law itself may create legal risks.

These two aspects are found in the field of EU social law. First, however, EU social law should been explained. Since it has been defined several times,[3] we just need to remind our readers that we will focus here on EU law and thus exclude

[1] Beck (1992).

[2] Giddens (1999).

[3] See for instance: Barnard (2012), p. 10.

national European laws as well as the work of the European Court of Human Rights. European social law encompasses a broad definition of labour law and social security law. It draws also on social policy issues.

Applying a prospective analysis of legal risks to EU social law implies understanding where these risks are located in EU labour and social law. The notion of legal risks is everywhere in EU law. The primary goal of EU law is to limit and multiply legal risks. We see a limit where a coordination or a harmonisation should in the long term simplify the relations between several legal orders and prevent legal risks thus allowing for more certainty. The process of simplification itself can lead to repetitions, contradictions, errors and comparison standards issues. The multiplication of legal orders and their combination creates legal risks by definition. This is even truer when we don't know to which legal order the judge will refer. In EU law, harmonising the interpretation of EU law is the main competence of the Court of Justice of the European Union. The question systematically raised here is if the national judge will make a preliminary reference to the EU judge? If the European Court of Justice (ECJ) is involved, will it give a wide margin of appreciation to the national level or will it give a very clear, unequivocal answer?

Beyond and from the point of view of the (physical or moral) individual, the multiplication of legal orders gives migrant citizens, residents, and enterprises a wider choice in terms of legal solutions. Moving—using the freedom of movement of persons, services, goods and capitals—opens the door to choosing a preferred legal order, a more convenient or legally satisfying one. Multinational companies often proceed to a cost/advantage analysis before settling in a State. Legal risks here are an important part of the test. Several studies on legal risk management concern Corporate Law and financial institutions and are led by management schools.

EU social law reflects this duality. One could go back to all the legislative developments of EU social law to show how legal risks were reduced by the mere creation and implementation of EU law or increased when a hiatus in the secondary legislation led to a cacophony of different interpretations. This exercise is too long and tedious to be relevant. We will limit this study to two examples. Each hypothesis will be studied in the light of general EU law and a factual/legal example drawn from three ECJ cases that I have chosen to study in this chapter. In order to illustrate the diversity of EU Social Law, two cases are about maternity leave whereas the third one is about the right to information, consultation and representation of workers.

The two cases are *CD versus ST*[4] and *Z*[5] of 18 March 2014. These two cases dealt with mothers asking their employers for maternity leave after the births of their children via surrogacy. More precisely, Ms D., who is employed in a hospital in the United Kingdom, and Ms Z., a teacher working in Ireland, both used surrogate mothers in order to have a child. Ms D. entered into a surrogacy agreement in

---

[4] Case C-167/12, *CD versus ST*, EU:C:2014:169.

[5] Case C-363/12, *Z.versus A Government Department and the Board of Management of a Community School*, EU: C: 2014:159.

accordance with UK law. The child was conceived using her partner's sperm and another woman's egg. Some months after the birth, a UK court, with the surrogate mother's consent, granted Ms D. and her partner full and permanent parental responsibility for the child in accordance with UK legislation on surrogacy. Ms Z. has a rare condition which has the effect that, although she has healthy ovaries and is otherwise fertile, she has no uterus and therefore cannot support a pregnancy. Ms Z. and her husband had a child as a result of an agreement with a surrogate mother in California. Genetically, the child is the couple's, and there is no reference to the surrogate mother's identity on the child's US birth certificate. Under Californian law, Ms Z. and her husband are considered the baby's parents.

Both women applied for paid leave equivalent to maternity leave or adoption leave. The applications were refused on the ground that Ms D. and Ms Z. had never been pregnant and the children had not been adopted by the parents. The national tribunals before which the two mothers brought actions have asked whether such a refusal is contrary to the Pregnant Workers Directive[6] or whether it constitutes discrimination on the ground of sex or disability (both types of discrimination being prohibited under the Equal Treatment Directive[7] and Employment Equality Framework Directive[8] respectively)? In its judgments, the Court of Justice replies that EU law does not provide for commissioning mothers to be entitled to paid leave equivalent to maternity leave or adoption leave.

The last case I want to focus on is the *Association de médiation sociale* (AMS) case of 15 January 2014.[9] It deals with the horizontal effect of the Charter of Fundamental Rights of the European Union.[10] More precisely, the AMS is an association governed by the Law of 1 July 1901 on the Contract of Association. This association participates in the implementation of social mediation measures and measures for the prevention of crime in the city of Marseille (France). On 4 June 2010, the *Union départementale CGT des Bouches-du-Rhône* appointed Mr Laboubi as representative of the trade union section created within the AMS. The AMS challenged that appointment. It took the view that it had staff numbers of fewer than 11 and, a fortiori, fewer than 50 employees and that, as a result, it is not required, under the relevant national French legislation, to take measures for the representation of employees, such as the election of a staff representative. The

[6] Council Directive 92/85/EC of 19 October 1992. on the introduction of measures to encourage improvements in the safety and health at work of pregnant workers and workers who have recently given birth or are breastfeeding (tenth individual Directive within the meaning of Art 16(1) of Directive 89/391EEC), OJ L 348, 28.11.1992, as amended by Directive 2007/30/EC, OJ L 165, 27.6.2007.

[7] Directive 2006/54/EC (recast) of the European Parliament and of the Council of 5 July 2006 on the implementation of the principle of equal opportunities and equal treatment between men and women in matters of employment and occupation [2006] OJ L 204/23.

[8] Council Directive 2000/78/EC of 27 November 2000 establishing a general framework for equal treatment in employment and occupation [2000] OJ L 303/16.

[9] Case C-176/12, *Association de médiation sociale*, EU:C:2014:2.

[10] Charter of Fundamental Rights of the European Union, OJ C 326/391 of 26 October 2012.

Tribunal d'instance de Marseille (Marseille District Court) referred a priority question on constitutionality to the *Cour de cassation* (Court of Cassation) concerning the provisions of Article L. 1111-3 of the Labour Code. The Cour de cassation referred that question to the *Conseil constitutionnel* (Constitutional Council). On 29 April 2011, the *Conseil constitutionnel* declared that Article L. 1111-3 of the Labour Code was not unconstitutional. Before the *Tribunal d'instance de Marseille*, Mr Laboubi and the *Union locale des syndicats CGT des Quartiers Nord* supported by the *Union départementale CGT des Bouches-du-Rhône* and the CGT as intervening party submitted that the provisions of Article L. 1111-3 of the Labour Code are nevertheless contrary to European Union law and to the French Republic's international commitments.[11] In these circumstances, the *Cour de cassation* decided to stay the proceedings and to refer questions to the Court for a preliminary ruling: Can Article 27 of the Charter about the fundamental right of workers to information and consultation be invoked in a dispute between private individuals in order to assess the compliance [with European Union law] of a national measure implementing the Directive? If so, does it preclude the application of a national legislative provision? The Court determined that Article 27 of the Charter cannot be invoked in a litigation between individuals because of the non-unconditional nature of this Article.

These two examples will be a basis for identifying legal risks. They will provide for a study of the context and the actors: On the one hand, it is the multiplication of legal orders which leads to legal risks (I). On the other hand, it is the actors' choices and first of all the choice of the judge of Luxembourg (II).

2 Social Legal Risks in a Context of a Tangled Web of Legal Orders

In the field of EU social law, the risk is not related to an earthquake or pollution, to a factual change. It is related to the pace of legal and regulatory change at national and EU level. These changes limit and increase legal uncertainty at the same time. According to the subsidiarity principle, in so far as the objectives cannot be sufficiently achieved by the Member States, the European Union is pressed to elaborate appropriate answers to this global occurrence of social disasters. Thus EU law creates new obligations and massive regulations: over 1500 regulations, 132 directives and 1600 decisions in 2014.[12] Public authorities and private entities

---

[11] Ruling again on 7 July 2011, the *Tribunal d'instance de Marseille* upheld these arguments and did not apply Article L. 1111-3 of the Labour Code on the ground that it did not comply with European Union Law. The tribunal thus declared the appointment of Mr Laboubi as trade union section representative to be valid, after finding that, without the exclusions established by Article L. 1111-3 of the Labour Code, the staff numbers of the association in question would be far above the threshold of 50 employees. The AMS brought an appeal before the *Cour de cassation* against that judgment.

[12] According EUR-Lex database.

are increasingly looking for effective monitoring of EU law. The adjunction of national legal orders and a superior one leads to a theoretical coordination (Sect. 2.1) and in practice a mess (Sect. 2.2).

2.1 Between Coordination of Laws

2.1.1 History of Social Law in the Treaties: Directives and Regulations

The first thing to recall is that the social sphere was initially excluded from the Treaties. This exclusion did not aim to deny the importance of this dimension, but to leave to States the choice as to the best protection of their workers, citizens and residents. The diversity of welfare state models and social protections led to a simple coordination of social securities of the different Member States and no harmonization. The progressive apparition of a social protocol and then a social chapter led to a more intense collaboration between Member States in the development and protection of social and labour rights. The EU (or in other words the Members States together in the Council) seem nowadays ready to adopt a broader vision of EU social law and propose more unified solutions to their common problems of employment, discrimination and social inclusion or the restrictions of EU social law. A certain federalism has been reached. It must be remembered, however, not only that Member States keep their sovereignty in the social field, but also that European and national answers deal with pragmatic issues far from a symbolic declaration of federalism: A practical approximation of national social policies even though they keep their own characteristics.

The EU has a competence in the social field that is not exclusive. It is a shared competence with the Member States.[13] The EU does not have its own budget.[14] This situation is original, *sui generis*. Some have qualified it as a recomposed integration.[15]

2.1.2 Two Examples

Two examples of these developments can be taken from the three cases presented in the introduction. In the *AMS* case,[16] the judges relied on several texts beyond the Treaties themselves. The Charter of Fundamental Rights is primary law. It is used in this instance to protect the right to information and consultation and to determine how this right should be implemented within a small French association. This is a

---

[13] Maitrot de la Motte (2015).

[14] Brunessen et al. (2015).

[15] Brunessen et al. (2015).

[16] Case C-176/12, *Association de médiation sociale*, EU:C:2014:2.

particularly interesting example as it shows already how difficult it can be to determine what belongs to the EU social field and what remains the State's realm. The question is raised here because this right which is in the Charter—an EU primary law text which has been added to the Lisbon Treaty[17] as a protocol and which thus has the same legal value—is not in the social chapter of the Treaty itself. The only information and consultation does not concern French entities, but European social dialogue or maybe the European Works Council.[18] The principle of subsidiarity justifies that EU law is supposed to be devoted only to European matters. Directive 2002/14 is also mentioned in this case as it provides a good example of implementation of EU law in the field of employment legislation in the EU. The Directive establishes a general framework for informing and consulting employees in the European Community, creates general and flexible obligations promoting high trust relationships between workers and employers—workplace partnership—and improves risk anticipation, employability, adaptability and competitiveness.

In the *Z* case,[19] Directives 92/85[20] and 2006/54[21] also provide good examples of social protection in the field of maternity leave and equality between men and women.

2.1.3 Supranational Organisation Which Does not Prevent the Limitation of Legal Risks

The EU appears to be a complex supranational organisation which does not prevent the limitation of legal risks. Indeed, coordination and workability are encouraged. Four techniques of coordination have been identified by scholars[22]:

a) The coordination of economic and budgetary policies imposes strong constraints on the financing of social protection, especially in periods of financial crisis. The States are limited in the way they can use social protection to stabilise their

---

[17] Treaty of Lisbon amending the Treaty on European Union and the Treaty establishing the European Community, OJ C 306 of 17 December 2007.

[18] Available at: http://ec.europa.eu/social/main.jsp?catId=329&langId=fr and Directive 94/45/CE.

[19] Case C-363/12, *Z.versus A Government Department and the Board of Management of a Community School*, EU: C: 2014:159.

[20] Council Directive 92/85/EC of 19 October 1992. on the introduction of measures to encourage improvements in the safety and health at work of pregnant workers and workers who have recently given birth or are breastfeeding (tenth individual Directive within the meaning of Art 16(1) of Directive 89/391EEC), OJ L 348, 28.11.1992, as amended by Directive 2007/30/EC, OJ L 165, 27.6.2007.

[21] Directive 2006/54/EC (recast) of the European Parliament and of the Council of 5 July 2006 on the implementation of the principle of equal opportunities and equal treatment between men and women in matters of employment and occupation [2006] OJ L 204/23.

[22] Blot et al. (2014), no. 134.

activities. They are encouraged (or sometimes obliged) to go down the path of social dumping[23];

b) Free movement of persons, freedom of establishment and competition law create constraints relating to the subjugation of workers to national laws. Interim work and posted workers from one country to another are a way to circumvent national labour laws and choose the location of contributions according to a specific social protection model;
c) Competition law and Treaty interpretation by the ECJ create the limits of public intervention in the field of social insurance: for an insurance to benefit from an exclusion of EU competition obligations, it has to fulfil numerous strict conditions regarding its social objects, its beneficiaries, its purposes, etc.
d) Citizens' rights and the non-discrimination principle create primary law and secondary law obligations (for instance about retirement age or family advantages).

2.2 *And Confusion of Laws*

Coordination takes place at all levels and in many different fields. This is also why this multiplication can lead to a certain confusion.

2.2.1 Taking Other Legal Orders into Account: Which Ones?

The judge is systematically confronted with transnational situations. For instance, he will be asked to take into account the work relations in a multinational enterprise. The cases mostly involve situations of mobility of workers or transnational norms. Most litigations involve directly or indirectly several legal orders. Often, though, the conflicts will appear at a national level. The litigation will depend on national as well as international laws. Even in the *AMS* case,[24] where a French worker is hired in a French association, the situation becomes transnational when one wonders about the implementation of non-French, i.e., EU law rules.

The judge is thus put in a situation where he should take into account other national norms (from other States) and international norms. Taking into account international norms will have a double effect on the judgement to be given in the case and in the procedure. This is true, for instance, with regard to the impact of the International Labour Organisation or the OECD director principles.

Within the EU, two elements are relevant: the association of supranational treaties and national constitutional traditions as well as the reliance on the European Convention of Fundamental Rights. There is also an attempt to extend

[23] Marzo et al. (2015).

[24] Case C-176/12, *Association de médiation sociale*, EU:C:2014:2.

these tendencies outside the EU, for instance, to associate states like Turkey. In this case, the judge will have a smaller role as association agreements will be more relevant.

In the EU, judges are keen to choose a comparative approach. Not only do they want to be aware of the differences between the Member States, but they also try to identify what an acceptable compromise could be in the light of the Treaties. This has led to talk about multilevel constitutionalism.

2.2.2 Two Examples

In the *Z* case,[25] the Court applies Articles 5, 6, 27(1)(b) and 28(2)(b) of the United Nations Convention on the Rights of Persons with Disabilities, which was approved on behalf of the European Community by the Council Decision 2010/48/EC of 26 November 2009.[26] The Court states that "the primacy of international agreements concluded by the European Union over instruments of secondary law means that those instruments must as far as possible be interpreted in a manner that is consistent with those agreements",[27] but also that "in so far as the obligations imposed by that Convention are addressed to Contracting Parties, that international agreement is 'programmatic'".[28] More generally, it must be borne in mind that, by virtue of Article 216(2) TFEU,[29] where international agreements are concluded by the European Union, they are binding on its institutions and, consequently, they prevail over acts of the European Union.[30]

In the *CD versus ST* case,[31] the transnational situation is less obvious as it appears that the surrogacy and maternity leave took place in the same country within the EU. The question of application of EU law still remains relevant.

In the *AMS* case,[32] a reference is made by the claimants to the French Republic's international commitments. Not only is French Law scrutinised in the light of EU

[25] Case C-363/12, *Z.versus A Government Department and the Board of Management of a Community School*, EU: C: 2014:159.

[26] Council Decision 2010/48/EC of 26 November 2009 concerning the conclusion, by the European Community, of the United Nations Convention on the Rights of Persons with Disabilities OJ 2010 L 23, p. 35.

[27] Joined Cases C-320/11, C-330/11, C-382/11 and C-383/11 *Digitalnet and Others* [2012] ECR, para. 39, and *HK Danmark*, para. 29.

[28] Case C-363/12, *Z.versus A Government Department and the Board of Management of a Community School*, EU: C: 2014:159, para. 88.

[29] Consolidated version of the Treaty on the Functioning of the European Union (TFEU), OJ C 326 of 26 October 2012.

[30] Case C-366/10 *Air Transport Association of America and Others* [2011] ECR I-13755, para. 50, and Joined Cases C-335/11 and C-337/11 *HK Danmark* [2013] ECR, para. 28.

[31] Case C-167/12, *CD versus ST*, EU:C:2014:169.

[32] Case C-176/12, *Association de médiation sociale*, EU:C:2014:2.

law, but also other international commitments. This does not appear as a surprise, but it shows the difficulty for the judge to identify the relevant applicable law.

2.2.3 The Difficult Identification of the Decisive Judge

Another difficulty for the judges is to manage to dialogue with each other. The example of AMS is striking. With the quite recent procedure of preliminary reference made to the *Conseil Constitutionnel*, it is quite difficult to determine which judge (a national supreme court, a national constitutional council or the EU judge) speaks first and/or last. Is the ECJ's ruling facilitated by a previous decision made by the *Conseil Constitutionnel*? Can one conclude that the solution given in AMS was tainted by the French appraisal? It is very difficult to say. Other cases have shown the willingness of the EU judge to give a broader field of application to the Charter, but it is possible that the field of social rights remains one where the Court does not want to go too far, especially in light of the UK's and Poland's refusal to participate.[33] This comment constitutes a prefect transition between the multiplying legal orders and the hesitating judge caught in the middle of them.

3 Social Legal Risks in the Hands of the European Court of Justice

In this context of entangled legal orders and norms, the European judge appears creative (Sect. 3.1) and at the same time frightened (Sect. 3.2).

3.1 Creative Judge

3.1.1 An Innovative Judge

The ECJ has proved very active since its creation. It has changed the face of EU law. EU social law has often been a field of experimentation. A transnational space of action is legitimised by the judge. The *Van Gend en* Loos[34] and *Costa*[35] cases have been commented on so many times that we tend to forget what a revolution they engendered. The direct access to the court of individuals from all Member States has now become a routine and is used regularly in most countries. This

[33] See the relevant protocol to the Treaty as well as the *Laval* and *Viking* cases where the reference to the Charter did not lead to a strong protection of social rights.

[34] C-26/62 *Van Gend en Loos v Administratie der Belastingen* [1963] ECR 1.

[35] Case C-6/64, *Costa v. E.N.E.L.* [1964] ECR I-585.

massive change has not been limited to EU social law, but it has contributed to its evolution.

Non-discrimination law has also been radically changed. We will only briefly remind our readers about the *Marshall* case[36] and many others which have reversed the burden of proof of the discrimination. The whole equality package has a case law origin. It now constitutes one of the strongest developments of EU law and dozens of cases are judged by the ECJ on a yearly basis on all grounds of discrimination. The discrimination on the ground of nationality was recognised in 1957.

The *AMS* case[37] shows again the power of the judge to create and change the law in an unexpected way. The Court considers, and this is not exactly a surprise, that Directive 2002/14[38] and Article 27 of the Charter of Fundamental Rights are directly applicable to national law. What is most remarkable in the current state of EU law and what most commentators, especially constitutional lawyers, have noticed is that Directive 2002/14 and Article 27 of the Charter are applicable to the case, but they cannot be invoked in a dispute between individuals in order to rule out a national provision implementing that Directive, such as Article L. 1111-3 of the French Labour Code. The *Kücükdeveci* case[39] exception remains where applicable.

The evolution shows law in action. It also reveals that legal risks are everywhere. The ECJ feels the need to make law evolve in an unexpected way. It pushes further integration in one case and then takes a step back in the following case. Although this attitude is fascinating to academics, it is a bit more difficult in terms of legal risks. It makes it quite difficult to determine where the new battles will be and what can be relied on.

To come back to the case, since its solution does not help the claim, the Court proposes an alternative solution which consists in a new damages claim against France (on the ground of the *Francovich* case[40]). This is interesting as it shows that there always is a way to ensure the application of EU law. It is a new type of action that creates a new opening. Legal risks are thus important. They are increased even more by the wide margin of appreciation that the principle of proportionality gives to the judge.

---

[36] Case C-409/95, *Marshall* [1997] ECR I-06363.

[37] Case C-176/12, *Association de médiation sociale*, EU:C:2014:2.

[38] Directive 2002/14/EC of the European Parliament and of the Council of 11 March 2002 establishing a general framework for informing and consulting employees in the European Community – Joint declaration of the European Parliament, the Council and the Commission on employee representation, OJ L 80, 23.3.2002, pp. 29–34.

[39] Case C-555/07, *Seda Kücükdeveci* [2010] ECR I-00365.

[40] Joined cases C-6/90 and C-9/90, *Francovich and Bonifaci v Italy* [1991] ECR I-05357.

3.1.2 Proportionality: A Judge with a Wide Margin of Appreciation

In general terms proportionality is the flexibility tool of the Court. Even though it is theoretically framed in two rational questions (Is the measure necessary? Could it be achieved in another way?), the answers to these questions require a very pragmatic and practical analysis of the cases. They sometimes need a technical analysis too, which is difficult for the judge to obtain. They also give the judge a margin of appreciation. It is a way to ascertain fundamental principles of EU law and still to reach an opposite solution (than the one which would be dictated by the application of these principles) because it seems more appropriate on non-legal grounds. In other words, proportionality is a non-legal tool hidden in the middle of a legal analysis and it has a defining influence.

In our examples, the judge is given a very open choice. In the *Z* case,[41] the Court can freely, consciously, morally decide whether or not refusing maternity leave to an intended mother after a surrogacy is a violation of EU law. It is a question of interpretation. We could have easily imagined that the Court would use exactly the same legal basis in order to reach an opposite solution. More precisely, in this case, the Court considers that Directive 2006/54/EC of the European Parliament and of the Council of 5 July 2006 on the implementation of the principle of equal opportunities and equal treatment of men and women in matters of employment and occupation,[42] in particular Articles 4 and 14 thereof, must be interpreted as meaning that a refusal to provide paid leave equivalent to maternity leave to a female worker who as a commissioning mother has had a baby through a surrogacy arrangement does not constitute discrimination on the ground of sex. It adds that Council Directive 2000/78/EC of 27 November 2000 establishing a general framework for equal treatment in employment and occupation[43] must be interpreted as meaning that a refusal to provide paid leave equivalent to maternity leave or adoptive leave to a female worker who is unable to bear a child and who has availed of a surrogacy arrangement does not constitute discrimination on the ground of disability.

On the one hand, the Court considers that the situation of the commissioning mother as regards the grant of adoptive leave is not within the scope of this Directive. On the other hand, there is no discrimination on the ground of disability. It would have been easy to imagine opposite outcomes. In the *Coleman* case[44] for instance, the Court has agreed to extend the category of victims of discrimination

---

[41] Case C-363/12, *Z.versus A Government Department and the Board of Management of a Community School*, EU: C: 2014:159.

[42] Directive 2006/54/EC (recast) of the European Parliament and of the Council of 5 July 2006 on the implementation of the principle of equal opportunities and equal treatment between men and women in matters of employment and occupation [2006] OJ L 204/23.

[43] Council Directive 2000/78/EC of 27 November 2000 establishing a general framework for equal treatment in employment and occupation [2000] OJ L 303/16.

[44] Case C-303/06, *Coleman* [2008] ECR I-05603.

thus creating a new collateral beneficiary of the non-discrimination Directives. This was a creative interpretation which illuminates the refusals here.

In the *AMS* case,[45] again, the judge has an open choice as to whether the application of the Charter of Fundamental Rights should be recognised or not. Whatever his decision is, it is easy to find a legal argument to justify it. The choice not to apply the Charter is in this case justified by its final Articles and the respect for the Member States' sovereignties, but a contrary decision might have been based on the necessity to ensure a uniform application of EU law. This analysis can be found, for instance, in the recent opinion 2/14 where the Court does not hesitate to remind us about the specific nature of EU law and its need to be differentiated from other legal systems. This is in a context of rejecting the proposal of association between ECJ and ECHR, but it shows the political relevance of the judge of Luxembourg. The *AMS* case[46] must be compared with the *Laval*[47] and *Viking*[48] cases where the Court had decided to go forward in the recognition of fundamental social rights and in the proclamation of the Charter's effect. This was more than 10 years ago, but it shows how non-legal elements shape the Court's decision-making. In these cases again, the Court had ascertained the principles to then have recourse to the proportionality principle and finally give the last word and more weight to the economic freedoms.

These analyses might give the impression of a very active judge, very aware of globalisation. Still, these three cases taken all together give a very dismissive overall stand of EU law. One could contend that it is this mere freedom which has led to making the EU judge not only a creative judge, but also a frightened judge. Too much power requires limitation. The judge is thus put in a situation of self-censorship. The Luxembourg judge is frightened especially in the social field. He tries not to disturb national preferences and sovereignties. He tries not to go too far in his interpretation of social rights (sometimes in opposition with economic rights).

3.2 Frightened Judge

The EU judge is caught between subsidiarity and national sovereignty on the one hand and his own power in the light of a horizontal separation of powers between EU institutions on the other hand.

[45] Case C-176/12, *Association de médiation sociale*, EU:C:2014:2.

[46] Case C-176/12, *Association de médiation sociale*, EU:C:2014:2.

[47] Case C-341/05, *Laval un Partneri* [2007] ECR I-11767.

[48] Case C-438/05, *The International Transport Workers' Federation and The Finnish Seamen's Union* [2007] ECR I-10779.

3.2.1 Between Subsidiarity and Sovereignty

According to the subsidiarity principle, in so far as the objectives cannot be sufficiently achieved by the Member States, the European Union is pressed to elaborate appropriate answers to the global occurrence of social disasters.

This can lead to a limited transnational *lex laboris*. The judge tries shyly to determine a minimal protection in very limited fields. Global analysis of the reactions to the financial crisis in the framework of multilevel constitutionalism has been an opportunity to rethink the EU social model and its functioning.

In the *CD versus ST* case,[49] the Court gives a wide margin of appreciation to the Member States. Its use of the principle of proportionality is probably justified by the attempt not to interfere with national social preferences since surrogacy is a very hot subject and more EU countries refuse to recognise it than to accept it. It is likely that the Court was simply trying to avoid misunderstandings. One can already imagine titles in legal journals and press such as ‘the ECJ recognises the legitimacy of surrogacy’. This is unfortunate as it was not the question of the case. The point was to recognise workers’ rights in countries which have agreed to make surrogacy legal. The Court could have concluded that maternity leave should be given and that there is a discrimination between men and women in the light of EU law, but it chose not to do so in order not to force Member States to have to take into account surrogacy that is recognised in other States. Similarly, in the *AMS* case,[50] the Court considers that Article 27 of the Charter cannot be applied since it has a programmatic character.

3.2.2 Towards an Accentuation of Inequalities in Order to Respect the States’ Sovereignties

The role of judges in the field of EU social law has long been to fight and limit inequalities. This role might be diminished today because the Court is more willing to listen to the states thus increasing legal risks.

In the *Z* case,[51] the Court considers that there is no discrimination because the father of the surrogate child would be treated in the same way. The States are not obliged to give maternity leave to intended mothers. The Court ruled that Directive 92/85[52] “must be interpreted as meaning that Member States are not required to

[49] Case C-167/12, *CD versus ST*, EU:C:2014:169.

[50] Case C-176/12, *Association de médiation sociale*, EU:C:2014:2.

[51] Case C-363/12, *Z.versus A Government Department and the Board of Management of a Community School*, EU: C: 2014:159.

[52] Council Directive 92/85/EC of 19 October 1992. on the introduction of measures to encourage improvements in the safety and health at work of pregnant workers and workers who have recently given birth or are breastfeeding (tenth individual Directive within the meaning of Art 16(1) of Directive 89/391EEC), OJ L 348, 28.11.1992, as amended by Directive 2007/30/EC, OJ L 165, 27.6.2007.

provide maternity leave pursuant to Article 8 of that directive to a female worker who as a commissioning mother has had a baby through a surrogacy arrangement, even in circumstances where she may breastfeed the baby following the birth or where she does breastfeed the baby".[53] The Court refuses to identify discrimination as such, but still distinguishes between breastfeeding mothers and birth mothers which is surprising. In the same case, the Court also refuses to identify a handicap since "the concept of 'disability' within the meaning of Directive 2000/78 presupposes that the limitation from which the person suffers, in interaction with various barriers, may hinder that person's full and effective participation in professional life on an equal basis with other workers".[54] Here again one could have expected a more avant-garde analysis since work makes the welcoming of the surrogate child more difficult.

In the *CD versus ST* case,[55] we find again a scared judge who does not prevent the national legislator to go further thus opening the door to legal risks. The judge considers "that directive does not in any way preclude Member States from applying or introducing laws, regulations or administrative provisions more favourable to the protection of the safety and health of commissioning mothers who have had babies through a surrogacy arrangement by allowing them to take maternity leave as a result of the birth of the child".[56] Here, the judge refuses to impose his interpretation of fundamental rights. A dialogue of judges is identified even if this discourse involves self-limitation. This can be explained by a strong controversy regarding the Charter which has led to the adoption of two protocols, one giving the Charter the same value as the Treaties, the other allowing for the non-application of this Charter to the UK and Poland.

Another justification comes from the refusal to recognise the social parent or the social role of the parent. This is particularly surprising since the Court tries to use its protective role. It says that "the right to maternity leave granted to pregnant workers must be regarded as a particularly important mechanism of protection under employment law".[57] Also that "a maternity leave from which the female worker benefits is intended, first, to protect a woman's biological condition during and after pregnancy and, secondly, to protect the special relationship between a woman and her child over the period which follows pregnancy and childbirth, by preventing that relationship from being disturbed by the multiple burdens which would result from the simultaneous pursuit of employment".[58] It would have been very easy to

---

[53] Case C-363/12, *Z.versus A Government Department and the Board of Management of a Community School*, EU: C: 2014:159, para. 58.

[54] Ibid., para. 80.

[55] Case C-167/12, *CD versus ST*, EU:C:2014:169.

[56] Ibid., para. 42.

[57] Ibid., para. 32.

[58] Ibid., para. 34 and see, in particular, Case 184/83 *Hofmann* [1984] ECR 3047, para. 25; Case C-116/06, *Kiiski* [2007] ECR I-07643, para. 46; Case C-5/12, *Betriu Montull*, EU:C:2013:571, para. 50.

construct an interpretation widening the access to maternity leave. This difficulty for the judge to accept his priorities and the will to satisfy all parties increase legal risks. The situation is also influenced by a parallel attempt to respect political decisions.

3.2.3 The Respect of Political Decisions

The will for the ECJ to respect political decisions comes from a traditional distinction between legal affairs and political affairs and should be praised. A balance, however, should always be attained. This will in the EU social context lead to uncertainty as to the ability of the judge to solve conflicts. A very good example is provided by a refusal of the ECJ to recognise its competence to answer a case about Greek social protection.[59] The claimants want, like several authors before them,[60] a better recognition of fundamental rights. In the Greek case, the claimants ask for the recognition of their patrimonial rights on the ground of Article 1 Protocol 1 of the European Convention of Human Rights.[61] Their rights are infringed by measures imposing pensions' and salaries' reduction.[62] Also, these measures go beyond the competences given to the European Commission and the Council by the Treaty, specifically Articles 4 and 5 TEU[63] about the principle of subsidiarity[64] and proportionality and Article 5, paragraph 2 TEU, which states that all competences not given to the Union in the Treaties belong to the Member States. Finally, according to Article 126 and following TFEU, the measures which can be decided upon by the Council in the framework of an excessive deficit procedure cannot be "concrete, absolute of without exceptions", and this is not the case here.[65]

4 Conclusion

The general impression is that the EU social context makes it more likely to fear uncertainty. Its main actor, the ECJ, has recently had an attitude which does not allow claimants and defendants to expect a definite answer.

---

[59] Case T-541/10, *Anotati Dioikisi Enoseon Dimosion Ypallilon (ADEDY) versus Council of the European Union*, EU:T:2012:626.

[60] Costamagna (2012), p. 7.

[61] European Convention for the Protection of Human Rights and Fundamental Freedoms (ECHR).

[62] Case T-541/10, *Anotati Dioikisi Enoseon Dimosion Ypallilon (ADEDY) versus Council of the European Union*, EU:T:2012:626.

[63] Consolidated version of the Treaty on European Union (TEU), OJ C 326 of 26 October 2012.

[64] Clément-Wiltz et al. (2015).

[65] The legal basis, according to the claimants, should not have been Article 126, paragraph 9, and Article 136 TFEU, but the bilateral agreement.

More generally, legal risks are numerous in any given legal order. This is even truer in the EU. Legal certainty is scarce in the EU, and more specifically in European social law. The numerous levels of jurisdiction, the multitude of actors and the unclear hierarchy between sources, powers, legislators and judges create a frightening picture.

Still, this black scenario should not lead to extreme concern. The European Union has proved resilient on many occasions and its lack of clarity might as well be an asset of its long-lasting judgements. Similarly, the difficulties of implementation can correspond with the needs for certain countries to be given more time to allow for a legal adaptation. More generally, legal uncertainty is probably one of the most common characteristics of law.

Another reason not to be overwhelmingly worried is that this whole analysis should be nuanced. The judges' hesitations depicted here are framed within a whole solid legal order, a general framework of hard and soft law, which pushes forward EU social law and ascertains its overall stability when details remain unpredictable.

Having started to analyse EU social law in terms of the risks created, the next step is to focus on limiting these risks and determining a viable way to tackle them. Thus, "risk is not the same as catastrophe, but the anticipation of the future catastrophe in the presence". In that sense, legal risk management anticipates the social threats through precaution and prevention. The legal approach shall focus on identifying legal responsibilities from the (EU) law making process to the (EU) law compliance.

As a conclusion, legal risk management may become a key scientific and practical approach for the European Union to assess the impact of its current and potential social legislation. As part of the better regulation policy, the European Commission itself stated that "decision-makers are often faced with the need to reduce or eliminate the risk of adverse effects to the environment or to health. When the problem you are dealing with is affected by risk, i.e. you can attach probabilities to different possible outcomes, the impact assessment will have to include a risk assessment as a tool to determine the best policy to deal with this" (Impact Assessment Guideline, 2009). Legal risks management is a tool to improve the quality of the EU legislation and case law.

Consequently, managing legal risks requires knowledge, methodology, assessment and social acceptance. The objective is not to eliminate the legal risks, but rather to anticipate their impact on public authorities and private entities.

References

Barnard C (2012) EU Employment Law. OUP

Beck U (1992) Risk society: towards a new modernity. Sage, New Delhi (Translated from the German Risikogesellschaft, 1986)

Blot Ch, Rozenberg O, Saraceno F, Streho I (eds) (2014) Réformer l'Europe, OFCE, Débats et Politiques, n° 134, available at: http://www.ofce.sciences-po.fr/pdf/revue/134/revue-134.pdf

Brunessen B, De la Rosa S, Dubout E, Maitrot de la Motte A (2015) L'Union européenne et le fédéralisme économique. Bruylant

Clément-Wiltz L, Dubout E, Maitrot de la Motte A (2015) L'Union européenne et le fédéralisme économique. Bruylant

Costamagna F (2012) Saving Europe 'Under Strict Conditionality': A Threat for EU Social Dimension?, Working Paper-LPF n. 7, Centro Einaudi, Laboratorio di Politica Comparata e Filosofia Pubblica

Giddens A (1999) Runaway world: how globalization is reshaping our lives. Profile, London

Maitrot de la Motte A (2015) In: de la Rosa S, Dubout E, Maitrot de la Motte A (eds) L'Union européenne et le fédéralisme économique. Bruylant

Marzo C, Dubout E, Maitrot de la Motte A (2015) L'Union européenne et le fédéralisme économique. Bruylant

Legal Risks from, to, and within EU Migration Law: An Inventory

Moritz Jesse

Contents

Abstract This chapter argues that European or national legislation seeking to regulate, steer or limit migration out of itself gives rise to risks. It is difficult to imagine an area of law, which is more susceptible to political interventions and heated public debates than the regulation of immigration. On the national level, migration and EU migration rules are perceived as a risk to welfare, social cohesion and national sovereignty. The binding character of EU legislation indeed limits the discretion of Member States significantly. This leads to a continuous struggle between Member States and the EU about the scope of application, effectiveness, and limits of EU migration rules on the national level. In turn, this constellation gives rise to three categories of risks: First, abstract risks such as the lack of legal certainty and undermining of objective and purpose of legislation. Second, institutional risks such as preventing the achievement of political promises or destabilizing national systems of governance. Third and final, individual risks to

M. Jesse (✉)
Europa Institute, Leiden Law School, University of Leiden, Leiden, The Netherlands
e-mail: m.jesse@law.leidenuniv.nl

E. Miščenić, A. Raccah (eds.), *Legal Risks in EU Law*,
DOI 10.1007/978-3-319-28596-2_9

individual immigrants who might suffer from denial of rights, insecurity and marginalization as an effect of the struggle between the EU and its Member States.

1 Introduction: Why is European Migration Law Special?

Engaging in immigration regulation as a politician in the European Union is a risky thing to do. In fact, it is hard to think of any issue today that is as sensitive and burdened with public emotion than immigration. Often, people fall into extremes and plead for utopian reactions to immigration, such as to completely ban immigration from certain parts of the world.[1] An easy way to make discussions about immigration even tenser is to link them to the European Union and its rules and regulations. Immediately, immigration and the regulation of it turns into an issue closely linked to national sovereignty. The decision who is allowed to cross the national border and to stay in a country is often perceived as *the* expression of national sovereignty.[2]

Currently, EU rules and regulations, not only govern the free movement of persons on the EU's internal market, the status of EU citizens, but also entry and residence of the majority of non-EU citizens, also known as third-country nationals.[3] These EU measures drastically limit the room for Member States to install their own policies governing migration. In a time when some national governments want to make immigration regulation stricter, EU regulation functions as a minimum norm and limits the Member States. This leads to tensions not only between the EU and the national level, but also between immigrants and national authorities in situations where the latter do not apply EU norms and regulations correctly resulting in the denial of EU rights to individuals. Naturally, this exposes the field of EU migration law to risks that put the stability and certainty of national migration and EU rules in peril.

This chapter will throw some light on the question how far the legal, social, and political context implies risks threatening as well as emanating from the system created by EU migration law. As such, it will reflect on what exactly the effects are of the tense situation within which EU migration regulation has to function. The effects will then be presented through an inventory of potential risks on the national and European level as well as the level of individual persons.

---

[1] See, for example, the election programme of the Dutch right wing populist party *PVV*, the party of Geert Wilders, categorically wanting to ban immigration from 'all Islam countries', Partij voor de Vrijheid (PVV) 2012, pp. 34–37.

[2] Dauvergne (2004), pp. 288–290.

[3] See the overview of the EU acquis on free movement and migration regulation, http://eur-lex.europa.eu/summary/chapter/justice_freedom_security.html?root_default=SUM_1_CODED%3D23, SUM_2_CODED%3D2301&obsolete=false, accessed 21 April 2015.

For the purposes of this chapter, the following shall be understood as EU migration law and the following shall be contained in the system created by EU migration law: *Firstly*, there are the rules governing the free movement of economically active persons on the EU's internal market. Traditionally, primary law, i.e. the founding Treaties, more specifically the TFEU, allows for free movement of workers, the freedom to provide services and to establish oneself in another Member State.[4] These rights have been specified by secondary legislation.[5] *Secondly*, there is primary and secondary law governing the rights of EU citizens at large when they move to another Member State for economic or non-economic purposes.[6] The first two categories basically provide equal rights to EU citizens with the local population when moving to another Member State as a matter of principle. *Thirdly*, there is a large *acquis* of rules and regulations that provides rights and procedures for admitting third-country nationals, such as EU rules on family reunification, long-term residence, or the admission of highly qualified workers.[7] EU rules on asylum and those seeking to combat irregular migration also fall within this third category of EU migration law.[8] *Fourthly*, the Charter of Fundamental Rights of the EU also contains rights which do and will influence the legal situation of migrants in the EU, regardless of their nationality and status.[9]

All of these rules bind the Member States. They contain provisions, which have a direct effect on the national legal orders of the Member States and on which individuals can rely in cases against the State when they feel that their EU rights are violated.[10] The European Court of Justice has interpreted these rules in many cases, upholding the rights provided for individuals, and struck down national legislation restricting the *effet utile* of EU rules in a disproportionate manner.[11] During these proceedings about the legality of national legislation the tense character of this field of law has been most tangible.

This contribution is not meant to be an elaborate treatise of the issues and risks mentioned. It cannot be. Others have dwelled upon the various aspects in much more detail and better than this contribution ever could.[12] In this chapter, individual

[4] Arts. 45, 49, 56 TFEU.

[5] For example, in Regulation (EU) 492/2011 of 5 April 2011 on freedom of movement for workers within the Union, codifying Regulation (EEC) 1612/68 and its successive modifications (Council Regulations 312/76 and 2434/92, and Article 38(1) of Directive 2004/38/EC).

[6] Arts. 20, 21, 22 TFEU, and Directive 2004/38/EC of 29 April 2004 on the right of citizens of the Union and their family members to move and reside freely within the territory of the Member States.

[7] See for legislation, http://europeanmigrationlaw.eu/en, accessed 21 April 2015.

[8] *Ibid.*

[9] For example, Arts. 6, 7, 45 Charter of Fundamental Rights of the European Union (OJ 2010 C83/02).

[10] See for more information on this issue, de Witte (2011), pp. 323–361.

[11] See Case C-578/08 *Rhimou Chakroun v Minister van Buitenlandse Zaken* [2010] ECR I-01839 for Directive 2003/86; or for Directive 2004/38 Case C-127/08 B*laise Baheten Metock and Others v Minister for Justice, Equality and Law Reform* [2010] ECR I-06241.

[12] See for example Shaw (2011), pp. 575–609.

legislation and case law is only referred to as examples and not as items of analysis themselves. However, what this chapter will provide is a brief inventory of risks to the system of EU migration law and of risks presumed to emanate from it. It will be shown that these risks derive from a complex web of interdependent issues. The following structure has been chosen: *The next section* will be looking at EU migration law from the national perspective. Issues such as the national debate on migration, the limitation of sovereign prerogatives in the field of migration and the resulting risks to coherence and legal certainty of national and EU law will be elaborated upon. Section 3 will deal with the specific nature of EU migration law and the risk arising from it. Section 4 will chart some of the risks posed to stakeholders, i.e. individual migrants, but also national policy makers. Section 5 will provide a schematic overview of the interdependencies of risks. The objective is to show that while there are abstract risks for the legal systems involved, and there are also certain risks for actors in the field of immigration, the most tangible risks are those of individual immigrants who are likely to suffer from the risks circling around EU migration law first.

2 Putting EU Migration Law at Risk: The National Perspective and Its Consequences

There are certain risks that directly stem from the nature of the political debate about migration in the EU. These are risks national politicians think come from EU migration law, which would go against national policies and interests. Trying to protect these national interests, however, inevitably puts the functioning and coherence of EU migration law at risk. The instinct of protecting national interests has also had direct effects on the very nature of EU migration legislation. Generally, these legal measures are full of undefined terminology and ample exceptions designed to protect existing national legislation. This, in turn, gives rise to the risk to legal certainty and *effet utile* of EU migration measures. This network of issues, which makes EU migration law a rather special affair, will be introduced in this section there under.

2.1 Risks Allegedly Stemming from Open EU Borders and EU Migration Policies

It is no secret that an increasing number of national governments and politicians in the EU look at EU migration and EU migration law critically. Several risks are regularly presented in this regard as intrinsically linked to immigration at large and the movement of people in the EU in particular. *Firstly*, there are economic risks migrants are allegedly posing. Often, migration from outside, but also the free movement of EU citizens from one Member State to another, is portrayed as a threat to public safety, public order, and social welfare. As a matter of fact, election campaigns are fought largely over the issue of immigration and the economic threat it is posing. Welfare tourism is high up the political agenda and the objective limitation of migration of EU citizens as well as third-country nationals for the sake of protecting the national welfare system has become mainstream politics, regardless of the fact that migration does not put economic development at peril.[13]

Secondly, and even more emotionally, is the risk migrants are thought to be posing to the social fabric of the nation state itself. Often, one hears allegations that immigrants are culturally so different that they would pose a threat to the good functioning of the receiving society because they would undermine the social homogeneity and cohesion of the receiving society.[14] These risks are frequently felt because of the mere presence of migrants, irrelevant of what they do and why they are there. Despite the fact that the alleged homogeneity of national societies is fiction,[15] in order to counter this perceived threat, immigrants have to fulfil the mandatory integration conditions in many European countries.[16] These integration conditions often consist of language courses and civic orientation exams before a secure residence permit is granted.[17] Following this logic, secure residence rights are a reward for integration and no longer a tool for achieving it.[18] The objective of such formal integration trajectories is to allow migrants to integrate more smoothly into the new society and to bring them closer to the mainstream of society.[19] In other words, these measures are installed to protect what is thought to be a reflection of cultural and social homogeneity of the receiving society. The new trend to force migrants to follow integration trajectories has even been called 'best practice' for integration on the EU level.[20] However, EU law only allows these measures to a limited extent for third-country nationals and they are absolutely forbidden for any EU citizen or their family members moving to another Member State.[21]

In conclusion, these two risks emanating from EU migration law identified on the national level have one thing in common as they both circle around the feeling

---

[13] See the publication OECD 2014 titled '*Is migration good for the economy?*' on this matter, available at http://www.oecd.org/migration/mig/OECD%20Migration%20Policy%20Debates%20Numero%202.pdf, accessed 13.08.2015.

[14] Groenendijk (2004), pp. 111–126.

[15] Lübbe-Wolff (2007), p. 121.

[16] See the elaborate study Carrera and Faure (2011), available at http://www.ceps.eu/system/files/book/2011/07/Integration%20as%20a%20Two-way%20Process.pdf, accessed 13.08.2015.

[17] de Vries (2014), pp. 417–420.

[18] Groenendijk (2004), pp. 111–114.

[19] See arguments of the Dutch governments as reported by AG Kokott in the Opinion of Advocate General Kokott delivered on 19 March 2015 in Case C-153/14 *Minister van Buitenlandse Zaken v K and A*, not yet reported.

[20] *Common Basic Principles of Immigration Integration*, Justice and Home Affairs Council Conclusions, 19 November 2004.

[21] See Jesse (2011), p. 173.

of disempowerment of the national regulators to react to these risks because they have to obey EU regulation. Due to EU law, they cannot prevent the entry and residence of certain groups of individuals. Moreover, because of rights attached to EU citizenship, they cannot push back migrants from other EU Member States, or deny them access to the national social welfare systems if conditions of EU law, not national law, are met.[22] Member States cannot deny entry and residence of third-country nationals without accepting the limits set to their actions by EU law, even to protect social cohesion.[23] All action on the national level regarding migration control has to be within the scope of what is allowed under EU law. This can be perceived as a risk.

2.2 *Risks for National Immigration Legislation Arising from the Duty to Obey EU Law*

Apart from the anecdotal risks introduced above, there are some technical legal risks EU (migration) law poses to the national legal system, which have to be acknowledged. In this instance, EU migration law is not special, because the mechanism set out thereunder applies for all national regulations. What is different, however, is the heated debate about immigration on the national level and the perception that migration is the expression of national sovereignty. Cases stating that national laws violate EU regulations inevitably heat up discussions on whether the limitation of sovereign national prerogatives to control immigration by EU law is appropriate and acceptable.

Since the seminal cases of *van Gent en Loos* and *Costa v ENEL* in the 1960s, it has been established that EU law has direct effect on the national legal order of the Member States and that, in case of conflict with national norms, EU law is supreme. This means that individuals can rely on directly effective EU law in national procedures and that national authorities and judges *have to* set aside national law, including immigration regulations that violate EU rules.[24]

Such orders to setting aside and no longer applying national rules will always be the result of individual cases concerning individual rules of EU and national law and have the potential effect of cutting out specific provisions of national law. This poses the general risk of disrupting a formerly coherent system in national legislation.

A good example is the ongoing limitation of mandatory integration conditions Member States are allowed to install for immigrants. These measures ideally prepare immigrants for a life in the host society through language training and civic orientation courses. Currently, such conditions are in place in Germany,

---

[22] Case C-333/13 *Elisabeta Dano, Florin Dano v Jobcenter Leipzig*, not yet reported.

[23] Jesse (2014), pp. 88–89.

[24] See de Witte (2011), pp. 323–361.

France, the Netherlands, Austria, Denmark, and the UK.[25] From the national perspectives, of course, one should subject all immigrants to such integration conditions to avoid an incoherent system and to maximize the effect such integration courses potentially have on all immigrants. However, such general application of integration measures is not allowed under EU law. At this moment in time, the illegality of integration conditions is established for family members of EU citizens,[26] and Turkish nationals.[27] Most of the Directives governing the immigration of third-country nationals allow for the introduction of integration measures and/or conditions.[28] However, this does not mean that Member States can now introduce such measures for an unlimited period. They will only be allowed to do so, when the *effet utile* of the Directives is preserved and when the objective and purpose of the Directives, which is allowing family reunification,[29] or the attainment of a permanent residence status,[30] for example, is not made impossible. Integration conditions also have to be proportionate to the objective of integration[31]; they are limiting the rights granted in the Directive and have to be interpreted narrowly.[32] To cut a long story short, for third-country nationals, the room for manoeuvre for the Member States to introduce integration conditions is also severely limited by EU law.[33]

If integration conditions for specific groups are taken out of the national legislation one by one, as it has happened in Germany and the Netherlands,[34] it is not hard to imagine that coherence of the national law is slowly vanishing. Needless to say that such case-by-case cutting out of specific conditions not only happened with regard to integration conditions, but also other conditions set by national law and even expressly allowed by EU law, such as financial conditions for family migration.[35] Even though the author agrees with the assessment of legality of the Court regarding the illegality of (integration) conditions, the disruptive effects EU law unfolds on the national level have to be acknowledged.

Moreover, it could be argued that the at times rather progressive interpretation of EU law by the European Court of Justice potentially poses a risk to legal certainty on the national level. The Court is often accused of judicial activism at the expense

---

[25] de Vries (2014), pp. 417–418.

[26] See on this Jesse (2011), pp. 172–178.

[27] Case C-138/13 *Dogan*, not yet reported.

[28] For example art. 7(2) Directive 2003/86/EC, Arts. 5(2), 15(3) Directive 2003/109/EC.

[29] Case C-578/08 *Rhimou Chakroun v Minister van Buitenlandse Zaken* [2010] ECR I-01839.

[30] Case C-571/10 *Servet Kamberaj v Istituto per l'Edilizia sociale della Provincia autonoma di Bolzano (IPES) and Others* [2006] ECR I-6057.

[31] Opinion of Advocate General Kokott delivered on 19 March 2015 in Case C-153/14 *Minister van Buitenlandse Zaken v K and A*, not yet reported.

[32] Opinion of Advocate General Mengozzi delivered on 30 April 2014 in Case C-138/13 *Naime Dogan v Federal Republic of Germany*.

[33] Confirmation of these arguments was recently provided in Case C-153/14 *K and A*, not yet reported.

[34] Klaassen and Lodder (2014), pp. 34–39.

[35] Case C-578/08 *Rhimou Chakroun v Minister van Buitenlandse Zaken* [2010] ECR I-01839.

of national interests. A recent example of such a progressive ruling leading to many discussions on the national level is the Court's decision in the *Zambrano* case. Contrary to the former state of the law, the Court decided that EU citizens could rely on the rights contained in the Treaty in proceedings against their own Member States even though no cross-border effect was present in the case.[36] In the event that national rules would put in danger 'the genuine enjoyment' of rights connected to the status of EU citizen, such as the threat that the citizen would have to leave the territory of the EU altogether, the citizen can rely on his EU rights also against his/her own Member State.[37] This was something new and disruptive to existing national legislation.

It was unclear in how far the Court would allow individuals to argue that their 'genuine enjoyment' of citizenship rights would be in peril. Before *Zambrano*, it was assumed that citizens could only rely on Union Citizenship rights against their own Member State when a crossborder element was present in their case, such as the return to the home state from another Member State. Now the world seemed open to a full internal application of Citizenship rights. In later cases the Court of Justice tried to contain the impact of *Zambrano* and to limit the application of the genuine enjoyment formula.[38] However, the case still creates significant insecurities on the national level and is therefore a good example for the risks EU law and its interpretation by the Court of Justice poses on the national level to legal certainty.

2.3 Risks to the (EU)-Migration Regulation by Member States' Actions

The two last sections introduced the tension that exists between the national and the EU level. It was shown how national legislators and governments perceive EU migration law as a risk to public welfare, public security and social cohesion. Also, it was acknowledged that the direct effect and supremacy of EU law has the potential to disrupt the coherency of national legislation. When looked upon from the EU perspective, this tense relationship with the national level poses a risk in itself. National governments, especially those where discussions of immigration take place prominently within society, will seek to limit the influence of EU migration law on national policies. More precisely, rights provided for in EU migration law will be under permanent attack from the national level. In turn, the

---

[36] Case C-34/09 *Gerardo Ruiz Zambrano v Office national de l'emploi (ONEM)* [2011] ECR I-01177.

[37] Case C-34/09 *Gerardo Ruiz Zambrano v Office national de l'emploi (ONEM)* [2011] ECR I-01177.

[38] Case C-256/11 *Murat Dereci* [2011] ECR I-11315; Case C-434/09 *Shirley McCarthy* [2011] ECR I-03375.

EU level will be in a permanent state of defence against the ongoing calls to restrict EU rights.

There are indeed propositions by some governments to limit rights for EU citizens and even the free movement of workers.[39] Moreover, rights of third-country nationals, especially those of family migrants, are often the target for campaigns to restrict them.[40] Asylum and how to deal with asylum seekers is another issue where Member States consistently try to limit rights that must be granted because of EU legislation. Moreover, borderless travel within the EU's area of freedom, security and justice, i.e. in the absence of border controls, is also questioned and portrayed as a security risk.[41]

Many of these initiatives will not be successful, or were already unsuccessful. However, it is not ruled out that the increasing political pressure, especially in the area of migration, will lead to restrictions of rights in the future. It has happened before with the restriction of free movement of workers from the new Eastern Member States. Their rights to free movement as workers could be restricted by Member States for a certain period after accession for the sake of protecting the labour markets of the old Member States.[42] It was the first time that such selective restrictions based on nationality to a fundamental freedom of the internal market were installed.

It should be remarked here that the national governments, who are advocating for the restriction of EU rights, are co-legislators on the EU level. They are the ones who have adopted all secondary legislation in its current form together with the European Parliament. Regarding primary legislation, i.e. the Treaties, the Member States are even considered the Masters of the Treaties. They have signed and ratified the treaties in their current form. It is slightly ironic that they permanently complain about the risks emanating from their own creations and, on the other hand, put the legislation they have adopted themselves in risk through their actions.

---

[39] See, for example, the plan of British PM David Cameron to cut access to social welfare for EU citizens, http://www.theguardian.com/politics/2014/nov/27/david-cameron-european-union-immigration, accessed 21 April 2015.

[40] See the Dutch government's initiative to amend Directive 2003/86/EC to allow for stricter policies, http://www.rijksoverheid.nl/regering/regeerakkoord/immigratie-integratie-en-asiel, accessed 21 April 2015. This initiative was not successful.

[41] See the ideas of Germany's Minister of the Interior, http://www.zeit.de/politik/deutschland/2015-04/sicherheit-passkontrolle-germanwings, accessed 21 April 2015.

[42] See European Commission, Communication from the Commission to the Council, the European Parliament, the European Economic and Social Committee and the Committee of the Regions, Report on the Functioning of the Transitional Arrangements set out in the 2003 Accession Treaty (COM/2006/0048 final); for the current restrictions for Croatian workers, see http://ec.europa.eu/social/main.jsp?catId=466&langId=en, accessed 21 April 2015.

3 The Nature and Effect of EU Migration Law: Risks from *Within*

3.1 The Nature of EU Migration Law: 'Reverse Harmonization' Par Excellence

The above mentioned tension between the national and the European level led to a rather special and problematic nature of EU immigration legislation. The strong sentiments of Member States and their hesitation to surrender sovereign power to the EU has undoubtedly left its mark on EU legislation itself. First of all, it took the Member States four full years to adopt measures in the field of regular migration,[43] even though the competences were available since 1999 with the legislative changes of the entry into force of the Treaty of Amsterdam. In other areas of migration law, such as the fight against irregular immigration, or measures regulating asylum,[44] it took less time to adopt legislation. For instance, already in 2000 the Council was able to agree on a Directive on the mutual recognition of expulsion decisions.[45] The decision-making procedures in place after the Treaty of Amsterdam provided for unanimity voting in the Council.[46] This amounted to a great bargaining power of each Member State, which partially explains the delay in the adoption of the legal migration measures.

Moreover, this huge bargaining power, in a situation where Member States are hesitant to hand over too much sovereign power to the EU, also resulted in a rather unique character of legislation that was eventually adopted. Member States used negotiations of the draft legislation in the Council as well as with Parliament to insert 'custom-made' exceptions. These exceptions are inserted to protect existing national legislation and to avoid significant changes of national law when the end product has to be implemented on the national level. Another way of protecting national legislation was to leave key terminologies within the Directive without definition while allowing Member States to rely on exactly these terminologies to install policies restricting the rights of the Directive on the national level. These terms will be defined in all Member States individually afterwards often in rather different ways leading to a rather inharmonious implementation and application of the Directive. It will need years for the Court of Justice to clarify these matters and terminology.

One could call these mechanisms *reverse harmonization*. Here, the draft legislation on the EU level is adapted in the light of existing national legislation rather

---

[43] See Laeken and Seville Council Conclusions 2001 and 2002; (Peers 2006, p. 6); also Conclusions of Laeken European Council, Presidency conclusions – Laeken, 14 and 15 December 2001. SN 300/1/01 REV 1. 8. EN. 24.

[44] See for an overview of these measures 'fighting' illegal immigration, Peers (2006), pp. 10–12.

[45] See Directive 2001/40/EC of 28 May 2001 on the mutual recognition of decisions on the expulsion of third-country nationals. OJ L 149, 2.6.2001.

[46] See Art. 63 TEC, since ToL ordinary legislative procedure.

than the other way around. One could call this behaviour of the Member States 'active risk aversion' bearing their perspective on the matter, as introduced above, in mind.

By way of example, a couple of typical articles taken from Directive 2003/86 will be introduced thereunder. The Directive was adopted to create a conditional positive right for third-country nationals to family reunification in the EU. As such, the Directive goes further than the pre-existing legal situation under the ECHR, which did not contain a positive right to family life in the Member States of the ECHR in general.[47] The objective of the Directive is to create a right to family reunification. This is thought to be beneficial to social cohesion because it contributes to the integration of immigrants from third countries.[48] The Directive, of course, provides for conditions and requirements, which have to be fulfilled in order to be able to rely on the right to family reunification. It is important to realize that these conditions are binding upon the Member States. They may not install other conditions than those mentioned in the Directive itself.[49] Here, the vague nature of terminology and exceptions in the Directive becomes problematic.

Article 3 Dir. 2003/86/EC, for example, determines that the Directive is only applicable in cases where a sponsor is legally resident and in possession of a residence and work permit in one Member State for at least 1 year or longer. In addition, the sponsor must have the reasonable prospect of obtaining a right of permanent residence. The latter formulation is vague, but placed at the very core of the Directive, i.e. the provision determining when the right to family reunification does arise. The study of the Directive will not tell the reader when the sponsor 'has a reasonable prospect of obtaining a right to permanent residence'. This is a quasi-open door for Member States to implement a restrictive interpretation, which the Court of Justice will have to deal with in the years to come.

Article 4 of Dir. 2003/86/EC prescribes which 4 groups of family members of the sponsor's family 'shall' be allowed to enjoy family reunification. However, the article itself provides a derogation: Member States may require that children over 12 years who arrive independently have to meet '[...] a condition for integration provided for by [...] existing legislation on the date of implementation of this Directive'. What a 'condition for integration' would be is not defined anywhere. In addition, Member States may, if they want to, authorize entry and residence for 'first-degree relatives in the direct ascending line of the sponsor or his or her spouse, where they are dependent on them and do not enjoy proper family support in the country of origin, and adult unmarried children [...], where they are objectively unable to provide for their own needs on account of their state of health'. It is not

---

[47] Case C-540/03 *European Parliament v Council*.

[48] Recital 4 Directive 2003/86/EC.

[49] See Case C-578/08 *Rhimou Chakroun v Minister van Buitenlandse Zaken* [2010] ECR I-01839; or Case C-127/08 *Blaise Baheten Metock and Others v Minister for Justice, Equality and Law Reform* [2008] ECR I-06241.

clear what the Member States have to do or what they should omit according to this article.

The Member States, according to article 4 (3) may also decide whether registered, long-term partners enjoy a right to family reunification, and they may, in order to ensure better integration and to prevent forced marriages, require the sponsor's spouse to be of a minimum age, and at maximum 21 years before the right to family unity arises under the Directive. In order to make this article of Directive 2003/86 clearer, the Directive finally adds that, by way of derogation, Member States may request that the applications concerning family reunification for minor children have to be submitted before the age of 15. Article 4 accounts for up to 7 possible derogations and facultative provisions ['may clauses'] to add to a basic rule that provides for four groups that should be allowed to be covered by the right to family reunification.

These are only a few examples taken from one important article of one of the most important pieces of European immigration law, Directive 2003/86 on family reunification. A rough and quick count reveals 18 'may clauses', 12 allowed derogations to rules, and 10 instances where they occur in combination with this Directive alone. The Directive, *nota bene*, only contains 28 articles.

Unfortunately, from the perspective of the Member States, this strategy of attempting to keep certain issues out of the realm of EU law through the very way legislation is drafted will not work. The Court will eventually deal with legislation and will interpret exceptions not in the light of the intentions of the Member States, but in the light of the objective and purpose of the legislative measure itself while seeking to uphold the *effet utile* of it. Often, the Court will act against the expressed will of the Member States and severely limit the room for manoeuvre of Member States under the exceptions allowed in the legislation. This will not only render the attempts of Member States to pre-empt risks deriving from EU legislation less effective over time, but it will also additionally increase the tension at the national and European level because Member States will fundamentally oppose the interpretation of EU legislation by the Court.

3.2 Risks Arising from the Nature of EU Migration Law

While the nature of EU migration law can be explained by the risks the Member States see in the adoption of these measures, one must not underestimate the risks arising from the resulting nature of this legislation. As a rule of thumb and quite logically, the higher the number of facultative provisions, exceptions and undefined terminology in legislation, the bigger the threat on legal certainty and uniform interpretation and application throughout the European Union. It will take time until the Court of Justice of the EU has interpreted the scope and meaning of all the dubious articles, facultative provisions and undefined terminology. Until then, or until a general line of interpretation is developed by the Court, the effectiveness of all measures of EU migration law is in danger and their divergent implementation and application is very likely to occur.

At this moment in time, the situation differs when comparing the situation of EU citizens and third-country nationals in this regard. Things are solidly defined or the European Citizenship and the market freedoms of workers, service providers and those who want to establish themselves in another Member State.[50] The judicial discussion in these areas is at the margins of the respective areas of law and mainly concerns the definition of rights citizens can rely on against their own Member State in the absence of a crossborder effect as well as the limits of equal treatment in access to specific welfare benefits for economically inactive citizens. The clarification of law is, on the other hand, only slowly developing for all measures governing the situation of third-country nationals. It will take years before legal certainty and effectiveness are taken care of through the case law of the Court.

Until then, the very nature of EU migration law itself gives rise to the risk of wrongful implementation and application with and without bad intentions on behalf of the Member States. It is simply not clear what is called for, what is allowed, and what not. Until a solution is found, it will be unavoidable that EU law is not implemented and applied correctly. This is worrying because immigration legislation is not dealing with things, goods, capital, or services, which are crossing the border, but with human beings. It is quite a different thing if the wrongful implementation of EU law leads to, for example, the denial of market access of a new product or the denial of a refugee status or family reunification.

4 Risks for Individual Stakeholders Stemming from EU Migration Law

In the preceding sections relatively abstract risks were introduced. These were mainly linked to the heated political debate on migration and the nature of EU migration law resulting therefrom. Hereafter, some risks arising for individual stakeholders shall be charted.

4.1 Risks for Individual Immigrants

The abstract risks of wrong implementation and wrongful application of EU migration law are easily translated in direct individual risks for immigrants. The problem here is the denial of rights, which, to be made available, was the objective and purpose of EU legislation. The denial of rights because of faulty implementation and/or application is, of course, nothing new and in no way limited to EU

---

[50] See Shaw (2011), pp. 575–609.

migration and asylum law. However, one has to recall that migration law and asylum law deal with people, their right to stay, and their future in a certain geographical space. Migration law determines the very delimitations of life within which the migrants legally can operate. Individually, life plans, a secure future, the willingness to integrate, or life in safety might be destroyed by the (wrongful) application of migration law to the detriment of immigrants. This is a big risk felt by immigrants, the provision of secure residence and legal certainty in the application of the regulations is therefore one of the biggest factors influencing integration and the willingness to integrate by immigrants.

4.2 Risk to National Policy Makers

A risk national policy makers might discover in EU migration law is that it potentially undermines the achievement of goals and objectives governments have set themselves in elections and put at the basis of their list of objectives for the period they are in government. If a government promises to bring down immigration numbers by a well-defined amount, EU migration law can put the achievement of this goal at risk. This is because the necessary competence to change laws and regulations to achieve a limitation of migration is no longer in the hands of the national governments themselves, but situated on EU level. EU citizens, but also many immigrants from third countries *can* derive rights directly from EU law, which national governments will have to obey. Denying them entry and residence directly violates EU law and will make the Member State liable. The fact that national governments, however, pledge and promise to reduce the migration of certain immigrants, leads to permanent attacks on EU regulation from the national level causing instability on the EU level.

The best example at the moment is the current British government under Prime Minister David Cameron. This government not only pledged a referendum about the United Kingdom's future in the European Union itself, but it also promised to bring numbers of immigration, including numbers of EU citizens, moving to the UK, down.[51] Such promises are a risky gamble for national politicians. The achievement of these objectives is largely dependent on the interpretation of the European legal framework, which Member States have to obey, but cannot change unilaterally, because it was introduced as an abstract risk above. Admittedly, the UK has an opt-in to EU migration law in place for third-country nationals, and is therefore not bound by EU measures concerning the legal situation of third-country nationals unless it positively decides not to opt out.

[51] See for the problem of David Cameron, who pledged to bring net immigration in the UK below 100.000 per year during his term, http://www.telegraph.co.uk/news/uknews/immigration/11436403/David-Cameron-immigration-pledge-in-tatters-as-net-immigration-stands-at-298000.html, accessed 22 April 2015.

However, the UK *is* bound by all rules and regulations concerning the movement of EU citizens for economic *and* non-economic purposes. It cannot unilaterally limit the rights of EU citizens to move to the UK and live there. This would amount to an outright violation of EU law. The individual risk the UK government and David Cameron are facing is that the only chance to realize the objective of bringing down immigration numbers, is either closing the UK off for third-country nationals, including wanted immigrants, such as highly qualified workers or students, something that cannot be in the interest of the UK, or to either persistently breach EU law, or to leave the EU altogether.

Given the sensitivity and intensity of the political debate about migration on the national level and the huge temptation to score presumably easy points with voters, many national legislators and governments repeatedly step into this trap of making promises that depend on EU legislation beyond their unilateral control. Apart from the individual risks posed to those politicians making these promises, these unattainable goals promised in national elections often, as is very likely in the example of the UK, have the potential risk of leading to further political shake-ups not only at the national, but also at EU level.

5 Conclusion

The following scheme seeks to show the web of risks connected to EU migration law in its interplay with national regulations, policies, and legislators (Fig. 1).

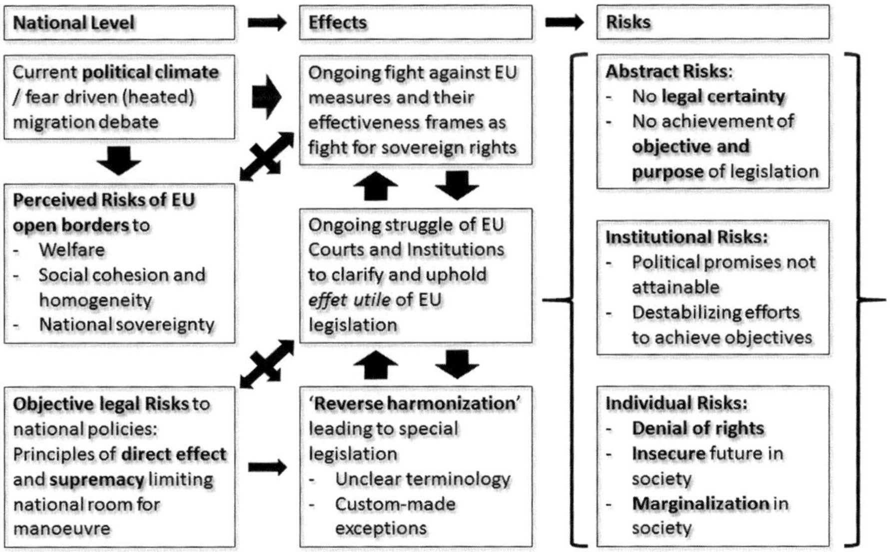

Fig. 1 (Legal)-risk from, to, and within EU migration law – an inventory

As is visible, the interdependencies of factors create a spider's web of issues and risks ranging from abstract and general risks to individual risks, all intertwined. The red line that keeps the issues and risks together, however, is the clash between the national and EU level in this delicate field of law. However, and this should be emphasized here, the highest costs are borne by the individual immigrants, who might see their rights denied and their future in a society severely jeopardized by the wrongful implementation and application of EU immigration regulations. The uncertainty created by the whole spider's web of interests and the resulting legislation has a direct impact on the reality of life of concrete individuals. Their individual stories, which lawyers usually know only from the facts section in judicial decisions, should be the prime reason to reconsider, whether immigration regulation is in need of an overhaul. It is too risky for all parties involved to keep it as it is.

References

Carrera S, Faure A (2011) Integration as a two-way process in the EU. Centre for European Policy Studies, Brussels

Dauvergne C (2004) Sovereignty, migration and the rule of law in global times. Mod Law Rev 67 (4):588–615

de Vries K (2014) Vreemde Verwanten: Inburgering in het buitenland en het recht op gezinsleven. Nederlands Tijdschrift voor de Mensenrechten 39(4):417–436

de Witte B (2011) Direct effect, primacy, and the nature of the legal order. In: Craig P, de Burca G (eds) The evolution of EU law, 2nd edn. Oxford University Press, Oxford, pp 323–361

Groenendijk K (2004) Legal concepts of integration in EU migration law. Eur J Migr Law 6 (2):111–126

Jesse M (2011) The value of integration in European law: the implications of the Förster case on legal assessment of integration conditions for third-country nationals. Eur Law J 17 (2):172–190

Jesse M (2014) The selection of migrants through law - a closer look at regulation governing family reunification. In: Anthias F, Pajnik M (eds) Contesting integration, engendering migration. Palgrave Macmillan, Houndmills, Basingstoke, pp 86–101

Klaassen M, Lodder G (2014) EU-recht en nationale ontwikkelingen – Kroniek gezinshereniging. Asiel en Migrantenrecht: 34–43

Lübbe-Wolff G (2007) Homogenes Volk - Über Homogenitätspostulate und Integration. Zeitschrift für Ausländerrecht und Ausländerpolitik 27(4):121–127

Peers S (2006) EU justice and home affairs law, 2nd edn. Oxford University Press, Oxford

Shaw J (2011) Citizenship: contrasting dynamics at the interface of integration and constitutionalism. In: Craig P, de Burca G (eds) The evolution of EU law, 2nd edn. Oxford University Press, Oxford, pp 575–609

Risks Relating to the Protection of Cultural Heritage: From Climate Change to Disasters

Alessandro Chechi

Contents

Abstract Climate change is one of the major environmental challenges of the twenty-first century. This chapter analyses the different ways climate change threatens cultural heritage, and examines the policy and legal measures that have been adopted by the European Union to enhance the protection of the European cultural heritage from the consequences of the accelerating degradation of the global climate. Its aim is twofold. First, to demonstrate that the existing EU regulatory framework may permit, to a certain extent, to reduce exposure and vulnerability of cultural assets and to increase their resilience to the adverse impacts of the changing climate. Second, to signal that, however, the measures put in place are not entirely effective as they entail significant legal risks. This chapter argues that EU institutions, together with EU Member States, should strive to operationalize the principles of 'common good' and 'sustainable development' in order to transform the current piecemeal response to the climate change-related

A. Chechi (✉)
Art-Law Centre, Faculty of Law, University of Geneva, Geneva, Switzerland
e-mail: alessandro.chechi@unige.ch

E. Mišćenić, A. Raccah (eds.), *Legal Risks in EU Law*,
DOI 10.1007/978-3-319-28596-2_10

weather events and disasters that threaten the cultural heritage into a coherent and effective regulatory framework.

1 Introduction

The recognition that climate change is one of the major environmental challenges of the twenty-first century has steadily gained momentum in the past few years. One of the most authoritative acknowledgments arrived in 2014 from the Fifth Assessment Report of the Intergovernmental Panel on Climate Change (IPCC).[1] With this comprehensive and up-to-date document, the IPCC stressed that '[h]uman influence on the climate system is clear',[2] and that a direct link can be established between anthropogenic greenhouse gases (GHGs) emissions[3] and the adverse effects of climate change occurring in Europe and around the world[4]: surface mean temperature has increased and precipitation patterns have changed; glaciers, ice sheets, and Arctic sea ice have decreased; seas are affected through acidification and increasing water temperatures; coastlines face rising sea levels, erosion, and more powerful storms; freshwater ecosystems are affected by a decrease in river flows and an increase in the frequency and intensity of droughts; finally, agriculture is affected by shifts in suitable cropping areas and changes in yields.[5]

Furthermore, the Fifth Assessment Report emphasised that limiting climate change requires cooperation at the international level in order to advance simultaneous and effective adaptation and mitigation measures.[6] As is well known, adaptation refers to 'the process of adjustment to actual or expected climate and its effects, in order to moderate harm or exploit beneficial opportunities',[7] whereas mitigation corresponds to any 'human intervention to reduce the sources or enhance the sinks of greenhouse gases'.[8] Regarding mitigation, the Fifth Assessment Report stated that 'substantial emissions reductions [. . .] can reduce climate risks [. . .] and contribute to climate-resilient pathways for sustainable development'.[9] Turning to adaptation, the IPCC underlined a general deficit in both developed and developing

[1] Available at: <http://www.ipcc.ch/report/ar5/index.shtml>, accessed 31 August 2015.

[2] IPCC (2013), p. 15.

[3] Human activities perturb the natural filtering effect of the atmosphere by adding GHGs (such as carbon dioxide and methane), which lead to an overall warming of the planet and to the disruption of the climate.

[4] IPCC (2014b).

[5] IPCC (2014a).

[6] IPCC (2014a), pp. 17–34.

[7] IPCC (2012), p. 556.

[8] IPCC (2012), p. 561.

[9] IPCC (2014b).

countries[10] and that there is robust evidence that climate change threatens international peace and security,[11] the stability of nation States,[12] and the enjoyment of human rights, including the individual rights to health, life, food, water, shelter, property, and culture.[13]

Having said that, it should be borne in mind that adaptation efforts can be truly effective only if based on the understanding that the risk of disasters is determined not only by weather or climatic events (the hazards), but also by two factors of risk: exposure and vulnerability. Exposure refers to the elements—such as human beings, their livelihoods, and assets—in an area in which hazard events may occur. Vulnerability refers to the propensity of exposed elements to suffer major harm and damage when impacted by hazards.[14]

The topic of this chapter concerns the impact of climate change on cultural heritage. In particular, it aims to analyse the policy and legal instruments that may permit to reduce exposure and vulnerability of cultural assets and increase their resilience[15] to the adverse impacts of the changing climate. This chapter concentrates on the European Union (EU)—though it is well known that, as climate change is a global phenomenon that transcends territorial boundaries, any action taken at the European level would be useless if not accompanied by decisive efforts at the international level. The reason for this focus on EU law is threefold. First, the EU is one of the largest economic and commercial blocs in the world having a vast impact on the global environment. Second, the EU is at the forefront of the international negotiations to advance climate change mitigation and adaptation. Third, the EU institutions have recently and repeatedly acknowledged that '[g]lobal warming and climate change [...] can put cultural heritage at risk'.[16]

This chapter proceeds in four stages. It begins by looking at the ways in which climate change impacts cultural heritage, both tangible—such as antiquities, monuments, and archaeological sites—and intangible—such as expressions, knowledge, and skills (Sect. 2). Then the chapter explores the most relevant EU policies that address—directly or indirectly—the degradation of the environment and global climate conditions and the protection of cultural heritage (Sect. 3). This analysis aims at demonstrating that cultural heritage protection cuts across several

[10] IPCC (2014b), pp. 6–8.

[11] See also UN General Assembly, 'Climate Change and Its Possible Security Implications', Report of the Secretary-General, 11 September 2009, A/64/350.

[12] See also Rayfuse and Scott (2012), p. 3; and McAdam (2012).

[13] See also UN Human Rights Council, Resolution 10/4 on Human Rights and Climate Change, 25 March 2009.

[14] Cardona et al. (2012), pp. 69–71.

[15] This is the ability of a community or society to resist, accommodate and recover from the effects of a hazard in a timely and efficient manner. See United Nations Office for Disaster Risk Reduction, 'Terminology: Resilience', available at: <http://www.unisdr.org/we/inform/terminology>, accessed 31 August 2015.

[16] See e.g. EU Commission, 'Towards an Integrated Approach to Cultural Heritage for Europe' COM (2014) 477 final, 22 July 2014, p. 5.

EU policies, the main reason being that culture is recognized as an important resource for economic growth and social cohesion. Next, this chapter looks at the concepts of 'common good' and 'sustainable development' and suggests that they should be employed to cope with the legal risks that stem from the piecemeal approach adopted by the EU (Sect. 4). The chapter concludes by offering a plea to rethink EU policies and normative instruments for the sake of the protection of the cultural and natural environment for present and future generations (Sect. 5).

2 The Impacts of Climate Change on Cultural Heritage

The alteration of the climatic equilibrium of the planet severely affects the environment and biodiversity in Europe and around the world. However, it has an impact also on the products of human creativity. The study of the UNESCO World Heritage Centre[17] examines the potential effects of climate change on 26 monuments and sites inscribed in the List set under the UNESCO Convention Concerning the Protection of the World Cultural and Natural Heritage (WHC).[18] These case studies demonstrate that the potential impacts of climate change on cultural heritage range from direct physical effects to effects on social structures.

In order to identify the most important direct physical effects of climate change, the World Heritage Centre has distinguished archaeological heritage from built heritage. With regard to the former, the following are some of the changes that have been considered: increased soil temperature in response to increased atmospheric temperature, which may provoke subsoil instability and landslides; sea-level rise, which threatens coastal areas with coastal erosion and permanent submersion of low-lying areas; and changes in wetting and drying cycles, which may affect wall paintings, frescos, rock art and other decorated surfaces. Essentially, these changes may jeopardize the conservation of archaeological evidence—even those not known today—and exacerbate decay mechanisms.[19] Regarding historic buildings, the study of the World Heritage Centre evidences that they have a great connection with the ground. They are more porous and draw water from the ground into their structure and lose it to the environment by surface evaporation. Their wall surfaces and floors are the point of exchange for these reactions. Therefore, increases in soil moisture might result in greater salt mobilisation and consequent damaging crystallisation on decorated surfaces through drying. Moreover, extreme and sudden variations or changes in the amplitude of the diurnal or seasonal variation of

---

[17] UNESCO World Heritage Centre, 'Case Studies on Climate Change and World Heritage' (2007), available at: <http://whc.unesco.org/en/activities/473>, accessed 31 August 2015.

[18] 16 November 1972, 1037 UNTS 151.

[19] UNESCO World Heritage Centre, 'Case Studies on Climate Change and World Heritage' (2007), pp. 52–53, available at: <http://whc.unesco.org/en/activities/473>, accessed 31 August 2015.

temperature and humidity can cause the splitting, cracking, and flaking of materials and surfaces. Timber and other organic building materials may be subject to increased biological infestation due to the migration of pests. Flooding is another concern. Buildings may be damaged due to the erosive character of rapid flowing water or because they were not designed to withstand prolonged immersion.[20]

Another serious threat for cultural resources is desertification. This phenomenon is not the product of natural causes only. Anthropogenic factors such as deforestation, pollution and poor land management play a significant part. Climate change also plays an important role. In the peripheral areas of deserts, sand dunes are normally stabilised by vegetation. Higher temperatures and reduced rainfall contribute to droughts in these areas, leading to the decline of vegetation and hence to the migration of dunes. Once the sand dunes become mobile, all vegetation in their vicinity is at risk and a chain reaction begins. Windstorms, which are increasing in number, extension and frequency due to climate alteration, further exacerbate the situation.[21]

With regard to social structures, climate change alters the way people relate to the buildings, sites, landscapes, and habitats where they live, work, worship, and socialize. For instance, under the pressure of desertification, flooding, or sea-level rise, populations are forced to migrate, leading to the abandonment of property.[22] This abandonment raises an important concern in contexts where traditional knowledge and skills are essential to ensure a proper maintenance of these properties. For example, the desertification in the region of Timbuktu, a regional capital in Mali, might lead to the migration of the local population, including the local craftsmen that are involved in the restoration of the mud structures of the ancient mosques of Djingareyber, Sankoré, and Sidi Yahia.[23] Moreover, the migration of people leads to the break-up of communities and thus to the eventual loss of cultural identity, rituals, and the cultural memory of former inhabitants.[24] This is the case with countries in high northern latitudes, where the melting of ice caps and the arctic ground ice as a result of temperature increase has had an impact on the traditional livelihoods and means of survival of the local indigenous peoples.[25] The same is happening with several islands in the Southern Pacific Ocean, which have been abandoned after the rising ocean flooded parts of their shorelines and saltwater seeped into the ground water.[26]

---

[20] Ibid., pp. 64–65.

[21] Gruber (2008), pp. 15–16.

[22] Gruber (2008), p. 12.

[23] UNESCO World Heritage Centre, 'Case Studies on Climate Change and World Heritage' (2007), pp. 74–75, available at: <http://whc.unesco.org/en/activities/473>, accessed 31 August 2015.

[24] Ibid., p. 65.

[25] Mutter and Barnard (2010), pp. 275–276.

[26] See also Hee-Eun (2011).

The following climate change-related impacts have not been reported by the World Heritage Centre. First, climate change-related events may lead to conditions suitable for the recrudescence of thefts, illicit excavations, and exportations of cultural objects. Just as in times of war and political disorder, the opportunity for illicit trafficking in art objects increases with the impoverishment of the local population or its departure due to environmental degradation, slow-onset disasters—such as desertification and reduced water availability—and the increase of hydro-meteorological disasters—such as flooding, hurricanes, and typhoons. Second, geophysical changes resulting from climate change could lead to armed conflicts over increasingly scarce but essential resources that sustain livelihoods.[27] In turn, these conflicts might impact on cultural sites and properties—as either unwanted or premeditated consequences. Third, extreme weather events in major art trade hubs like New York and London jeopardize the preservation of movable works of art.[28] These are not unlikely events. In 2012, New York was hit by hurricane Sandy and in 2011 by hurricane Irene, two of the most devastating hurricanes in recent history.[29] During hurricane Sandy, Christie's Fine Art Storage Services, a wholly owned subsidiary of the auction house that stores and protects artworks for private and institutional owners in Brooklyn, New York, was hit by at least one storm surge. Christie's storage facility is not the only one to have clients' works damaged. The storm damaged manifold businesses, including Chelsea's art galleries. It is impossible to know the exact loss as most sources requested anonymity. It has been estimated, however, that total losses run in the hundreds of millions.[30] Christiane Fischer, President of AXA Art in the Americas, observed that 'Sandy was the costliest event for the art insurance industry by far. We all will need to adjust our disaster planning strategies to protect important works [. . .] from becoming victims of water damage'.[31]

---

[27] See e.g. Ban (2007); and Homer-Dixon (2007).

[28] On London, see UNESCO World Heritage Centre, 'Case Studies on Climate Change and World Heritage' (2007), pp. 66–69, available at: <http://whc.unesco.org/en/activities/473>, accessed 31 August 2015.

[29] These can be related to climate change because, in a warming world, tropical climate conditions expand toward the poles. Consequently, storm tracks that have been associated with the tropics are moving northward and areas that previously experienced very few hurricanes and cyclones will start to experience them in greater numbers. Mutter and Barnard (2010), pp. 275–277.

[30] Gilbert (2013).

[31] AXA ART Group, 'Water – A Serious Peril to Works of Art' (4 April 2013), available at: <http://www.axa-art-usa.com/news-events/detail/detail/water-a-serious-peril-to-works-of-art.html>, accessed 31 August 2015.

3 EU Policies Having an Impact on Cultural Resources

The World Heritage Centre's case studies demonstrate that climate change is increasingly posing dangers and risks that threaten the enjoyment, preservation, and transmission of cultural heritage to future generations.[32] This notwithstanding, these case studies only led the WHC Committee to issue three policy documents[33] and a guide for site managers,[34] and to revise the Operational Guidelines for the Implementation of the World Heritage Convention. As the Operational Guidelines stand now, climatic factors should be mentioned in the nomination format for inscription on the WHC List,[35] and as a potential danger leading to the inscription on the List of World Heritage in Danger.[36] Thus the Operational Guidelines contain the only provisions taking into account the deleterious impact of climate change on cultural resources. This means that the WHC Committee opted for a soft approach. This has been motivated by the alleged primary role of the IPCC and of the UN Framework Convention on Climate Change (UNFCCC)[37] in addressing the problem of climate change.[38] However, neither the UNFCCC nor its Kyoto Protocol address the impacts of climate change on cultural heritage or contain references to UNESCO treaties.

In the face of this gloomy picture, this section aims at analysing the instruments adopted by the EU to enhance the protection of the European cultural heritage from the accelerating degradation of the global climate. Specifically, it focuses on the following EU policy areas: culture, environment, climate action, humanitarian aid and civil protection.[39] This study does not claim to offer a full catalogue of the legal risks and challenges at work in these areas. Nor does it offer a detailed analysis of

---

[32] See also the survey in 'Report on Predicting and Managing the Effects of Climate Change on World Heritage' (2006), which indicates that of 'the 110 responses received from 83 States Parties, 72 % acknowledged that climate change had an impact on their natural and cultural heritage', and that a 'total of 125 World Heritage sites were mentioned specifically as threatened by Climate Change' (paras. 39–46).

[33] These are the 'Report on Predicting and Managing the Effects of Climate Change on World Heritage' (2006); the 'Strategy to Assist State Parties to Implement Appropriate Management Responses' (2006); and the 'Policy Document on the Impacts of Climate Change on World Heritage Properties' (2007).

[34] Perry and Falzon (2014).

[35] See Annex 5, 4.b (ii).

[36] A WHC property can be inscribed on the List of World Heritage in Danger due to a potential danger 'threatening impacts of climatic, geological or other environmental factors' (para. 179(b) (vi)).

[37] Adopted 9 May 1992, 1771 UNTS 107.

[38] The 'Strategy to Assist State Parties to Implement Appropriate Management Responses' (2006) states that the 'UNFCCC is the UN instrument through which mitigation strategies at the global and States Parties level is being addressed' (para. 18).

[39] Due to space restrictions, this chapter will not dwell on the other policy areas listed in the document 'Mapping of Cultural Heritage Actions in European Union Policies, Programmes and Activities', available at: <http://ec.europa.eu/culture/library/>, accessed 31 August 2015.

the legal instruments adopted in these fields. Rather, the objective is to demonstrate that: (1) cultural heritage protection cuts across several EU policies; (2) the cultural heritage-related measures adopted by EU institutions offer strong potential for the achievement of the goals pursued in other fields of EU law; and (3) cultural heritage protection in connection with climate change-related weather events and disasters is taken into consideration by the EU legal order.

3.1 Culture

The EU action in the field of culture is envisaged by Article 167 of the Treaty on the Functioning of the European Union (TFEU).[40] This article establishes that the EU 'shall contribute to the flowering of the cultures of the Member States, while respecting their national and regional diversity and at the same time bringing the common cultural heritage to the fore'. It also states that EU action 'shall be aimed at encouraging cooperation between Member States and, if necessary, supporting and supplementing their action in the [. . .] conservation and safeguarding of cultural heritage of European significance'.

The TFEU contains other references to culture. Article 6 states that the EU 'shall have competence to carry out actions to support, coordinate or supplement the actions of the Member States' in the area of culture. Article 36 allows prohibitions or restrictions on imports, exports, or goods in transit for 'the protection of national treasures possessing artistic, historic or archaeological value'. Article 107(3)(d) TFEU establishes that aid granted to Member States, if meant to promote culture and heritage conservation, can be considered to be compatible with the internal market 'when it does not affect trading conditions and competition in the Union to an extent that is contrary to the common interest'.

Moving to the Treaty on European Union (EU Treaty), its preamble refers to 'the cultural, religious and humanist inheritance of Europe', and Article 3 provides that one of the EU's aims is to 'respect its rich cultural and linguistic diversity, and [. . .] ensure that Europe's cultural heritage is safeguarded and enhanced'. Finally, it is worth taking a look at the Charter of Fundamental Rights of the European Union (EU Charter).[41] Apart from the preamble—where it is established that the EU undertake to respect 'the diversity of the cultures and traditions of the peoples of Europe'—two provisions are relevant: Article 13 stipulates that 'the arts and

[40] Pursuant to the Treaty of Lisbon (OJ C 115, 9 May 2008), the Treaty of Rome was replaced by the TFEU (OJ C 115/47, 9 May 2008) and the Treaty on European Union (TEU) was amended.

[41] The EU Charter (OJ EC C 364/1, 18 December 2000) became legally binding on the EU institutions and on national governments on 1 December 2009 with the entry into force of the Treaty of Lisbon.

scientific research shall be free of constraint'; and Article 22 lays down the requirement that 'the EU shall respect cultural, religious and linguistic diversity'.

It emerges from this brief overview that, while cultural heritage protection is primarily a matter for Member States, the EU has a role to play in keeping with the principle of subsidiarity. There is no contradiction between national responsibilities and EU action: heritage is always both local and European. As a result, it is possible to identify various policy developments and action programmes with which the EU supplements the States' intervention and enhances the protection of Europe's cultural heritage.

The European Agenda for Culture, which was adopted in 2007 by the EU Council,[42] was centred on the promotion of: (a) cultural diversity and intercultural dialogue; (b) culture as a catalyst for creativity; and (c) culture as a vital element in the Union's international relations.[43] The Agenda opened a new chapter of cooperation on cultural policy. For the first time, all partners—EU institutions, Member States, and the civil society—pooled their efforts on explicitly defined goals. Moreover, the Agenda reaffirmed the importance that culture has for the European project. Not only is it the anchor on which the EU's 'unity in diversity' is founded, it also constitutes an indispensable factor towards achieving the EU's strategic objectives of sustainable and inclusive growth, solidarity, security, mutual understanding, and cooperation worldwide.[44]

Two Work Plans for Culture have been adopted under the European Agenda for Culture. The most recent Work Plan, which will be operative in the period 2015–2018, will focus on four priority areas: (a) accessible and inclusive culture; (b) cultural heritage; (c) cultural and creative sectors; and (d) promotion of cultural diversity. Importantly, with respect to cultural heritage, the EU Commission will conduct a study on 'risk assessment and prevention for safeguarding cultural heritage from the effects of natural disasters and threats caused by human action'. The factors that will be considered are 'over-exploitation, pollution, unsustainable development, conflict areas and natural catastrophes'.[45] In this respect, it should be mentioned that the Commission has already highlighted that '[g]lobal warming and climate change [...] can put cultural heritage at risk', and that 'research and innovation is [...] needed to enable a dynamic and sustainable cultural heritage in Europe in response to climate change and natural hazards and disasters'.[46]

---

[42] Resolution of the EU Council of 16 November 2007 on a European Agenda for Culture (OJ C 287/1, 29 November 2007).

[43] One of the priorities for cooperation between the EU and Africa is the fight against illicit trafficking. Heritage-related topics are also addressed in policy dialogues with strategic partners such as Brazil, China and India. See EU Commission, 'Towards an Integrated Approach to Cultural Heritage for Europe' COM (2014) 477 final, 22 July 2014.

[44] EU Commission, 'Report on the Implementation of the European Agenda for Culture' COM (2010) 390 final, 19 July 2010.

[45] Conclusions on a Work Plan for Culture (2015–2018) OJ C 463/4, 23 December 2014.

[46] EU Commission, 'Towards an Integrated Approach to Cultural Heritage for Europe' COM (2014) 477 final, 22 July 2014, p. 13.

Moreover, it is important to consider that one of the objectives of the Work Plan for Culture 2015–2018 is to mainstream culture in other policy areas in accordance with Article 167(4) TFEU. This enables the recollection that the Work Plan explicitly states that heritage can generate innovation and contribute to smart, sustainable and inclusive growth—in line with the objectives of the Europe 2020 Strategy.[47]

Finally, it should be mentioned that the EU has operationalized its cultural policy with a series of programmes, the latter being the Creative Europe 2014–2020 programme.[48] These programmes led to the adoption of various pan-European actions: the European Heritage Days,[49] the European Union Prize for Cultural Heritage/Europa Nostra Awards,[50] the European Capitals of Culture,[51] and the European Heritage Label.[52] The overall objective of these actions is to inform European citizens about the richness of Europe's cultural heritage and the efforts to protect it. Accordingly, they contribute significantly to the implementation of Article 167(2) TFEU, which states that the Union action should focus on improving 'the knowledge and dissemination of the culture and history of the European peoples', and on the 'conservation and safeguarding of cultural heritage of European significance'. By way of example, the European Heritage Label was established to 'strengthen European citizens' sense of belonging to the European Union, based on shared elements of history and heritage', and to bring them closer to the EU by enhancing 'the value and the profile of sites which have played a key role in the history and the building of the European Union'.[53]

The foregoing discussion demonstrates that EU institutions are aware of the dangers posed by the natural and human-induced disasters that threaten the enjoyment and protection of cultural heritage. However, it is also clear that no enforceable provision regarding the protection of cultural heritage from the effects of natural disasters and weather events exists. More effective measures have been established pursuant to other EU policies. It is to these policy areas we now turn.

---

[47] See also EU Council Conclusions of 21 May 2014 on Cultural Heritage as a Strategic Resource for a Sustainable Europe (OJ C 183, 14 June 2014).

[48] The 'Creative Europe' programme was established with Regulation 1295/2013 of 11 December 2013 and has a budget of €1.46 billion. It was preceded by the 'Culture 2000' and 'Culture 2007–2013' programmes.

[49] See at: <http://pjp-eu.coe.int/en/web/ehd-jep/home>.

[50] Launched in 2002 by the EU Commission, since then it has been organised by Europa Nostra, a non-governmental organization based in The Hague. See at: <http://www.europanostra.org/heritage-awards/>.

[51] Decision 445/2014/EU of 16 April 2014 establishing a Union Action for the European Capitals of Culture for the years 2020 to 2033 and repealing Decision No. 1622/2006/EC.

[52] Established with Decision 1194/2011/EU of 16 November 2011.

[53] Proposal for a Decision of the European Parliament and of the Council Establishing a European Union Action for the European Heritage Label COM (2010) 76 final, p. 2.

3.2 Environment

The EU's competence on environmental matters is firmly established by the TFEU. Article 4 states that the 'Union shall share competence with the Member States' in the area of environment. Under Article 36 Member States are allowed to pursue the protection of the environment provided that their measures do not constitute a means of arbitrary discrimination or a disguised restriction on trade. Title XX TFEU (Articles 191–193) contains the EU environmental objectives and principles as well as the legislative procedure by which environmental measures are adopted. Article 191 lists the reduction of climate change among the objectives of the Union.[54] This explicit reference was introduced by the 2009 Treaty of Lisbon. Previously, climate change was (implicitly) covered by Article 191(1) as a 'world-wide environmental problem'. Accordingly, the new formulation of Article 191—together with the fact that today the EU is a major global force in pushing for tighter environmental standards—makes it less likely that the climate change issue will disappear from the EU environmental agenda.[55]

The EU Treaty contains other relevant provisions. The preamble affirms that the Member States are 'determined to promote economic and social progress for their peoples, taking into account the principle of sustainable development and within the context [...] of reinforced [...] environmental protection'. Article 3 affirms that the EU internal market 'shall work for the sustainable development of Europe based on [...] a high level of protection and improvement of the quality of the environment'.

Since the 1970s, a substantial and diverse range of programmes and legal instruments have been put in place to protect, conserve, and enhance ecosystems. The current environmental programme—the 7th Environment Action Programme (EAP)—was adopted in 2013 and covers the period up to 2020.[56] Through the EAP, the EU has envisioned that '[i]n 2050, we live well, within the planet's ecological limits'. In order to move towards this ambitious vision, the EAP sets out a framework for environmental action—uniting the short, medium and long terms—and focuses on key priority objectives, including: protecting Europe's ecosystems; safeguarding people's health and well-being; improving environmental integration; and increasing the Union's effectiveness in addressing environmental and climate-related challenges.[57] The following instruments have been enacted to achieve these objectives.

---

[54] 'Union policy on the environment shall contribute to pursuit of the following objectives: [...] promoting measures [...] to deal with [...] environmental problems, and in particular combating climate change'.

[55] Lee (2014), p. 4.

[56] Decision 1386/2013/EU of 20 November 2013 on a General Union Environment Action Programme to 2020 'Living Well, within the Limits of Our Planet' (OJ L 354/171, 28 December 2013).

[57] Ibid., Article 2.

The Environmental Impact Assessment (EIA) Directive[58] provides for the assessment of the effects of certain public and private projects on the environment. However, it also aims to ensure 'the protection and promotion of cultural heritage [. . .] in accordance with Article 167(4) TFEU' (preamble). In this respect, Article 3 (d) EIA Directive states that the 'environmental impact assessment shall identify, describe and assess [. . .] the direct and indirect significant effects of a project on [. . .] material assets, cultural heritage and the landscape'. In the same vein, under the Strategic Environmental Assessment (SEA) Directive,[59] the likely significant effects on 'cultural heritage including architectural and archaeological heritage' must be taken into consideration.

The Habitats Directive 92/43/EEC[60] provides the cornerstone of Europe's nature conservation policy as well as the legal foundation of the Natura 2000 Network. This is an EU wide system of protected areas ('Special Areas of Conservation' and 'Special Protection Areas') that aims to ensure the survival of Europe's most valuable and threatened species and habitats. However, the Natura 2000 also encompasses—tangible and intangible—cultural heritage. In effect, it includes areas which are the outcomes of the interaction between people and the environment through time, and which include physical remains of past human activity and extensive agricultural practices. Article 2 of the Habitats Directive establishes that the measures taken to ensure 'bio-diversity through the conservation of natural habitats and of wild fauna and flora in the European territory [. . .] shall take account of economic, social and cultural requirements [. . .]'. It is interesting to mention here the 2009 White Paper on Adapting to Climate Change.[61] In this document the EU Commission recognised the importance of biodiversity preservation—especially, but not exclusively of Natura 2000 areas—as a means to help society to adapt to, and mitigate the impacts of climate change. Ecosystems can help limit atmospheric GHGs concentrations because forests and other habitats are major stores of carbon. Moreover, they can help mitigate climate change impacts by absorbing excess flood water or buffering inhabited areas against extreme weather events. Of course, only healthy ecosystems can be truly resilient to climate change and thus effectively instrumental to the well-being of the human society and to the conservation of tangible as well as intangible cultural resources. Stated differently, this document emphasises that Europe's prosperity and human well-being are inherently linked to the protection of the natural environment from traditional sources of pollution.

[58] Directive 2014/52/EU (OJ L 124/1, 16 April 2014) on the assessment of the effects of certain public and private projects on the environment. This Directive has amended Directive 2011/92/EU of 13 December 2011, which codified the initial Directive 85/337/EEC of 27 June 1985 and its three amendments (Directive 97/11/EC, Directive 2003/38/EC, Directive 2009/31/EC).

[59] Directive 2001/42/EC of 27 June 2001 on the assessment of the effects of certain plans and programmes on the environment (OJ L 197, 21 July 2001).

[60] Directive 92/43/EEC of 21 May 1992 on the conservation of natural habitats and of wild fauna and flora (OJ L 206, 22 July 1992).

[61] White Paper 'Adapting to Climate Change: Towards a European Framework for Action' COM (2009) 147 final, 1 April 2009.

3.3 Climate Action

The EU has developed a vast patchwork of legislation in matters of climate change based on Articles 191–193 TFEU. Needless to say, all EU climate change legislation sits in the international legal framework which includes the UNFCCC or the Kyoto Protocol. The UNFCCC sets the 'ultimate objective' to achieve the 'stabilization of greenhouse gas concentrations in the atmosphere at a level that would prevent dangerous anthropogenic interference with the climate system [...] within a time-frame sufficient to allow ecosystems to adapt naturally to climate change, to ensure that food production is not threatened and to enable economic development to proceed in a sustainable manner'. However, the UNFCCC does not contain binding obligations. One of the reasons is that various States refused to accept legally binding reduction targets for GHG emissions. Consequently, the UNFCCC merely calls on the (industrialized) States Parties to 'aim' to return their GHG emissions back to 1990 levels without setting precise targets. In 1997, the UNFCCC was supplemented by the Kyoto Protocol, which set binding obligations. The Protocol called 37 industrialized States and the EU to reduce 'their overall emissions [...] [of GHGs] by at least 5 per cent below 1990 levels in the commitment period 2008 to 2012'.[62]

The EU was instrumental in the adoption of the UNFCCC and the Kyoto Protocol. Furthermore, since the beginning of the 1990s, the EU has consistently set the pace in tackling climate change. On the one hand, a new round of negotiations is ongoing on the initiative of the EU (and of certain developing countries). This time the objective is to conclude a comprehensive and legally binding treaty for all countries.[63] The EU's leadership in the global fight against climate change is further confirmed by the fact that the EU is the biggest provider of overseas development aid and climate finance. At the Doha Climate Change Conference in 2012, the EU (and a number of Member States) announced voluntary climate finance contributions to developing countries.[64]

On the other hand, the EU has set up a series of measures to tackle climate change and to encourage moves towards a low-carbon economy. First, the structural policies implemented in the field of climate and energy between 1990 and 2012 have contributed significantly to the reduction of GHG emissions by 19 %.[65] As a result, the EU is well on track towards meeting its targets for cutting GHG

---

[62] Under the Kyoto Protocol, States must meet their reduction targets for GHG emissions primarily through national measures. In addition, the Protocol introduced three market-based mechanisms: (1) Joint Fulfilment of Commitments and Implementation; (2) the Clean Development Mechanism; and (3) Emissions Trading. For an analysis of these mechanisms see Leal-Arcas (2013), pp. 227 ff.

[63] This new agreement is due to be adopted at the 21st session of the Conference of the Parties to the UNFCCC, which will take place in December 2015 in Paris.

[64] EU Commission, 'Building a World We Like, with a Climate We Like', 2014, p. 14, available at: <http://europa.eu/pol/clim/index_en.htm>, accessed 31 August 2015.

[65] Ibid., p. 5.

emissions under the Kyoto Protocol.[66] Second, the EU has set specific targets under the Europe 2020 Strategy. These targets set three objectives for 2020: (1) a cut by 20 % in EU GHG emissions from 1990 levels; (2) raising the share of EU energy consumption produced from renewable resources to 20 %; and (3) a 20 % improvement in the EU's energy efficiency.[67] Four legislative initiatives have been taken to implement this 'EU climate and energy package': (1) the revision of the Emissions Trading Directive in order to reform the EU Emissions Trading System (EU ETS)[68]; (2) the adoption of Decision 406/2009,[69] which sets up binding national targets for reducing GHG emissions from the sectors not covered by the EU ETS; (3) the adoption of the Renewable Energy Directive,[70] which establishes binding national targets for raising the share of renewable energy in their energy consumption by 2020; and (4) the adoption of Directive 2009/31 on carbon capture and storage,[71] which regulates the safe use of the technologies employed to capture the carbon dioxide emitted by industrial processes and to store it in underground geological formations. Third, the EU has strengthened its commitment to make the EU's economy and energy system more competitive and sustainable by adopting the 'Climate and Energy Policy Framework' for 2030[72] and a 'Roadmap for Building the Low-Carbon European Economy' for 2050.[73] Fourth, in 2013 the EU Commission has developed an Adaptation Strategy with a view to strengthen Europe's resilience to the impacts of climate change and to complement mitigation actions.[74] As said, adaptation means anticipating the adverse effects of climate

---

[66] EU Commission, 'Report Progress towards Achieving the Kyoto and EU 2020 Objectives', October 2014. However, it seems that reductions are largely due to: reduced output during the post-2008 recession; earlier unrelated reductions such as a shift from coal to gas and migration of industry out of the EU; mild winters; and high energy prices. Lee (2014), p. 146.

[67] EU Commission, '20 20 by 2020: Europe's Climate Change Opportunity' COM (2008) 30 final.

[68] Directive 2003/87/EC of 13 October 2003 establishing a scheme for greenhouse gas emission allowance trading within the Community and amending Directive 96/61/EC. The EU ETS is the centrepiece of the EU's policy to combat climate change. It aims at reducing industrial GHG emissions by setting up: limits (caps) to the amount of GHGs that can be emitted by the installations covered; tradable emission allowances; and fines in case of non-compliance.

[69] Decision 406/2009/EC of 23 April 2009 on the effort of Member States to reduce their greenhouse gas emissions to meet the Community's greenhouse gas emission reduction commitments up to 2020.

[70] Directive 2009/28/EC of 23 April 2009 on the promotion of the use of energy from renewable sources and amending and subsequently repealing Directives 2001/77/EC and 2003/30/EC.

[71] Directive 2009/31/EC of 23 April 2009 on the geological storage of carbon dioxide and amending Directives 85/337/EEC, 2000/60/EC, 2001/80/EC, 2004/35/EC, 2006/12/EC, 2008/1/EC, and Regulation 1013/2006.

[72] EU Council, Conclusions – 23/24 October 2014.

[73] 'Roadmap for Moving to a Low-Carbon Economy in 2050' COM (2011) 112 final, 8 March 2011.

[74] EU Council, 'An EU Strategy on Adaptation to Climate Change' COM (2013) 216 final, 16 April 2013, available at: <http://ec.europa.eu/clima/policies/adaptation/what/documentation_en.htm>, accessed 31 August 2015.

change and taking appropriate action to prevent or minimise the damage they can cause, or taking advantage of opportunities that may arise. Among the instruments that can be employed to achieve the objectives of the Strategy, the EU Commission highlighted the importance of the EIA Directive, the SEA Directive and the Flood Directive.[75] As said, the EIA and SEA Directives address the challenges posed by climate change-related events and the protection of cultural resources. Likewise, the Flood Directive recognizes that the likelihood and adverse impacts of flood events could increase because of human activities and climate change, and that floods may have adverse consequences not only for human health, life and the environment, but also for cultural heritage. Accordingly, the Directive establishes that cultural heritage protection should be taken into account by Member States in the preparation of the framework for the assessment and management of flood risks.

3.4 *Humanitarian Aid and Civil Protection*

The TFEU contains various provisions referring to the EU action in response to natural and human-induced disasters.[76] Article 6(f) TFEU states that civil protection is one of the areas of 'complementary' EU competence. Pursuant to Article 214, the EU provides assistance to victims of disasters and conflicts around the world and also works to prevent humanitarian crises. In this sense, a key role is played by the EU Commission's Humanitarian Aid and Civil Protection Department (ECHO), which was established in 1992 as a result of a series of large-scale humanitarian crises. Specifically, ECHO was created in order to increase the EU's capacity to respond to the full cycle of natural and man-made disaster management: prevention, preparedness, response, and recovery. Today, ECHO is part of the EU External Relations and Foreign Affairs policy.

Title XXIII of the TFEU, entitled 'Civil Protection' and consisting of Article 196, constitutes the legal basis for the actions carried out by the EU in the field of civil protection. This norm stipulates that the EU shall enhance Member States' cooperation 'in order to improve the effectiveness of systems for preventing and protecting against natural or man-made disasters'. Another relevant provision is Article 222 TFEU. This contains the so-called 'solidarity clause': 'The Union and its Member States shall act jointly in a spirit of solidarity if a Member State is [...] the victim of a natural or man-made disaster'. This provision has been interpreted as

---

[75] Directive 2007/60/EC of 23 October 2007 on the assessment and management of flood risks.

[76] Apart from the provisions described in what follows, the TFEU contains two other relevant norms: Article 107 stipulates that 'aid to make good the damage caused by natural disasters [...]' is compatible with the internal market; Article 122 says that '[w]here a Member State is in difficulties or is seriously threatened with severe difficulties caused by natural disasters or exceptional occurrences beyond its control, the Council, on a proposal from the Commission, may grant, under certain conditions, Union financial assistance to the Member State concerned [...]'.

entailing a legal obligation for the EU and its Member States to intervene in favour of the Member State hit by a disaster, provided that their assistance is explicitly requested.[77] The implementation of Articles 196 and 222 TFEU is currently ensured by the Union Civil Protection Mechanism (UCPM).[78] This can be regarded as 'a visible expression of European solidarity by ensuring a practical and timely contribution to prevention of and preparedness for disasters and the response to disasters' occurring inside or outside the Union.[79]

Since 2010, humanitarian aid and civil protection are administered by ECHO to streamline and improve the effectiveness of EU's crisis response. More importantly, the 2013 Decision establishing the UCPM instituted the Emergency Response Coordination Centre (ERCC) within the ECHO. This Centre collects and analyses real-time information on disasters, monitors hazards, prepares plans for the deployment of experts and equipment, and coordinates the disaster response by matching offers of assistance by the EU and the Member States to the needs of the disaster-stricken country.

At this juncture, it is worth pausing to consider the scope of application of the EU action in the field of disaster risk reduction and preparedness. On the one hand, according to Decision 1313/2013, the UCPM's main objective is 'to facilitate coordination in the field of civil protection in order to improve the effectiveness of systems for preventing, preparing for and responding to natural and man-made disasters' (Article 1(1)). Decision 1313/2013 affirms that disasters are 'any situation which has or may have a severe impact on people, the environment, or property, including cultural heritage', and that the protection to be ensured by the Union 'shall cover primarily people, but also the environment and property, including cultural heritage, against all kinds of natural and man-made disasters, including the consequences of acts of terrorism, technological, radiological or environmental disasters, marine pollution, and acute health emergencies, occurring inside or outside the Union' (Article 1(2)).[80] On the other hand, Decision 1313/2013 establishes a causal link between disasters and climate change.[81] The preamble underlines that climate change is one of the causes of 'the significant increase in the

---

[77] Gestri (2012), p. 109.

[78] Established with Decision 1313/2013/EU of 17 December 2013 on a Union Civil Protection Mechanism (OJ L 347/924, 20 December 2013). The UCPM replaced the Civil Protection Mechanism, which was established with Decision 2001/792/EC Euratom of 23 October 2001 (OJ 2001 L 297/7, 15 November 2001).

[79] Decision 1313/2013/EU of 17 December 2013 on a Union Civil Protection Mechanism (OJ L 347/924, 20 December 2013), preamble, fifth recital.

[80] Another explicit reference to the protection of cultural heritage is contained in EU Parliament Resolution of 21 September 2010 on the Commission Communication 'A Community Approach on the Prevention of Natural and Man-Made Disasters' (2009/2151 (INI)).

[81] The nexus between climate change and the increased frequency and intensity of extreme weather events and disasters was also recognized by the European Environmental Agency with the document 'Mapping the Impacts of Natural Hazards and Technological Accidents in Europe: An Overview of the Last Decade', Copenhagen, 2011.

numbers and severity of natural and man-made disasters in recent years' and of 'future disasters [that] will be more extreme and more complex with far-reaching and longer-term consequences'. The preamble of Decision 1313/2013 also maintains that the Union should aim at 'achieving a higher level of protection and resilience against disasters [...] by fostering a culture of prevention, including due consideration of [...] the need for appropriate adaptation action'. Moreover, Article 5 states that 'the Commission shall [...] (c) establish and regularly update a cross-sectoral overview and map of natural and man-made disaster risks the Union may face, by taking [...] due account of the likely impacts of climate change'.

The foregoing analysis leads to observe that disaster risk management and climate change adaptation have come to focus on the same variables, namely exposure and vulnerability. As said, exposure refers to the elements—such as human beings, their livelihoods, and assets—in an area in which hazard events may occur, whereas vulnerability refers to the propensity of exposed elements to suffer major harm and damage when impacted by hazards. This convergence should not be surprising given that extreme climate events, interacting with exposed and vulnerable human and natural systems, can lead to disasters. On the one hand, efforts towards disaster risk reduction and climate change adaptation should concentrate on identifying and reducing: (1) the processes by which persons, property, and the environment are exposed to potentially damaging events, and (2) the factors that determine or contribute to the vulnerability of persons, property, and the environment. [82] Arguably, the following are the most probable factors and processes of risk: environmental mismanagement and degradation,[83] rapid and inappropriate urban development, international financial pressures, and increases in socio-economic inequalities.[84] On the other hand, in order to ensure the well-being of populations, the security of assets, and the maintenance of ecosystem's goods, functions and services, any action should aim at increasing resilience vis-à-vis the potential adverse impacts of both short-lived climate extremes and long-lived, slow events.

Finally, it should be mentioned that the EU seeks to increasingly incorporate disaster risk reduction and climate change assistance into its development cooperation activities with the most vulnerable developing countries.[85] As such, the EU has come to support the achievement of the Millennium Development Goals,[86] and

---

[82] IPCC (2014b).

[83] From the cultural heritage perspective, the direct and indirect effects of air pollution in urban areas represent the most serious risks. Direct effects consist in the deterioration of monuments and artworks: recession of façades in limestone or marble, soiling of stone surface, chemical leaching of stained glass, and metal corrosion. Indirect effects stem from the slow deterioration and extreme weather events originating from the warming of the planet.

[84] Cardona et al. (2012), pp. 69–71.

[85] See e.g. EU Commission, 'Action Plan for Resilience in Crisis Prone Countries' SWD (2013) 227 final; and 2007 EU Global Climate Change Alliance Flagship Initiative 2014–2020.

[86] See e.g. EU Commission, 'A Decent Life for All: From Vision to Collective Action' COM (2014) 335 final.

the objectives envisaged by the United Nations Office for Disaster Risk Reduction through the 'Sendai Framework for Disaster Risk Reduction 2015–2030'[87] and the campaign 'Making Cities Resilient: My City Is Getting Ready!'.[88]

4 Coping with Legal Risks: The Role of the Concepts of 'Common Good' and 'Sustainable Development'

The foregone analysis demonstrates that EU regulation in the fields of culture and environment has expanded dramatically over the past decades. Regarding cultural heritage, policy initiatives and legislation have developed not only to ensure its protection, but also to capitalise on its economic values. The reason is that cultural heritage has a great capacity to promote the regeneration of neglected areas and the creation of jobs.[89] Concerning the environment, EU legislation has permitted to significantly reduce air, water, and soil pollution. EU actions have also stimulated innovation and investments in low-carbon technologies which generate jobs and export opportunities.[90] Furthermore, it has been shown that the EU does not regard the cultural and environmental policies as self-contained areas. On the contrary, the policy and legal instruments analysed thus far reflect a holistic conceptualization of the environment that covers ecosystems and man-made cultural spaces. Moreover, the above examination offers considerable evidence that the EU actions carried out within the environmental, climate, and humanitarian policy areas may have a positive effect on cultural heritage protection as they bring about a multiplication of adaptation and mitigation measures and hence a reduction of the conditions that may lead to disaster situations.[91]

Yet, the EU regulation in the fields of culture and environment is far from satisfactory. This is testified by the continuous depletion of ecosystems and biodiversity and the glaring failures to tackle the effects of the changing climate.[92] The same mixed trends emerge with respect to cultural heritage. This is demonstrated by the fact that cultural resources in many areas are threatened by neglect, neoliberal development models, growing and unfettered urbanization, unregulated tourist

---

[87] Adopted in 2015 at the Conference on Disaster Risk Reduction (Sendai, Japan), it is the successor of the 'Hyogo Framework for Action 2005–2015: Building the Resilience of Nations and Communities to Disasters'.

[88] See : <http://www.unisdr.org/campaign/resilientcities/>.

[89] For instance, tourism is estimated to contribute €415 billion to the EU GDP and 3.4 million tourism enterprises account for 15.2 million jobs. See EU Commission, 'Towards an Integrated Approach to Cultural Heritage for Europe' COM (2014) 477 final, 22 July 2014, p. 4.

[90] European Environmental Agency, 'Mapping the Impacts of Natural Hazards and Technological Accidents in Europe: An Overview of the Last Decade', Copenhagen, 2011, pp. 21–22.

[91] EU Commission, 'Towards an Integrated Approach to Cultural Heritage for Europe' COM (2014) 477 final, 22 July 2014, p. 5.

[92] Ibid.

influxes, and, as shown, loss and damage associated with climate change.[93] One of the reasons is that States—even the wealthiest in terms of art and culture—look at the national patrimony mostly as a driver for the economy and disregard its intrinsic and intangible functions—such as its social value as a significant element of a cultural community and as an expression of the creative spirit and identity of such a community.[94]

However, although the European cultural and natural heritage remains vulnerable to the increasing incidence of weather events and disasters, there is a small glimmer of hope. The policy and legal measures that have been discussed in this chapter contain manifold references to two important concepts, namely 'common good' and 'sustainable development'. These principles may be used to reinvigorate and steer the proper implementation of the EU's normative response to the climate change-related phenomena that threaten cultural and natural resources.

4.1 Common Good

The concept of common good is used in international law discourse to refer to values that are fundamental for the international community as a whole and that transcend the individual self-interests of States.[95] Such a notion is also a strong indicator of the transformation of international law from a regime designed to preserve States' sovereignty to a system that aims at bringing about increased cooperation between nations in order to address global problems and to ensure the survival for all, i.e. the States and the human communities that live therein.[96]

There is no authoritative list of common goods in international law. However, a number of international binding and non-binding texts and documents refer explicitly to the protection of common goods—or to some variations of the term, such as 'global commons', 'common interests', 'common heritage of humankind' and 'common concerns'.

The recognition of fundamental problems in the fields of environment and cultural heritage has been a crucial catalyst for the affirmation of this concept in the international law discourse. The 1972 Stockholm Declaration on the Human Environment constitutes the first body of rules with the goal of safeguarding the essential elements of the environment—including the climate and the biosphere—as a 'global public good'. Resolution 43/53 of the General Assembly underlined that 'emerging evidence indicates' that the effects of global warming 'could be

[93] Bevan (2013).

[94] Francioni (2012a), p. 722.

[95] In economic literature, a common good is one that is characterized by non-rivalry (anyone can use a good without diminishing its availability to others) and non-excludability (no one can be excluded from using the good). See Kaul et al. (1999).

[96] Voigt (2014), p. 11.

disastrous for mankind if timely steps are not taken at all levels' and that climate change is a 'common concern of humankind'.[97] Likewise, the UNFCCC acknowledged that 'change in the Earth's climate and its adverse effects are a common concern of humankind'.[98] The idea of cultural heritage as a 'public good' can be traced back to the Convention for the Protection of Cultural Property in the Event of Armed Conflict,[99] according to which 'damage to cultural property belonging to any people whatsoever means damage to the cultural heritage of all mankind, since each people makes its contribution to the culture of the world'.[100] The same idea was echoed by the UNESCO Declaration Concerning the Intentional Destruction of Cultural Heritage of 2003. This establishes that 'cultural heritage is an important component of the cultural identity of communities, groups and individuals [. . .]',[101] and that '[t]he international community recognizes the importance of the protection of cultural heritage and reaffirms its commitment to fight against its intentional destruction in any form [. . .]'.[102] Finally, it is worth considering Article 6(1) of the WHC, which states that 'the cultural and natural heritage [of outstanding universal value] constitutes a world heritage for whose protection it is duty of the international community as a whole to co-operate'. In sum, natural and cultural resources have emerged as common goods a long time ago.

Having said this, it must be recognized that the idea of common goods stems, albeit indirectly, from two distinct developments. First, it represents a logical deduction from the affirmation that certain international obligations by their very nature have an *erga omnes* character—in the sense that they are owed to the international community as a whole and not simply to another State or a group of States.[103] Second, the idea of common goods emerges by way of inductive reasoning from the incremental use of the principles of 'common heritage of humankind' and 'common concern' in international legal documents.[104] These principles are thus expressions of the different degrees of normativity that the idea of common good, as an umbrella term, may produce in international law.

The concept of 'common heritage of humankind' has found expression in the legal frameworks regulating, inter alia, the environmental resources of the seabed, ocean floor and the subsoil thereof. By way of example, Article 136 of the United Nations Convention on the Law of the Sea (UNCLOS)[105] establishes that the

[97] Preamble, first, second and third recitals. Adopted 6 December 1988.

[98] Preamble, first recital.

[99] Adopted 14 May 1954, 249 UNTS 240.

[100] Preamble, second recital.

[101] Preamble, fifth recital.

[102] Article I.

[103] This idea was articulated for the first time by the International Court of Justice in *Barcelona Traction, Light and Power Company, Limited (Belgium v. Spain)*, 5 February 1970, ICJ Reports 1970, 3, para. 33.

[104] Francioni (2014), p. 444.

[105] 10 December 1982, 21 ILM 1261 (1982).

seabed and ocean floor beyond the limits of national jurisdiction 'are the common heritage of mankind'. The UNCLOS and other international instruments reiterate the four basic implications of the common heritage of humankind: (1) it cannot be appropriated; (2) it requires the establishment of an international system of management and supervision in which all users have a right to share and use; (3) it should be reserved for peaceful uses; and (4) it implies an active sharing of benefits.[106]

The different concept of 'common concern' indicates the presence of urgent issues having potentially devastating, possibly irreversible and wide-ranging environmental impacts that inevitably transcend the boundaries of a single State and require collective action in response.[107] This concept embodies universal solidarity, emphasises the interests of future generations, reflects the basic values of the international community, and becomes relevant where the four basic elements of the principle of common heritage of humankind are not available altogether. More importantly, this concept can be seen as a legal basis for legitimising forms of intervention within the jurisdiction of individual States.[108] This holds true with respect to one of the domains where this principle has been recognized, namely the cultural heritage of outstanding universal value that falls under the scope of application of the WHC. This convention does not affect the sovereignty of the States Parties. However, the State where a WHC site is situated cannot invoke the exception of reserved domain to justify any use or regulation of that site that can jeopardize its outstanding universal value. The reserved domain of States must give way to the interest in the conservation and enjoyment of properties that present such outstanding universal value.[109] Stated differently, States retain sovereignty subject to no legal constraints except those imposed by international law.[110]

4.2 Sustainable Development

In 1987, the World Commission on Environment and Development ('Brundtland Commission') defined sustainable development as the '[d]evelopment that meets the needs of the present without compromising the ability of future generations to meet their own needs'.[111] Today, this concept—which is regarded as a general

[106] See e.g. Joyner (1986).

[107] Shelton (2009), p. 34.

[108] Francioni (2006), pp. 3, 8–9, 15.

[109] Francioni (2012b), pp. 19–20.

[110] Shelton (2009), p. 38.

[111] Report of the World Commission on Environment and Development, 'Our Common Future' (1987).

principle of environmental law, along with the precautionary principle and the polluter pays principle—has become relevant in the field of cultural heritage law.[112]

One of the fundamental characteristics of general principles is that they cannot be defined in precise terms, yet they are indispensable for the design and assessment of policy and normative initiatives.[113] This means that, as sustainable development is perceived as one of such principles, the normative process at the domestic and international levels has to take this into consideration. In this respect, it is important to note that the principle of integration is the most central procedural principle relevant to the operationalization of sustainable development.[114] Integration requires that environmental factors are taken into account in the formulation and implementation of all sectoral policies. This is motivated by the fact that many environmental problems, such as climate change and the loss of biodiversity, necessitate tackling the multiple causes and sources of pollutant emissions and natural resource mismanagement across sectors. Stated differently, the principle of integration requires taking account of environmental factors in the formulation and implementation of the policies that regulate economic activities and social organization in order to achieve the objective of sustainable development.

The principle of integration is a basic principle and objective of EU environmental law and policy. The TFEU contains three important references to this principle. Article 11 reads: '[e]nvironmental protection requirements must be integrated into the definition and implementation of the Union policies and activities, in particular with a view to promoting sustainable development'. Article 13 states: '[i]n formulating and implementing the Union's agriculture, fisheries, transport, internal market, research and technological development and space policies, the Union and the Member States shall [. . .] pay full regard to the welfare requirements of animals, while respecting the legislative or administrative provisions and customs of the Member States relating in particular to religious rites, cultural traditions and regional heritage'. Article 167(4) affirms that the EU 'shall take cultural aspects into account in its action under other provisions of the Treaties, in particular in order to respect and to promote the diversity of its cultures'. The latter provision coins the protection and promotion of culture as a horizontal policy principle. In addition, Article 167(4) signals that the EU is not simply bound to refrain from interfering with the enjoyment of culture ('to respect'), but it is also under duty to take appropriate measures to further encourage it ('to promote'). The principle of integration is mentioned also in the EU Charter[115] and in most of the legal instruments adopted in the policy areas examined above.

---

[112] This is proved by the Hangzhou Declaration (adopted at UNESCO's Congress 'Culture: Key to Sustainable Development', 15–17 May 2013), which represents the culmination of UNESCO's long-standing advocacy to prove the link between culture and development.

[113] Bosselmann (2008), p. 63.

[114] Bosselmann (2008), p. 61.

[115] Article 37: 'A high level of environmental protection and the improvement of the quality of the environment must be integrated into the policies of the Union and ensured in accordance with the principle of sustainable development'.

A powerful manifestation of the application of the principle of integration within the EU is provided by the funding opportunities in the field of culture. Although the actions adopted under the 'Creative Europe 2014–2020' programme[116] entail limited or no funding at all, a range of other policies make important financial contributions to culture. By way of example, cultural heritage is one of the investment priorities under the Cohesion Policy—through the Regional Development Fund, the Social Fund, the Agricultural Fund for Rural Development, and the European Maritime and Fisheries Fund[117]—and the Research and Innovation Policy.[118]

5 Conclusions

The alarms launched by the scientific community about the worsening conditions of the planet's atmosphere are clear and consistent. Despite of the uncertainties associated with projections of future climate patterns, climate change-related phenomena are expected to increasingly threaten natural and cultural resources and to bring about disasters involving vulnerable human systems. These risks can be reduced by the prompt adoption of concrete steps, most notably meaningful mitigation and adaptation measures. Preventing global warming from exceeding the 2 °C threshold is technologically feasible. This certainly carries substantial economic, social, and institutional challenges. Doing nothing, however, would increase the likelihood of long-lasting changes in the climate system, which will lead to severe, widespread, and irreversible impacts for people and ecosystems globally.[119]

The efforts deployed thus far at the international and EU levels are far from satisfactory. This is testified by the fears that the forthcoming Conference of the

---

[116] See supra Sect. 3.1.

[117] From 2007 to 2013, the Regional Development Fund allocated €3.2 billion for the protection and preservation of cultural heritage, €2.2 billion for the development of cultural infrastructure, and €553 million for cultural services. In the 2014–2020 period, cultural heritage investments are possible under the specific regulations of the Cohesion Policy, whose overall budget is €325 billion. EU Commission, 'Mapping of Cultural Heritage Actions in European Union Policies, Programmes and Activities', available at: <http://ec.europa.eu/culture/library/>, p. 10, accessed 31 August 2015.

[118] The new Framework Programme for Research and Innovation, Horizon 2020, has a budget of €80 billion for the period 2014–2020, and supports heritage-related research under the three pillars of the programme: Excellent Science, Industrial Leadership, and Societal Challenges. In the latter, Challenge 6 ('Europe in a Changing World: Inclusive, Innovative and Reflective Societies') and Challenge 5 ('Climate Action, Environment, Resource Efficiency and Raw Materials') require the development of technology and multidisciplinary research for the preservation of cultural heritage resources. EU Commission, 'Mapping of Cultural Heritage Actions in European Union Policies, Programmes and Activities', p. 14, available at: <http://ec.europa.eu/culture/library/>, accessed 31 August 2015.

[119] IPCC (2014b).

Parties to the UNFCCC—which will take place in December 2015—will fail to achieve meaningful progress just like the meetings held in the past two decades. Another illustration is provided by the fact that the mechanisms introduced under the Kyoto Protocol and EU law to enable industrialized States to meet their emission targets have attracted several criticisms.[120] On the one hand, it has been argued that these market-based mechanisms reduce the natural world to a purely economic resource because they encourage profit from pollution and subject the development of green technologies to the approval of the market.[121] On the other hand, it can be said that the solution to climate change should not lie in the dogma of market freedom and price mechanism. The contemporary financial crisis and banking scandals testify that the market cannot be trusted to self-regulate.[122] Other problems specifically concern the protection of cultural heritage. As said, neither the UNFCCC nor the Kyoto Protocol address the impacts of climate change on cultural heritage, whereas the UNESCO bodies have failed to provide decisive responses. Moreover, EU actions to protect Europe's heritage from climate change-related phenomena are fragmented among diverse sectors and policies.

However, the main legal risk is that EU governance structures have failed to translate into practice the concepts of 'common good' and 'sustainable development'. As a result, the idea of 'common good' remains elusive—just as the related notions of 'common concern' and 'common heritage of humankind'[123] Therefore, it is difficult to derive concrete obligations from the provisions that employ these notions, as they mostly require States to cooperate with each other in order to address the identified issues.[124] Regarding sustainable development, it is regrettable that the Brundtland definition provided above is generally interpreted as promoting primarily human development, not necessarily limited or tempered by environmental or social considerations.[125] In other words, this principle is construed as entailing a mere economic dimension. Originally, however, this principle was based on the concept of ecological sustainability, which is essentially 'the duty of the human beings to protect and restore the integrity of the Earth's ecological systems'.[126]

In light of the magnitude of the risks posed by climate change and of the asymmetries of the existing regulatory framework, the EU and its Member States should, first, develop an understanding that the principle of sustainable development entails the respect of the ecological boundaries of the Earth, and, second, put

[120] The Kyoto Protocol introduced the following mechanisms: 'Joint Fulfilment of Commitments and Implementation', 'Clean Development Mechanism', and 'Emissions Trading' (see Sect. 3.3). As for EU Law, see the EU Emissions Trading System (see Sect. 3.3).

[121] Adelman (2010), p. 164.

[122] Francioni (2012c), p. 458.

[123] See Baslar (1998), pp. 108–109, 314; and Francioni (2006), p. 18.

[124] Voigt (2014), pp. 20–22; and Shelton (2009), p. 38.

[125] Bosselmann (2002), p. 84.

[126] Bosselmann (2008), p. 53; Brown Weiss (1989), p. 38; and Montini (2012), p. 280.

in place rational procedural arrangements and normative reforms to ensure the ecological integrity of ecosystems. These can be seen as the prerequisites for the realization of the primary common good—the long-term survival of humankind—and also for the transformation of the current piecemeal response to the climate change-related weather events and disasters that threaten the European cultural heritage into a coherent and effective regulatory framework.

References

Adelman S (2010) Rethinking human rights: the impact of climate change on the dominant discourse. In: Humphreys S (ed) Human rights and climate change. Cambridge University Press, Cambridge, pp 159–179

Ban K (2007) A climate culprit in Darfur. Washington Post (16 June 2007), available at: <http://www.washingtonpost.com/wp-dyn/content/article/2007/06/15/AR2007061501857.html>, accessed 31 August 2015

Baslar K (1998) The concept of the common heritage of mankind in international law. Martinus Nijhoff Publishers, The Hague

Bevan R (2013) Global heritage on the back foot. The Art Newspaper, No. 252, p 16

Bosselmann K (2002) The concept of sustainable development. In: Bosselmann K, Grinlinton D (eds) Environmental law for a sustainable society. New Zealand Centre for Environmental Law, Auckland, pp 81–96

Bosselmann K (2008) The principle of sustainability: transforming law and governance. Ashgate, London

Brown Weiss E (1989) In fairness to future generations: international law, common patrimony and intergenerational equity. Transnational Publishers, Dobbs Ferry, NY

Cardona OD et al (2012) Determinants of risk: exposure and vulnerability. In: IPCC – Field CB et al (eds) Managing the risks of extreme events and disasters to advance climate change adaptation. A Special Report of Working Groups I and II of the Intergovernmental Panel on Climate Change. Cambridge, pp 65–108

Francioni F (2006) International law for biotechnology: basic principles. In: Francioni F, Scovazzi T (eds) Biotechnology and international law. Hart Publishing, Oxford, pp 1–28

Francioni F (2012a) Public and private in the international protection of global cultural goods. Eur J Int Law: 719–730

Francioni F (2012b) The evolving framework for the protection of cultural heritage in international law. In: Borelli S, Lenzerini F (eds) Cultural heritage, cultural rights, cultural diversity: new developments in international law. Martinus Nijhoff Publishers, Leiden/Boston, pp 3–25

Francioni F (2012c) Realism, Utopia and the future of international law. In: Cassese A (ed) Realizing Utopia: the future of international law. Oxford University Press, Oxford, pp 442–460

Francioni F (2014) International common goods: an epilogue. In: Lenzerini F, Vrdoljak AF (eds) International law for common goods. Hart Publishing, Oxford, pp 443–448

Gestri M (2012) EU disaster response law: principles and instruments. In: de Guttry A et al (eds) International disaster response law. TMC Asser Press, The Hague, pp 105–127

Gilbert L (2013) An Exodus from Red Hook. The Art Newspaper (26 April 2013)

Gruber S (2008) The impact of climate change on cultural heritage sites: environmental law and adaptation. Sydney Law School-Legal Studies Research Paper 8/117, available at: <http://papers.ssrn.com/sol3/papers.cfm?abstract_id=1285741>, accessed 31 August 2015

Hee-Eun K (2011) Changing climate, changing culture: adding the climate change dimension to the protection of intangible cultural heritage. Int J Cult Prop: 259–290

Homer-Dixon TF (2007) Terror in the weather forecast. New York Times (24 April 2007), available at: <http://www.nytimes.com/2007/04/24/opinion/24homer-dixon.html?_r=0>, accessed 31 August 2015
IPCC (2012) Managing the risks of extreme events and disasters to advance climate change adaptation. In: Field CB et al (eds) A Special Report of Working Groups I and II of the Intergovernmental Panel on Climate Change. Cambridge
IPCC (2013) Summary for policymakers. In: Stocker TF et al (eds) Climate Change 2013: The Physical Science Basis. Contribution of Working Group I to the Fifth Assessment Report of the Intergovernmental Panel on Climate Change. Cambridge, pp 1–30
IPCC (2014a) In: Field CB et al (eds) Climate Change 2014: Impacts, Adaptation and Vulnerability. Part A: Global and Sectoral Aspects. Contribution of Working Group I to the Fifth Assessment Report of the Intergovernmental Panel on Climate Change. Cambridge
IPCC (2014b) Fifth Assessment Report, Climate Change 2014, Synthesis Report, Synthesis for Policymakers, available at: <http://www.ipcc.ch/report/ar5/syr/>, accessed 31 August 2015
Joyner CC (1986) Legal implications of the concept of the common heritage of mankind. Int Comp Law Q: 190–199
Kaul I, Grunberg I, Stern MA (eds) (1999) Global public goods. International cooperation in the 21st century. Oxford University Press, Oxford
Leal-Arcas R (2013) Climate change and international trade. Edward Elgar Publishing, London
Lee M (2014) EU environmental law, governance and decision-making, 2nd edn. Hart Publishing, Oxford
McAdam J (2012) Climate change, forced migration, and international law. Oxford University Press, Oxford
Montini M (2012) Revising international environmental law through the paradigm of ecological sustainability. In: Lenzerini F, Vrdoljak AF (eds) International law for common goods. Hart Publishing, Oxford, pp 271–287
Mutter JC, Barnard KM (2010) Climate change, evolution of disasters and inequality. In: Humphreys S (ed) Human rights and climate change. Cambridge University Press, Cambridge, pp 275–276
Perry J, Falzon C (2014) Climate change adaptation for natural world heritage sites. A practical guide. UNESCO World Heritage Series, Series No. 37
Rayfuse R, Scott SV (2012) Mapping the impact of climate change on international law. In: Rayfuse R, Scott SV (eds) International law in the era of climate change. Edward Elgar Publishing, London, pp 3–25
Shelton D (2009) Common concern of humanity. Iustum Aequum Salutare: 33–40
Voigt C (2014) Delineating the common interest in international law. In: Benedek B et al (eds) The common interest in international law. Intersentia, Antwerp, pp 9–27

Legal Risks in European Environmental Law and Policy

Harry H.G. Post

Contents

Abstract The theoretical framework for legal risk analysis is still in a rather preliminary state, but uncertainty may be called a prominent aspect in the definition of legal risk. Environmental law tends to be characterised by many uncertainties due to the nature of the environment as well as to its relative newness and its often innovative aspects. Two examples from European environmental law, where serious factual as well as legal uncertainty can be observed, are discussed in terms of legal risk analysis. The results for both the EU law on waste management and the legal norms for the exposure of PM 2.5 in the EU law on ambient air quality are evaluated as positive. This judgment, however, is qualified as 'cautiously' positive due to the less than fully elaborated theoretical state of legal risk analysis.

1 Introduction

'Legal risk' is a somewhat remarkable notion as we will soon hope to show. Although it might initially impress as an established instrumental concept, on somewhat closer scrutiny 'legal risk' appears to be rather indeterminate and still demanding complicated theoretical reasoning in order to provide it with meaning

H.H.G. Post (✉)
Faculty of Law, Catholic University of Lille, Lille, France
e-mail: hhg_post00@yahoo.com

E. Miščenić, A. Raccah (eds.), *Legal Risks in EU Law*,
DOI 10.1007/978-3-319-28596-2_11

that may make it relevant as a legal instrument, that is to say, in some areas. Here we will introduce legal risk beginning at one of its main 'official' sources, the EU Banking Directive 2006/48/EC. It appears that a major connotation of legal risk in the academic and institutional discussions is its relationship to uncertainty. Environmental law, including its European variety, is a field of law where uncertainty has found an expression in some important principles and, subsequently, legal instruments. The most notable and controversial example (it still is regarding its precise meaning) is undoubtedly the precautionary principle. Legal uncertainty in different forms also appears in other parts of Environmental law. Following the introduction, below, of the notion of legal risk in Sect. 1 are two sections where such different forms of uncertainty are important. The subject of Sect. 2, European law on waste management, almost from its initiation in the 1970s has been 'marred' by the rather impressive dynamics of the relevant technological developments regarding the treatment of waste. As a result, the applicable (European) law is also characterised by uncertainty and in almost constant need of adaptation to these changes. Judicial interpretation and explanation has become virtually endemic.

Section 3 discusses another part of European environmental law. A rather curious aspect of the EU law on air pollution (or better protection of ambient air) will be examined where measures have been decided upon that bring the lives of thousands, if not hundred thousands of EU citizens in jeopardy. The dangers involved are explicitly recognized, so that we might assume that a rather serious risk has been deliberately taken. However, the levels of uncertainty here may be said to have reached a rather new dimension due to the character of some of the objectives of the major legal instrument, the 'Framework' Directive 2008/50/EC on ambient air quality and cleaner air for Europe.

The subject of the concluding Sect. 4 is the question if the notion of 'legal risk' is helpful to understand or explain the uncertainties found in these two parts of European environmental law. On the basis of the excursus in the Sects. 2 and 3 a necessarily tentative assessment of the possible merits of legal risk analysis to these aspects of European environmental law will be undertaken.

2 The Notion of 'Legal Risk'

A risk is of a legal nature if its source involves a legal norm. The most authoritative definition of legal risk from a legal point of view is said to be the still 'rather loose' understanding the Basel Committee on Banking Supervision (or Basel II) used:

> Legal risk includes, but is not limited to, exposure to fines, penalties, or punitive damages resulting from supervisory actions, as well as private settlements.

The reason for its importance is that the notion will "[. . .] probably, have a major influence on the understanding of legal risk in the Basel II-related Banking Directive (Art. 4(22) of Directive 2006/48/EC), which provides no definition."[1]

This may be called a rather 'instrumental' definition: The risk of a particular behaviour is that fines, punitive damages or perhaps less formal penalties may be the consequence. The exposure to such potential 'sanctions' is the result of engaging in 'risky' behaviour.

The Basel II definition focuses solely on legal norms which are detrimental to the stakeholder as sources of risk. Legal risk is in this context understood as a type of operational risk. The latter term is defined in the same way in Basel II and in the Banking Directive:

> Operational risk means the risk of loss resulting from inadequate or failed internal processes, people and systems, or from external events, and includes legal risk (Art. 4(22) of Directive 2006/48/EC).[2]

In a recommendable paper, *Tobias Mahler* has attempted to lift the discussion of, in particular, 'legal' risk to a more general and also more sophisticated level, so that we may be able to work with a concept of legal risk that may find a more general and useful application than is so far the case.[3] Hence, using the Basel II notion of legal risk as a starting point, he sets out to analyse other definitions and classifications of legal risk with the ambitious objective 'to introduce a context-independent classification, based on norm theory'. In the process he convincingly demonstrates that 'legal risk' has not particularly developed into a clear concept that can easily be used in serious analysis and perhaps even less into a legal concept able to clarify or explain legal processes. The usefulness of the term seems, indeed rather 'context-dependent'. Whether or not legal risk has much significance in such other 'extra-legal' contexts is a question the answer to which is largely beyond the subject of this chapter.

In his effort to develop a more generally applicable concept of legal risk, *Mahler* takes us on a tour of philosophical and social science methodology. He makes choices, like favouring an Aristotelian approach to define via genus *et differentiam* which seem reasonable and helpful enough. Also, in order to explain risk in law, he chooses the well-known approach of *H.L.A. Hart* for a legal norm: Every legal norm consists of an antecedent (if A) and a consequent (then B). Antecedent and consequent are linked by a normative modality, which states how antecedent and

---

[1] Basel Committee on Banking Supervision, International Convergence of Capital Measurement and Capital Standards, BIS 2006, fn. 97, at p. 144; the definition of 'legal risk has disappeared from the Basel Committee on Banking Supervision,' Core Principles for Effective Banking Supervision, BIS 2012, although the definition of 'operational risk', Principle 25 of the Principles, has been maintained including the reference to legal risks—see the text—in fn. 79 at p. 58.

[2] Operational risk has been the subject of many discussions and arguments in the banking world. See for a useful overview, Moscadelli (2004); or Basel Committee on Banking Supervision, Core Principles for Effective Banking Supervision-Consultative Document, BIS 2012, Basel, in particular, Principle 15, Risk Management Process, and 25, Operational Risk, pp. 40–44.

[3] Mahler (2007), pp. 10–31.

consequent are related. For example, if A is the case, then there may be a legal obligation to perform B.[4]

What does the concept of risk add to this straightforward logical legal perspective? It seems that one connotation may be of particular interest for the field of (European) environmental law. *Mahler* explains this as follows. In his view, the contribution of the risk perspective to law consists of at least the following three elements:

First, risks involve (mostly) negative consequences of events. In order to know whether a legal norm has negative consequences, we need to apply the norm to a given set of facts and evaluate the result from the stakeholder's subjective perspective as either beneficial or detrimental for his assets or objectives.

Second, risks imply future events, i.e., we need to assume an ex-ante perspective, different from the ex-post perspective of, e.g., a judge.

The third, related, element is perhaps the most interesting one for our perspective, and one which lawyers often do not like too much:

Third, risks entail likely future events, obliging us to address matters of uncertainty.[5]

Risk is often distinguished from "true uncertainty" by understanding risk as probabilistically measurable uncertainty.[6] Notably, this probabilistic concept of risk differs from the understanding of risk in law. Lawyers do not typically assess probabilities when addressing risk. Instead, the question is "Whose risk is this?" The concept implies that the parties to a contract or agreement bear the consequences (losses) that result from certain contingencies. Unfortunately, *Mahler's* main examples and illustrations are from contract law and other less public legal areas than EU environmental law. Still, much of his discussion generally applies to public law as well, in particular the following three more general questions:

a) Can there be a legal risk in the absence of any uncertainty? For example, can we speak of legal risk if the law is "not sound," but is well-defined and predictable?
b) Does legal risk encompass solely normative uncertainty, or does it also cover factual uncertainty? For example, should liability for an accident be included, if the only uncertain factor is whether or not the accident will happen?
c) If we include factual uncertainty in relation to legal norms, where are the outer limits of legal risk? Should we include factually uncertain events which have consequences on an asset or objective for which the stakeholder holds some type of legal position? For example, should the breach of a contractual obligation by the other party be considered a legal risk?[7]

---

[4] Hart (1994).

[5] Mahler (2007), p. 10.

[6] Here he refers to Knight 1921: Houghton Mifflin. As a point of departure for the present paper, *Mahler* proposes to use the following ISO definition of risk, which is representative for the use of the term in risk management: Risk is the combination of the probability of an event and its consequences (ISO, Risk management – vocabulary – guidelines for use in standard; Geneva, 2002, ISO, definition 3.1.1).

[7] Mahler (2007), p. 18.

In respect to environmental 'risks', the discussion of legal uncertainty seems relevant. When we speak of legal uncertainty, we typically assume a given set of facts and focus on the uncertainty regarding the correct or likely legal judgement about these facts. This uncertainty is not related only to vague laws, but may arise from many different causes. Hence, the law's vagueness does not seem to be the only, and maybe not even the most important, source of legal uncertainty but vagueness, in addition to other factors, permits different legal decisions, and such decisions may lead to an unforeseen negative consequence for a stakeholder. Legal uncertainty, anyhow, can be considered a very relevant source of legal risk. The question remains if legal uncertainty should be understood as the only source of legal risk, or if a wider definition, which includes factual uncertainty, is more appropriate. Factual uncertainties need to be considered in any type of planning for the future. *Mahler* submits therefore a broad notion of the term "legal risk" including both legal and factual uncertainties,[8] and that seems relevant for the 'context' of (EU) environmental law. The same holds true for his discussion of what he calls 'the outer limits' of legal risk.

A legal norm may contribute to a loss for a stakeholder. In that case, the legal norm is one of the sources of the legal risk. This presumes that it must be possible for the norm to be applied in a manner detrimental to the stakeholder, and that the norm's existence and validity have an impact on the risk value.

In summary, risk is the combination of the probability of an event and its consequences. A risk is a legal risk if its source involves a legal norm. Thus, the risk needs to be the manifestation of a legal norm's potential detriment. Both factual and legal uncertainty may influence legal risk.

In conclusion, *Mahler* submits that, firstly, legal risk should address and cover events which are uncertain, based on both factual and legal uncertainty. Secondly, reference to a legal norm is not sufficient if this norm is beneficial solely to the stakeholder. Hence, a legal norm can constitute a legal risk only if the norm can be qualified as a source of risk.

From *Mahler's* discussion of legal risk we have thus concluded that there are two kinds of legal risks potentially relevant for environmental law: instrumental legal risk and legal risk as a consequence of legal or factual uncertainty.

Once the definition of legal risk has been clarified, we may be interested in understanding what types of legal risk there are. *Mahler* submits that a possible categorisation could be based on the distinction between legal and factual uncertainty. Most typologies suggested by practitioners are essentially context-dependent, non-exhaustive and do not consist of mutually exclusive types of legal risks. Hence, they may be very useful in their specific context, but they do not form a solid basis for a general theory of legal risk. This would be the case for the norm-theoretic approach *Mahler* proposes. Such a theory will enable the distinction between two types of legal risk, under the condition that we face a single relevant norm which is either deontic, or prescriptive, or a qualification norm. A deontic

[8] Mahler (2007), p. 20.

norm prescribes what is obligatory, prohibited or permitted for an actor. Deontic norms are sometimes referred to as "duty-imposing norms" or "prescriptive norms". "Qualification" or "secondary norms" (*Hart's* term) do not impose an obligation, prohibition or permission, they qualify a set of facts as something which has a legal meaning. The combination of the norm-theoretic approach with the distinction of normative and factual uncertainties renders a matrix of legal risk, which should be generally applicable for the identification of legal risks, independent of the context. *Mahler* provides the following table for such a perspective of legal risk.[9]

Norms	Legal	Factual
	Uncertainty	Uncertainty
Deontic or prescriptive norms	**I may have to pay taxes** (depending on interpretation of tax law).	**I may have to pay damages** (depending on whether I cause an accident while driving and drinking).
Qualification norms	**The contract may not be valid** (depending on uncertain validity rules).	**The contract may not be enforceable** (depending on whether a claim is submitted within the time limitation).

This first still rather basic typology of legal risk could be expanded by adding additional levels for sub-types of norms in each class and by applying it subsequently to different legal contexts. More practical risk identification needs to be done in a context-dependent approach.

In conclusion, apart from instrumental legal risk, taken as the quite straightforward starting point of the discussion, the norm-theory form of legal risk *Mahler* describes, should, firstly, address and cover events which are uncertain, based on both factual and legal uncertainty. Secondly, reference to a legal norm is not sufficient if this norm is beneficial solely to the stakeholder. Hence, a legal norm can constitute a legal risk only if the norm can be qualified as a source of risk. In the following two sections we will discuss two different subjects of European environmental law where norms seem to qualify.

3 The Regulation of Waste Management: A Continuous Race with Technology

In European Union policy and law, waste management has been all along marked by tension between trade interests and objectives, on the one hand ('waste as a product'), and environmental and health concerns, on the other hand. Now the latter can be said largely to prevail. Article 1 of the newest waste 'Framework' Directive 2008/98 expresses this shift when it says that the Directive "[...] lays down measures to protect the environment and human health by preventing and reducing

[9] Mahler (2007), p. 28.

the adverse impacts of the generation and management of waste and by reducing overall impacts of resource use and improving the efficiency of such use."

This ambivalent attitude towards waste management expresses itself even in the so-called 'waste hierarchy', also included in the 2008 Framework Directive.[10] Its implementation was to be determined by considering the best solutions for health and environment as well as economic and social costs.[11] The reality of implementation and execution of this policy can best be seen in terms of a balancing act between both kinds of objectives.

In addition to this ambivalence of choice, the EU lawmakers have had somehow through the years to face the most serious factual problem of the dynamic technological development in respect to waste. A multitude of judicial findings were needed to help with the meaning of terms used in the basic definitions, or in closely related ones. A good example is provided by the pivotal term 'discard', covering both disposal and recovery.[12] In the Inter-Environment case, the Court chose a broad approach deciding "[. . .] that the concept of waste does not in principle exclude any kind of residue, industrial by-product or other substance arising from production processes".[13] This led again to further differentiate between 'by-product' and 'waste', making by-products an important exception to waste. In the end, it, e.g., matters very considerably if a substance resulting from the refining of crude oil like petroleum coke, is to be considered a 'waste substance', a 'residue', or a 'by-product' which technically can be used as a fuel and is therefore excluded from the waste definition. After a number of Court decisions regarding various aspects of this important distinction,[14] the 2008 Directive in Article 5 stipulates considerable and cumulative conditions to be fulfilled for a 'secondary' substance from a production process to be a by-product and not waste. In addition, it is possible and legally acceptable under conditions set in Article 6 that a substance firstly classified as waste may cease to be waste when it is after all possible to recover it, including being recycled thus becoming a real product for the market.[15] Even the distinction

---

[10] Art. 4 of the 2008 Framework Directive formulate the waste hierarchy as: The prevention of waste production; preparation for re-use; re-cycling; other means of recovery, such as energy recovery; disposal. Art. 4.2 allows for certain waste streams a departure from the order if that leads to better environmental outcomes (Directive 2008/98/EC of the European Parliament and of the Council of 19 November 2008 on Waste and Repealing Certain Directives, OJ 2008 L 312/3). This section liberally makes use of my 'Waste Management in EU legislation-an Introduction', chapter I of Panoussis and Post 2014.

[11] SEC(89) 934 and the new Strategy presented by the Commission in 1996, COM(96) 399; see also the Council's Resolution of 24 February 1997 on a Community Strategy for Waste Management, OJ 1997 C 76/1.

[12] Telling is, perhaps, the reported amazement of an experienced judge of the European Court of Justice about the judicial effort put into defining the concept of waste. Tieman (2003), pp. 5 et seq. *Tieman's* book by itself provides ample illustration of Judge *Kapteyn's* finding.

[13] Case C-129/96, *Inter-Environnement Wallonie ASBL v. Waals Gewest* [1997] ECR I-7411.

[14] *Cf.* Cases C-1114/01, *Avesta Polarit Chrome* [2003] ECR I-8725 and C-235/02, *Saetti* [2004] ECR I-1005.

[15] Again *see* Case C-9/00, *Palin Granit and Vehmassalon kansanterveystyön kuntayhtymän hallitus* [2002] ECR I-3533 and Case C-444/00, *Mayer Parry* [2003] ECR I-6163.

between recovery and disposal can occasionally be complicated to make. An important more recent example is the new possibility that waste is now combusted to generate energy. Such a generation of energy is, according to the Court, in principle a lawful form of recovery.[16] Hence, as a result of technological development, constant modification and reclassification of substances is needed as the rules covering waste differ very considerably from those regarding marketable products and so do, e.g., the transport regulations that apply.

As a result of all this the EU law on waste management seems to be in constant flux, leaving an almost endemic legal insecurity caused by, primarily, the state of the relevant technology. The question can even seriously be raised if the EU law on waste management will ever be 'sound', that is in a state of adequate legal security.[17]

4 An Arbitrary Choice in the EU Regulation of the Protection of Ambient Air

Directive 2008/50/EC on ambient air quality and cleaner air for Europe was agreed upon on 14 April 2008; its transposition date is 11 June 2010.[18] This Directive provides the legal framework for the implementation of the EU policy regarding air quality until 2020. The Directive should be seen in the context of the EC Commission's 2000 "Better Regulation" initiative. However, as the Explanatory Memorandum to the Proposal for a Directive on ambient air quality and cleaner air for Europe of 21 September 2005[19] explains, simplifying and streamlining are not the only purposes of this 'Framework' Directive. Although the aim is to merge the provisions of five separate legal instruments into a single directive with the intention of simplifying, streamlining and reducing the volume of existing legislation, the objective is also to revise the substance of the existing provisions "[. . .] so as to incorporate the latest health and scientific developments and the experience of the Member States."[20]

In particular improved insight in the health risks involved in high levels of PM2,5 is a huge new challenge. Addressing these is the most important substantial

[16] Case C-228/00, *Commission v. Germany* [2003] ECR I-1439. Waste to energy processes are still very much in a state of technological development.

[17] This apart from other problems observed like the so-called 'Legal waste paradox'. See Raccah (2014), fn. 8, see, in particular Chapter 6, Section 6.2, 'Main reasons of the problems faced by the EU Waste Law', pp. 87 et seq.

[18] Directive 2008/50/EC on ambient air quality and cleaner air for Europe, 11 June 2008, OJ EU L 152/1. In this section I amply draw on my 'The Future of Ambient Air Management; concluding remarks'; in Post (2009), pp. 135–147.

[19] Explanatory Memorandum to the Proposal for a Directive of the European Parliament and of the Council on ambient air quality and cleaner air for Europe of 21 September 2005, SEC(2005)1133.

[20] Id.

innovation in the new 2008 instrument. On the basis of research carried out by the World Health Organisation (WHO) as well as in the framework of CAFE, the EU's own Cleaner Air for Europe Programme, it is estimated that in the EU, air pollution due to particulate matter causes around 350,000 premature deaths each year. Accepting this finding has made reducing PM levels the first priority in European air pollution policy. Whereas for the other air pollutants the 2008 Directive only brought some minor modifications not essentially altering the existing air quality standards, EU legislation now, for the first time, has also set binding limit values for PM2,5. With regard to PM2,5 the European Commission has proposed binding limits which are to be imposed from January 2010 on. For the 2008 Directive, however, Council and Parliament eventually decided that the PM2,5 limit value will not be binding law until January 2015. From 2010 till 2015 a 'mere' target value will apply.

This decision, and thus the Directive itself, is certainly remarkable. It seems also highly inopportune if not shocking in light of the huge number of almost 350,000 premature deaths per year caused in the EU by way of the current high levels of PM2,5. How is this delay of effective action for another 5 years to be explained and/or justified? After all no less than 100,000's (!) additional premature deaths will be the price to be paid according to the preparatory documentation.

It may be worthwhile taking a somewhat closer look at the objectives in respect to PM2,5 stated in the new EC legislation. In the first paragraph of its Preamble the new Directive puts an emphasis on human health right away. Referring to the Sixth EC Environment Action Programme adopted in 2002, it states "the need [...] to reduce [air] pollution to levels which minimise harmful effects on human health, paying particular attention to sensitive populations, and the environment as a whole [...]"[21]

After extensive research under the CAFE programme just mentioned, in 2005 the European Commission adopted the Thematic Strategy on Air Pollution. This Thematic Strategy was the first of seven thematic environmental strategies announced in the Sixth Environment Action Programme.[22]

As already said we are not talking minor matters here. The CAFE research has reported that the number of premature deaths in 2000 as a result of deteriorated air quality in the EU amounted to 370,000, about 20,000 caused by low-level (tropospheric) ozone or 'smog' and no less than 348,000 as a result of high levels of particulate matter, primarily PM2.5.[23]

---

[21] Directive 2008/50/EC on ambient air quality and cleaner air for Europe, see, op.cit., fn. 3. Its predecessor, the 1996 Framework Directive 62/96/EC says in its second preamble less specifically: "Whereas, in order to protect the environment as a whole and human health, concentrations of harmful air pollutants should be avoided, prevented or reduced [...]".

[22] Thematic Strategy on Air Pollution, COM (2005) 446, Communication of 21 September 2005 from the Commission to the Council and the European Parliament.

[23] Not to mention possible other harmful effects, see, e.g., the American Lung Association 2005 Research Highlights: Health Effects of Particulate Matter and Ozone Air Pollution, January 2006, reporting on studies conducted in 9 Californian Counties and in 22 European cities.

In addition to the human loss, poor air quality (in particular high levels of nitrogen) also has a very considerable negative effect in forest areas and on surface fresh water due to excessive acid deposition, and in ecosystems exposed to eutrophication.[24] In view of all these consequences the European Union has set ambitious goals to improve the quality of ambient air, and they are supposed to reflect the seriousness of the problem. The 2005 Thematic Strategy on Air Pollution already states that the EU has chosen:

> [. . .] health and environmental objectives and emission reduction targets for the main pollutants. These objectives will be delivered in stages, and will make it possible to protect EU citizens from exposure to particulate matter and ozone in air, and protect European ecosystems more effectively from acid rain, excess nutrient nitrogen, and ozone.

The Strategy sets out, in particular, to achieve a reduction of 47 % of the loss of life expectancy as a result of particulate matter, and a 10 % reduction in acute mortalities from exposure to ozone. This is to be achieved in comparison to 2000, and by the year 2020. To realize these objectives (and to fight acidification and eutrophication) by 2020, SO2 emissions will need to decrease by 82 %, NOx emissions by 60 %, volatile organic compounds (VOCs) by 51 %, ammonia by 27 %, and primary PM2.5, i.e. particles emitted directly into the air, by 59 %. However, of these goals the greatest challenge is undoubtedly involved in the reduction of PM2.5 concentrations as they have not been covered by the legislation before the new 2008 Directive. As the figures show, PM2.5 is also—by far—the most serious threat to human health. Obtaining all these reductions demands costs of up to €7.1 billion per year. This is in addition to the spending on existing measures. These costs although huge are nevertheless easily offset by the savings to be made as a result of the Strategy: an estimated €42 billion per year! Seen in this financial light only, it may be somewhat surprising to read that the 2005 Thematic Strategy does not aim to remove all these very serious dangers at all. The Strategy does not argue that such a result would be impossible to obtain but that

> it was impossible to determine a level of exposure to particulate matter and tropospheric ozone that does not constitute a danger to human beings. However, a significant reduction in these substances will have beneficial effects in terms of public health, and will also generate benefits for ecosystems.[25]

In its Preamble (11) the 2008 Directive repeats this argument for PM2,5 as follows: '(11) Fine particulate matter (PM2,5) is responsible for significant negative impacts on human health. Further, there is as yet no identifiable threshold below which PM2,5 would not pose a risk.'

Measures to fight high levels of PM 2.5 can be taken, albeit in a different way than for other pollutants. In the same Preamble (11) the new Directive says: 'As

[24] Eutrophication is defined as excess nutrient nitrogen (in the form of ammonia and nitrogen oxides) which disrupts plant communities, and leaches into fresh waters, leading in each case to a loss of biodiversity, in COM(2005) 446, Communication of 21 September 2005 from the Commission to the Council and the European Parliament – Thematic Strategy on Air Pollution, 2005.

[25] Id.

such, this pollutant should not be regulated in the same way as other air pollutants. The approach should aim at a general reduction of concentrations in the urban background to ensure that large sections of the population benefit from improved air quality'.[26]

According to the Thematic Strategy (the Directive does not provide such figures in its objectives) the result of this general reduction of concentrations is to be that "[. . .] the number of premature deaths should fall from 370,000 in 2000 to 230,000 in 2020" (compared with 293,000 in 2020 without the Strategy).

Hence, the Thematic Strategy's implementation will result in an extra reduction of premature deaths by 2020 of 63,000.

It seems that for this new episode in EU policy on air pollution in particular in respect to PM2,5—but perhaps also in respect to tropospheric ozone[27]—some important moral and ethical choices for more limited measures than are feasible have been made. It is of course not at all unusual to see (considerably) more limited objectives in policies than can be realised or are imaginable in an ideal world.

Financial grounds are the most common reasons for such restraint. However, in this case the choices made are difficult to explain by financial considerations, at least not by 'over all' financial reasons. In fact, according to the Thematic Strategy, investing in cleaner air saves huge sums of money. Why then has the threshold of a reduction to 'only' 230,000 premature deaths been chosen? Why not aim at a reduction to 200,000 or 100,000, or even 0 premature deaths by 2020? For answers to such rather important, but apparently delicate questions the documents here quoted do not offer much help.

The statement both in the Thematic Strategy and in the new Directive that there is as yet no identifiable threshold below which PM2,5 would not pose a risk to health, does not bring us any further. If anything, it only seems to emphasize the urgency of the matter.

No doubt implementing the reductions in PM2,5 as well as in the other pollutants covered always implies considerable incursions in the daily life of citizens, most notably in urban areas. Transport is the most sensitive of fields in this respect in particular where it includes the use of private cars. Politically, decision-makers tend to be very reluctant to impose limitations in this area, because it causes problems with various groups of citizens, from shopkeepers and bus passengers to private car owners. Implementing often controversial measures in respect to transport and mobility in general is quite a challenge for politicians and other decision-makers; the process does not usually increase their popularity.[28]

Perhaps the real costs EC decision makers were anticipating and reluctant to face were more of a 'political' than a financial nature or did they come from other

[26] 2008 Directive, Preamble (11).

[27] The measures will by 2020 lead to an expected reduction of about 10 % of premature deaths due to ozone.

[28] See, e.g., Orlando (2009), pp. 35–37.

sources? Anyway, there seems to be a form of legal uncertainty here, uncertainty at least for a part of the stakeholders.

Some consolation for those who are unhappy with the rather less than effective and curious 'road-map' set out in respect to PM2,5 (and ozone) may be found in the results of other reductions stemming from the Directive's implementation envisaged by 2020 for the environment at large. After warning that "[w]here the environment is concerned, there is no agreed way to assign a monetary value to ecosystem damage or the likely benefits resulting from the Strategy", the Thematic Strategy continues: "However, there should be a favourable impact as a result of reducing acid rain and nutrient nitrogen inputs, resulting among other things in better protection for biodiversity."[29] The reduction, mentioned above, in such substances as SO2, NOx, and ammonia in particular, will have a considerable positive effect on the levels of acidification and eutrophication. It is expected that by 2020 there will be a 74 % reduction in acid deposition in forest areas and a 39 % reduction regarding surface fresh water. The areas subject to eutrophication will be reduced by 43 %.

Of course, whether this reduction and the decrease in PM2,5 will all actually take place as envisioned depends in particular on whether the Member States adequately and speedily implement the new EC legislation on air pollution in their national law and, importantly, effectively enforce it. Here the alertness and awareness of the public, of NGO's and other groups of citizens is particularly important.

5 Legal Risk Management Analysis to Clarify Legal Uncertainty

Environmental law is perhaps the most appropriate field of law to apply the notion of legal risk to. It is after all marred with uncertainties due to the nature of the environment and the relative newness of the law applicable to it. The result is a field of law which does not stop changing and, as said above, is characterized by new and innovative instruments based on principles often unique for the field. The precautionary principle, the principle that preventive action should be taken, that environmental damage should be rectified at source, and that the polluter should pay as expressed in Article 191 of the Treaty on European Union are explicit examples from European Union law. In the previous sections we have briefly explained two examples from European environmental law where serious factual and legal uncertainty seems to exist. Of the two the example from the law on the protection of the air we breathe is much more dramatic than the one from the area of the law on waste management.

Can 'legal risk' management analysis as set out in Sect. 1 be helpful here? I think the answer should for both cases be 'cautiously' in the affirmative. Cautiously,

---

[29] See COM (2005) 446.

because the theoretical framework for legal risk and its typology are still in a rather preliminary state, and need considerable elaboration. Both examples seem to fit in well with the two preconditions that legal risk should address and cover: (a) events are uncertain both legally and factually, and (b), the legal norm at stake itself can be qualified as a source of risk.

In the section on EU law on waste management we pointed at the notorious problem of dynamic technological development. Changes in the technical possibilities to recycle or reuse materials continuously undermine the quality and certainty of the legal instruments. This leads then to endless judicial decisions explaining and interpreting the state of the law. The technologically induced factual uncertainty leads initially to a high level of legal uncertainty and, next, to an almost judicially governed field of environmental law. European waste law and the Framework Directive in particular, can be called an example of a set of deontic norms where factual uncertainty reigns. How could such a field legally be improved so that the legal risk diminishes? As technological change is not occasional but 'endemic' to the subject matter, a built-in 'technological modification mechanism' or even a 'self-regulating mechanism' capable of producing fast modes of legal change should be part of the legal instrument. Such a mechanism should of course contain adequate guarantees against inadequacy, inconsistency or misuse.

In Articles 15 and 16 and Annex XIV, Directive 2008/50/EC sets the legal norms for the exposure to PM 2,5 in respect to the protection of human health. The health risks involved here (also named 'risks' in the Directive) can be qualified as events that are uncertain to happen in a factual sense. Also, the standards set (notably the limit values to be attained from 2015 on—Annex XIV, section D and E) contain such a margin of tolerance (section E) that they can be labelled uncertain, notably in light of the objective to be obtained by them, i.e. a reduction in the number of premature deaths estimated to be of some 350,000 a year by 2020. Addressing these estimated events of 350,000 premature deaths in the EU as a result of high levels of PM2,5 in the way the Directive does can therefore be said to involve taking a considerable legal risk. This 'uncertainty' legal risk is the more serious if we consider that it can be assumed to coexist with the more traditional instrumental legal risk of sanctions by way of judicial judgments. Stakeholders, individuals/family members related to the numbers of premature deaths may take legal action against Member States in their national courts because of the inadequate results of the legal instrument created.[30] Member States who are unhappy with the way the PM 2,5 protection of the Directive is arranged and its equally vague implementation modus, may challenge that aspect before the European Court of Justice (ECJ).

We seem to face here a case of on the one hand factual uncertainty, and of a rather remarkable magnitude, and on the other hand of the explicit choice of legal norms that are inadequate in terms of saving the lives of thousands of people,

[30] Which nevertheless in view of the use of 'limit values' and 'alert thresholds' may lead to effective action in court along the way of the German *TA Luft* cases (Case C-361/88, *Commission v. Germany*, 1991 ECR 1-2567, paras. 28, 29).

therefore setting a legal regime of great and fundamental uncertainty. Furthermore, due to the nature of the objectives set, in particular in respect to the Framework Directive and its implementation, there are considerable instrumental legal risks involved.[31]

Acknowledgments I wish to thank Professor Ige F. Dekker for his valuable comments and suggestions.

References

Hart HLA (1994) The concept of law. Clarendon, Oxford

Mahler T (2007) Defining legal risk. Proceedings of the conference "Commercial Contracting for Strategic Advantage - Potentials and Prospects". Turku University of Applied Sciences. Available at SSRN: http://ssrn.com/abstract=1014364

Moscadelli M (2004) The modelling of operational risk: experience with the analysis of the data collected by the Basel Committee, Banca d'Italia-Temi di discussione del servizio studi, Nr. 517

Orlando GF (2009) The protection of air quality in the city of Modena. In: Post H (ed) The protection of ambient air in international and European law. Eleven International Publishing, The Hague

Post H (2009) The future of ambient air management. In: Post H (ed) The protection of ambient air in international and European law. Eleven International Publishing, The Hague

Post H (2014) Waste management in EU legislation – an introduction. In: Panoussis IK, Post H (eds) Waste management in European law. Eleven International Publishing, The Hague

Raccah A (2014) The legal paradox of EU waste management. In: Panoussis IK, Post H (eds) Waste management in European law. Eleven International Publishing, The Hague

Tieman J (2003) Naar een nuttige toepassing van het begrip afvalstof: over de betekenis en toepassing van kernbegrippen van international, Europees en Nederlands afvalstoffenrecht, (Towards a Useful Application of the Concept of Waste: on the Meaning and Application of Core Concepts of International, European and Dutch Waste Law) Kluwer, Deventer, The Netherlands

[31] What will be the future of the Ambient Air Legislation, including the Framework Directive is uncertain. The 'Clean Air Package' that contained more severe emission limits for the decade following 2020 was originally put on the 'kill list' of the new European Commission. Eventually, it has been decided to modify it. The results will be published in the course of 2015.

A Resilient EU Facing Global Environmental Risks

Leonardo Massai

Contents

Abstract International climate negotiations for the 2015 agreement started in 2005 in order to find an alternative solution to the fight against climate change. The international climate regime based on the UNFCCC and the Kyoto Protocol is not responding to the new world and the developments, which occurred since its creation. The reality of 1992 when the Convention was signed has changed and the evolution of climate negotiations, from Bali to Copenhagen to Cancún and Durban, has shown that all Parties are now ready to share their responsibility in the mitigation and adaptation to climate change. Since 2001, the EU has assumed a leading role in the global fight against climate change and has developed advanced legislation to reduce greenhouse gas emissions and to promote renewable energy

This chapter is an updated and revised version of Massai 2013. Views expressed in this chapter belong exclusively to the author and cannot be associated with the position of any Party in the multilateral negotiations on climate change under the UNFCCC.

L. Massai (✉)
Faculty of Law, Catholic University of Lille, Lille, France
e-mail: leonardo.massai@gmail.com

E. Miščenić, A. Raccah (eds.), *Legal Risks in EU Law*,
DOI 10.1007/978-3-319-28596-2_12

and energy efficiency. In this respect, the EU is seen by many as a pioneer and example, especially in consideration of the EU Emissions Trading System that introduced binding caps on private installations in many key economic sectors. EU climate diplomacy is therefore strongly committed to climate negotiations and has invested many resources in the run-up to Paris COP21. The EU is also aware of the many challenges of the UN climate negotiations and is trying to promote key reforms and more efficiency from not only an internal point of view, but also regarding improvements in the UNFCCC process.

1 International Climate Change Regime

The international climate change regime is founded on two major international conventions, notably the United Nations Framework Convention on Climate Change[1] (UNFCCC or Convention) and the Kyoto Protocol.[2]

The legal and institutional infrastructure created by the Convention and the Kyoto Protocol builds upon the classical frameworks of a multilateral environmental agreement where environmental concerns for the humankind are tackled by international law. Indeed, the major legal responses to modern global and transboundary environmental threats are provided as multilateral treaties, whatever form they may take.[3] Other sources such as soft law instruments, international principles and jurisdictional decisions traditionally play a less important role, in particular when complex problems such as climate change are to be tackled by the international community. However, it must be emphasized that decisions adopted by the supreme bodies of the Convention and the Kyoto Protocol are of great importance and create serious consequences and constraints for the Parties to the treaties.

At the moment of writing, climate change and global warming are clearly undisputed phenomena recognized as the major environmental hazards the global humanity is facing. According to the Intergovernmental Panel on Climate Change (IPCC), the main international scientific body dealing with global warming, climate change is principally caused by anthropogenic sources, such as the burning of fossil fuels or the emissions of other greenhouse gases. The negative impacts of climate change are, amongst others, sea level rise, ice melting, shifts in plant and animal ranges, and variations in the frequency of rains as well as the hydrological cycle. To

[1] United Nations Framework Convention on Climate Change (New York, 26 May 1992) (UNFCCC).

[2] Kyoto Protocol to the UNFCCC (Kyoto, 11 December 1997).

[3] Traditionally, this can be a convention, protocol, agreement or any other legal term recognized by International Law.

combat climate change and its consequences, the international community has decided to intervene both in terms of mitigation and adaptation.

The latest report of the IPPC demonstrates that scientific evidence about climate change is already a fact.[4]

1.1 Convention

The United Nations Framework Convention on Climate Change was opened for signature in 1992 in Rio de Janeiro during the Earth Summit, together with two other key international conventions on the environment (the Convention on Biological Diversity and the Convention to Combat Desertification). The UNFCCC is a perfect example of a multilateral framework treaty dealing with international environmental protection. It entered into force in 1994 and it now embraces 195 Parties (194 States and 1 regional economic integration organization—the EU). It set a broad and general objective, notably 'the stabilization of greenhouse gas concentrations in the atmosphere at a level that would prevent dangerous anthropogenic interference with the climate system'. Key principles of international environmental law are mentioned in the Convention under Article 3. These are the precautionary principle and the principle of sustainable development, and two other fundamental principles, which are at the foundation of the international climate change regime. They are the Principle of Common but Differentiated Responsibilities (CBDR) and the principle of equity. The CBDR principle in particular is at the foundation of the current division between Annex I and non-Annex I Parties, developed and developing countries respectively.

Differentiated commitments for Parties are included in the Convention under Article 4, which emphasizes the leadership role of developed countries both in terms of mitigating climate change and providing financial support.

The institutional structure of the Convention reflects the structure of all major international conventions on the environment, namely a pyramid where the Conference of the Parties (COP) is the supreme body responsible for the implementation and application of the Convention, and is supported by the subsidiary bodies, the Subsidiary Body for Scientific and Technological Advice (SBSTA) and the Subsidiary

[4] From the Fifth Assessment Report of the IPCC, Working Group I, Summary for policymakers: "Warming of the climate system is unequivocal, and since the 1950s, many of the observed changes are unprecedented over decades to millennia. The atmosphere and ocean have warmed, the amounts of snow and ice have diminished, sea level has risen, and the concentrations of greenhouse gases have increased", "Over the last two decades, the Greenland and Antarctic ice sheets have been losing mass, glaciers have continued to shrink almost worldwide, and Arctic sea ice and Northern Hemisphere spring snow cover have continued to decrease in extent", "Human influence on the climate system is clear. This is evident from the increasing greenhouse gas concentrations in the atmosphere, positive radiative forcing, observed warming, and understanding of the climate system".

Body for Implementation (SBI), and finally the Secretariat of the Convention located in Bonn, Germany. In addition to the permanent bodies embedded in the text of the Convention, Parties are free to establish other temporary auxiliary bodies. This is exactly what happened in the current negotiations on the future of the international climate change regime after 2012, as will be explained below.

The Kyoto Protocol is the related instrument to the Convention that Parties adopted in 1997 at COP3 in accordance with the procedure inscribed under Article 17 of the Convention. The Kyoto Protocol is therefore an international treaty in all effects and as such with no expiration date. The Kyoto Protocol shares the same infrastructure of the Convention, with the only difference that the COP is replaced by the Conference of the Parties serving as the Meeting of the Parties to the Protocol (CMP). Furthermore, the Protocol shares the main objectives and principles of the Convention as well as the division between developed and developing countries. The Kyoto Protocol established legally binding Quantified Emission Limitation and Reduction Commitments (QELRCs) for the developed countries listed in Annex B, expressed in percentages and valid for the period 2008–2012 (first commitment period). The Kyoto Protocol also established one of the most advanced and powerful compliance regimes for an environmental treaty. The Compliance Committee of the Kyoto Protocol is an ad hoc regime designed to ensure that the obligations created by the Protocol are fully respected by all Parties. Another important novelty created by the Kyoto Protocol are the flexibility mechanisms inscribed in Articles 6, 12 and 17, Joint Implementation (JI), Clean Development Mechanism (CDM) and Emissions Trading (ET) respectively. The flexibility mechanisms were designed to allow Annex I Parties to meet their reduction targets in the least costly manner possible by purchasing so-called carbon reduction units in the carbon market or through investments in climatefriendly projects.[5] Finally, under the Kyoto Protocol a special place is reserved for Land-Use, Land-Use Change and Forestry (LULUCF) activities that can be used by Annex I Parties as to their capacity to absorb greenhouse gas emissions from the atmosphere.[6]

1.2 Where Do We Stand?

On 11 November 2014 the president and prime minister of the US and China respectively announced a bilateral deal on climate change. For the US this means a reduction of 26–28 % by 2025 compared to 2005 levels and for China a peaking of greenhouse gas emissions by 2030. The two commitments are obviously not

[5] Units that can be used for compliance under the Kyoto Protocol are: Assigned Amount Units (AAUs), Removal Units (RMUs), Emission Reduction Units (ERUs), Certified Emission Reductions (CERs).

[6] For more background information about the UNFCCC and the Kyoto Protocol and the EU climate policy see Massai (2001, 2011), Grubb et al. (1999), Oberthür (2008), Oberthür and Pallemaerts (2010) and Schaik (2012), and Schunz S (2012).

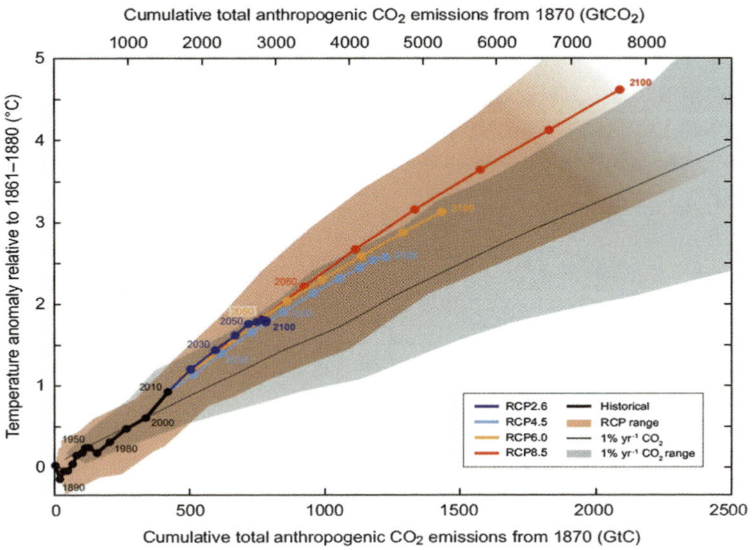

Fig. 1 Summary for policy makers of the fifth report of the IPCC, Working Group I

comparable. Still they show some political willingness from the two most powerful and influential Parties to the UNFCCC to converge and cooperate on the global solution to fight climate change. Most likely, the numbers indicated in the US-China deal are not sufficient to put the world on a path that will not go over the 2 degree target required by science. Below is a graph from the Summary for Policy Makers of the fifth report of the IPCC, Working Group I, indicating that half the global carbon budget has been used up already (Fig. 1).

2 Negotiating the Future International Climate Change Regime

2.1 The Mechanics

The international climate change talks on the future multilateral regime represent, since the early 2000s, one of the most important areas of international affairs and thus a good model to understand how sovereign States relate with each other on environmental issues at the international level. The Climate Change Summit of Copenhagen in 2009 gathered together for the first time in the history of environmental diplomacy the highest number of heads of State and government.[7]

[7] For a better understanding of what happened in Copenhagen at COP15 see Massai (2009), pp. 102–119.

The main actors taking part in international environmental negotiations are usually assembled in the following three main categories:

a. Groups of States;
b. Observers;
c. Conference officers and facilitators and secretariats.

Sovereign States are the key actor in environmental negotiations. They participate in formal and informal meetings and make decisions mainly through the supreme bodies of the international treaty to which they are bound. In international law, with Parties we refer to traditional sovereign States and Regional Economic Integration Organizations (REIO) like the European Union (EU). The EU participates in international treaties and multilateral negotiations as a single actor, with the same rights and obligations as sovereign States.

Parties negotiate under so-called negotiating groups. The most complex and numerous is the Group of 77 and China that by now encompasses 132 developing countries, including China. Apart from the G77, China and the EU (with its currently 28 Member States), in the field of climate change the Umbrella Group (USA, Canada, Australia, New Zealand, Norway, Russian Federation, Ukraine, Japan) and the Environmental Integrity Group (EIGs, consisting of Mexico, South Korea and Switzerland) are also worth mentioning. Several new groups have been formed since the beginning of the climate change talks in 2005.

The role of the international organizations, institutions and the civil society in multilateral environmental negotiations is secondary compared to States. International organizations active in the field of environmental protection are UN specialized agencies such as IMO, ILO, FAO and ad hoc bodies at the global level such as UNEP and UNDP. International organizations and institutions play a key role in environmental policy making and in the development of international environmental law. The latter is achieved either by facilitating international meetings and relations among States, or by producing some forms of binding or nonbinding documents, depending on the type of institution.

The role of civil society in international negotiations, usually participating through Non-Governmental organizations (NGOs) divided according to sectors such as environmental, research, business, etc., is limited. NGOs participate in the negotiations as observers only in open sessions. The participation of NGOs is regulated by an accreditation procedure based on specific modalities which can differ from one convention to another. An important way NGOs can influence the negotiations is by participating directly in national delegations or through the domestic process which, especially in developing countries, is often tailored to all ranges of local stakeholders.

Negotiations take place in both formal and informal settings. More precisely, most negotiations among Parties take place in informal settings, behind closed doors, where the participation of civil society is limited and government representatives can discuss and exchange views and ideas without any external influence.

The goal and outcome of the negotiations depend on the mandate and can take different forms, such as resolutions, treaties, declarations or decisions. The main difference between the adoption of international treaties, conventions or protocols and other results such as resolutions, declarations and decisions lies in the way they enter into force. While for the former a process of national ratification is required for their entry into force, for the latter there is no need for ratification and the result is directly applicable once adopted.[8]

2.2 *The Bali Action Plan*

The negotiations for the future international climate change regime are usually referring to the term 'post-2012'. Post-2012 is the period after the end of the first commitment period of the Kyoto Protocol and Article 3(9) of the Protocol requires negotiations for the future commitment periods to start at the latest in 2005. Indeed, the negotiations for the second commitment period of the Kyoto Protocol were launched by CMP1 in Montreal in 2005 with the establishment of a new subsidiary body under the Kyoto Protocol; the Ad Hoc Working Group on Further Reduction Commitments under the KP (AWG-KP).

The establishment of the AWG-KP was agreed to under the condition that another parallel track is to be established as soon as possible with a view to craft a future global international response to climate change embracing all Parties under the Convention. In other words, the launch of the negotiations on the second commitment period of the Kyoto Protocol by many important developed countries was subordinated to the start of a discussion on how to engage big emitters like the USA and some of the developing countries in similar greenhouse gas emission reduction commitments.

Consequently, in 2007 in Bali, COP13 decided to establish another subsidiary body under the Convention, the Ad Hoc Working Group on Long-Term Cooperative Action (AWG-LCA), to study and provide for a new international solution on mitigation and adaptation to climate change after 2012. Decision 1/CP.13 included the so-called Bali Action Plan (BAP), 'a comprehensive process to enable the full, effective and sustained implementation of the Convention through long-term cooperative action, now, up to and beyond 2012, in order to reach an agreed outcome and adopt a decision at its fifteenth session'.[9] The BAP identified the following 5 key areas of negotiation:

a. shared vision for long-term cooperative action, including a long-term global goal for emission reductions;
b. mitigation (including action by developed and developing countries, reducing emissions from deforestation and forest degradation, various approaches including market and response measure);

---

[8] For a better understanding of multilateral environmental negotiations see 'Guide for Presiding Officers, UNFCCC, November 2011' and 'Multilateral Environmental Agreement Negotiator's Handbook, UNEP, 2006' and Vanhoonacker (2010).

[9] Bali Action Plan, Decision 1/CP.13 (FCCC/CP/2007/6/Add.1, 14 March 2008).

c. adaptation;
d. finance;
e. technology and capacity-building.

Furthermore, in order to comply with the deadline set by COP13 (2009) the Bali Road Map was launched by COP13, including 2 years of intense negotiations, with 8 international high-level meetings under both tracks, the AWG-LCA and the AWG-KP. In 2008, Parties soon realised that four meetings in 2009 would not be sufficient to reach a meaningful agreement by COP15. Therefore, at the beginning of 2009 two additional sessions were added to the original schedule.[10]

2.3 Copenhagen Accord

From 7 to 18 December 2009, six bodies under the UNFCCC met simultaneously. These were the COP15, CMP5, SBI, SBSTA, AWG-LCA and AWG-KP, as well as the highlevel segment. The complexity of the Summit was reinforced by the multiplicity of issues to be resolved by the different bodies. Consequently, already months before the actual Summit took place, it appeared to many that a successful conclusion of the Summit was very unlikely.

In Copenhagen, the journey launched in 2005 in Montreal was supposed to terminate, with the two additional bodies created in 2005 and 2007 respectively, the AWG-KP and AWG-LCA, concluding their work and leave the formal decision on the new climate change regime to COP15 and CMP5.

Unfortunately, these two groups were unable to finish their business in the second week of the Summit, and no formal conclusion on the next steps was taken. The twotrack negotiations neither merged nor concluded in Copenhagen and this lack of clarity allowed for the political leaders present to step up and engage directly in intense negotiations behind closed doors that concluded with the Copenhagen Accord in the early hours of Saturday morning, 19 December 2009.

The Copenhagen Accord was negotiated, drafted and agreed in the final hours of COP15 by approximately 28 countries in representation of all major regional groups, but led in particular by the USA and the BASIC countries.

The Copenhagen Accord was formally presented to the plenary of COP15 and CMP5 after several procedural irregularities of the Danish presidency. Explicit objections were raised by a few Parties so that the plenary could not formally adopt the Accord as planned, but was forced to adjourn the meeting several times.

The Accord was finally rescued by Decision 2/CP.15, which reads: ‘the COP takes note of the Copenhagen Accord of 18 December 2009’. The Copenhagen Accord is not the result expected by the mandate given to the AWG-KP and

[10] The Bali Road Map, closing statement of Joint High-Level Segment by the President of the COP, Rachmat Witoelar (Bali, 15 December 2007), available at <http://unfccc.int/files/meetings/cop_13/application/pdf/close_stat_cop13_president.pdf>.

AWG-LCA respectively in 2005 and 2007, both in terms of contents and form. The Copenhagen Accord is more of a political declaration where all main elements of the Bali Action Plan are recognized.[11]

2.4 The Run: Up to Paris COP21

In Cancun (COP16, 2010) the main objective of all Parties, including the EU, was to restore trust in the multilateral process after what had happened in Copenhagen 1 year earlier. The main results of the Cancun meeting were the Cancun Agreements (Decision 1/CP.16) which integrated the Copenhagen Accord into the UNFCCC process.

The major results of the Durban Climate Change Conference (COP17, 2011) were:

a. Design of the Green Climate Fund;
b. Mandate for a new working group (Ad Hoc Working Group on the Durban Platform for Enhanced Action) to 'complete its work as early as possible but no later than 2015 in order to adopt this protocol, legal instrument or agreed outcome with legal force at COP21 and for it to come into effect and be implemented from 2020';
c. AWG-LCA to terminate its work by COP18.

The main results of CMP7 were:

a. Second commitment period under the Kyoto Protocol, although still uncertainty about the exact numbers of Annex B Parties' Objectives (QELROs) and the length of the commitment period (5 or 8 years?);
b. Parties took note of the quantified economy-wide emission reduction targets to be implemented and of the intention of these Parties to convert these targets to Quantified Emission Limitation or Reduction Objectives (QELROs) for the second commitment period under the Kyoto Protocol;
c. Parties information on QELROs for 2nd Commitment Period Kyoto Protocol by 1 May 2012;
d. CDM confirmed and no decision on JI;
e. New flexible mechanism to be elaborated in the near future.

In Doha (COP18, 2012) the second commitment period of the Kyoto Protocol was finally launched for a period of 7 years (2013–2020) with the adoption of the Doha Amendment to the Kyoto Protocol which also established specific limits on the use of the flexible mechanism and of surplus AAUs and carryovers, notably the possibility for Annex I Parties to use part of their surplus of emission reduction

[11] For more information on the Copenhagen Accord, please see Massai (2009), pp. 104–121.

units in subsequent commitment periods. At the COP level, important decisions were adopted on loss and damage, finance and mitigation.

In Lima (COP20, 2014) the COP adopted Decision 1/CP.20 that indicates that the negotiating text for the 2015 agreement was to be made available before May 2015. Another important decision adopted in Lima refers to the process for submitting and reviewing INDCs including their scope, upfront information and steps to be made by the Secretariat. Additional decisions were adopted on the operationalisation of the Warsaw International Mechanism for Loss and Damage, Work Programme on Gender as well as the Lima Declaration on Education and Awareness Raising.

The first iteration of the negotiating text for the 2015 agreement was formally published on the UNFCCC website on 25 February 2015 as the main result of the Geneva negotiations of February 2015. The negotiating text included the following sections:

a. Preamble;
b. Definitions;
c. General/Objective;
d. Mitigation;
e. Adaptation and Loss and Damage;
f. Finance;
g. Technology Development and Transfer;
h. Capacity Building;
i. Transparency of Action and Support;
j. Time Frames and Process Related to Commitments;
k. Facilitating Implementation and Compliance;
l. Procedural and Institutional Provisions;
m. Annex.

Still, the road to Paris includes the following set of meetings:

a. ADP 2–9, 1–11 Jun, Bonn;
b. ADP 3, 31 Aug–4 Sep, Bonn;
c. ADP 4, 19–23 Oct, Bonn;
d. COP21/CMP11, 30 Nov–11 Dec, Paris.

3 EU Climate Change Policy

3.1 Policies and Measures

Traditionally, since the early nineties, when scientific evidence emerged at the international level supporting the notion that climate change is a real threat for the planet, European climate policy and law is one of the strongest and most advanced areas of action of the EU.

One of the first documents of EU climate policy is the European Climate Change Programme (ECCP) launched in the year 2000 as the guiding instrument for the European Community and its Member States to tackle climate change. The main objective of the ECCP was to identify policies and measures aimed at the reduction of greenhouse gas emissions with the view to adopt specific legislation. The first phase of the ECCP I (2000–2001) focused on cost-effective policies and measures to reduce greenhouse gas emissions to be introduced in the energy, transport and industry sectors, while the second phase (2001–2003) studied the following themes: linking JI and CDM with the EU Emissions Trading System (ETS), agriculture, forest-related sinks, sinks in agricultural soils,[12] fluorinated gases, energy supply, energy demand, transport, industry, waste and research.

The clearest sign of EU leadership regarding the fight against climate change can be traced back to 2001 when the European Community[13] decided to take the lead after the declared intention of the United States to step out of the Kyoto Protocol.[14] In 2001 the following three proposals on climate change were issued by the European Commission:

a) Proposal for a Council Decision concerning ratification of the Kyoto Protocol by the European Community, COM (2001)579;
b) Communication from the Commission on the implementation of the first phase of the European Climate Change Programme, COM (2001)580;
c) Proposal for a Directive of the European Parliament and of the Council establishing a scheme for greenhouse gas emission allowance trading within the Community and amending Council Directive 96/61/EC, COM(2001)581.

The main instrument of EU climate policy, adopted on the basis of the proposal COM(2001)581 mentioned above, is Directive 2003/87/EC on the establishment of the European Allowance Trading System (EU Emissions Trading Scheme—EU ETS) and will be discussed in detail in the next paragraph.

Through the adoption of Council Decision 2002/358/EC of 25 April 2002 concerning the approval, on behalf of the European Community, of the Kyoto Protocol to the United Nations Framework Convention on Climate Change and the joint fulfilment of commitments thereunder, the Kyoto Protocol becomes part of the Acquis Communautaire.

In 2007, the EU heads of State and government decided to agree on the so-called 20 + 20 + 20 targets:

a. 20 % reduction of GHG emissions by 2020;
b. 20 % increase of share of renewable energy by 2020;
c. 20 % increase of energy efficiency by 2020.

---

[12] In the international climate change regime, sinks are defined as all activities in the agriculture and forestry sectors that result in a net reduction of greenhouse gas emissions.

[13] Thanks to the changes to the EU Treaties introduced by the Treaty of Lisbon since 2009 the European Community is superseded by the European Union.

[14] In order to know more about EU climate policy and law see Massai (2011).

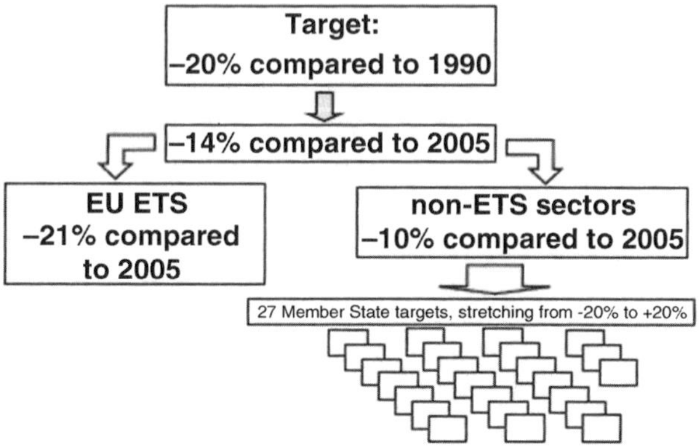

Fig. 2 EU climate and energy targets 2020

The core of the EU climate strategy to achieve the 2020 objectives is indicated in Fig. 2.

The 20 % GHG emissions reduction target is divided into main blocs: on the one side the sectors covered by the EU ETS and on the other all sectors that are excluded.

The 2007 targets were translated into the following legislative acts in 2009:

a. Directive 2009/28/EC on the promotion of the use of energy from renewable sources;
b. Directive 2009/29/EC so as to improve and extend the greenhouse gas emission allowance trading scheme of the Community;
c. Directive 2009/30/EC as regards the specification of petrol, diesel and gas oil and introducing a mechanism to monitor and reduce greenhouse gas emissions;
d. Directive 2009/31/EC on the geological storage of carbon dioxide;
e. Decision No. 406/2009/EC on the effort of Member States to reduce their greenhouse gas emissions to meet the Community's greenhouse gas emission reduction commitment up to 2020;
f. Regulation (EC) No. 443/2009 setting emission performance standards for new passenger cars as part of the Community's integrated approach to reduce CO2 emissions from light-duty vehicles.

On 23 October 2014 the European Council decided to increase the effort and mitigation ambition of the EU and move to a 40 % domestic reduction by 2030 compared to 1990 levels.

3.2 EU ETS

The EU ETS is the major tool adopted by the EU to reduce greenhouse gas emissions as required by the Kyoto Protocol. The first blueprint to develop a trading scheme was the Green Paper COM (2000)87 developed by the Working Group 1 of the European Climate Change Programme. The subsequent step was the legislative proposal presented by the European Commission in 2001.[15] Proposal COM(2001) 581 for a Directive establishing a scheme for greenhouse gas emission allowance trading within the Community and amending Council Directive 96/61/EC introduced the first regional capandtradescheme for the most energyintensive installations. The proposal of the European Commission became law on 13 October 2003 when European Parliament and the Council formally adopted Directive 2003/87/EC. The EU ETS is entitybased. Operators of the installations covered by the Directive, shall receive an authorization to operate from the national authority, usually the Ministry of Environment, as well as a specific amount of EU allowances (expressed in tonnes of equivalent CO_2) that represents the limit to the authorized emissions of greenhouse gases annually. The distribution of allowances fell under the responsibility of the Member States, which were required to submit to the European Commission a National Allocation Plan subject to reviews by the Commission. Directive 2003/87/EC also included specific rules for penalties in the event that operators did not surrender the EUAs accordingly, for opting in and out of installations and certain gases and, finally, for a system for monitoring, reporting and verification. Directive 2003/87/EC identified two phases: a 'learningbydoing' phase between 2005 and 2007 and a trading phase between 2008 and 2012, running parallel to the first commitment period of the Kyoto Protocol.

Through the amendment introduced by Directive 2004/101/EC of 27 October 2004 the EU ETS enabled the inclusion of reduction units from the Clean Development Mechanism (CDM) and Joint Implementation (JI) respectively, generating the Certified Emissions Reductions (CERs) and Emission Reduction Units (ERUs).

The implementation of the EU ETS in the first two phases showed that the environmental benefit of the caps imposed to the single installations was very limited. The overallocation of EUAs by the relevant national authorities not only generated a collapse of the prices for EUAs, but also did not create the necessary incentive for green investments by the various installations. Indeed, 99 % of installations fulfilled their obligations with regard to 2005 reporting emissions. Finally, the implementation of the EU ETS showed the need for greater harmonisation of national legislation in the future.

3.3 *The EU and the Post-2012 Negotiations*

Until the entry into force of the Treaty of Lisbon, legal personality was conferred to the European Community (EC) by Article 281 of the Treaty of the European Community (TEC). Thus, the EC had the power to conclude international agreements with one or more States and international organizations (as confirmed by

[15] In March of the same year the United States of America announced the decision to not ratify the Kyoto Protocol.

Article 300 TEC). These specific Articles in the Treaties were also supported by the jurisprudence of the European Court of Justice that referred to the legal personality of the EC and the capacity of the Community institutions to represent the EC in international treaties.[16] Since the changes introduced by the Treaty of Lisbon on 1 December 2009, the EU has replaced and succeeded the European Community (EC). As of that moment, it is the EU that 'shall have legal personality' (Article 47 TEU).

The external competence of the Union in the field of environmental protection is provided by Article 191(1) and Article 191(4) of the Treaty on the Functioning of the European Union (TFEU). Article 192 TFEU is also often used as legal basis for decisions regarding international agreements adopted by the EU. By assuming legal personality, the EU can, on behalf of the Member States, conclude an international agreement and consequently be subject to rights and obligations.

In international negotiations, the EU and its Member States act with one voice, and moreover work and cooperate very closely in the identification of a common strategy and position. Behind the formal representation of the EU in international negotiations, the division of power and work between the EU institutions and the Member States is, however, complex. Adequate balance must be struck between the interests of all actors involved in the EU process. It happens, especially when international meetings are at the highest political level (heads of State and government or ministry), that key Member States intervene in their national capacity. The pre-Lisbon practice is so far maintained in multilateral climate change negotiations, i. e. the Commission and the Member States (through the Presidency) still have an equal role in terms of EU representation in multilateral environmental affairs. Articles 17(1) and 27(2) that mandate the Commission to represent the EU externally are far from being concretely applied in the case of international climate change negotiations.

Historically, the position of the EU in international negotiations is based on the common position adopted by the Council prior to an international event. The common position of the EU agreed by the Environment Council representing the Member States is a compromise between the different interests of the Member States, but it is also influenced by other factors such as judgements of the Court of Justice or the lobbying activity of key stakeholders, such as industries. Nowadays, given the immense political importance of the climate change issues, the European Council gives the highest political importance to EU climate policy.

In the international climate regime, the negotiations on the different agenda items are left to key experts of the European Commission and the Member States. Behind the scenes, the principle of close cooperation is ensured through regular meetings between the representatives of the Member States and the EU institutions as well as regular EU coordination meetings held before, during and after the negotiations.

[16] Case 6/64 *Flaminio Costa v ENEL* [1964] ECR, 585.

Moreover, if we focus on the Copenhagen Summit of 2009, this meeting was, from a diplomatic point of view, at the highest level ever of political participation for a climate change conference with almost 200 heads of State and governments attending the event. EU diplomats were therefore committed to its preparation and held regular bilateral and similar highlevel meetings with the most important countries in the world.

On 28 January 2009 the European Commission released Communication COM (2009)39 'Towards a Comprehensive Climate Change Agreement in Copenhagen', which started to identify the EU position for the Copenhagen Summit at the end of the year. In particular, this Communication focused on mitigation and finance respectively, describing expected actions by developing and developed countries as well as the inclusion of aviation[17] and shipping in the final agreement, and a request for the creation of a global climate financing mechanism for developing countries.

Despite the differing interests of the Member States and the difficulties to reach a common agreement on the Copenhagen Summit during the Czech Presidency of the Council of the EU (January–June 2009), the EU position on the Copenhagen Climate Change Conference was outlined by the conclusions adopted by the Environment Council of 21 October 2009 in Luxembourg. The European Council of 10 and 11 December 2009 adopted its conclusions that reiterated the EU position agreed in the Council in October 2009. Most notably it was stated that '[t]he agreement should lead to finalizing a legally binding instrument, preferably within six months after the Copenhagen Conference, for the period starting on 1 January 2013'. Also, 'the need for a significant increase in public and private financial flows to 2020' was emphasized. Furthermore, the EU commitment to provide a fair share of international public support was confirmed.

In the follow-up to Copenhagen, on 28 January 2010, Spain and the European Commission on behalf of the EU and its Member States submitted a joint letter to the UNFCCC Secretariat as an expression of willingness to be associated with the Copenhagen Accord. The EU's 20 % quantified economy-wide emissions reduction targets for 2020 were discussed with the specification that 'the EU reiterates its conditional offer to move to a 30 per cent reduction by 2020 compared to 1990 levels, provided that other developed countries commit themselves to comparable emission reductions and that developing countries contribute adequately according to their responsibilities and respective capabilities'. Since the joint letter, a never-ending discussion on whether the move to a 30 % reduction in the future is somehow feasible started in the EU. The division among the Member States is clear as well as their different interests on the issue.

On 9 March 2010 the European Commission released the policy paper COM (2010)86 'International Climate Policy Post-Copenhagen: Acting now to Reinvigorate Global Action on Climate Change'. The paper was designed with the aim to maintain the focus of the international community on climate change.

[17] A topic covered by Ms S. Huber in this paper.

The Commission reiterated the call for the adoption of a legally binding agreement as soon as possible and the need to integrate the Copenhagen Accord into the UNFCCC process.

The European Council conclusions of 26 March 2010 referred to the post-2012 climate change talks and invited Parties to adopt a stepwise approach so that international negotiations could build on the Copenhagen Accord. The aim is the conclusion of a global and comprehensive legal agreement to reach the objective of staying below the 2 °C increase in global temperatures compared to pre-industrial levels.

On 26 May 2010 the European Commission released Communication COM (2010)265: 'Analysis of Options to Move Beyond 20 per cent GHG Emission Reductions and Assessing the Risk of Carbon Leakage', which showed that it is economically and technically affordable for the EU to move to a 30 per cent cut of GHG emissions by 2020.

On 6 March 2015 Latvia, on behalf of the European Union, submitted to the UNFCCC Secretariat the Intended Nationally Determined Contribution of the EU and its Member States as required by Decision 1/CP.20 adopted in Lima by COP20. The INDC of the EU indicated a target of at least 40 % by 2030 compared to 1990. The sectors covered are energy, industrial processes, agriculture and waste. No information on the adaptation and use of the market mechanism is provided in the INDC. The INDC of the EU is also vague on the policy to include the land sector (LULUCF).

4 The Way Forward

Some of the major institutional innovations introduced by the Treaty of Lisbon relate to the external relationships of the EU and its way to interact with third countries and international organizations. The creation of the positions of President of the European Council and High Representative of the Union for Foreign Affairs and Security Policy were designed specifically with the view to finally give to the European Union all necessary instruments to perform at the political level. Unfortunately, in the field of environmental protection, and in particular of climate change, the EU is still seen as a weak actor. Since Copenhagen the EU is often marginalized during negotiations. That is the case, for instance, of the Kyoto Protocol, whose second commitment period sees on board only the EU and a few other developed countries.

Strengthening the position and role of the EU in international law is what is needed if the EU wants to compete with all major economies and States in the world.

The focus of EU climate diplomacy is therefore very much oriented towards an independent long-term framework for climate and clean energy as well as the new international agreement to be agreed by 2015. After the failure of the Copenhagen summit in 2009, the European Commission has come forward with several policy documents designed to provide clarity on its vision about climate change.

The Commission's Communication COM (2013)167 'The 2015 International Climate Change Agreement: Shaping International Climate Policy beyond 2020', released on 26 March 2013, sheds some light on how the Commission sees the 2015 agreement. The latter should:

a. be inclusive, by containing commitments that are applicable to all countries, developed and developing alike;
b. focus on encouraging and enabling countries to take on new and ambitious commitments to cut their GHG emissions;
c. include commitments ambitious enough to limit global warming to 2 °C;
d. be effective, by enabling the right set of incentives for implementation and compliance;
e. be perceived as equitable in the way it shares the effort of cutting emissions and the cost of adapting to unavoidable climate change;
f. be legally binding;
g. learn from and strengthen the current international climate regime;
h. respond to scientific advances and be sufficiently dynamic and flexible to adjust as scientific knowledge develops further and as technology costs and socio-economic circumstances change;
i. see a broader range of countries share responsibility for providing financial support to help poor countries tackle climate change.[18]

The Communication COM(2013)167 touches upon the shortcomings of the UN negotiating process thus representing one of the first official documents where considerations on how to promote the efficiency of the UN model are expressed so openly. The Communication refers, in particular, to the UN negotiating process as an 'open-ended participation and decision-making by consensus [that] often results in only agreeing on the lowest common denominator'. The Communication provides some ideas on how to strengthen the effectiveness and efficiency of UN negotiations[19]:

a. developing rules of procedure to better facilitate reaching decisions than through the consensus rule applied under the Convention;
b. revisiting the frequency of the annual COPs, where the Convention is one of the few that provides for an annual conference. In doing so, it will be important to find a balance between the continued need for political attention for climate change and avoiding the expectation of ground breaking new progress at every meeting;

[18] Commission Communication COM (2013)167, The 2015 International Climate Change Agreement: Shaping International Climate Policy beyond 2020, Brussels, 26 March 2013, p. 3.

[19] See COM (2013)167, pp. 9 and 10.

c. rather than working with a single annually rotating COP Presidency, options such as grouping countries into joint Presidencies over more than 1 year or having 2 year Presidencies;
d. keeping the current frequency of formal meetings for technical work, the intensity of which is likely to increase in the coming years;
e. streamlining and consolidation of the large number of specific agenda items, more informal exchanges ahead of formal technical meetings as well as setting clear priorities in order to contain the overall cost of meetings;
f. opportunities to further strengthen the contributions of stakeholders, including expert views from business and non-governmental organisations;
g. a strengthened role for the Convention Secretariat.

The newest document is the EU INDC presented by Latvia on 6 March 2015 on behalf of the European Union. The EU INDC formalizes the agreement of the EU heads of State and government of October 2014, but also leaves many uncertainties in relation to important issues such as the use of land sector or the accounting principles.

Clearly, COP21 in Paris is the last call for the EU. The contents and rules of the 2015 agreement will tell the world whether the European climate policy has been a success or a failure.

References

Grubb M et al (1999) The Kyoto protocol - a guide and assessment. The Royal Institute of International Affairs, London

Massai L (2001) The Kyoto Protocol in the EU: legal obligations of the European Community and the Member States under International and European Law. Asser Press/Springer, The Hague

Massai L (2009) The long way to the Copenhagen accord: climate change negotiations. RECIEL 19(1):104–121

Massai L (2011) European Climate and Clean Energy Law and Policy (ECCE) – texts and materials. Earthscan Publishing, London

Massai L (2013) Is there anybody out there? EU climate diplomacy before and after Copenhagen. In: Douma WT, van der Velde S (eds) EU environmental norms and third countries: the EU as a global role model? CLEER Working Papers No. 5

Oberthür S (2008) EU leadership on climate change: living up to the challenges. In: European Commission, the European Union and world sustainable development: visions of leading policy makers & academics. Office for Official Publications of the European Communities, Luxembourg, pp 41–54

Oberthür S, Pallemaerts M (2010) The new climate policies of the European Union: internal legislation and climate diplomacy. VUB Press, Brussels

Schaik L (2012) The EU and the progressive alliance negotiating in Durban: saving the climate? ODI and CDKN, Working Paper 354

Schunz S (2012) Explaining the evolution of European Union foreign climate policy: a case of bounded adaptiveness. EIoP 16(6). Available at: http://eiop.or.at/eiop/texte/2012-006a.htm

Vanhoonacker S (2010) The EU's impact in international climate change negotiations – the case of Copenhagen, Diplomatic System of the European Union (DSEU). Loughborough University

ISBN 978-3319285955 -5

9 783319 285955

Printed in Japan

G0095776